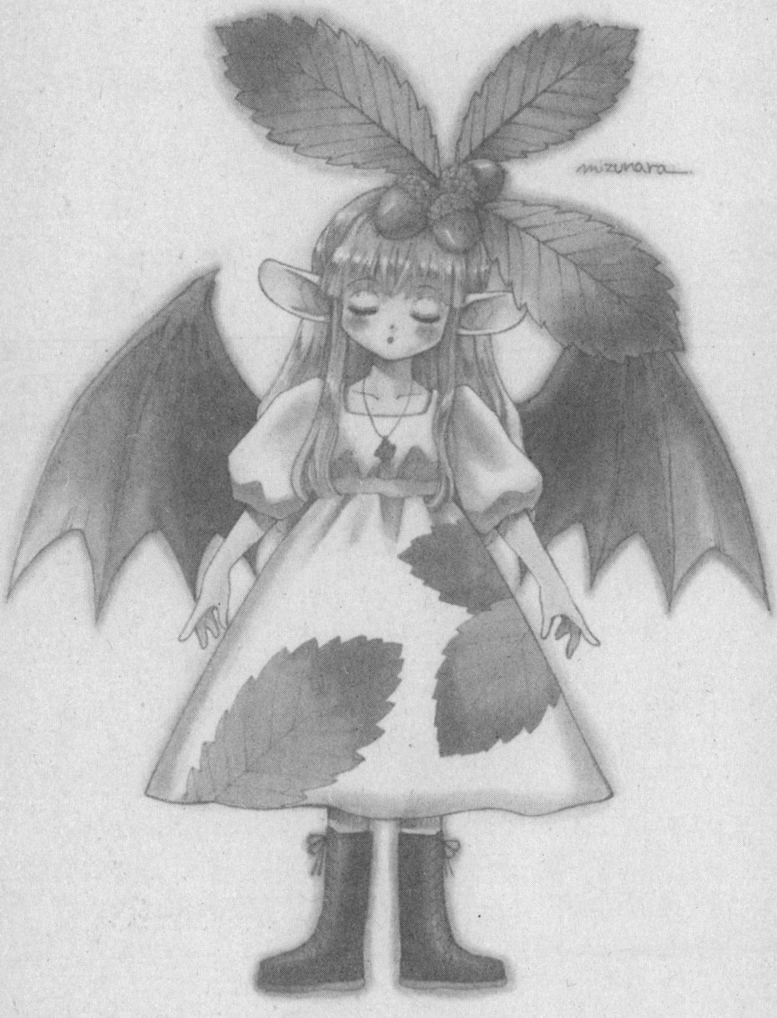
mizunara

nana

+ANIMA Volume 7
Created by Natsumi Mukai

Translation - Alethea & Athena Nibley
English Adaptation - Karen S. Ahlstrom
Copy Editor - Sarah Mercurio
Retouch and Lettering - Star Print Brokers
Production Artist - Courtney Geter
Graphic Designer - James Lee

Editor - Troy Lewter
Digital Imaging Manager - Chris Buford
Pre-Production Supervisor - Erika Terriquez
Production Manager - Elisabeth Brizzi
Managing Editor - Vy Nguyen
Creative Director - Anne Marie Horne
Editor-in-Chief - Rob Tokar
Publisher - Mike Kiley
President and C.O.O. - John Parker
C.E.O. and Chief Creative Officer - Stuart Levy

A  Manga

TOKYOPOP Inc.
5900 Wilshire Blvd. Suite 2000
Los Angeles, CA 90036

E-mail: info@TOKYOPOP.com
Come visit us online at www.TOKYOPOP.com

ISBN: 978-1-59816-353-7

First TOKYOPOP printing: March 2008
10 9 8 7 6 5 4 3 2 1
Printed in the USA

Volume 7
by Natsumi Mukai

HAMBURG // LONDON // LOS ANGELES // TOKYO

+ANIMA

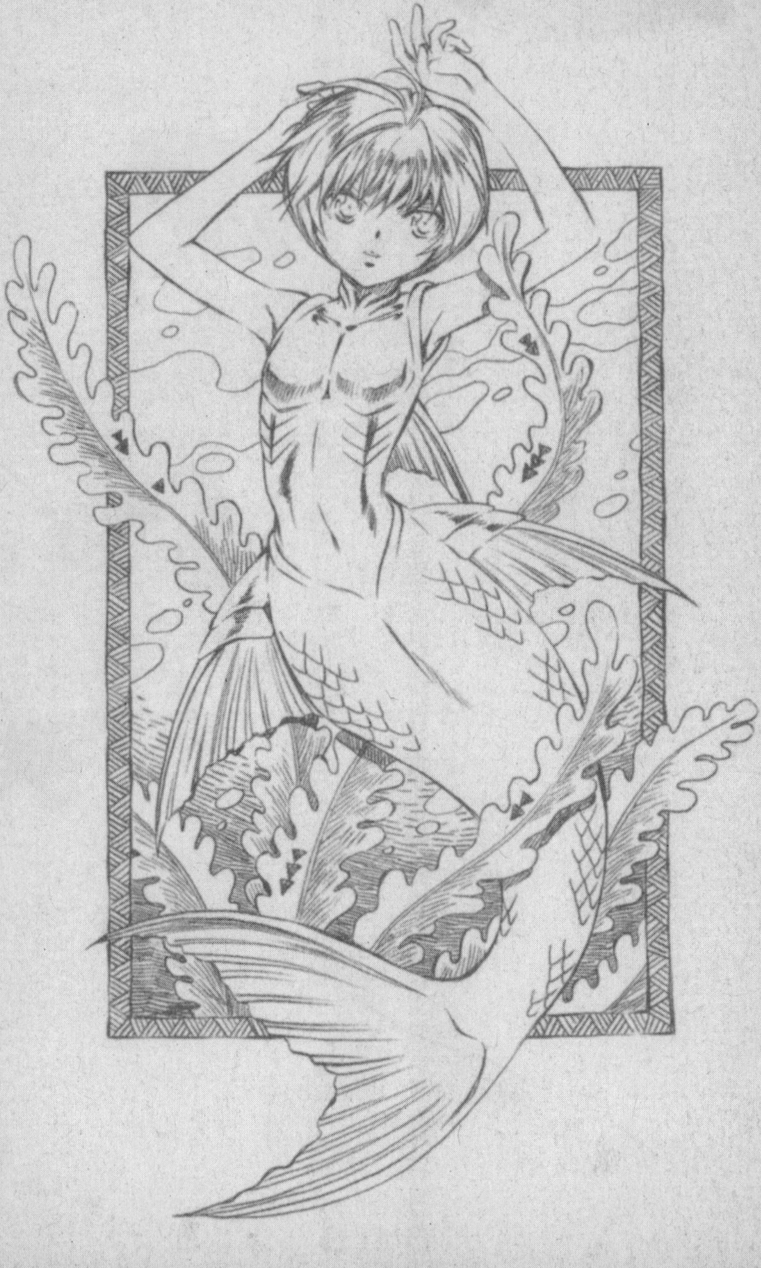

プラスアニマ
+ANIMA

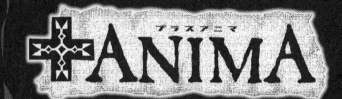

迎夏生
NATSUMI MUKAI

STORY & CHARACTERS

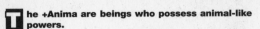

The +Anima are beings who possess animal-like powers.

Cooro, a crow +Anima, meets Husky, a fish +Anima, at the circus. The two of them travel together and are soon joined by new companions: Senri, a bear +Anima, and Nana, a bat +Anima. And so, the four children's adventures begin...

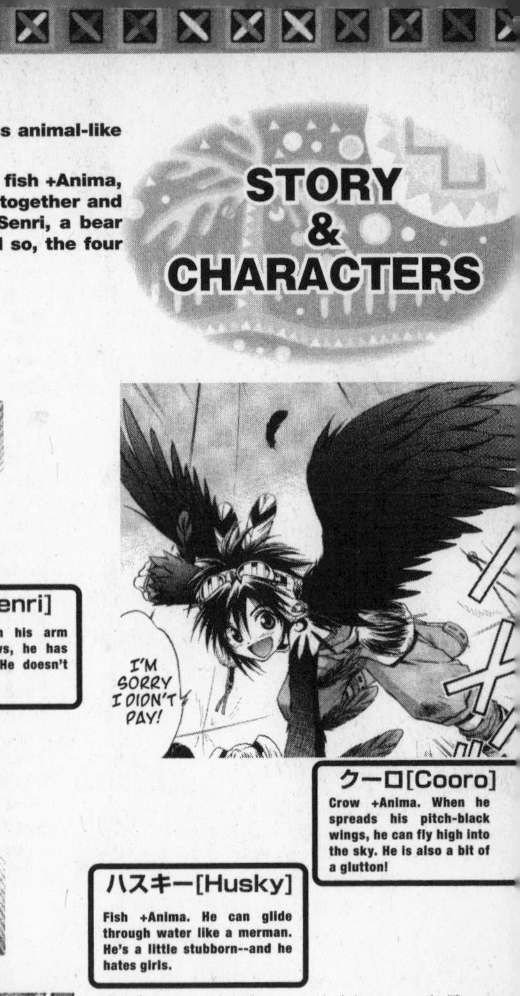

I'M SORRY I DIDN'T PAY!

クーロ[Cooro]

Crow +Anima. When he spreads his pitch-black wings, he can fly high into the sky. He is also a bit of a glutton!

ハスキー[Husky]

Fish +Anima. He can glide through water like a merman. He's a little stubborn--and he hates girls.

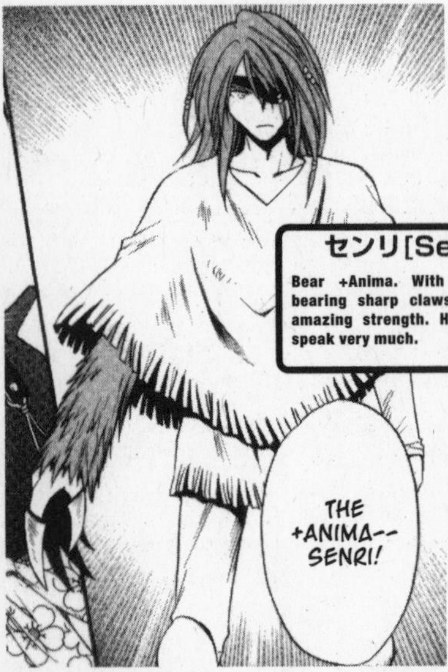

THE +ANIMA-- SENRI!

センリ[Senri]

Bear +Anima. With his arm bearing sharp claws, he has amazing strength. He doesn't speak very much.

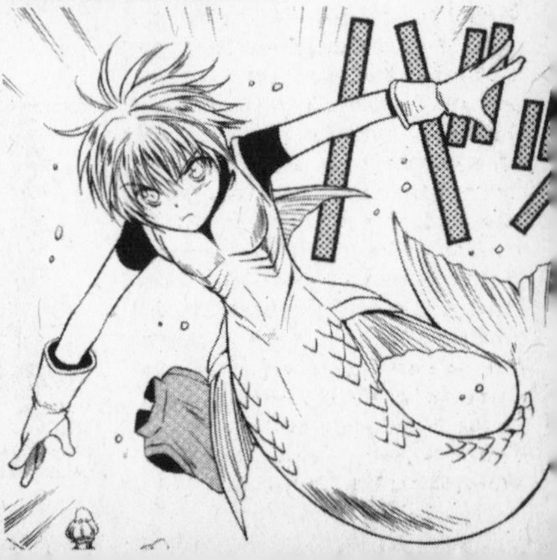

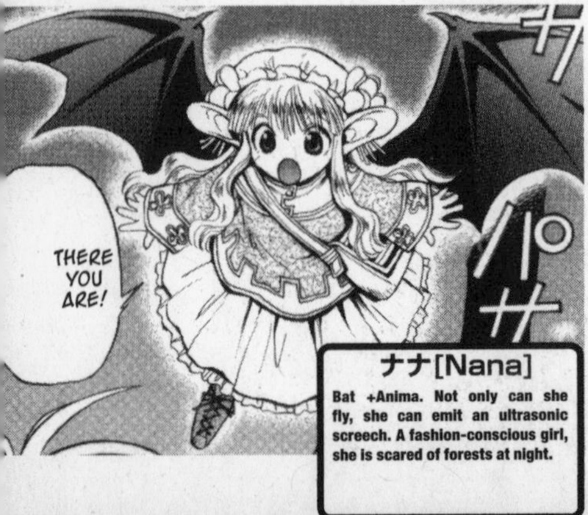

THERE YOU ARE!

ナナ[Nana]

Bat +Anima. Not only can she fly, she can emit an ultrasonic screech. A fashion-conscious girl, she is scared of forests at night.

SENRI...

...PREPARE TO DIE!!

Igneous leads a troop of Astarian soldiers on a mission to form an alliance with the Kim-un-kur to oppose the warmongering country of Sailand. But due to a long history of ill-feeling between the groups, the Kim-un-kur refuse. Igneous then asks Senri, a Kim-un-kur, to act as an emissary. He agrees, and Cooro and the others have to travel with the Astarian military to the negotiations. Along the way they are confronted by a large bear, which activates Senri's anima power. He then faints....

When he awakens, Senri has forgotten Cooro and the others. Then, Upas, who had been best friends with Senri's late father, takes Senri and Igneous onto a treacherous mountain path in order to retrieve Senri's memories. But along the way, Upas attacks Senri and tries to kill him!

Senri is a +Anima with ferocious strength, having taken in the anima of the mad bear Amurui. Years ago, when Senri's father was about to die, he passed his anima onto Senri, but Amurui's mad anima came with it. Senri goes feral while fighting Upas, but thanks to Cooro and the others, he is able to return to normal, promptly ending the battle.

Cooro and company are uncertain where to go next. Nana suggests they go back to Sandra, but Husky seems to have his hopes on Sailand, which is west of Moss Mountain. But the path there is treacherous, and they may not ever be able to come back. This doesn't deter Husky, though, and Cooro and the others decide to go with him (as if it were the obvious choice). What is the real reason Husky wants to go to Sailand? What will greet them there? A new adventure has begun...

DO YOU WANT TO GO TO SAILAND THAT MUCH?

C O N T E N T S

Chapter 33
Dark Tunnel

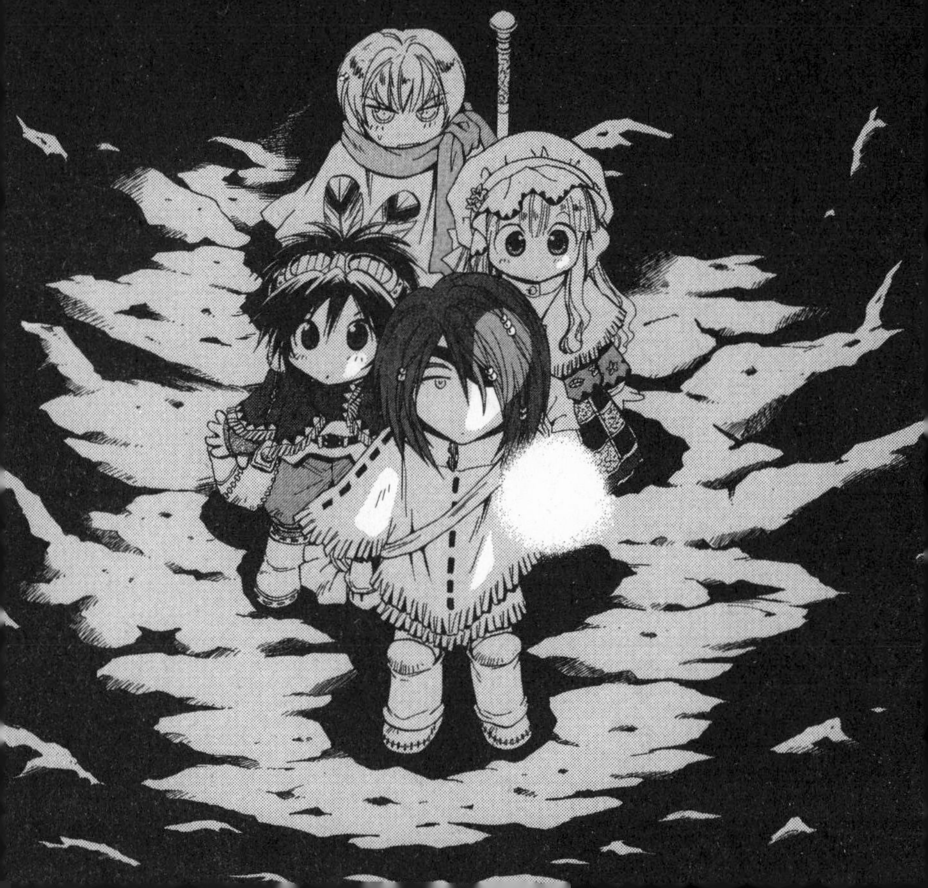

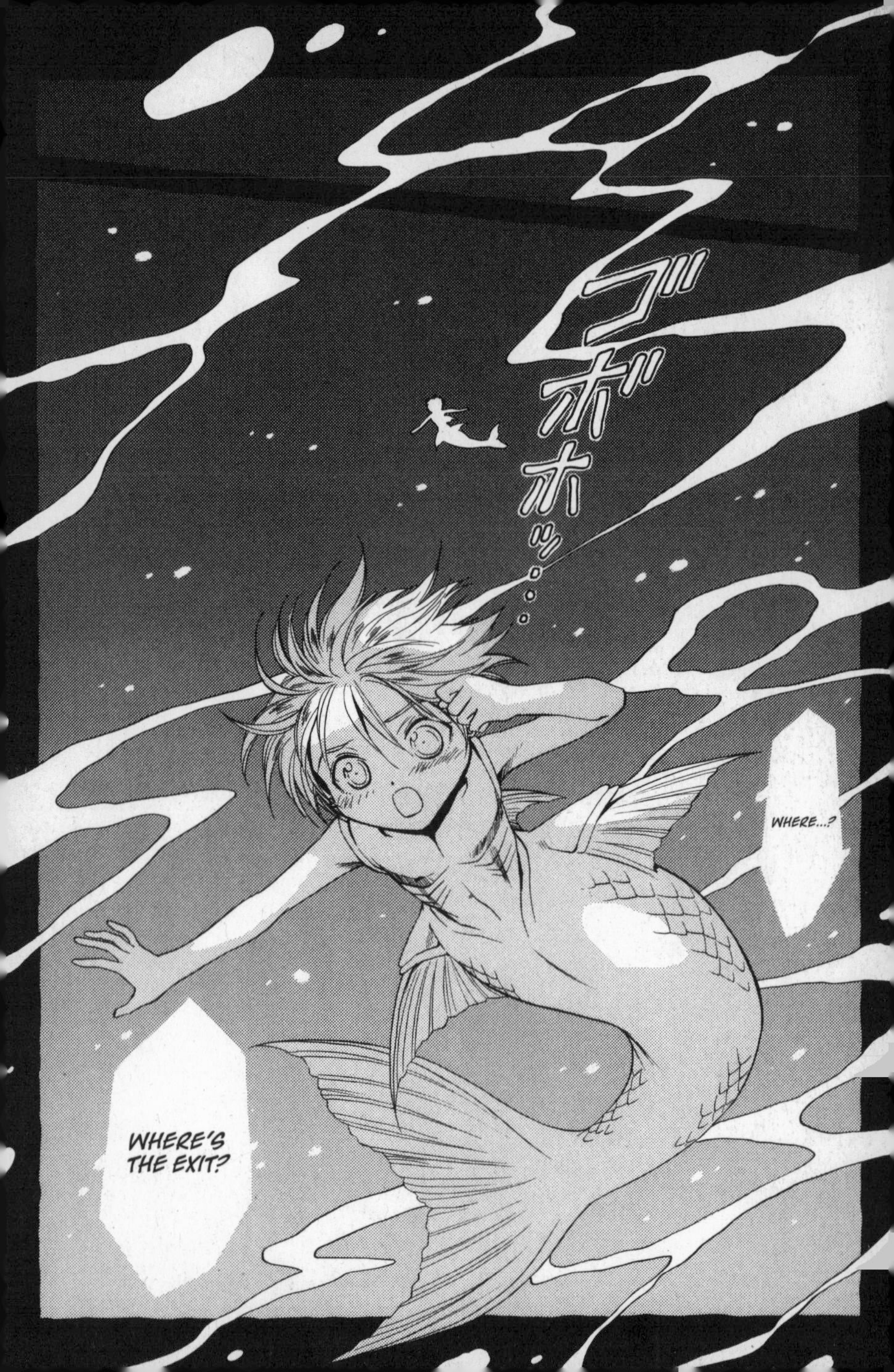
ゴボホッ…
WHERE...?
WHERE'S THE EXIT?

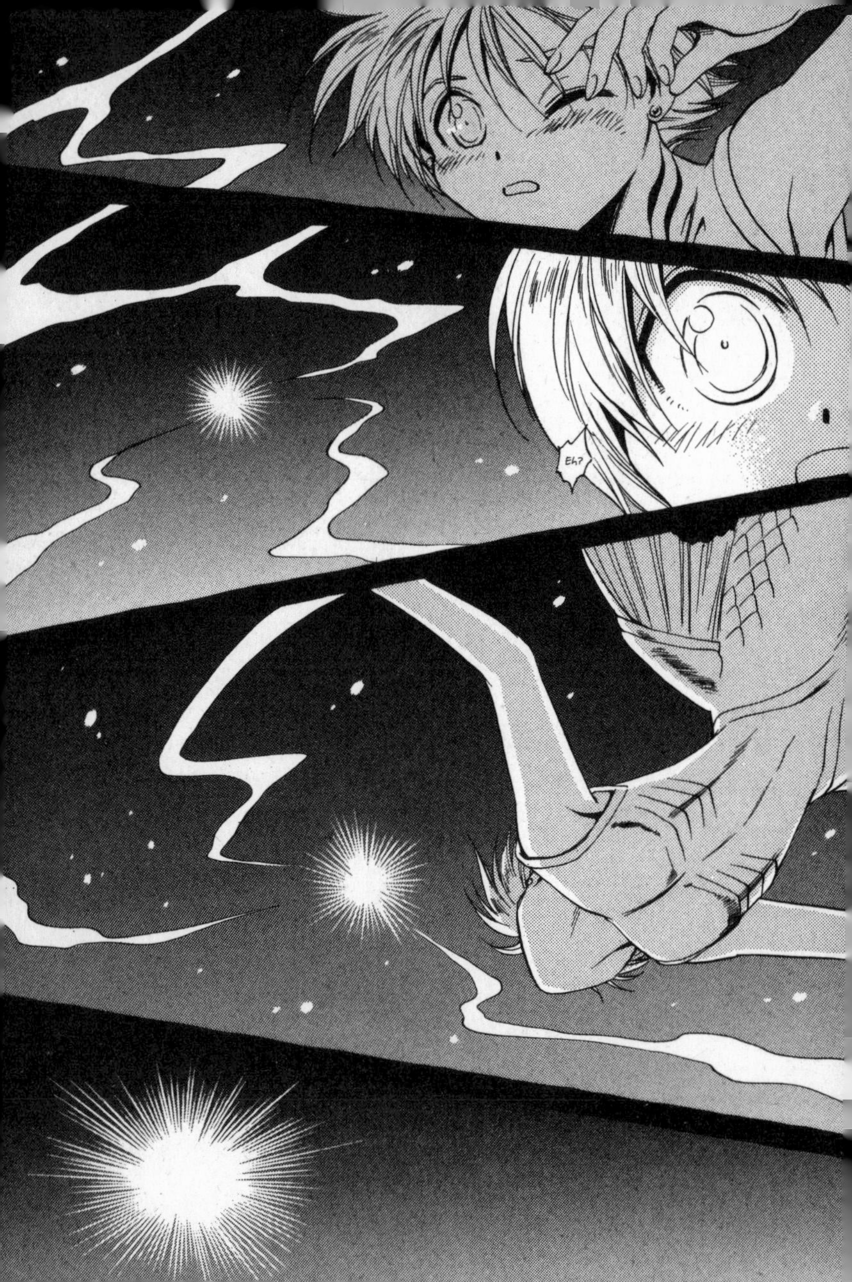
Eh?

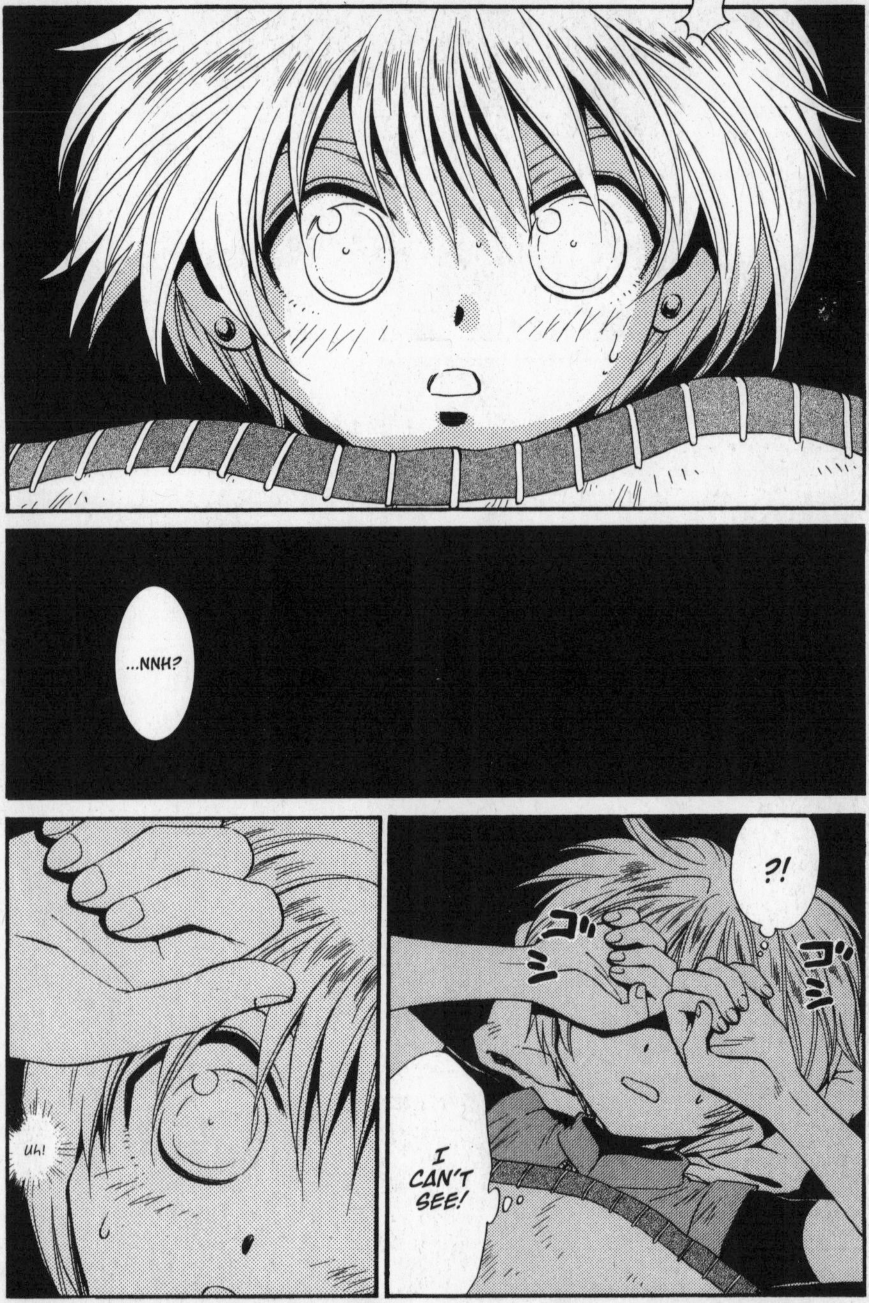
...NNH?
?!
ゴシ
ゴシ
I CAN'T SEE!
uh!

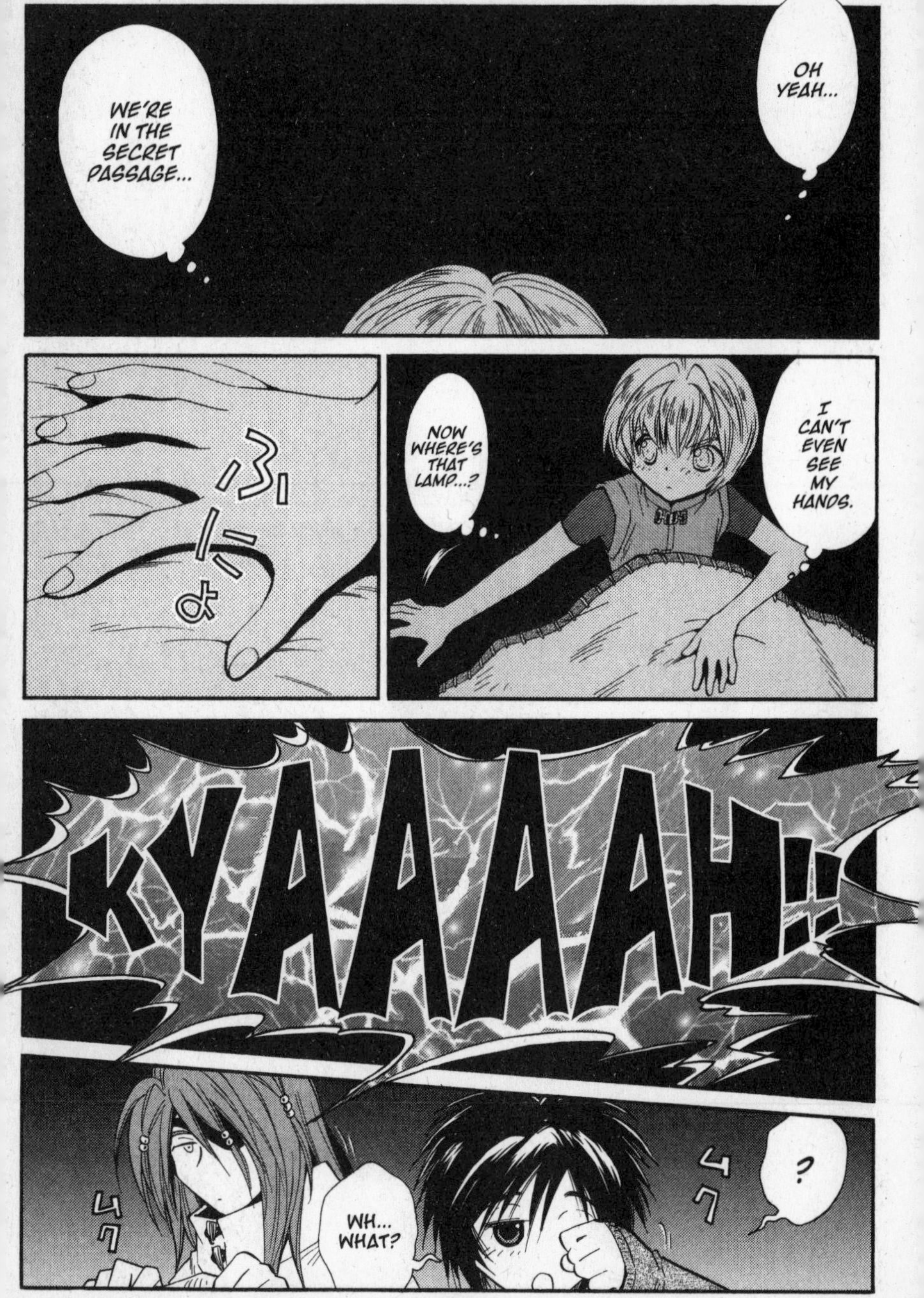
OH YEAH...
WE'RE IN THE SECRET PASSAGE...
I CAN'T EVEN SEE MY HANDS.
NOW WHERE'S THAT LAMP...?
ふにゅ
KYAAAAH!!
?
ムク
WH... WHAT?
ムク

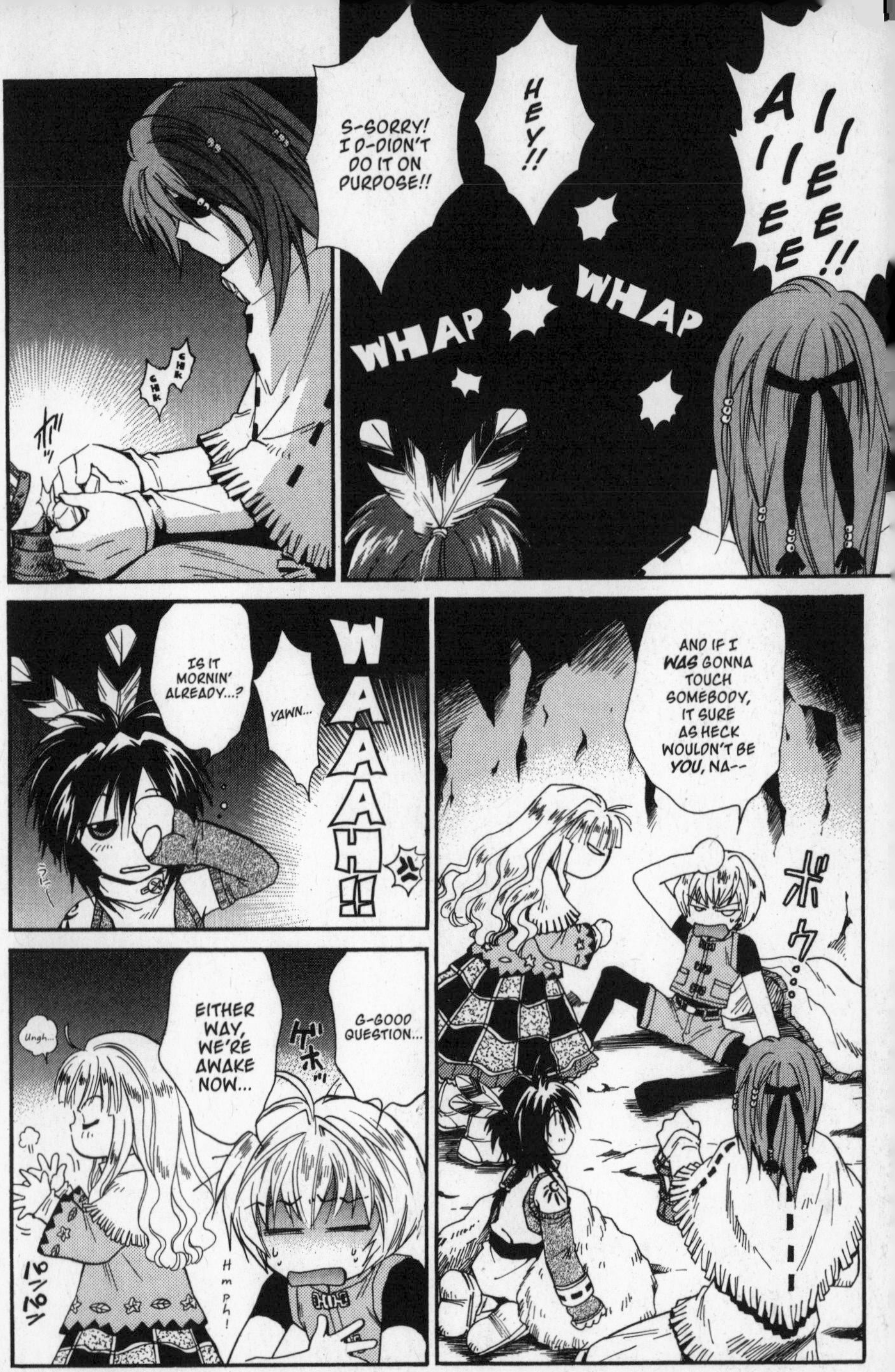
AIIIIEEEEEE!!
HEY!!
WHAP
WHAP
S-SORRY! I D-DIDN'T DO IT ON PURPOSE!!
CHK CHK CHK
AND IF I WAS GONNA TOUCH SOMEBODY, IT SURE AS HECK WOULDN'T BE YOU, NA--
WAAAAH!!
YAWN...
IS IT MORNIN' ALREADY...?
G-GOOD QUESTION...
EITHER WAY, WE'RE AWAKE NOW...
Ungh...
Hmph!

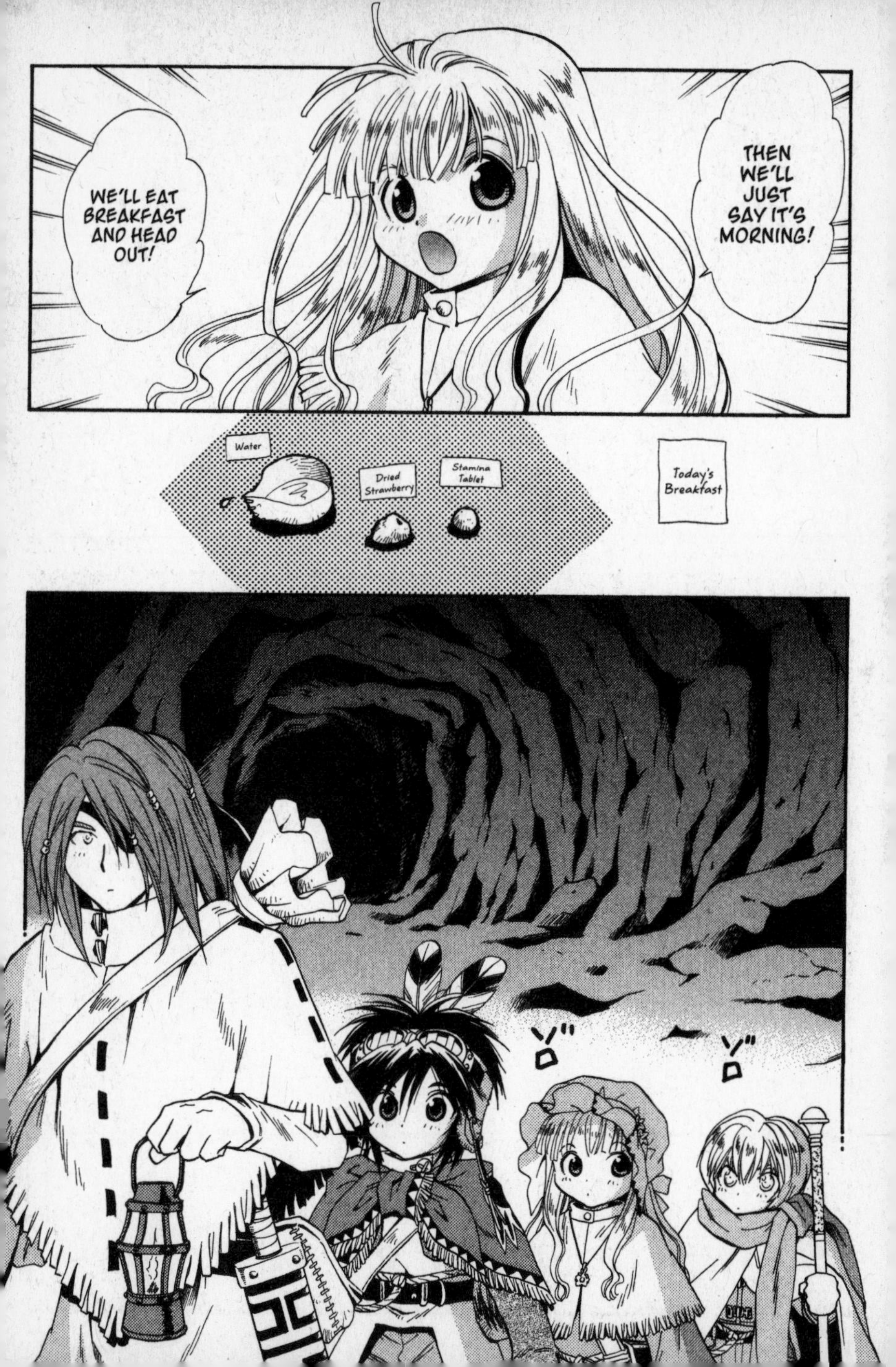
THEN WE'LL JUST SAY IT'S MORNING!
WE'LL EAT BREAKFAST AND HEAD OUT!
Today's Breakfast
Stamina Tablet
Dried Strawberry
Water
ゾロ
ゾロ

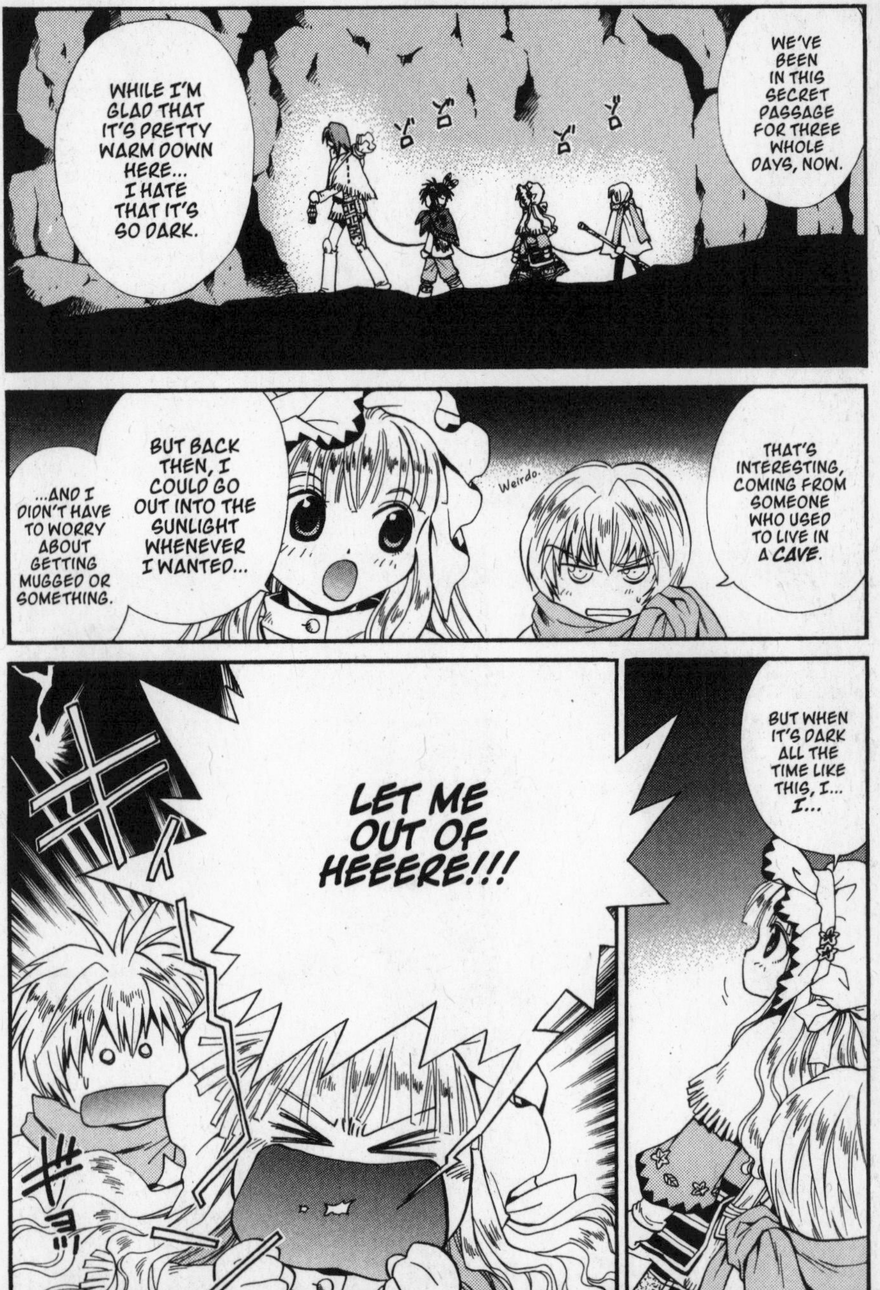

WE'VE BEEN IN THIS SECRET PASSAGE FOR THREE WHOLE DAYS, NOW.
WHILE I'M GLAD THAT IT'S PRETTY WARM DOWN HERE... I HATE THAT IT'S SO DARK.
THAT'S INTERESTING, COMING FROM SOMEONE WHO USED TO LIVE IN A *CAVE*.
Weirdo.
BUT BACK THEN, I COULD GO OUT INTO THE SUNLIGHT WHENEVER I WANTED...
...AND I DIDN'T HAVE TO WORRY ABOUT GETTING MUGGED OR SOMETHING.
BUT WHEN IT'S DARK ALL THE TIME LIKE THIS, I... *I*...
LET ME OUT OF HEEERE!!!

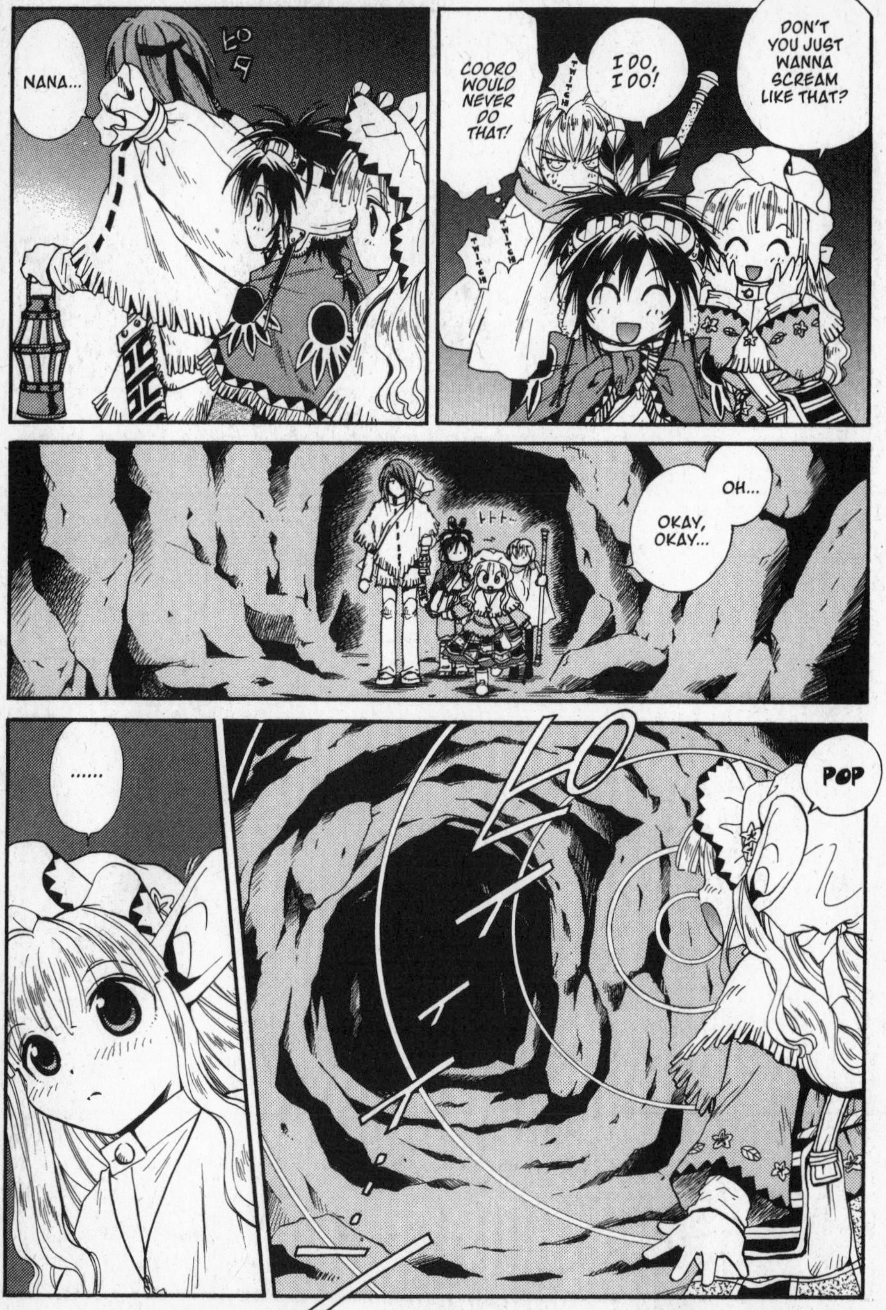
DON'T YOU JUST WANNA SCREAM LIKE THAT?
I DO, I DO!
TWITCH
COORO WOULD NEVER DO THAT!
TWITCH TWITCH
NANA...
OH... OKAY, OKAY...
POP
......

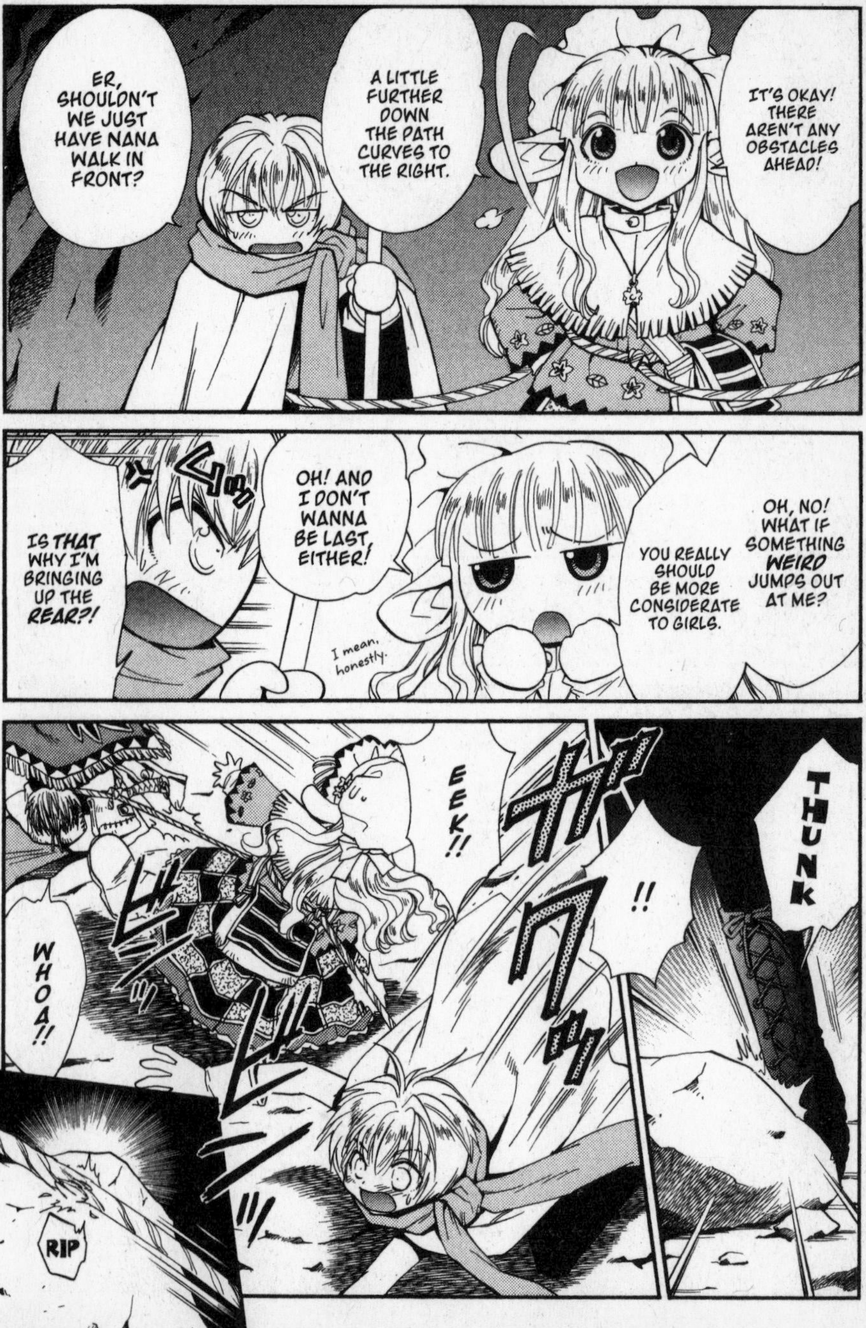
IT'S OKAY! THERE AREN'T ANY OBSTACLES AHEAD!
A LITTLE FURTHER DOWN THE PATH CURVES TO THE RIGHT.
ER, SHOULDN'T WE JUST HAVE NANA WALK IN FRONT?
OH, NO! WHAT IF SOMETHING WEIRD JUMPS OUT AT ME?
YOU REALLY SHOULD BE MORE CONSIDERATE TO GIRLS.
I mean, honestly.
OH! AND I DON'T WANNA BE LAST, EITHER!
IS THAT WHY I'M BRINGING UP THE REAR?!
THUNK
!!
EEK!!
WHOA!!
RIP

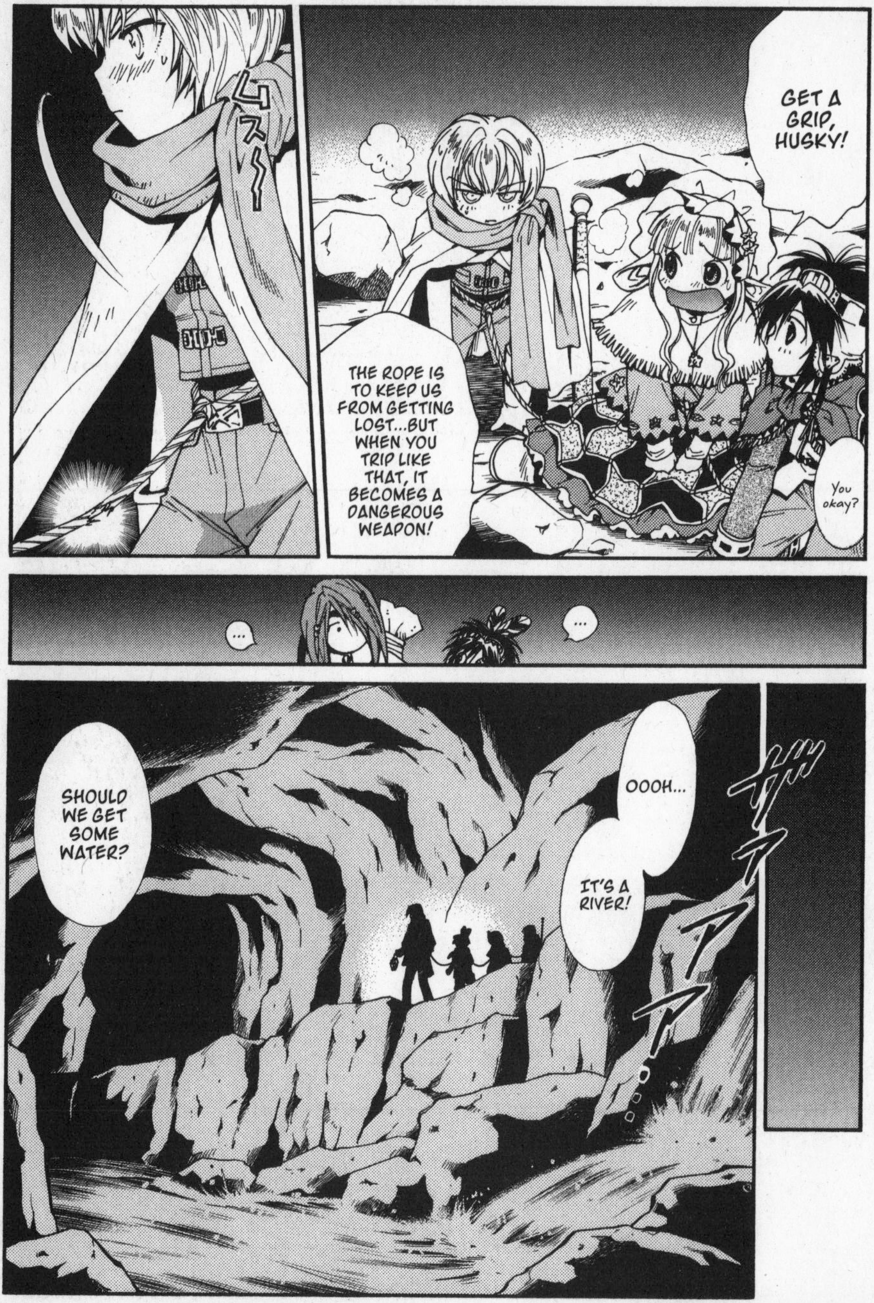
GET A GRIP, HUSKY!
You okay?
THE ROPE IS TO KEEP US FROM GETTING LOST...BUT WHEN YOU TRIP LIKE THAT, IT BECOMES A DANGEROUS WEAPON!
...
...
OOOH...
IT'S A RIVER!
SHOULD WE GET SOME WATER?

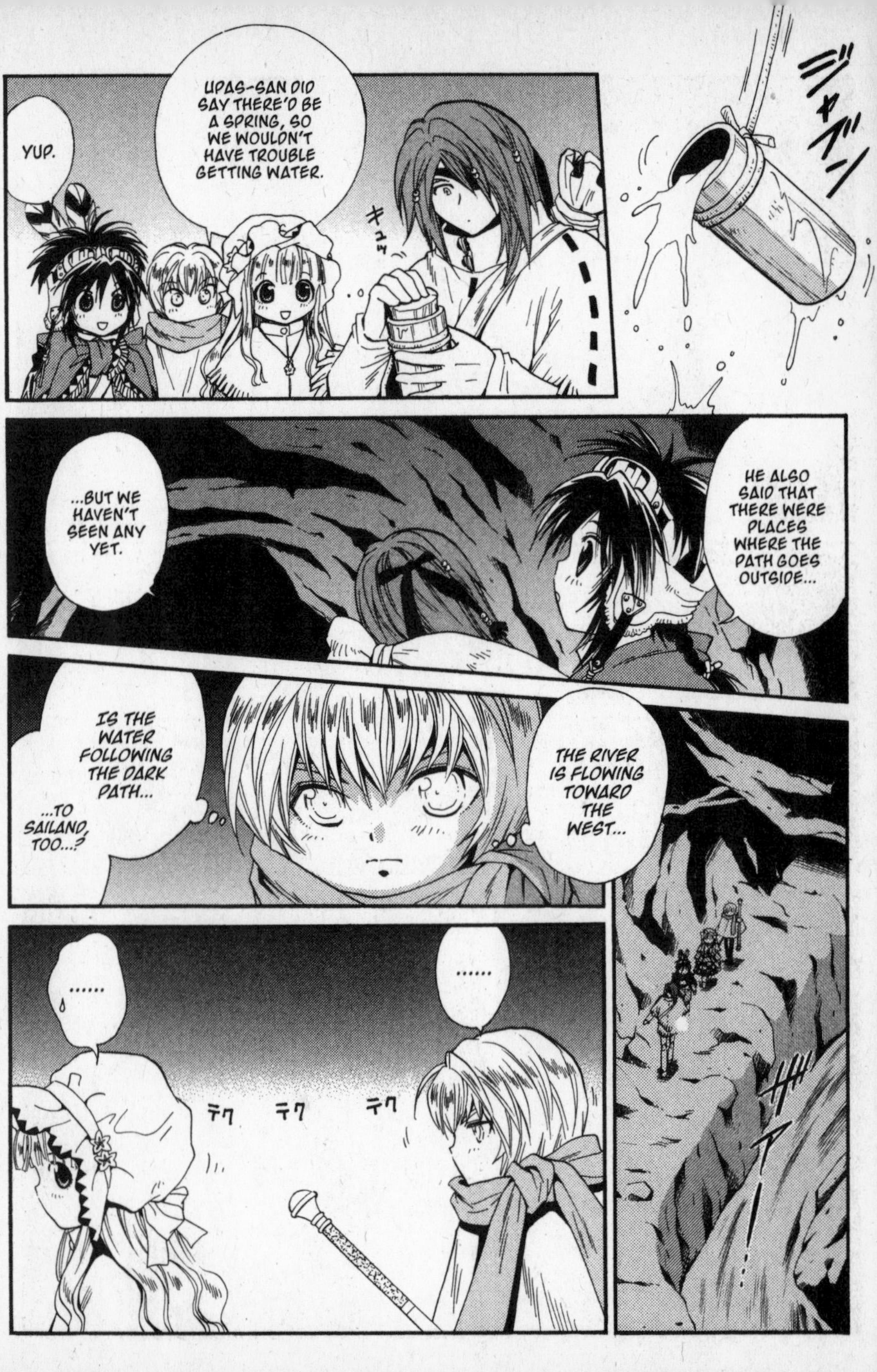
ジャブン
UPAS-SAN DID SAY THERE'D BE A SPRING, SO WE WOULDN'T HAVE TROUBLE GETTING WATER.
YUP.
キュッ
HE ALSO SAID THAT THERE WERE PLACES WHERE THE PATH GOES OUTSIDE...
...BUT WE HAVEN'T SEEN ANY YET.
THE RIVER IS FLOWING TOWARD THE WEST...
IS THE WATER FOLLOWING THE DARK PATH...
...TO SAILAND, TOO...?
......
......
テク テク テク

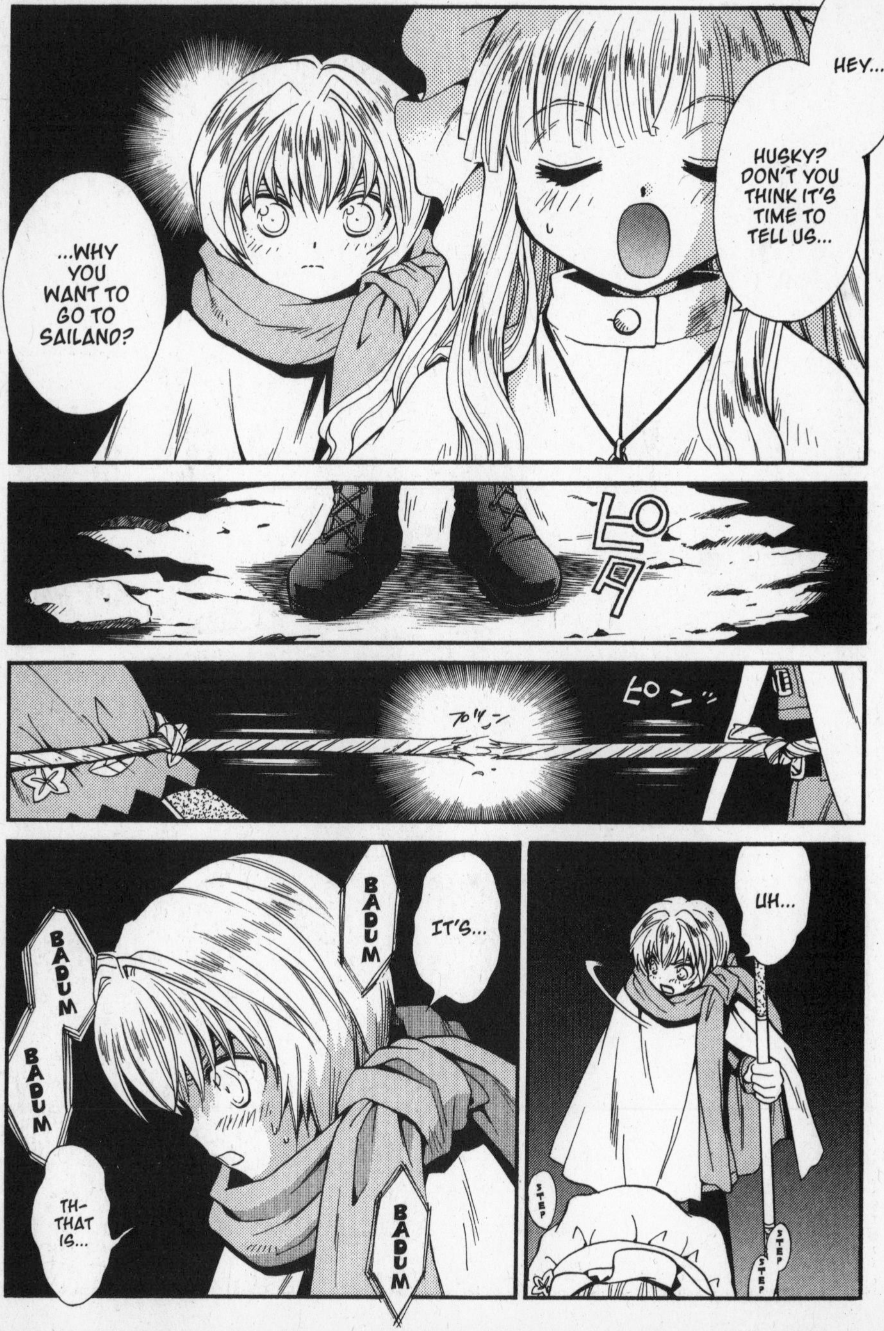
HEY...
HUSKY? DON'T YOU THINK IT'S TIME TO TELL US...
...WHY YOU WANT TO GO TO SAILAND?
UH...
STEP
STEP
STEP
BADUM
IT'S...
BADUM
BADUM
BADUM
TH-THAT IS...
BADUM

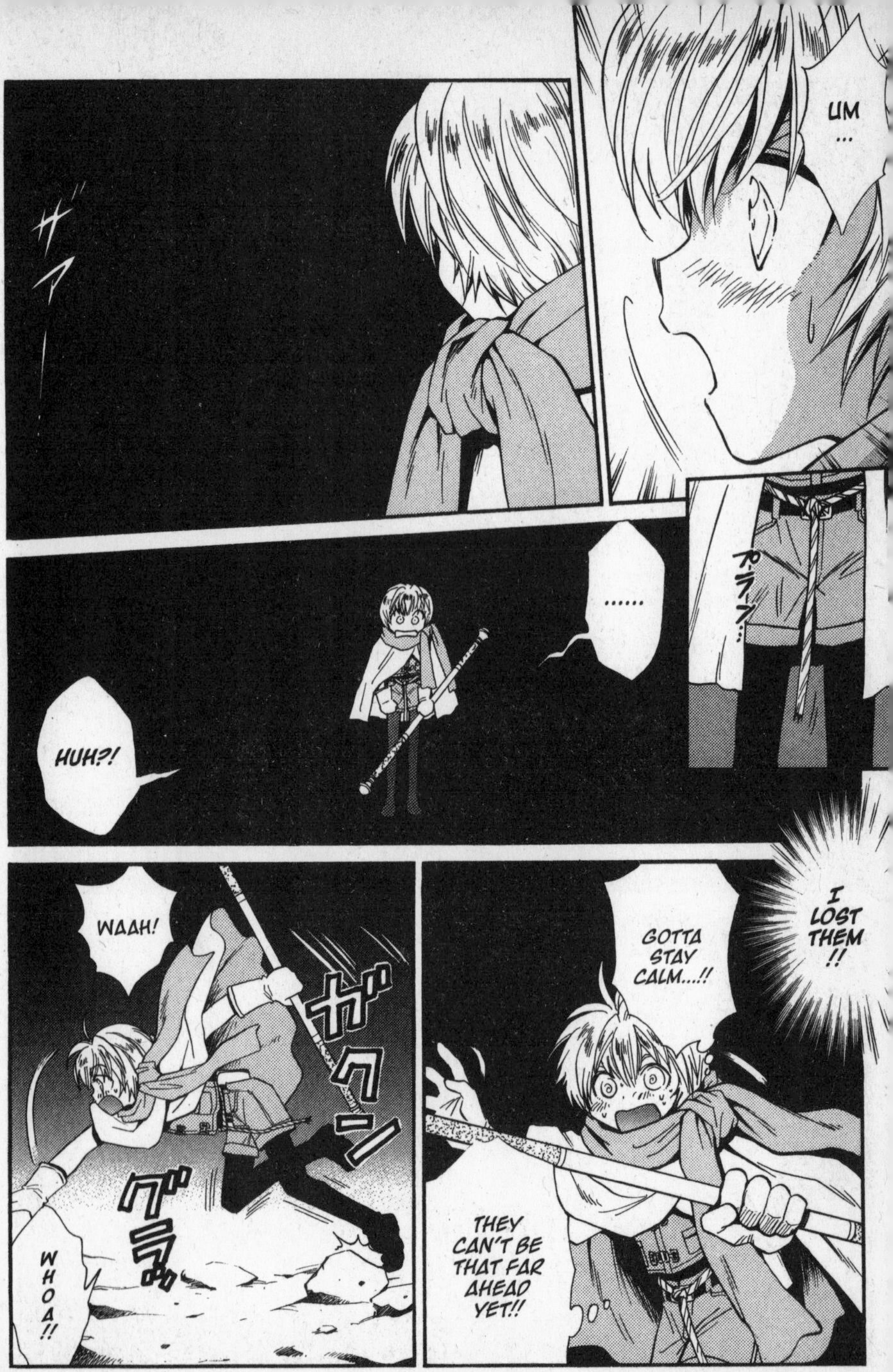
UM ...
......
HUH?!
I LOST THEM!!
GOTTA STAY CALM....!!
THEY CAN'T BE THAT FAR AHEAD YET!!
WAAH!
WHOA!!

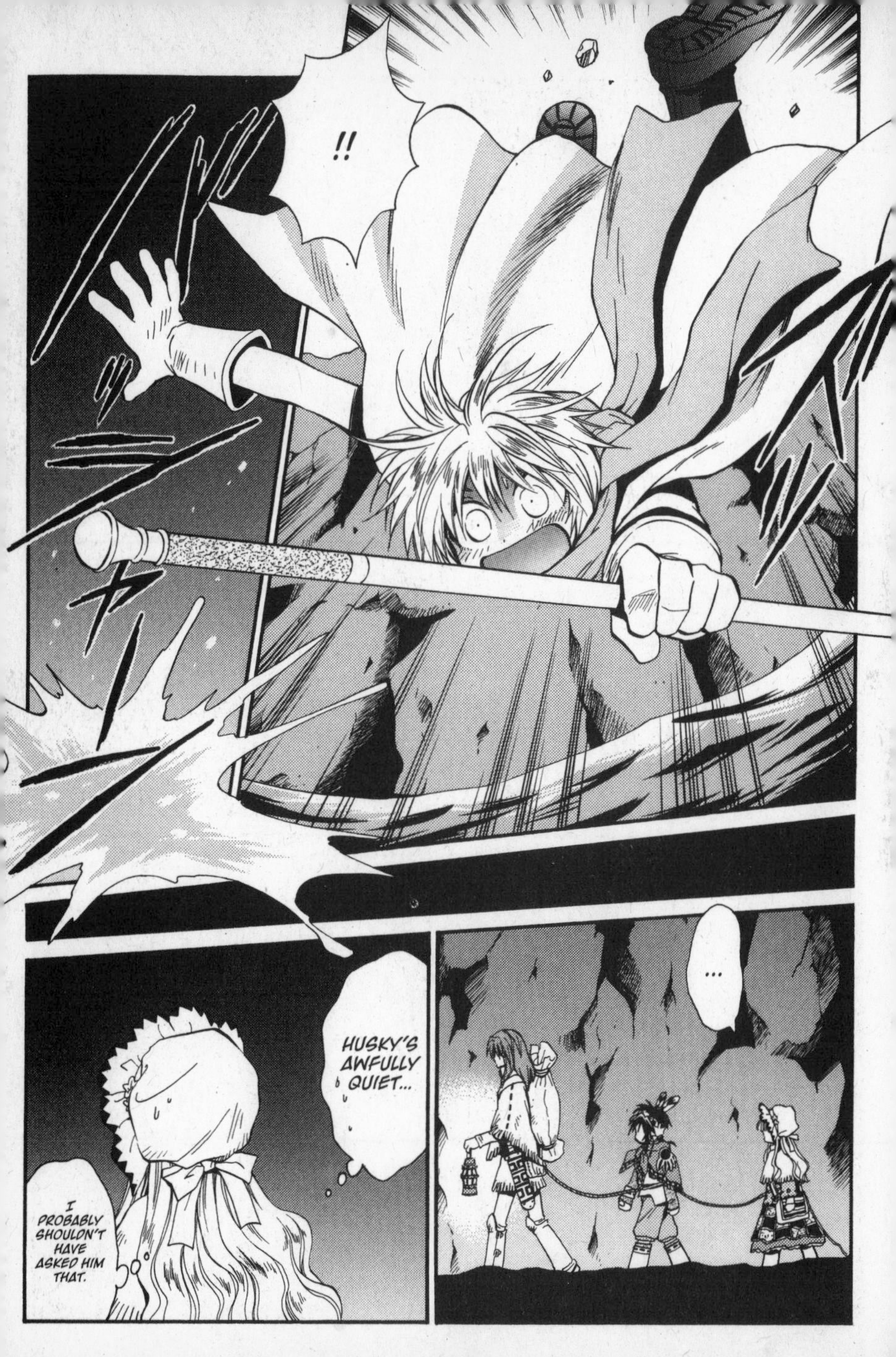
!!
...
HUSKY'S AWFULLY QUIET...
I PROBABLY SHOULDN'T HAVE ASKED HIM THAT.

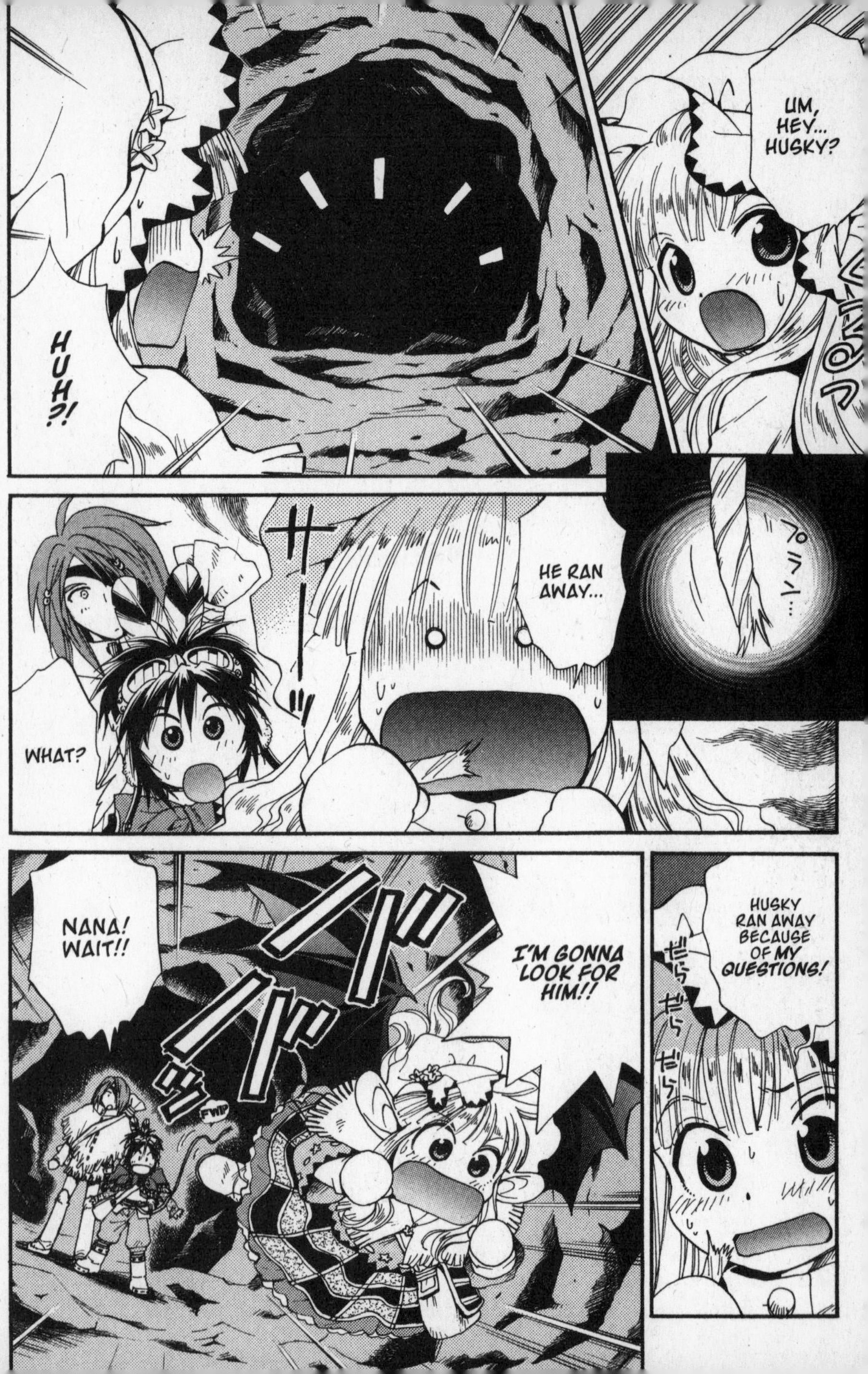
UM, HEY... HUSKY?
HUH?!
HE RAN AWAY...
WHAT?
HUSKY RAN AWAY BECAUSE OF MY QUESTIONS!
だら だら だら
I'M GONNA LOOK FOR HIM!!
FWIP
NANA! WAIT!!

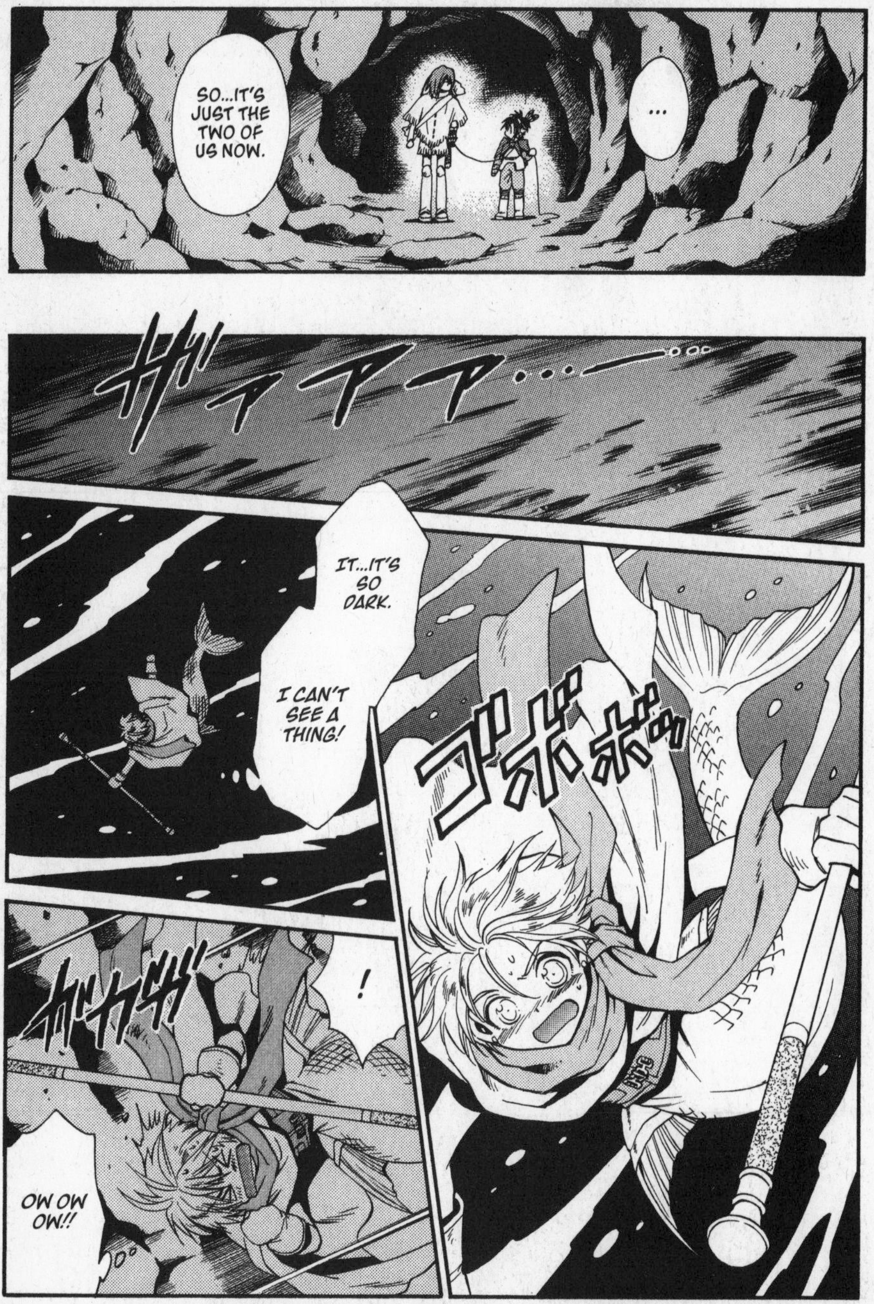
...
SO...IT'S JUST THE TWO OF US NOW.
ザァアア…—
IT...IT'S SO DARK.
I CAN'T SEE A THING!
ゴボボ
!
OW OW OW!!

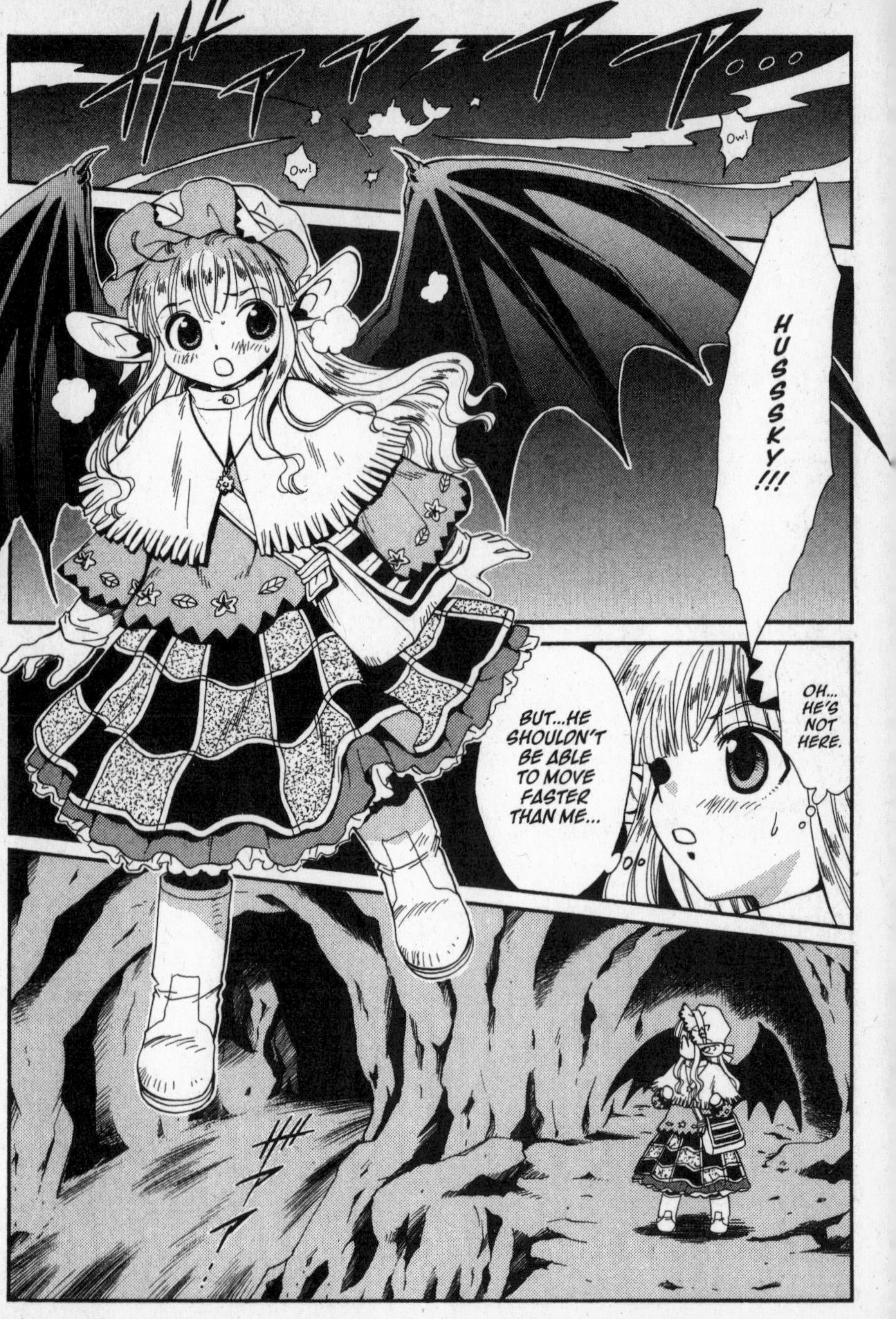
Ow!
Ow!
HUSSSKY!!!
OH... HE'S NOT HERE.
BUT...HE SHOULDN'T BE ABLE TO MOVE FASTER THAN ME...

OKAY...

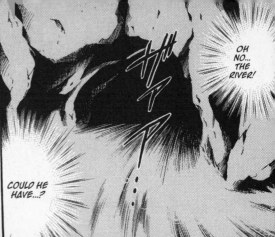

OH NO... THE RIVER!

COULD HE HAVE...?

HERE GOES!!

GOSH... I WONDER HOW FAR NANA WENT?

...

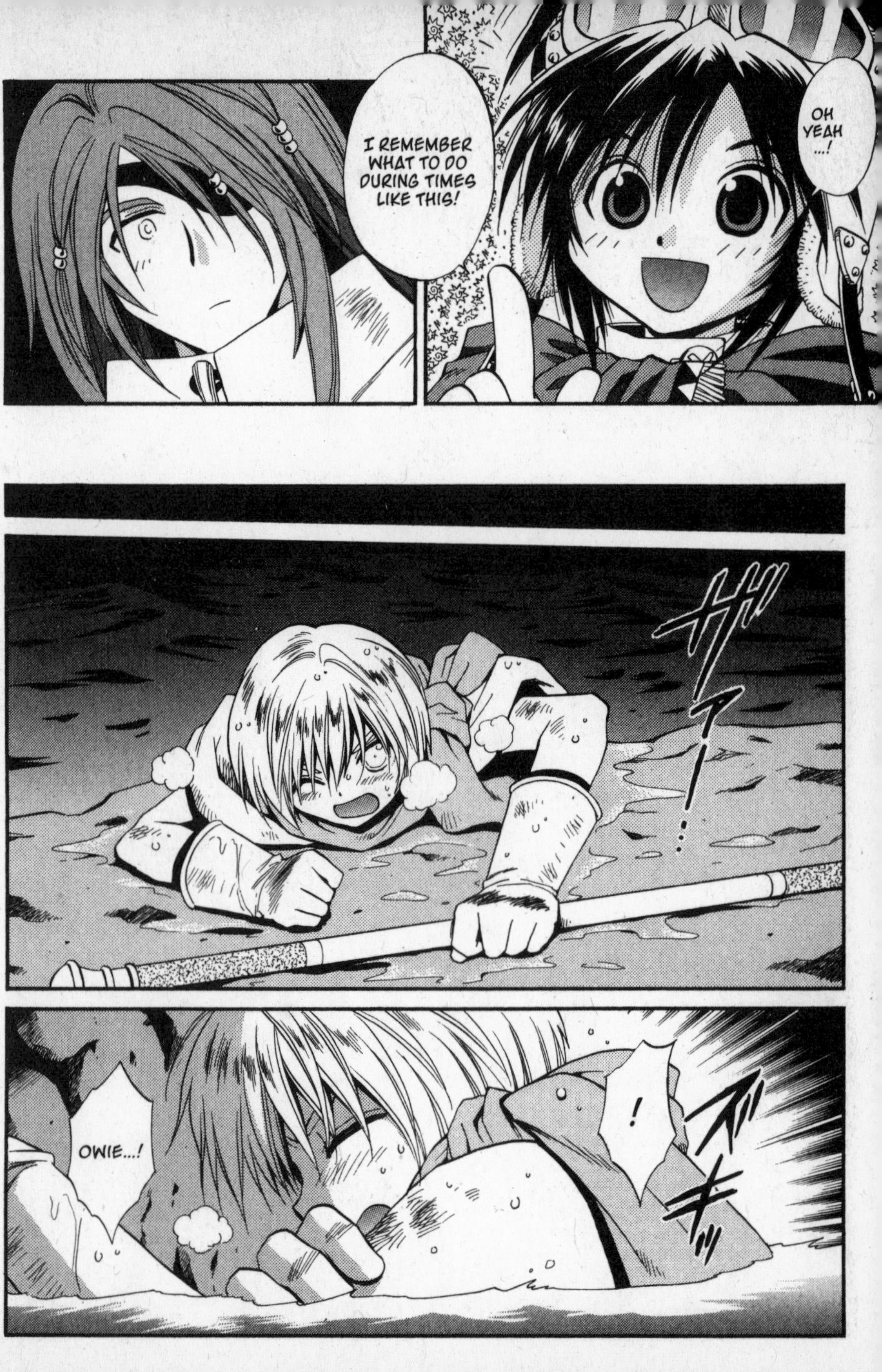
OH YEAH ...!
I REMEMBER WHAT TO DO DURING TIMES LIKE THIS!
!
OWIE...!

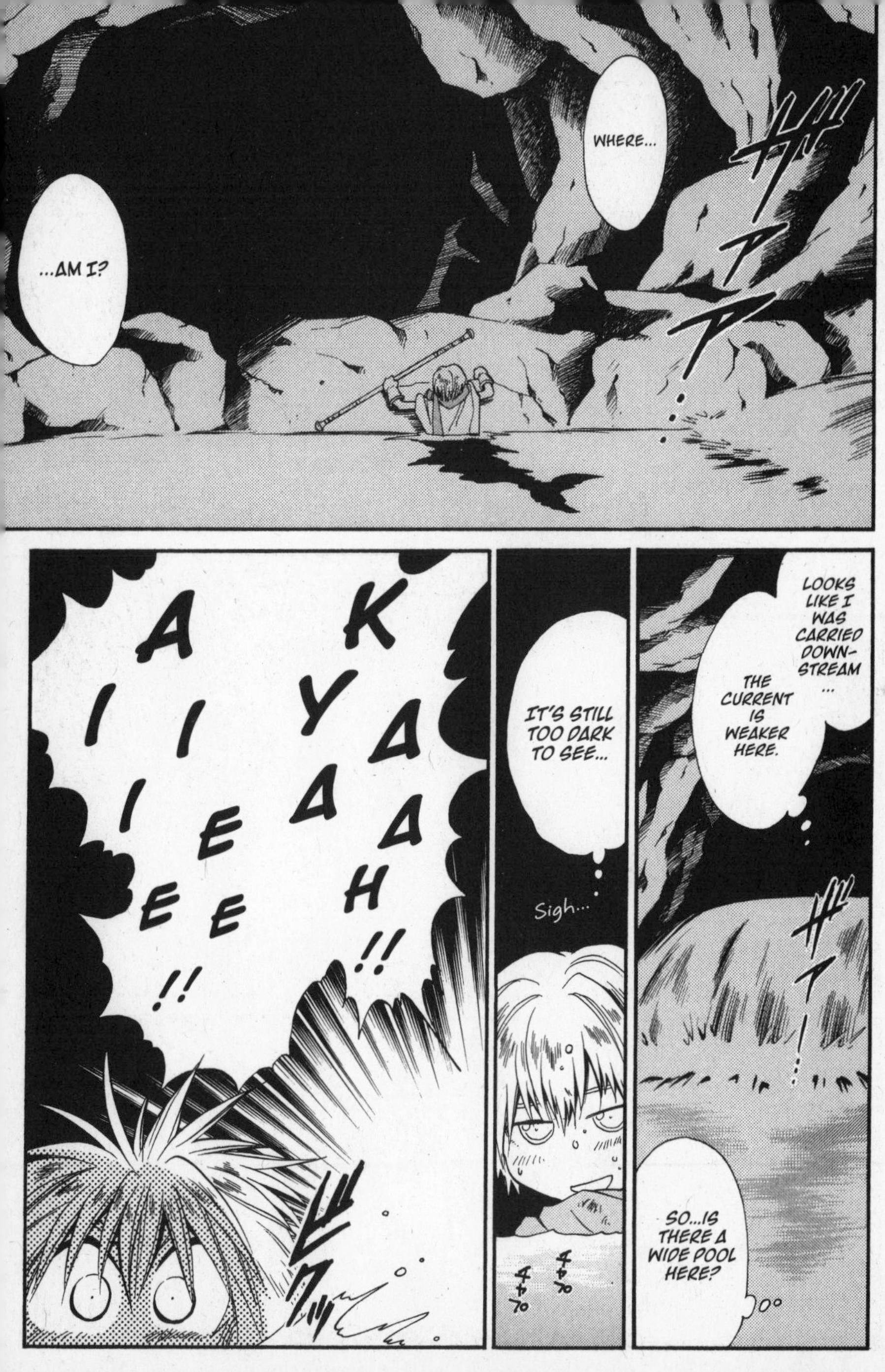
WHERE...
...AM I?
LOOKS LIKE I WAS CARRIED DOWN-STREAM... THE CURRENT IS WEAKER HERE.
SO...IS THERE A WIDE POOL HERE?
IT'S STILL TOO DARK TO SEE...
Sigh...
KYAAAH!!
AIIIEEE!!

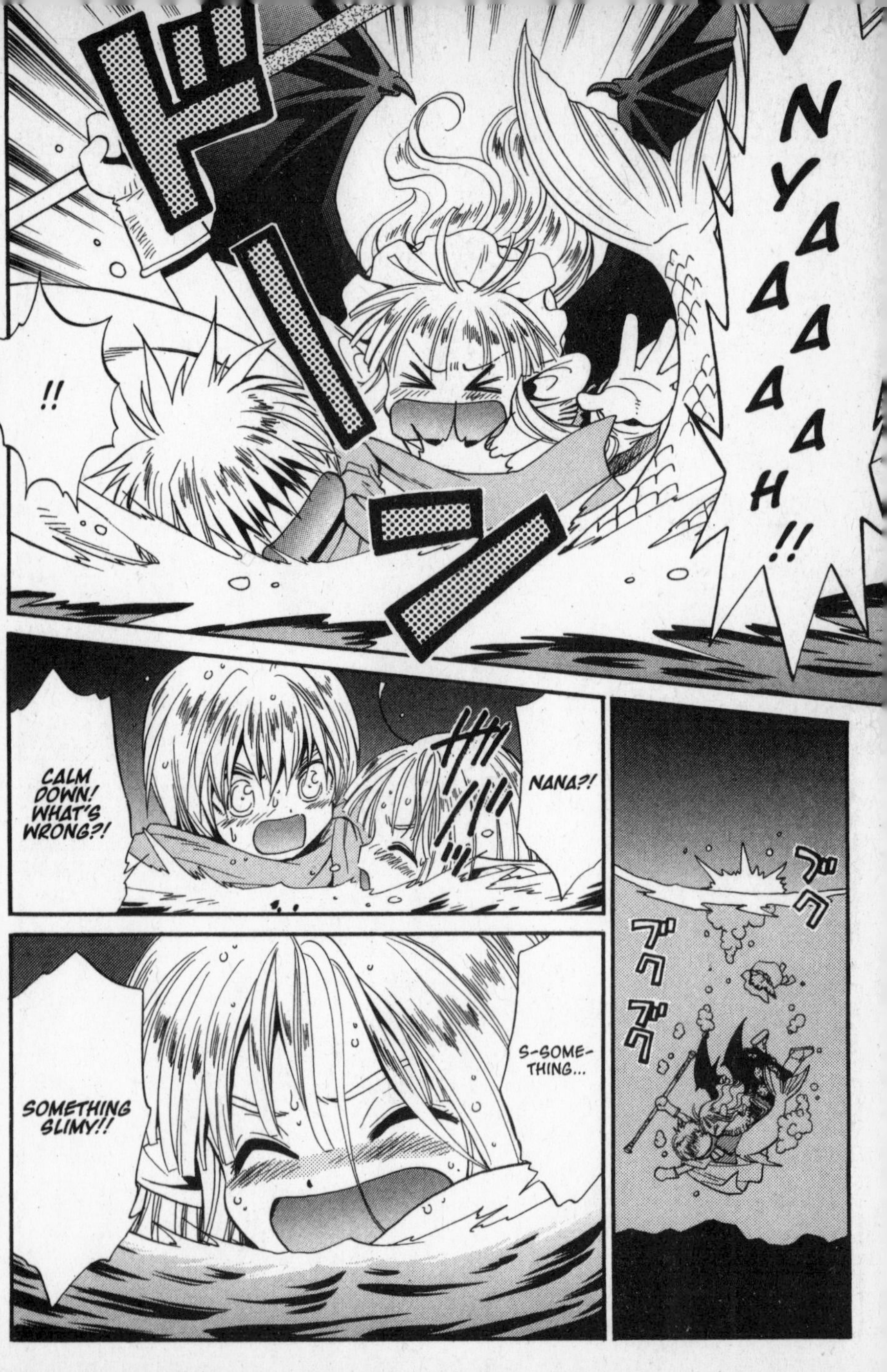

NYAAAAAH!!
ドーン
!!
ブク
ブク
ブク
ブク
ザバ
NANA?!
CALM DOWN! WHAT'S WRONG?!
S-SOME-THING...
SOMETHING SLIMY!!

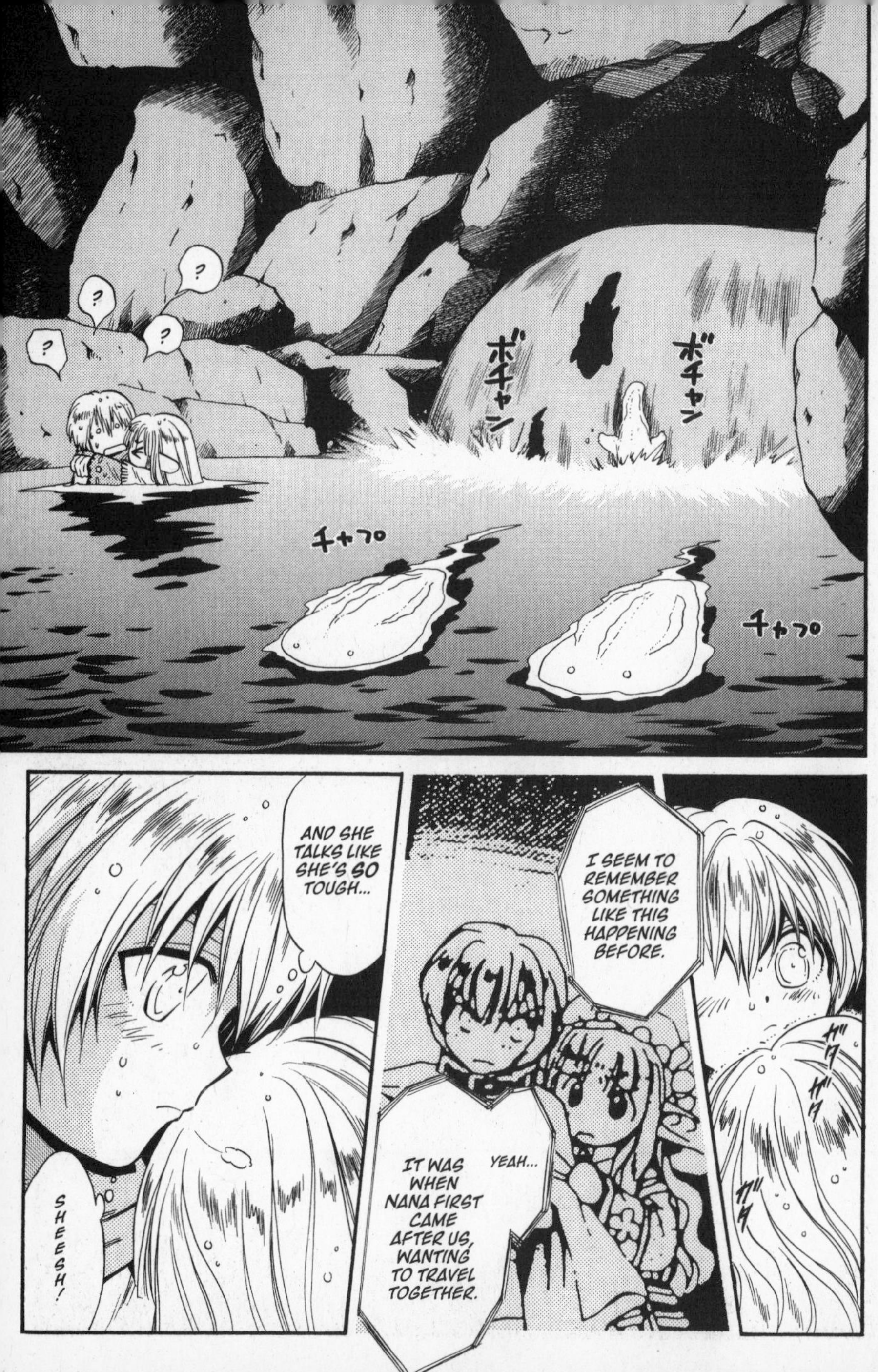
?
?
?
?
ボチャン
ボチャン
チャプ
チャプ
I SEEM TO REMEMBER SOMETHING LIKE THIS HAPPENING BEFORE.
ガクガク
ガク
YEAH...
IT WAS WHEN NANA FIRST CAME AFTER US, WANTING TO TRAVEL TOGETHER.
AND SHE TALKS LIKE SHE'S SO TOUGH...
SHEESH!

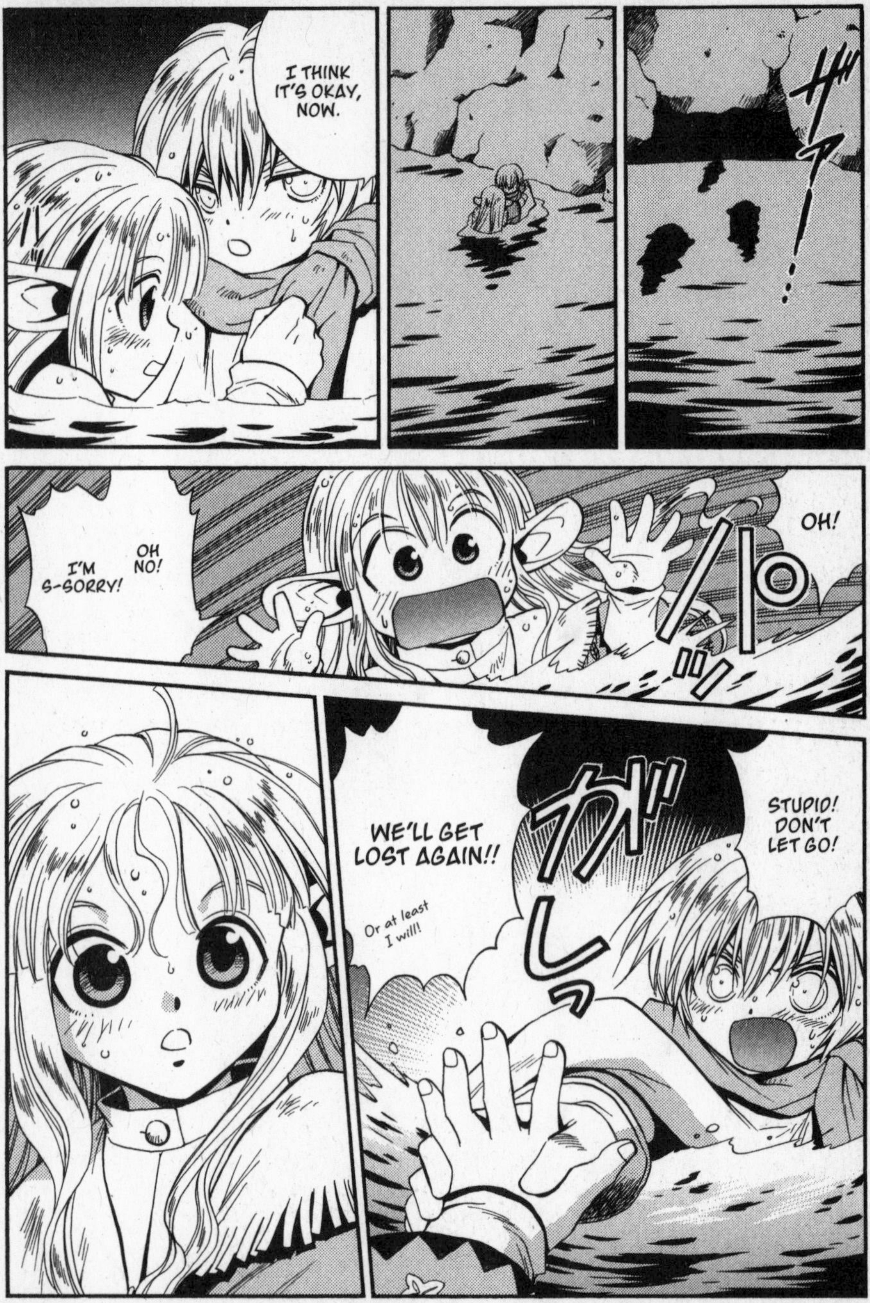
I THINK IT'S OKAY, NOW.
OH!
OH NO!
I'M S-SORRY!
STUPID! DON'T LET GO!
がしっ
WE'LL GET LOST AGAIN!!
Or at least I will!

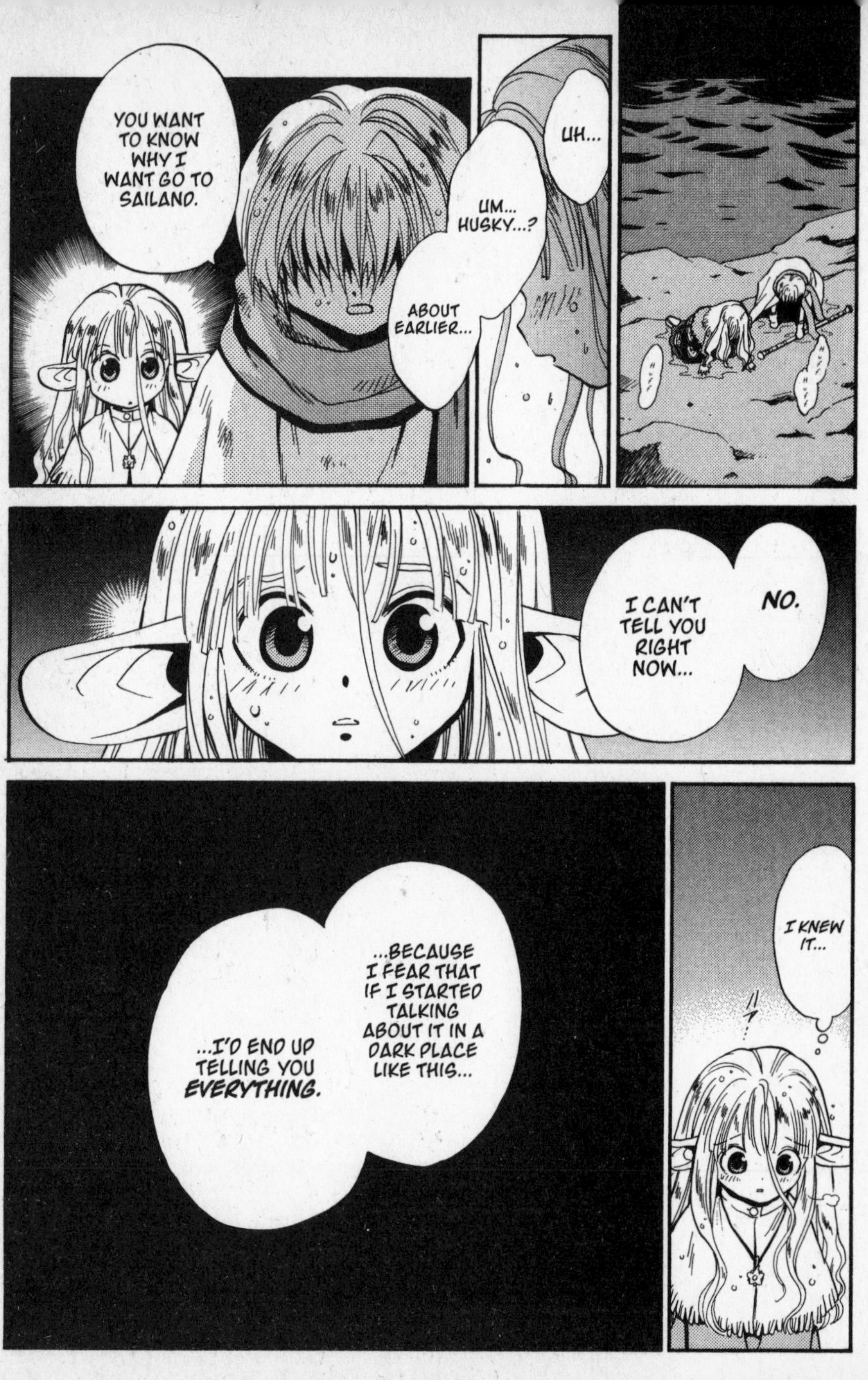
UH...
UM... HUSKY...?
ABOUT EARLIER...
YOU WANT TO KNOW WHY I WANT GO TO SAILAND.
NO.
I CAN'T TELL YOU RIGHT NOW...
I KNEW IT...
...BECAUSE I FEAR THAT IF I STARTED TALKING ABOUT IT IN A DARK PLACE LIKE THIS...
...I'D END UP TELLING YOU EVERYTHING.

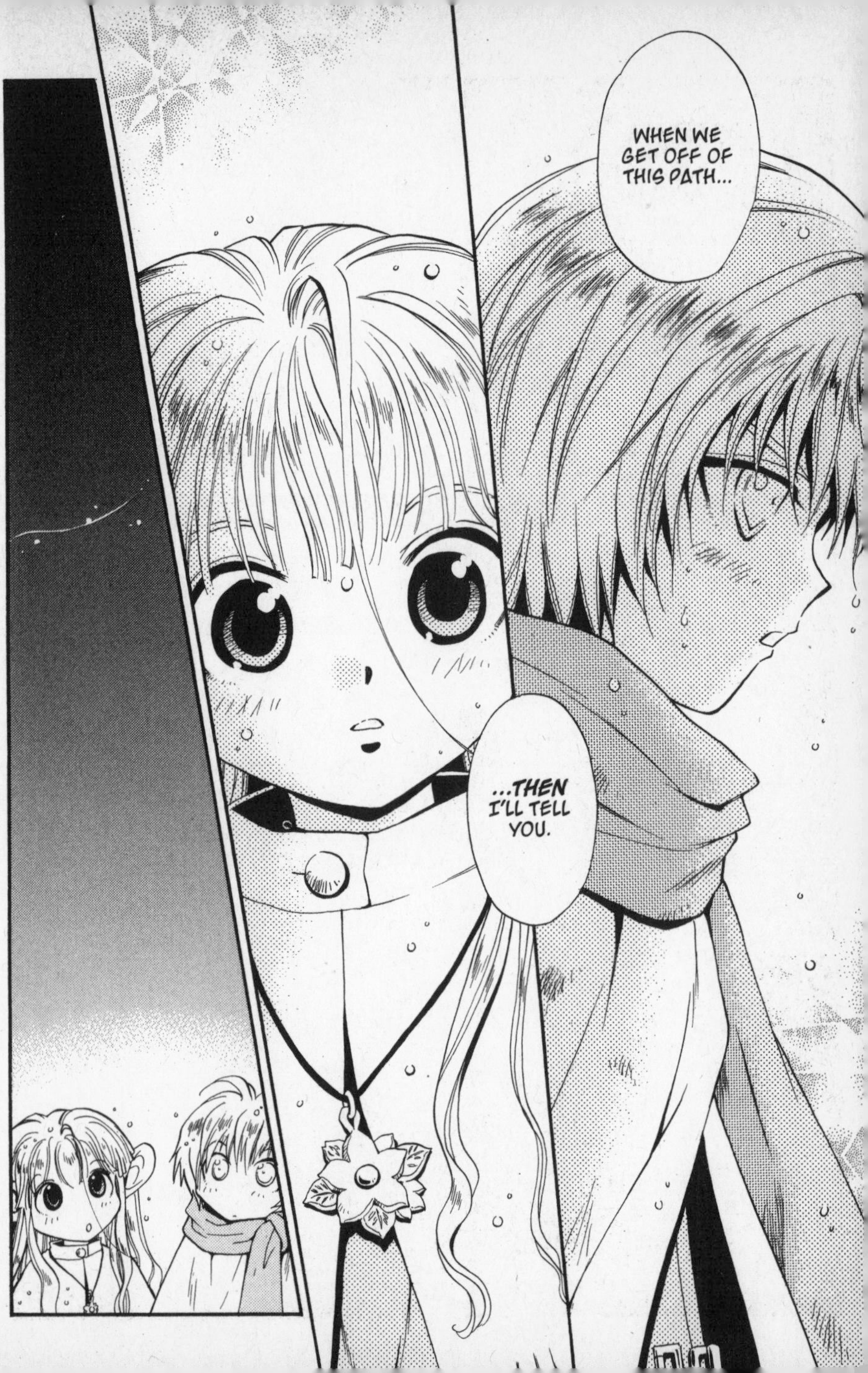
WHEN WE GET OFF OF THIS PATH...
...THEN I'LL TELL YOU.

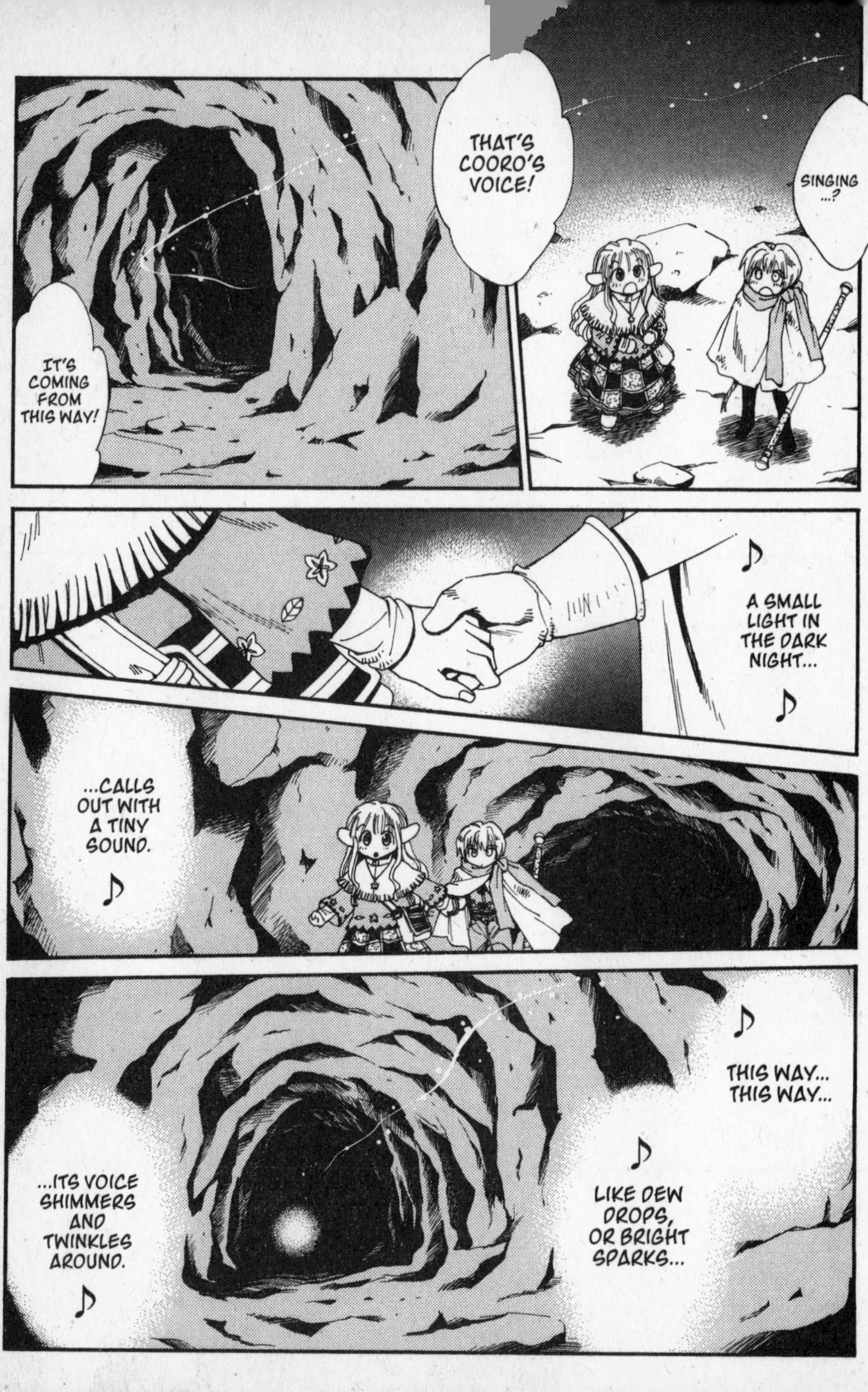
SINGING ...?
THAT'S COORO'S VOICE!
IT'S COMING FROM THIS WAY!
A SMALL LIGHT IN THE DARK NIGHT...
...CALLS OUT WITH A TINY SOUND.
THIS WAY... THIS WAY...
LIKE DEW DROPS, OR BRIGHT SPARKS...
...ITS VOICE SHIMMERS AND TWINKLES AROUND.

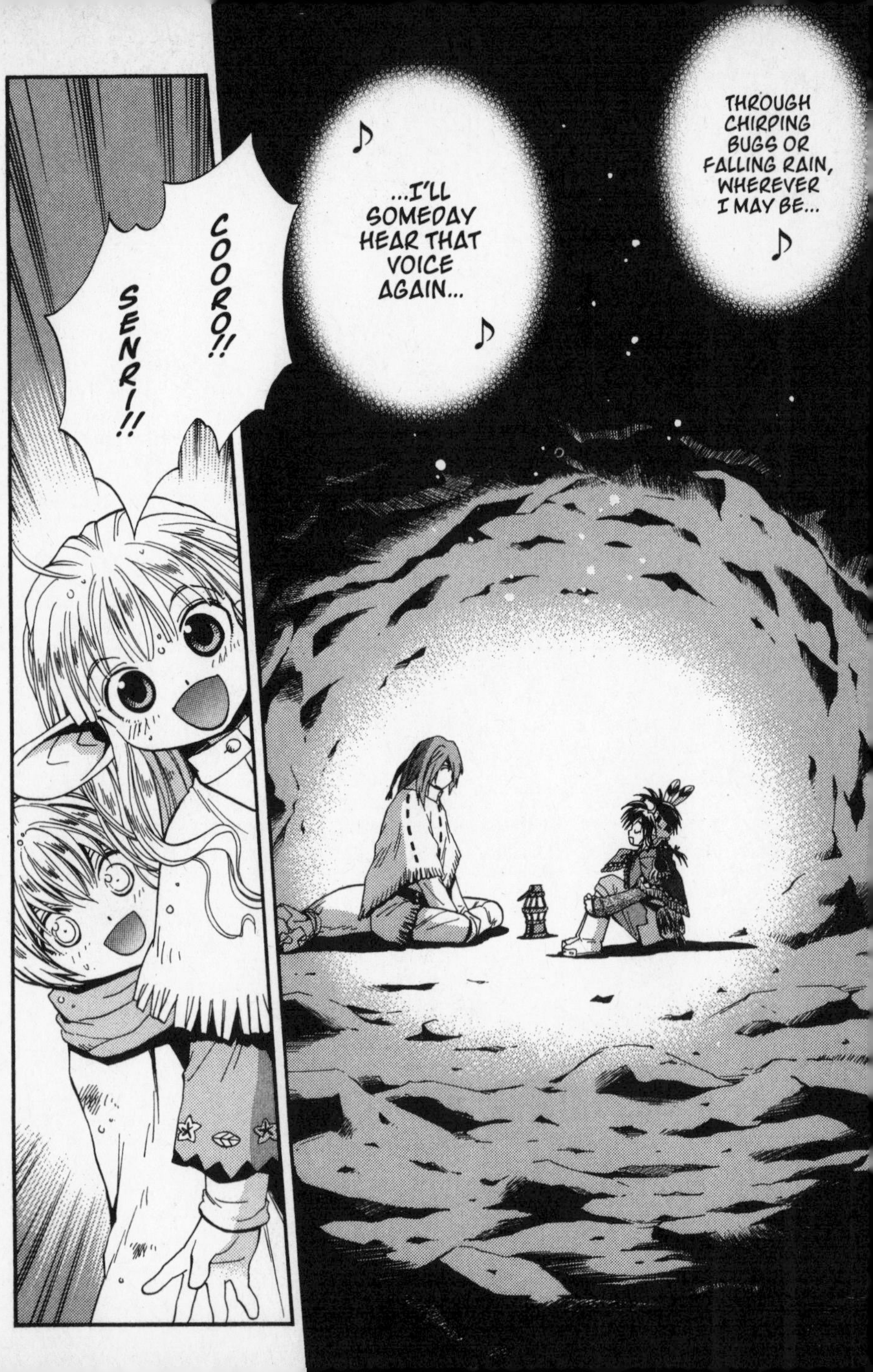
THROUGH CHIRPING BUGS OR FALLING RAIN, WHEREVER I MAY BE... ♪
♪ ...I'LL SOMEDAY HEAR THAT VOICE AGAIN... ♪
COORO!! SENRI!!

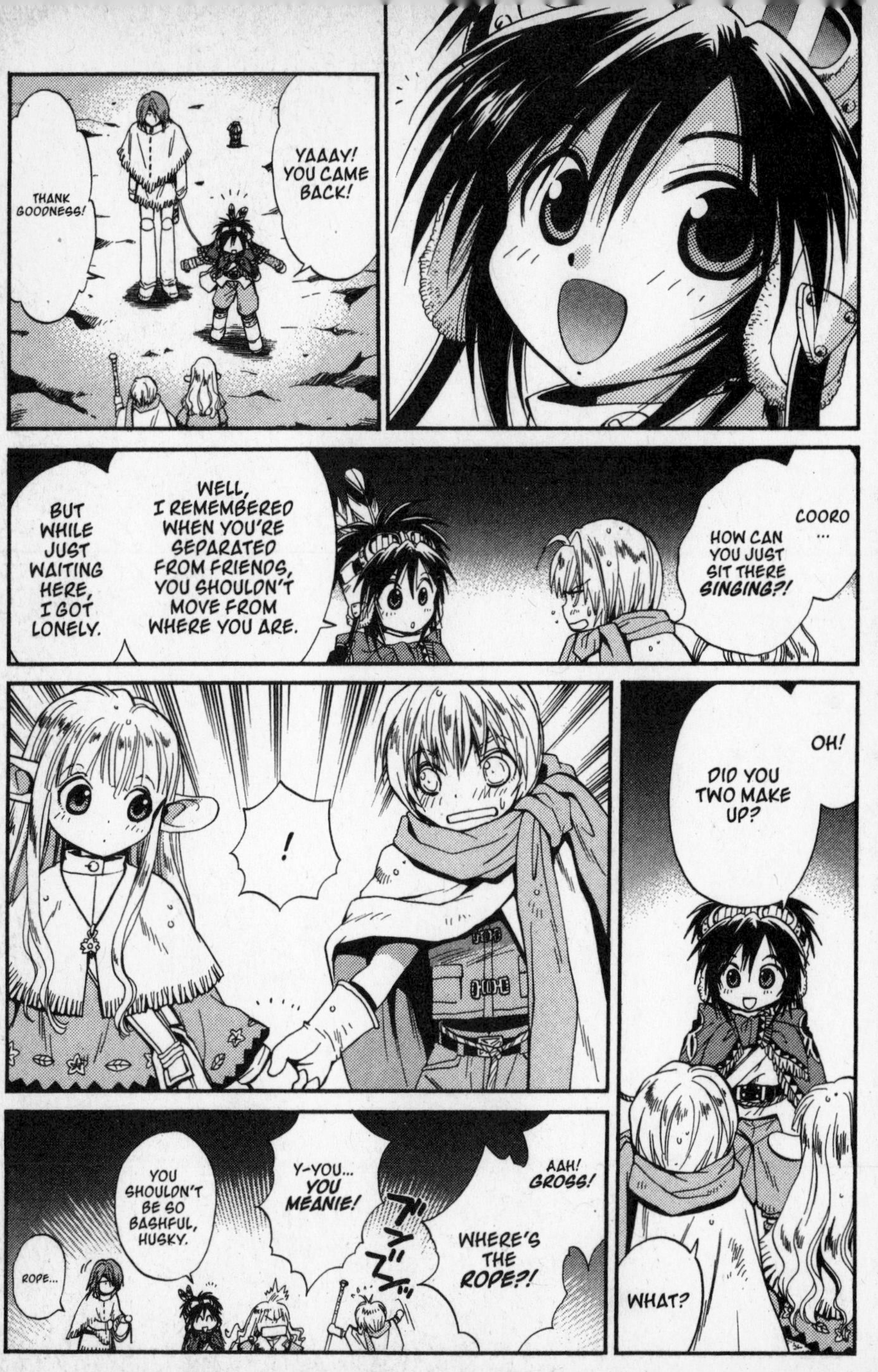
YAAAY! YOU CAME BACK!
THANK GOODNESS!
COORO ...
HOW CAN YOU JUST SIT THERE SINGING?!
WELL, I REMEMBERED WHEN YOU'RE SEPARATED FROM FRIENDS, YOU SHOULON'T MOVE FROM WHERE YOU ARE.
BUT WHILE JUST WAITING HERE, I GOT LONELY.
OH!
DID YOU TWO MAKE UP?
WHAT?
!
AAH! GROSS!
WHERE'S THE ROPE?!
Y-YOU... YOU MEANIE!
YOU SHOULON'T BE SO BASHFUL, HUSKY.
ROPE...

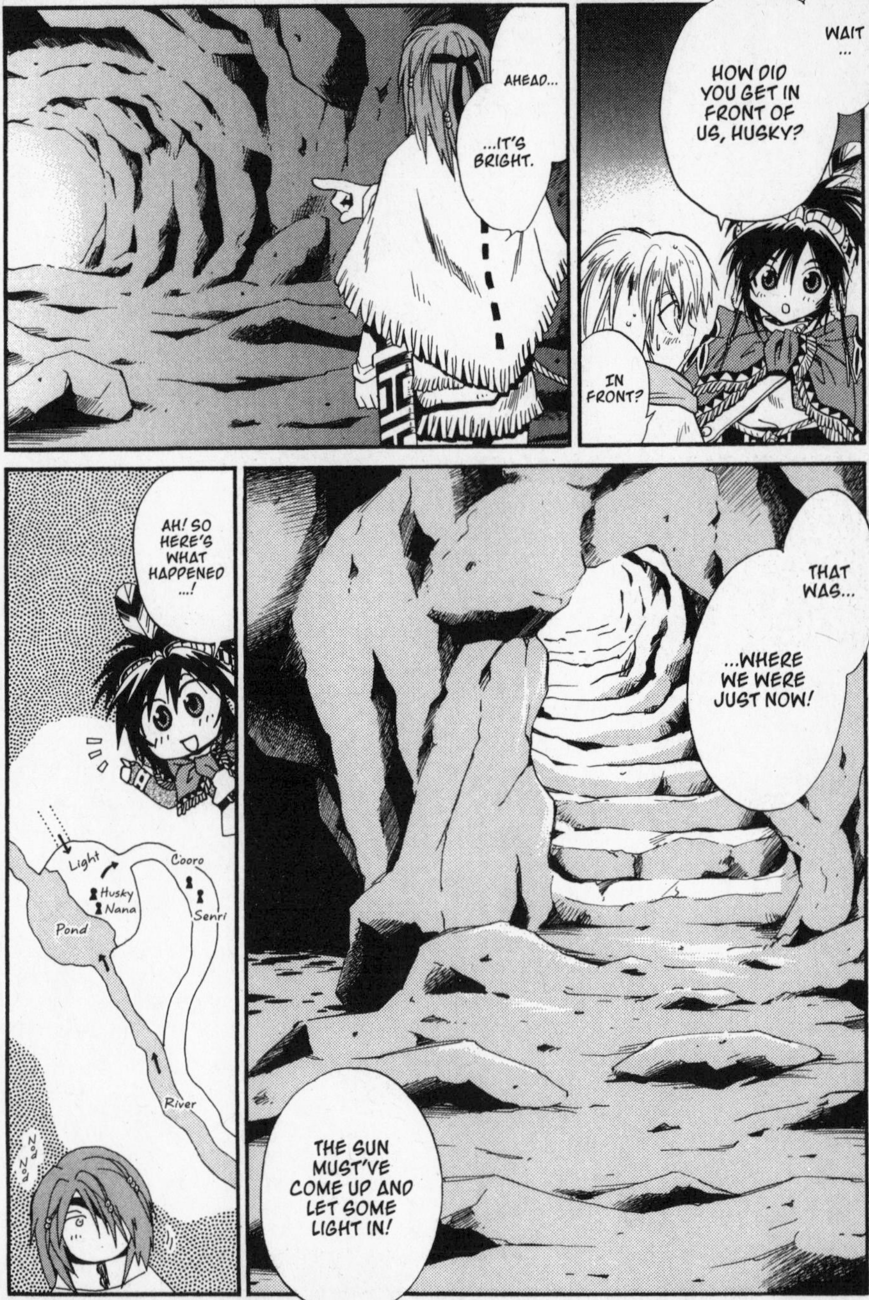
WAIT ...
HOW DID YOU GET IN FRONT OF US, HUSKY?
IN FRONT?
AHEAD...
...IT'S BRIGHT.
THAT WAS...
...WHERE WE WERE JUST NOW!
THE SUN MUST'VE COME UP AND LET SOME LIGHT IN!
AH! SO HERE'S WHAT HAPPENED ...!
Light
Cooro
Husky
Nana
Senri
Pond
River
Nod Nod

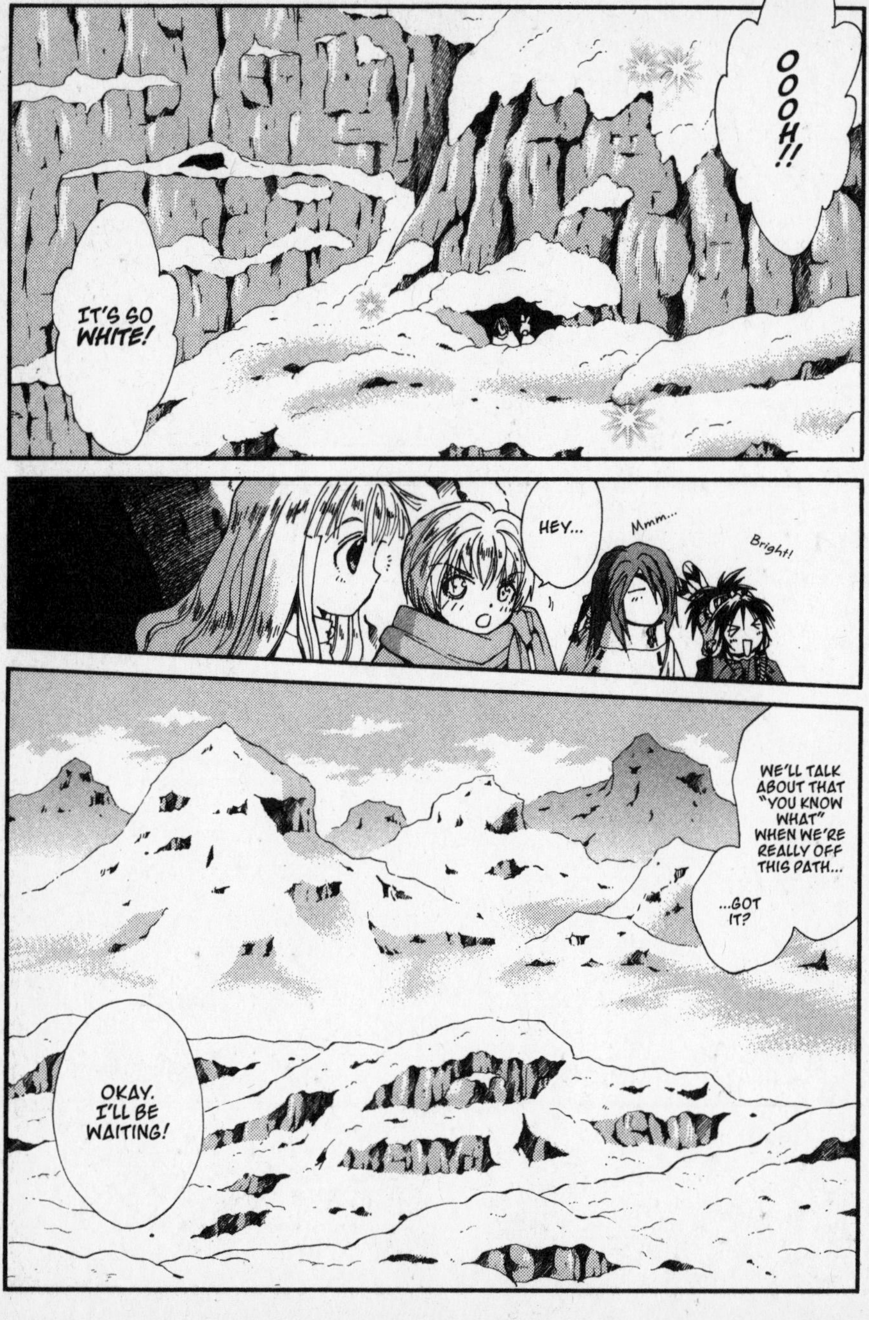
OOOOH!!
IT'S SO WHITE!
Bright!
Mmm...
HEY...
WE'LL TALK ABOUT THAT "YOU KNOW WHAT" WHEN WE'RE REALLY OFF THIS PATH...
...GOT IT?
OKAY. I'LL BE WAITING!

Many terrible fish...

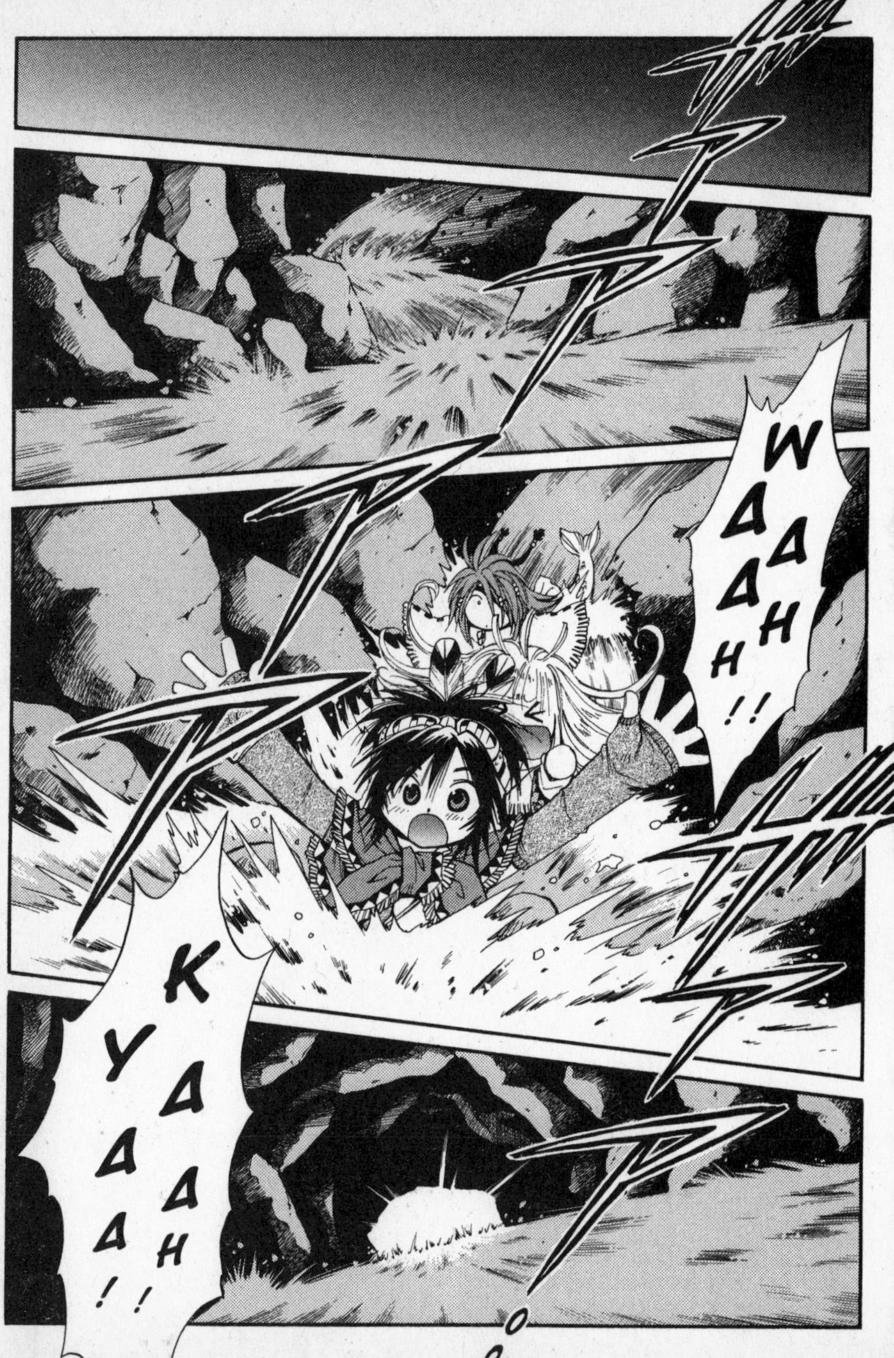
WAAAHH!!
KYAAAAH!!

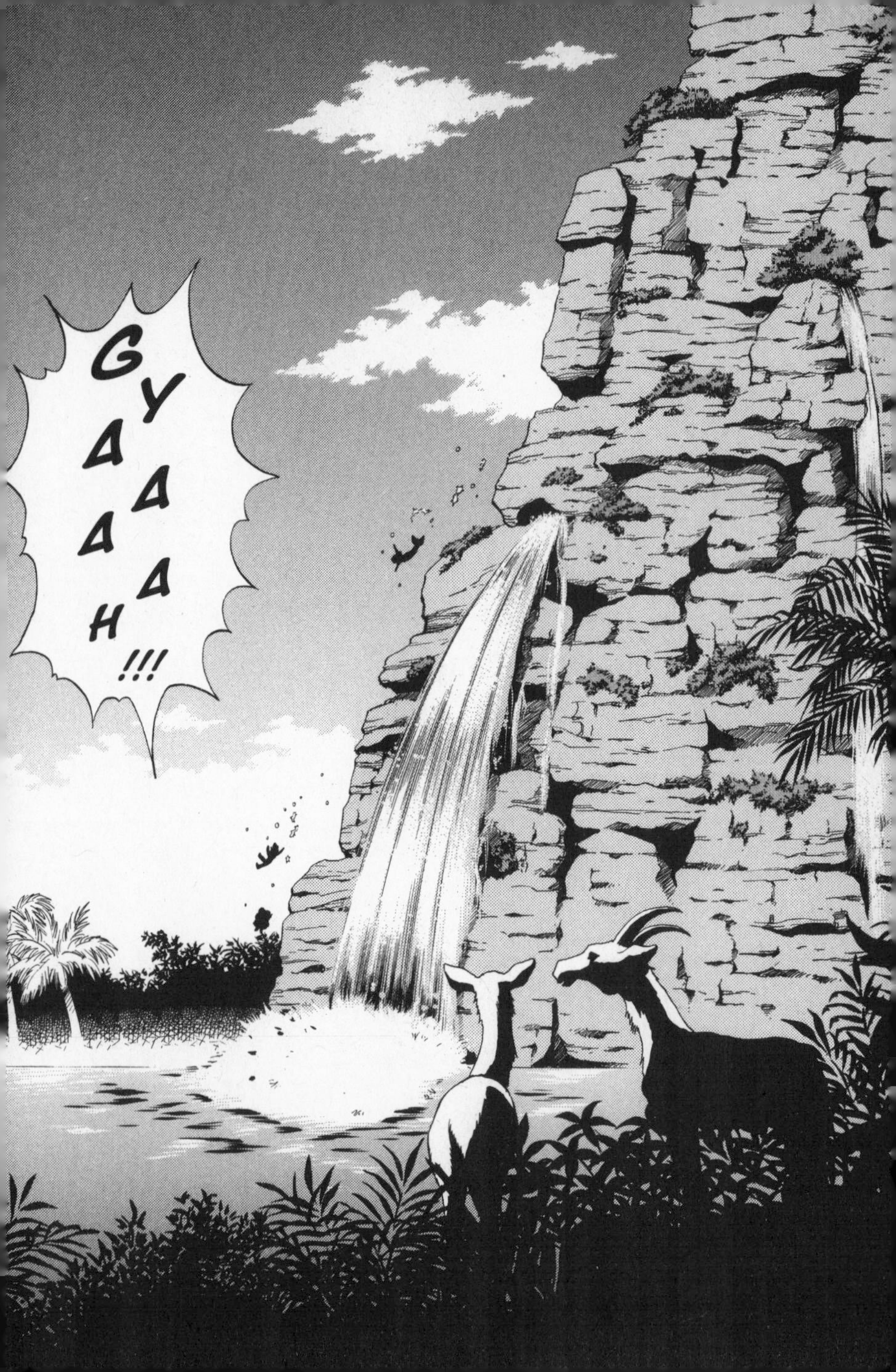
GYAAAAAH!!!

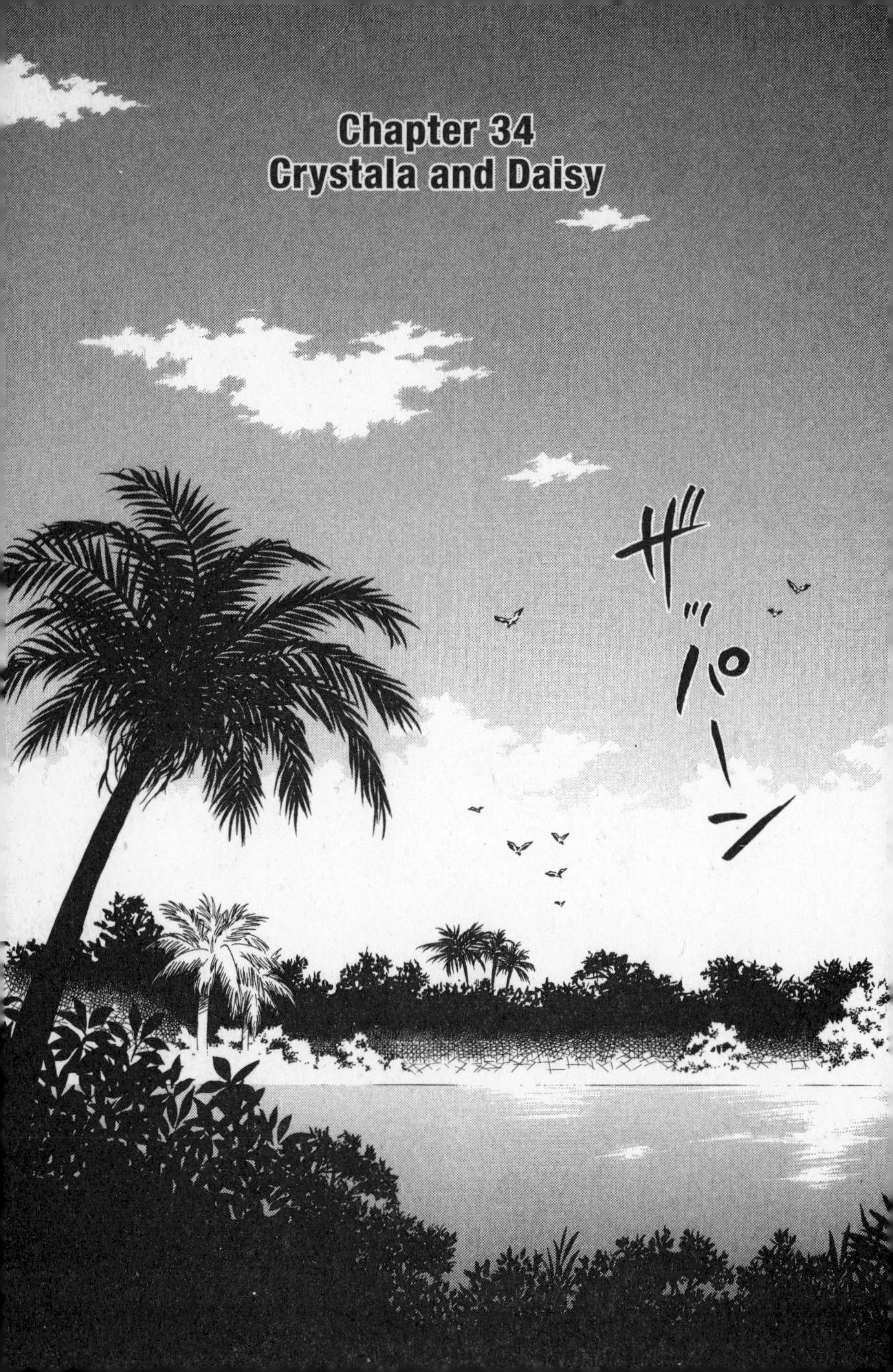
Chapter 34
Crystala and Daisy
ザパーン

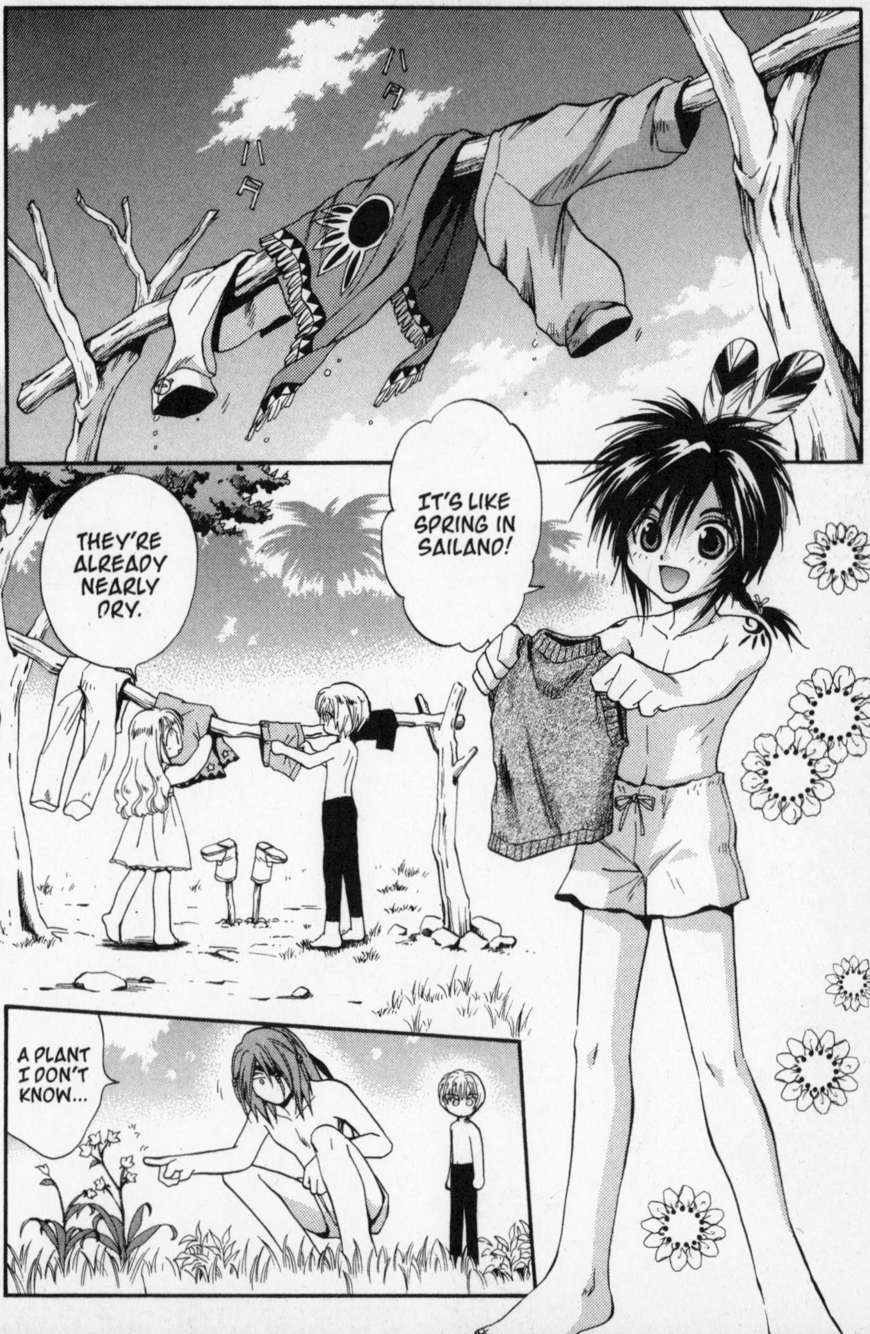
ハタ
ハタ
IT'S LIKE SPRING IN SAILAND!
THEY'RE ALREADY NEARLY DRY.
A PLANT I DON'T KNOW...

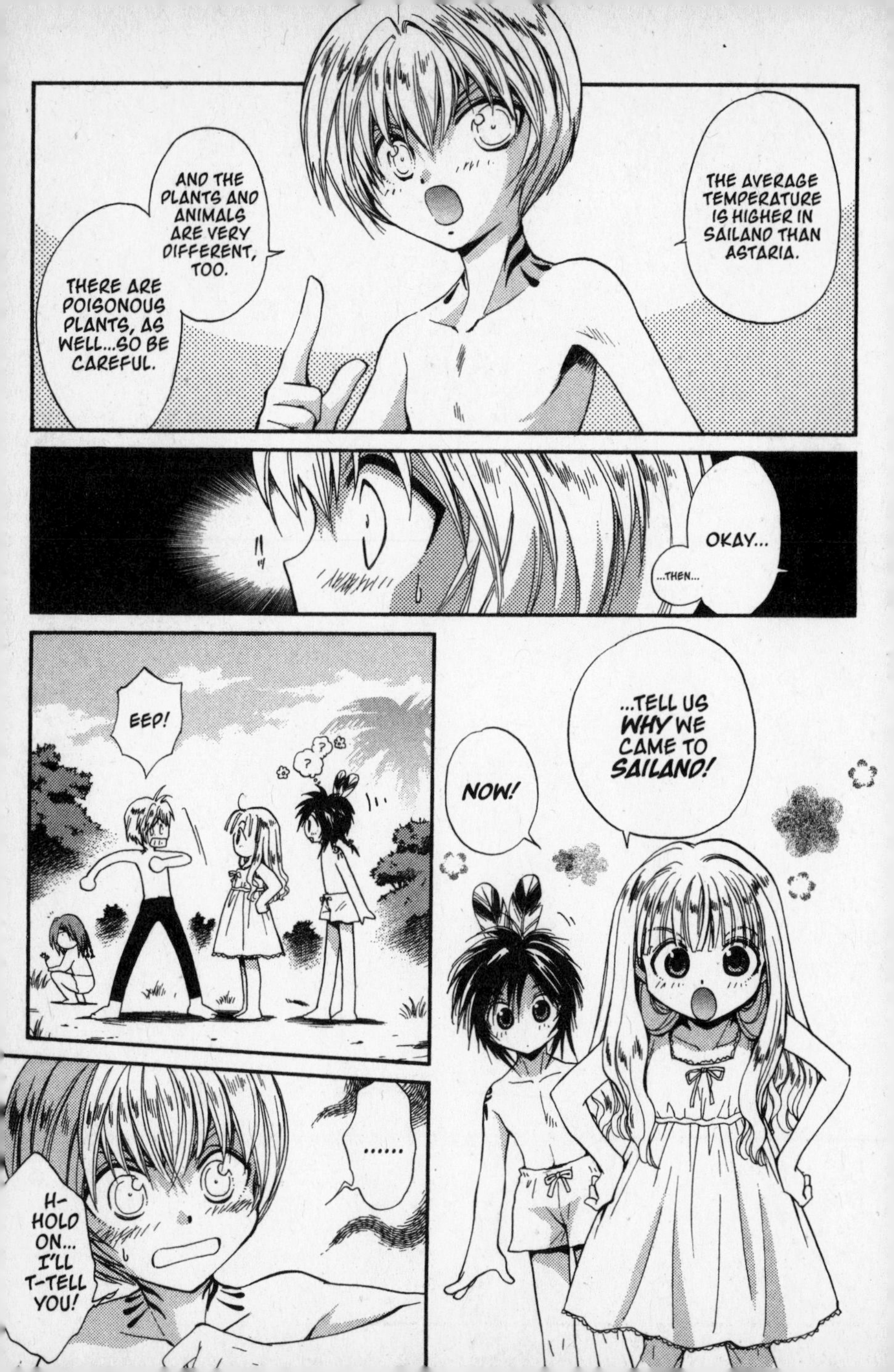
THE AVERAGE TEMPERATURE IS HIGHER IN SAILAND THAN ASTARIA.
AND THE PLANTS AND ANIMALS ARE VERY DIFFERENT, TOO.
THERE ARE POISONOUS PLANTS, AS WELL...SO BE CAREFUL.
OKAY...
...THEN...
!!
...TELL US WHY WE CAME TO SAILAND!
NOW!
EEP!
......
H-HOLD ON... I'LL T-TELL YOU!

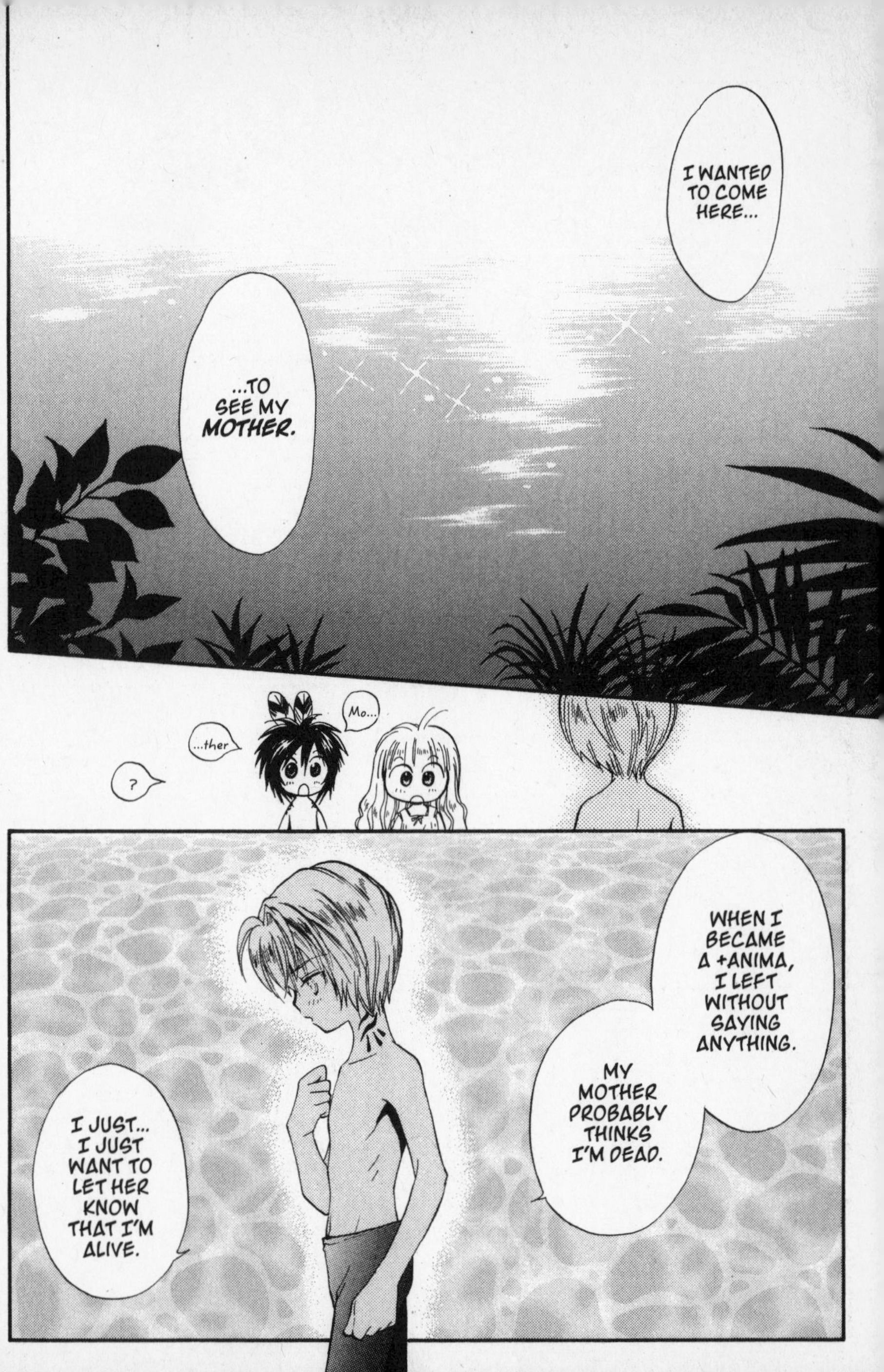
I WANTED TO COME HERE...
...TO SEE MY MOTHER.
Mo...
...ther
?
WHEN I BECAME A +ANIMA, I LEFT WITHOUT SAYING ANYTHING.
MY MOTHER PROBABLY THINKS I'M DEAD.
I JUST... I JUST WANT TO LET HER KNOW THAT I'M ALIVE.

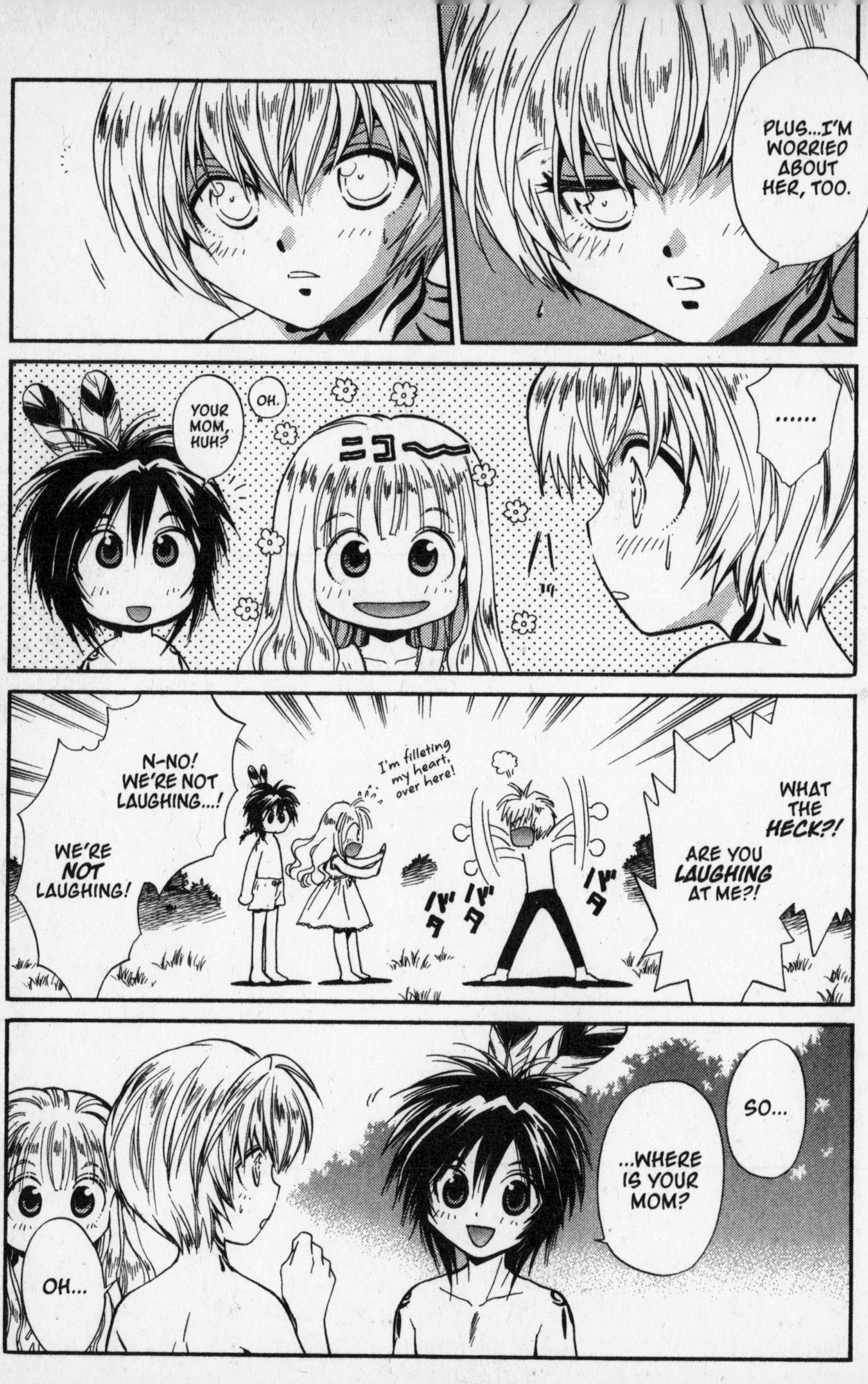
PLUS...I'M WORRIED ABOUT HER, TOO.
......
OH.
YOUR MOM, HUH?
ニコ〜〜
WHAT THE HECK?!
ARE YOU LAUGHING AT ME?!
バタ
バタ
バタ
I'm filleting my heart, over here!
N-NO! WE'RE NOT LAUGHING...!
WE'RE NOT LAUGHING!
SO...
...WHERE IS YOUR MOM?
OH...

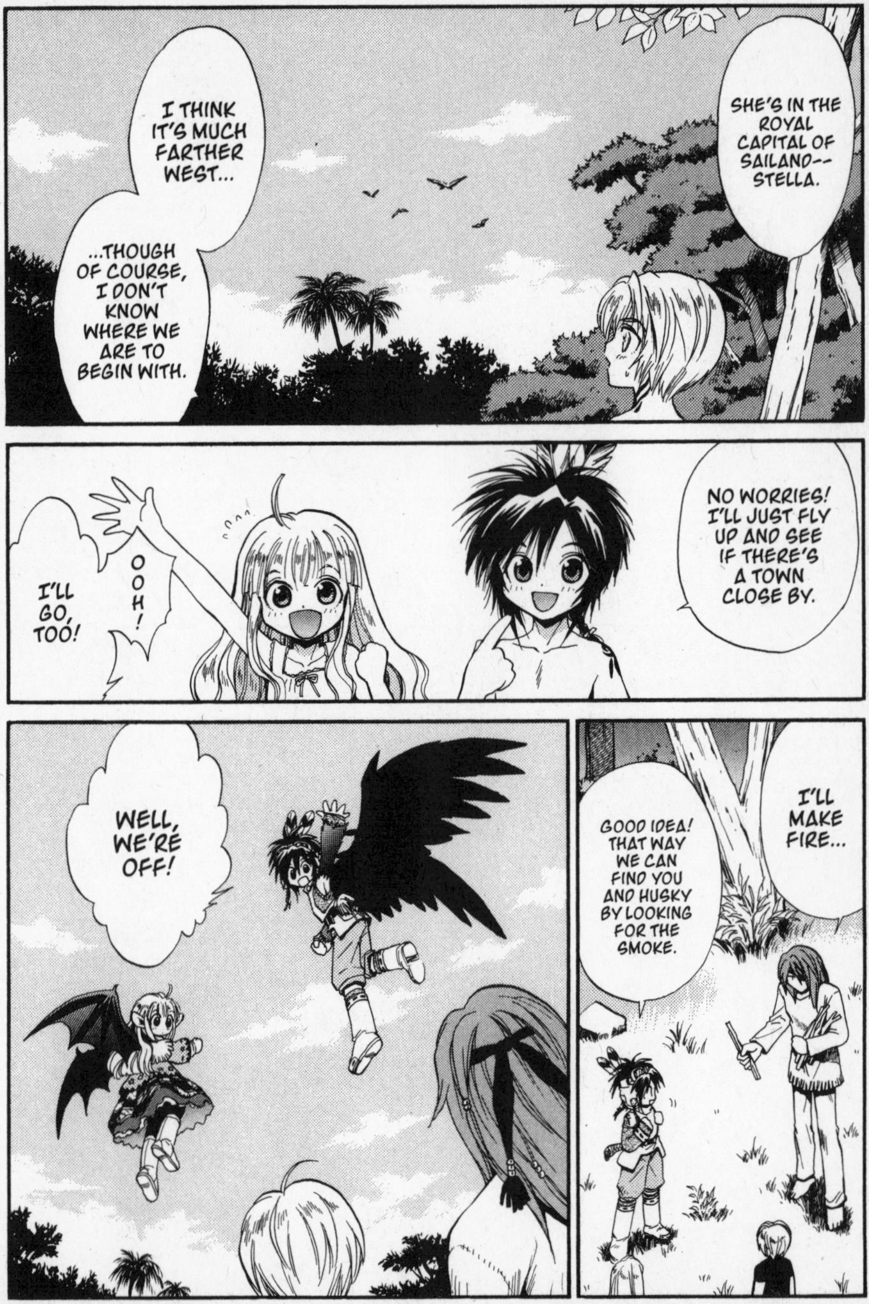
SHE'S IN THE ROYAL CAPITAL OF SAILANDO--STELLA.
I THINK IT'S MUCH FARTHER WEST...
...THOUGH OF COURSE, I DON'T KNOW WHERE WE ARE TO BEGIN WITH.
NO WORRIES! I'LL JUST FLY UP AND SEE IF THERE'S A TOWN CLOSE BY.
OOOH!
I'LL GO, TOO!
I'LL MAKE FIRE...
GOOD IDEA! THAT WAY WE CAN FIND YOU AND HUSKY BY LOOKING FOR THE SMOKE.
WELL, WE'RE OFF!

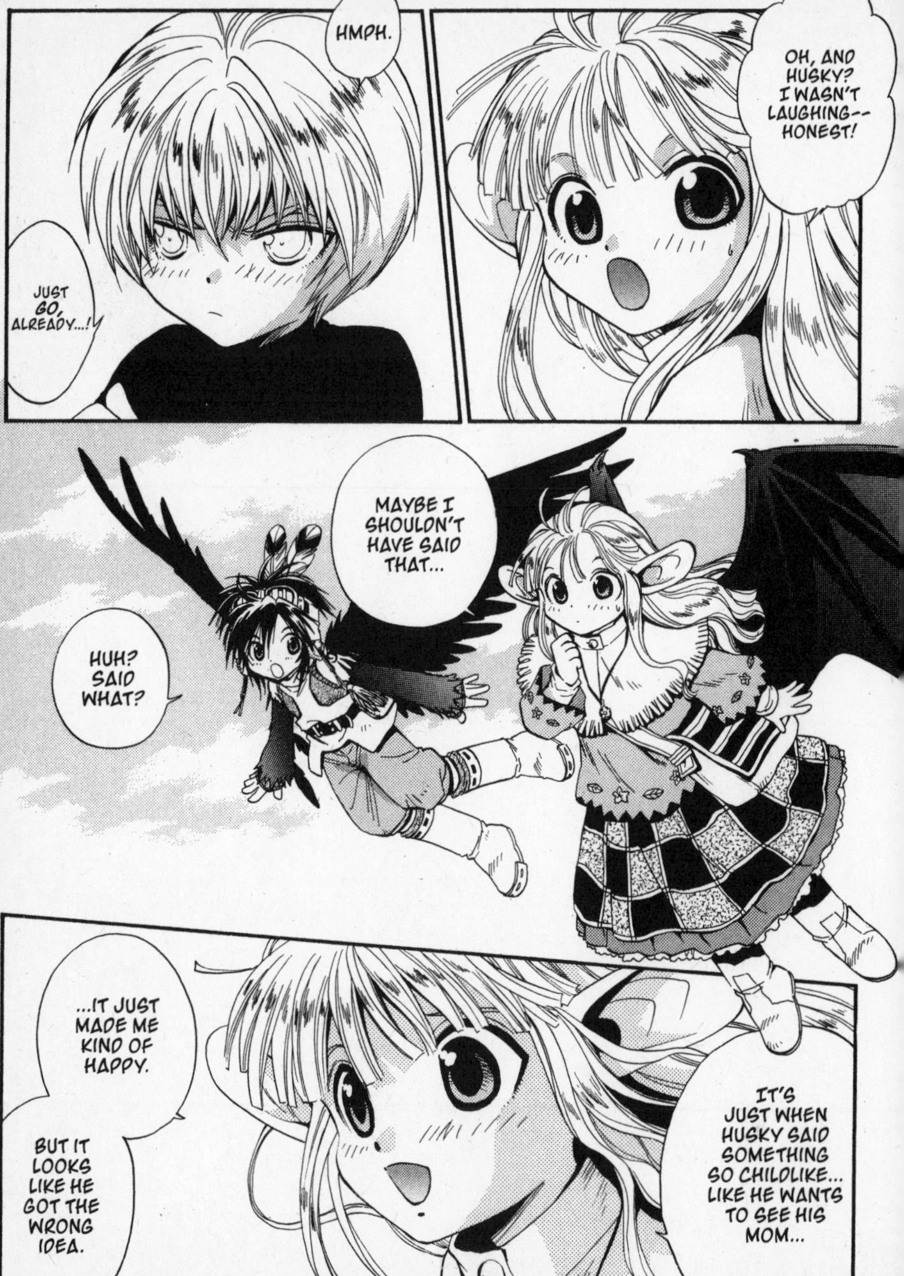
OH, AND HUSKY? I WASN'T LAUGHING--HONEST!
HMPH.
JUST GO, ALREADY...!
MAYBE I SHOULDN'T HAVE SAID THAT...
HUH? SAID WHAT?
IT'S JUST WHEN HUSKY SAID SOMETHING SO CHILDLIKE... LIKE HE WANTS TO SEE HIS MOM...
...IT JUST MADE ME KIND OF HAPPY.
BUT IT LOOKS LIKE HE GOT THE WRONG IDEA.

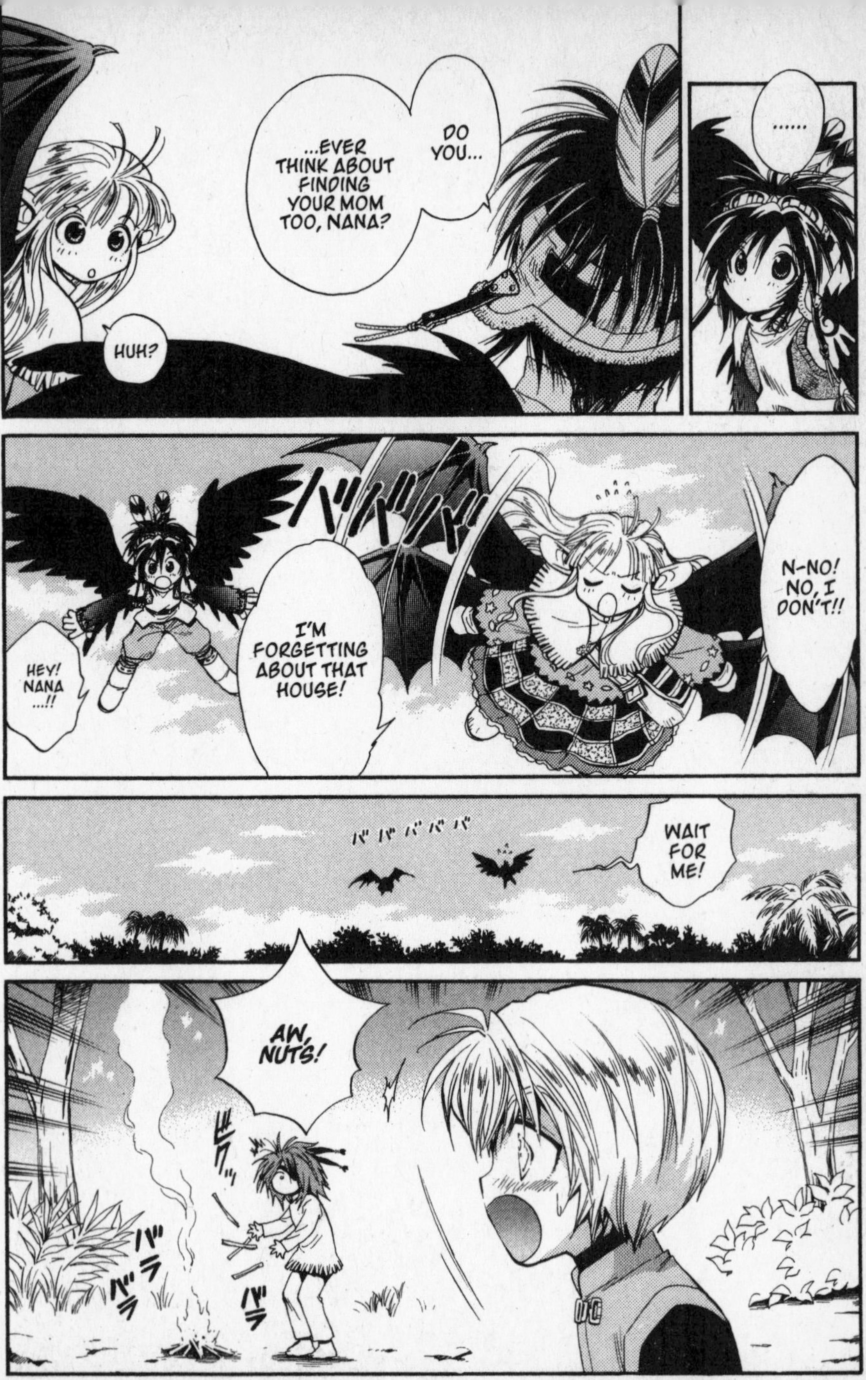
......
DO YOU...
...EVER THINK ABOUT FINDING YOUR MOM TOO, NANA?
HUH?
N-NO! NO, I DON'T!!
I'M FORGETTING ABOUT THAT HOUSE!
HEY! NANA ...!!
WAIT FOR ME!
AW, NUTS!

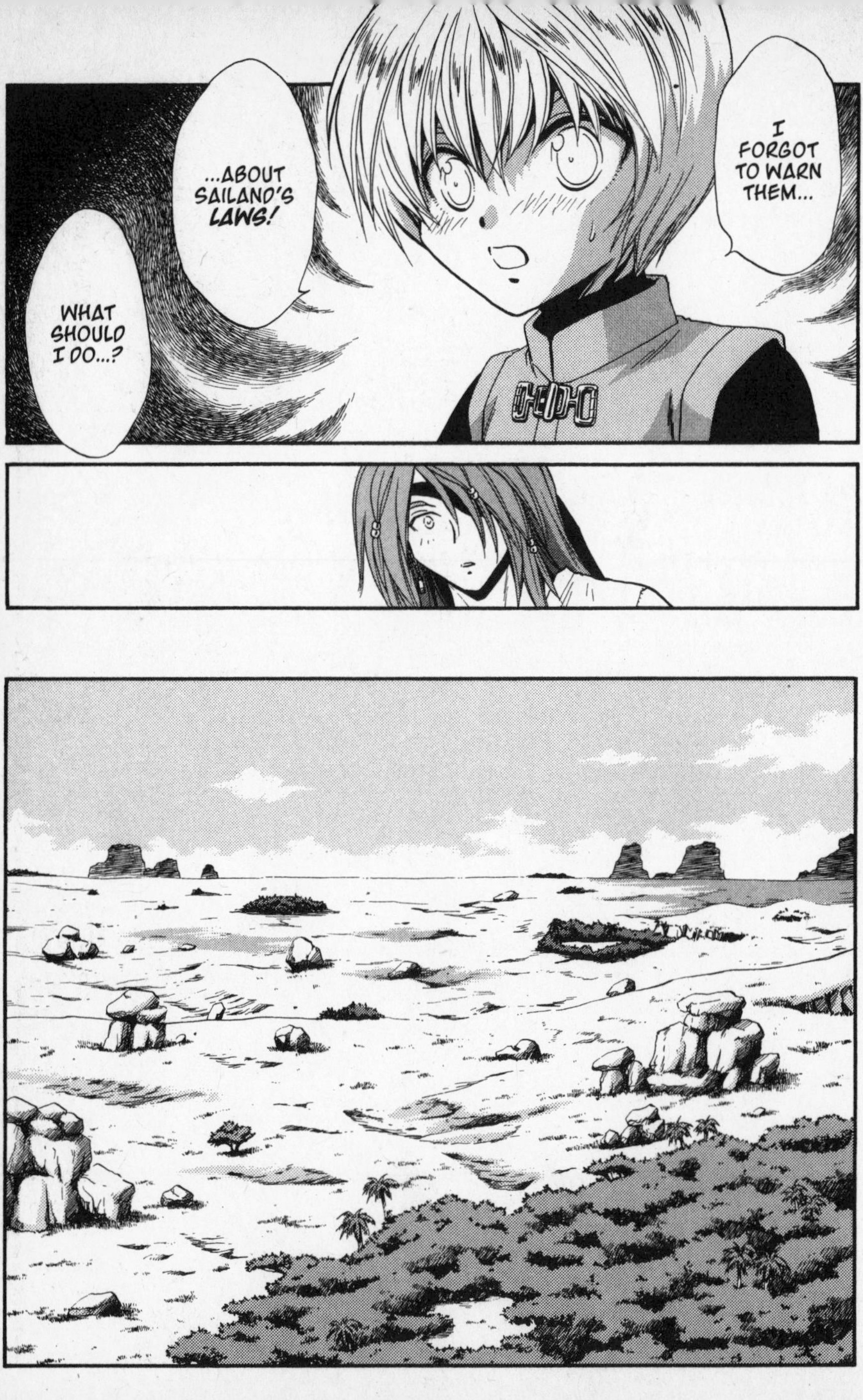
I FORGOT TO WARN THEM...
...ABOUT SAILAND'S **LAWS!**
WHAT SHOULD I DO...?

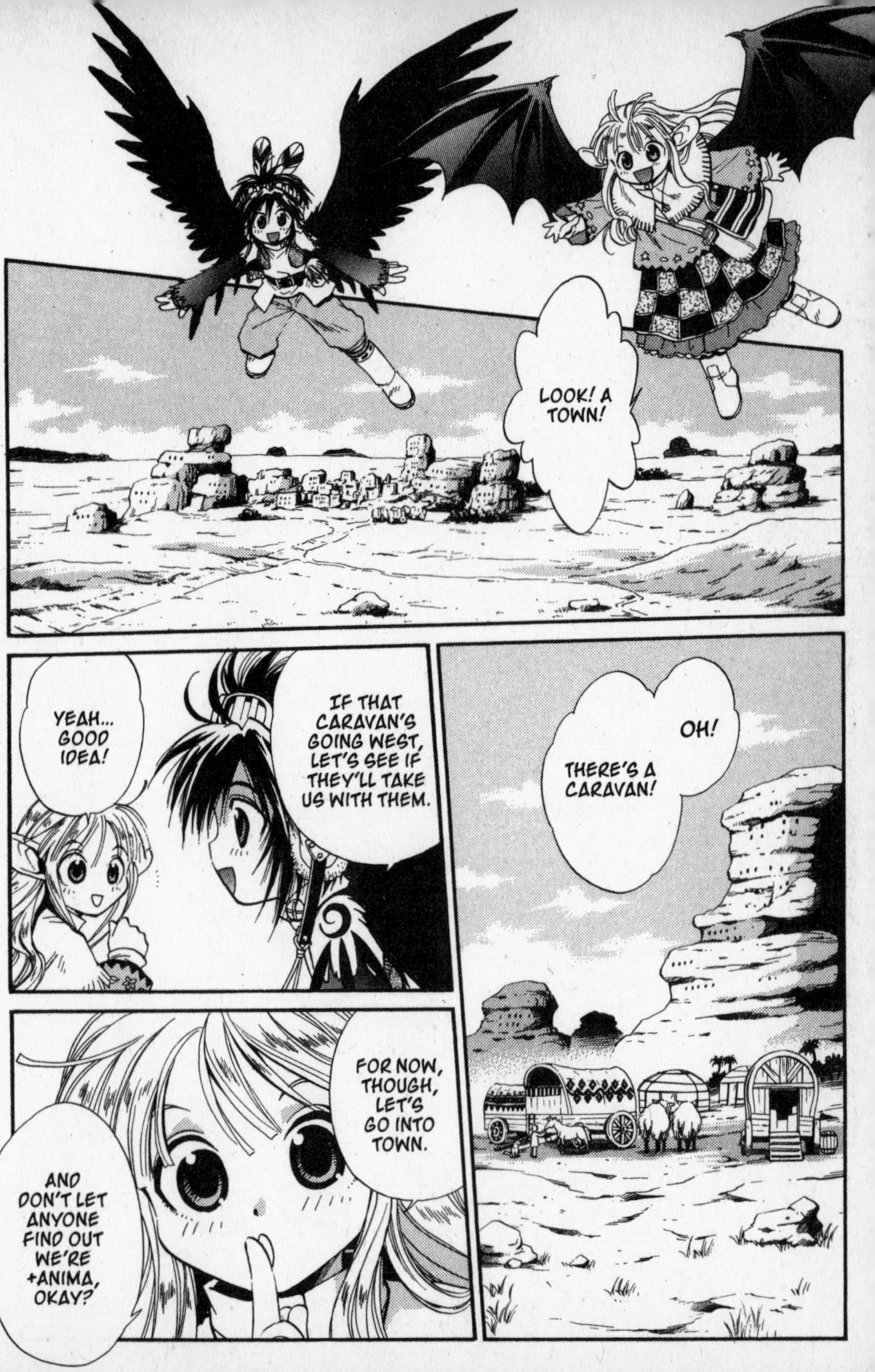

LOOK! A TOWN!
OH!
THERE'S A CARAVAN!
IF THAT CARAVAN'S GOING WEST, LET'S SEE IF THEY'LL TAKE US WITH THEM.
YEAH... GOOD IDEA!
FOR NOW, THOUGH, LET'S GO INTO TOWN.
AND DON'T LET ANYONE FIND OUT WE'RE +ANIMA, OKAY?

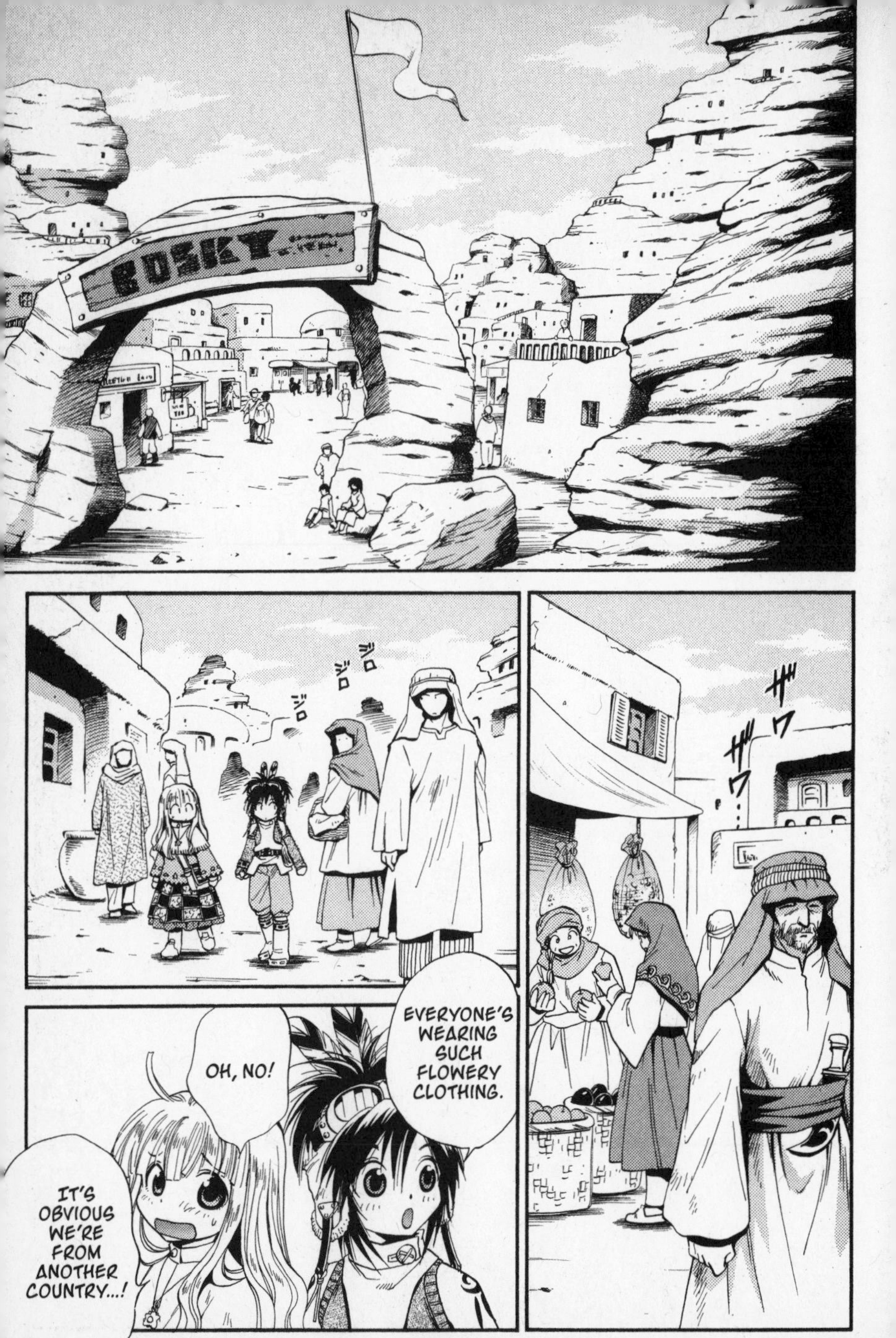
BOSKY
ザワ
ザワ…
ジロ
ジロ
ジロ
EVERYONE'S WEARING SUCH FLOWERY CLOTHING.
OH, NO!
IT'S OBVIOUS WE'RE FROM ANOTHER COUNTRY...!

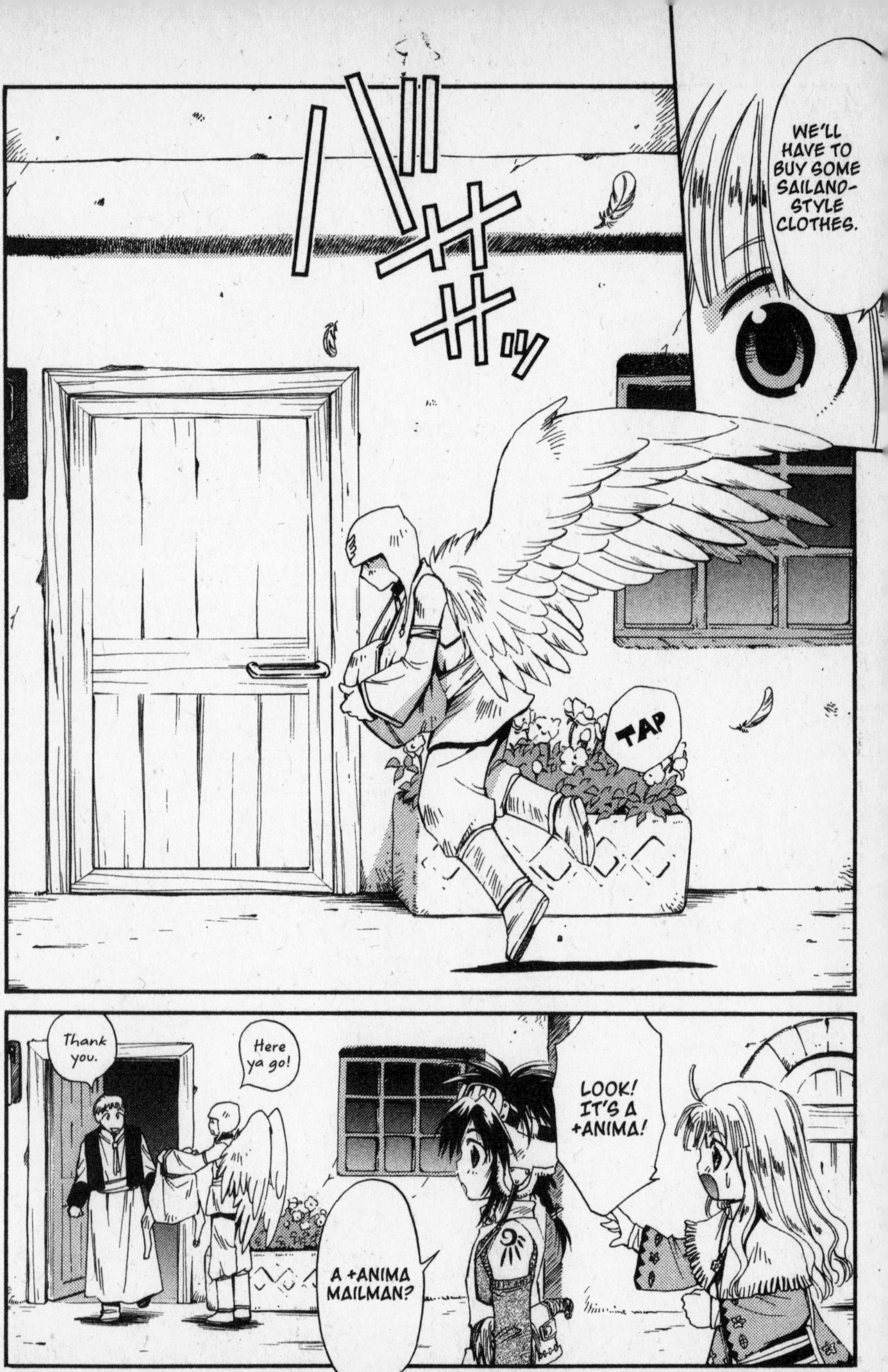
WE'LL HAVE TO BUY SOME SAILAND-STYLE CLOTHES.
バササッ
TAP
LOOK! IT'S A +ANIMA!
A +ANIMA MAILMAN?
Here ya go!
Thank you.

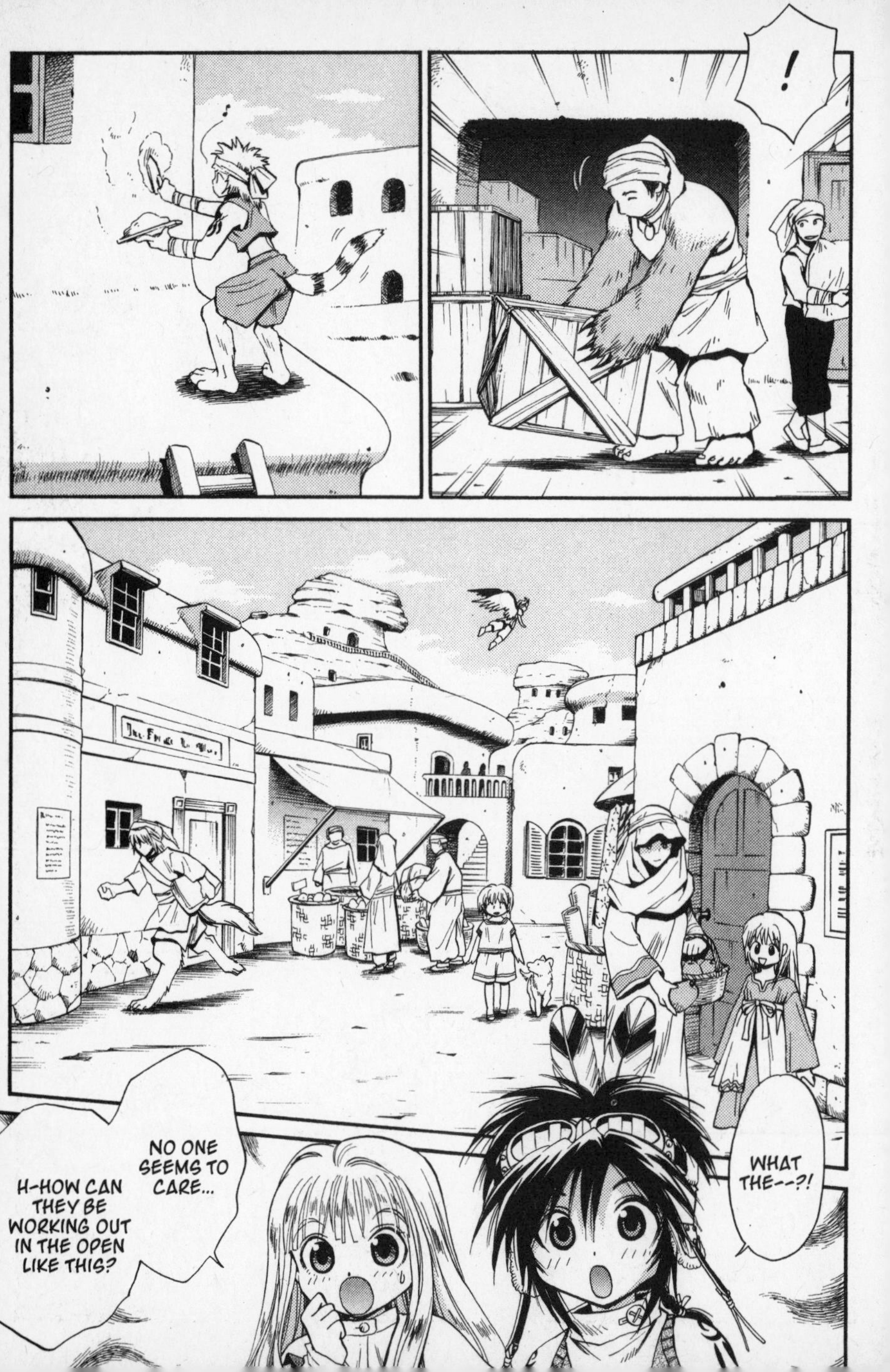
!
WHAT THE--?!
NO ONE SEEMS TO CARE...
H-HOW CAN THEY BE WORKING OUT IN THE OPEN LIKE THIS?

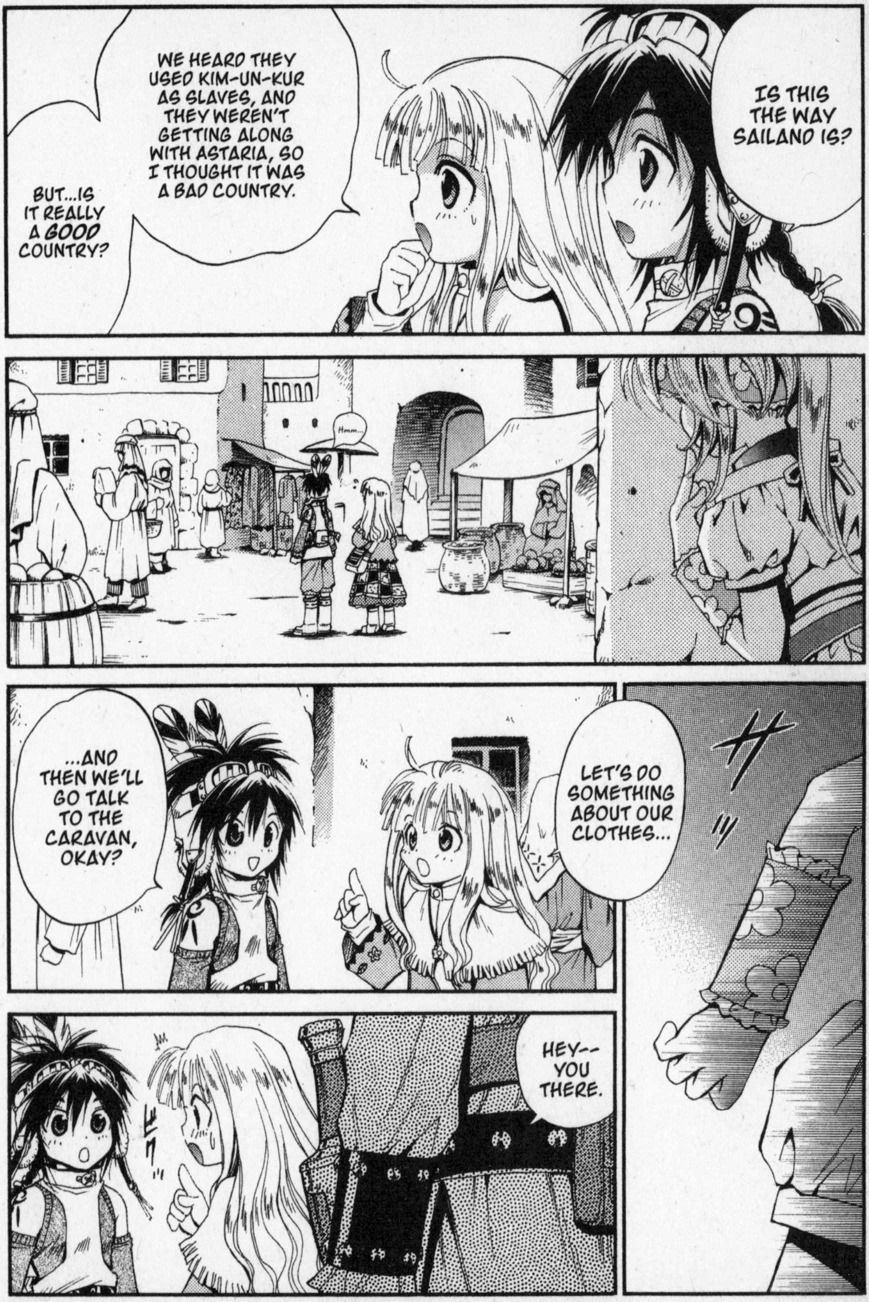
IS THIS THE WAY SAILAND IS?
WE HEARD THEY USED KIM-UN-KUR AS SLAVES, AND THEY WEREN'T GETTING ALONG WITH ASTARIA, SO I THOUGHT IT WAS A BAD COUNTRY.
BUT...IS IT REALLY A GOOD COUNTRY?
Hmm...
LET'S DO SOMETHING ABOUT OUR CLOTHES...
...AND THEN WE'LL GO TALK TO THE CARAVAN, OKAY?
HEY-- YOU THERE.

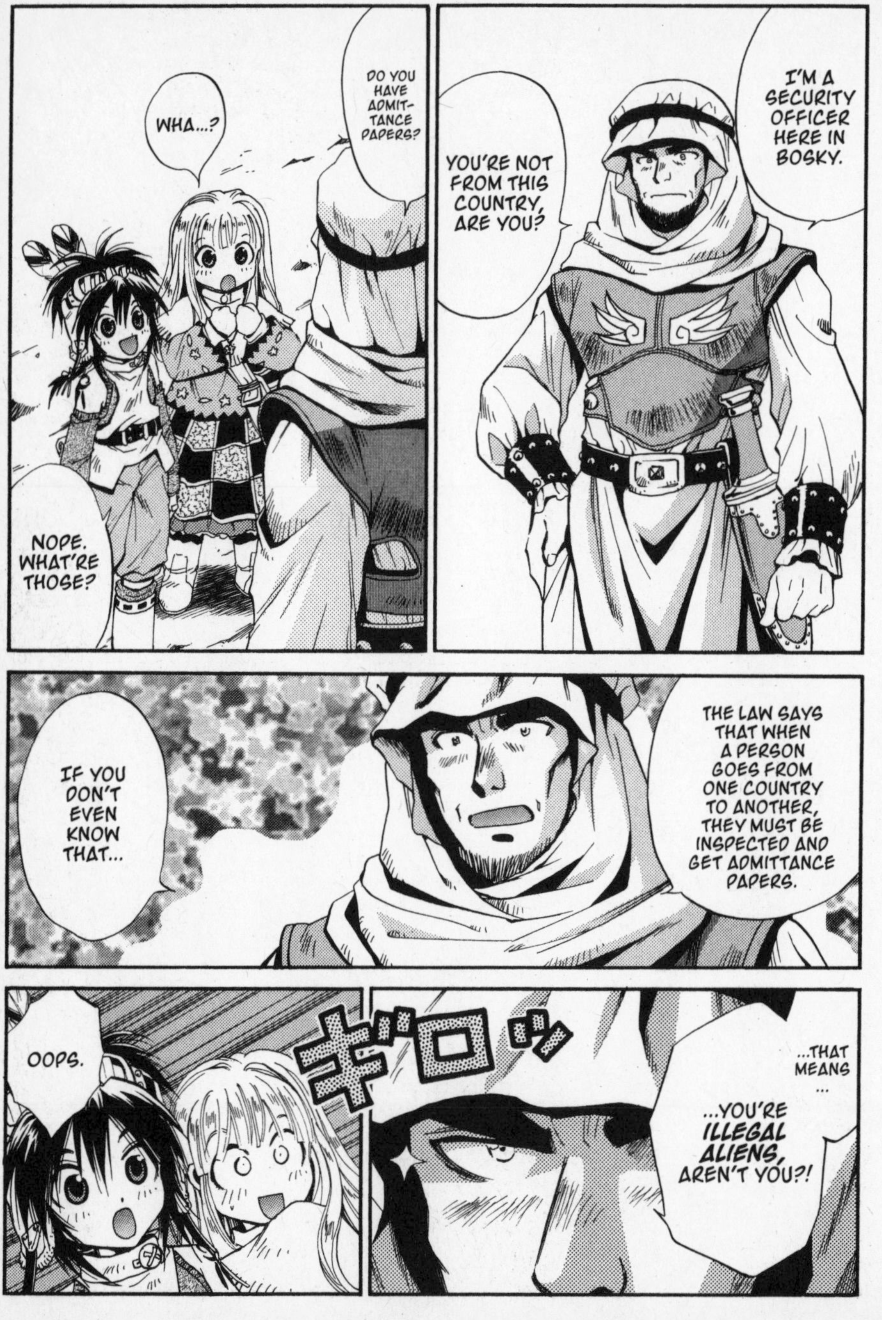
I'M A SECURITY OFFICER HERE IN BOSKY.
YOU'RE NOT FROM THIS COUNTRY, ARE YOU?
DO YOU HAVE ADMIT-TANCE PAPERS?
WHA...?
NOPE. WHAT'RE THOSE?
THE LAW SAYS THAT WHEN A PERSON GOES FROM ONE COUNTRY TO ANOTHER, THEY MUST BE INSPECTED AND GET ADMITTANCE PAPERS.
IF YOU DON'T EVEN KNOW THAT...
...THAT MEANS ...
...YOU'RE ***ILLEGAL ALIENS***, AREN'T YOU?!
ギロッ
OOPS.

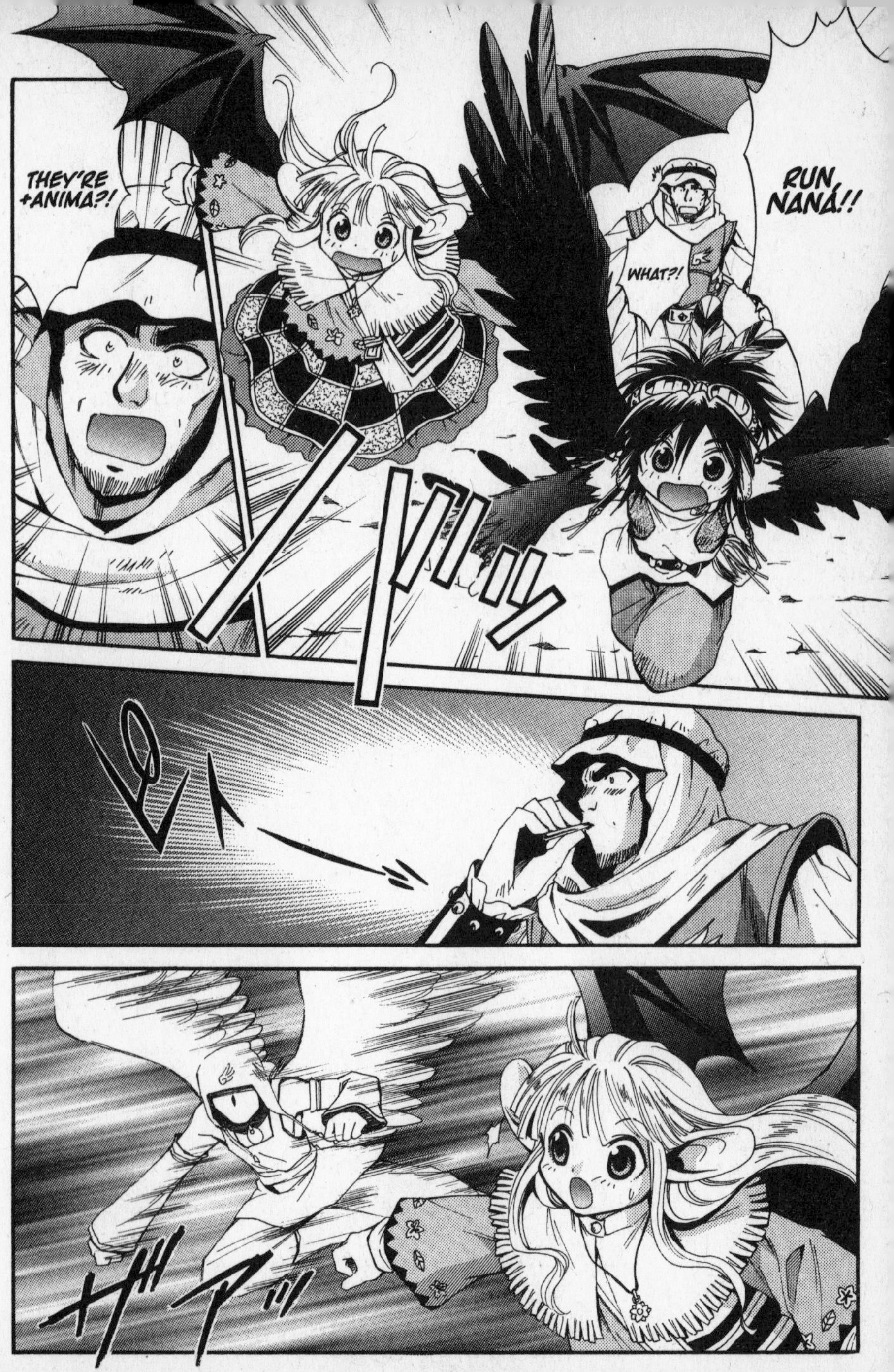
RUN, NANA!!
WHAT?!
THEY'RE +ANIMA?!

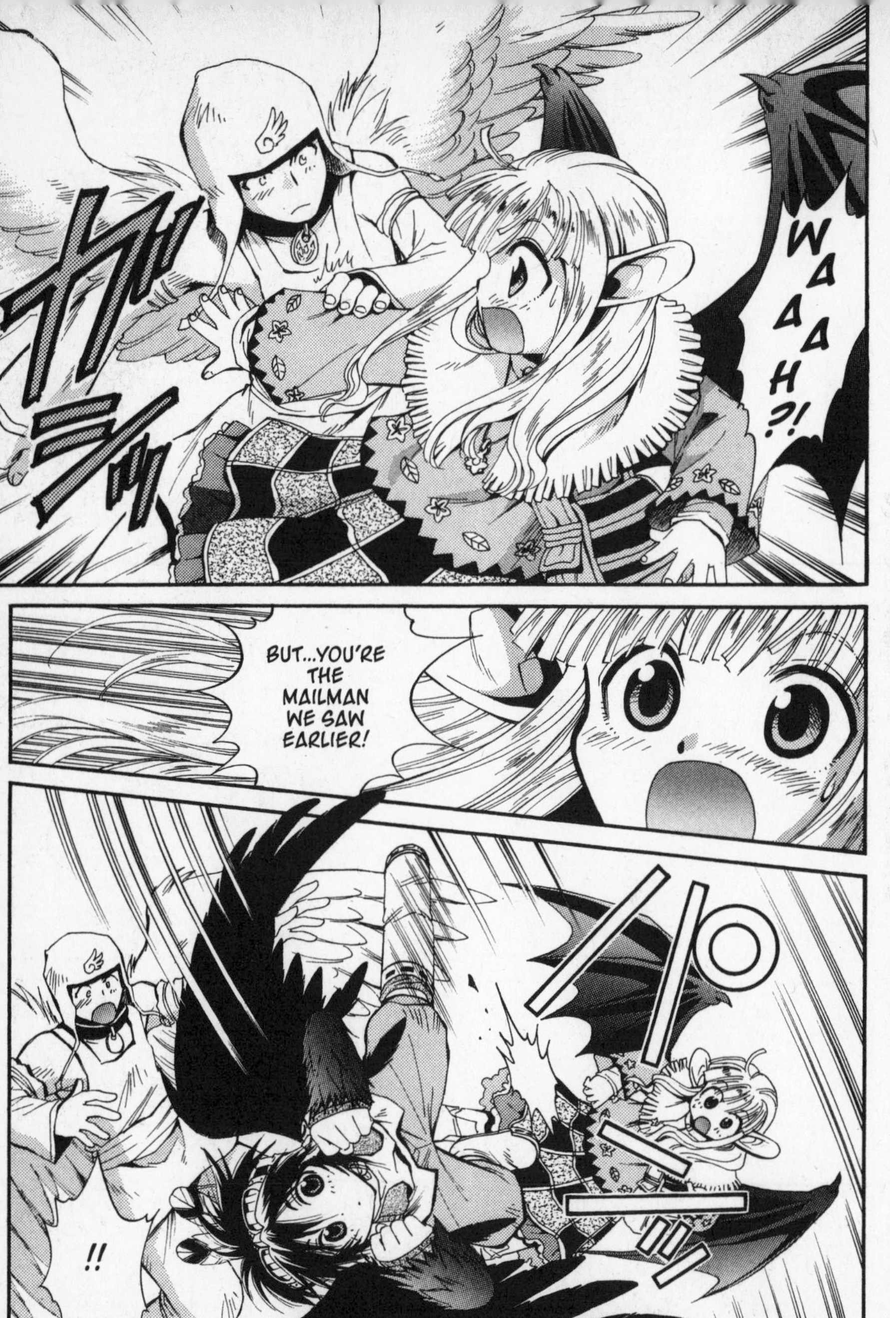
WAAAAH?!
BUT...YOU'RE THE MAILMAN WE SAW EARLIER!
!!

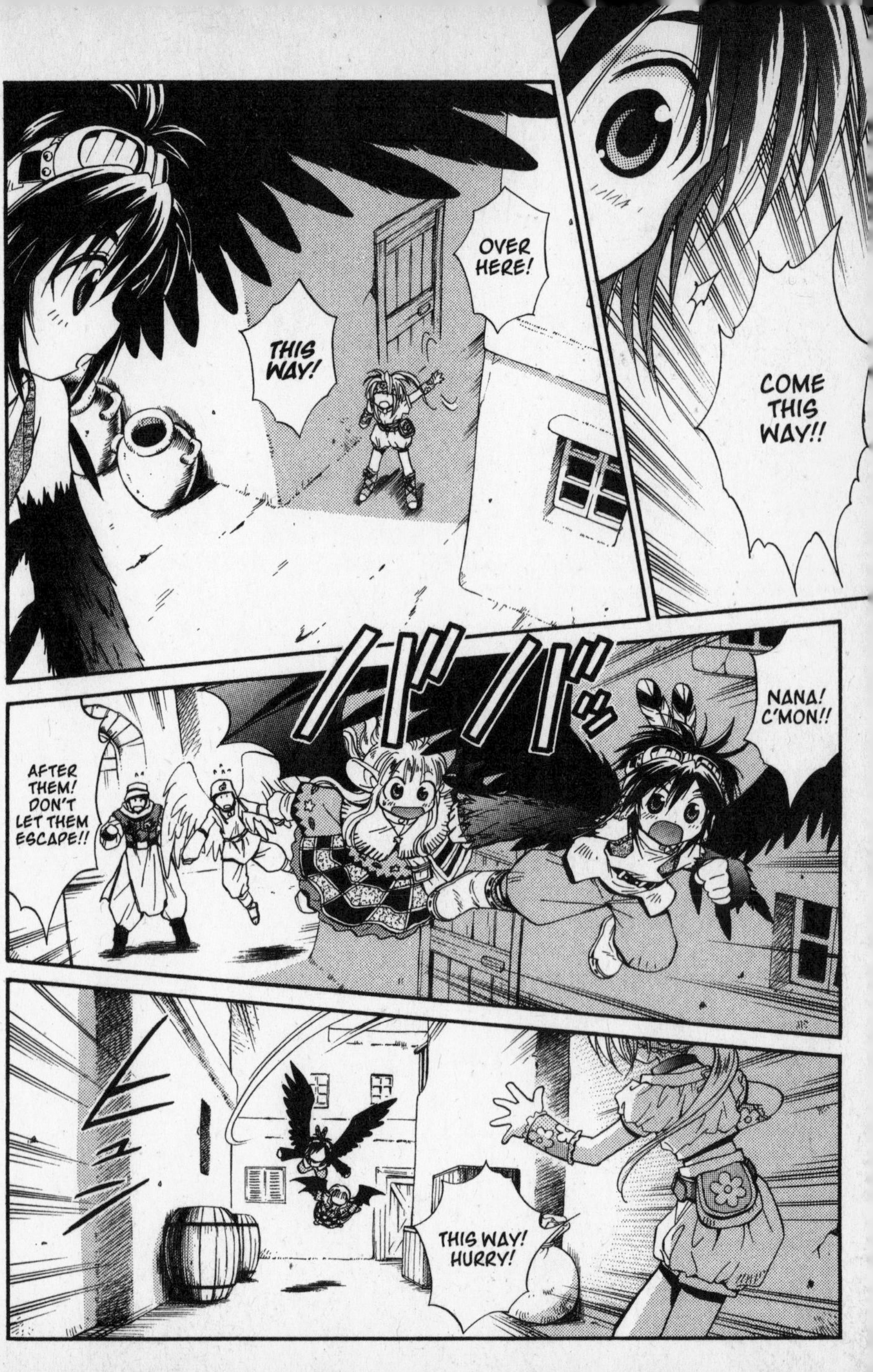
COME THIS WAY!!
OVER HERE!
THIS WAY!
NANA! C'MON!!
AFTER THEM! DON'T LET THEM ESCAPE!!
THIS WAY! HURRY!

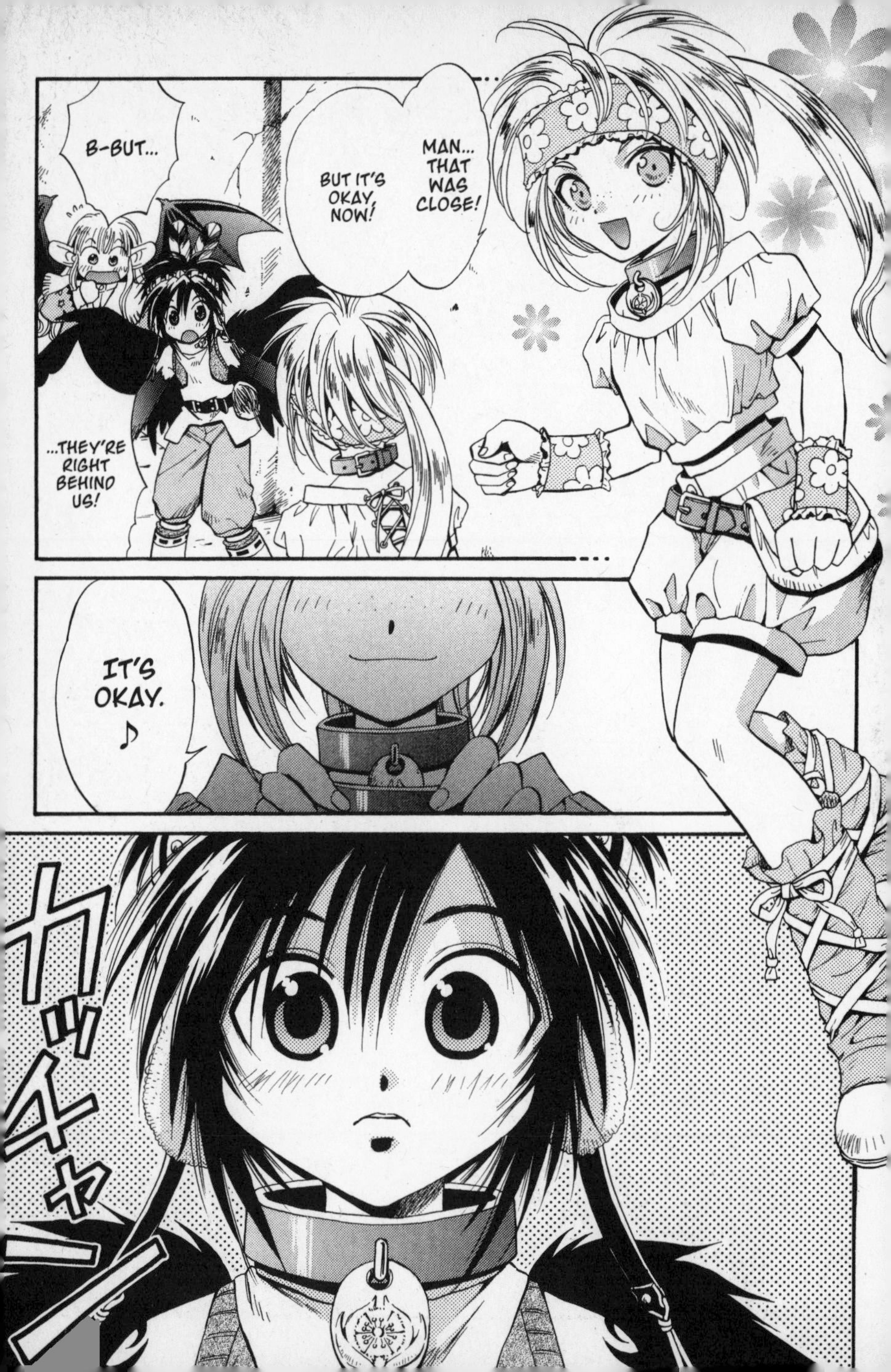
MAN... THAT WAS CLOSE!
BUT IT'S OKAY, NOW!
B-BUT...
...THEY'RE RIGHT BEHIND US!
IT'S OKAY. ♪

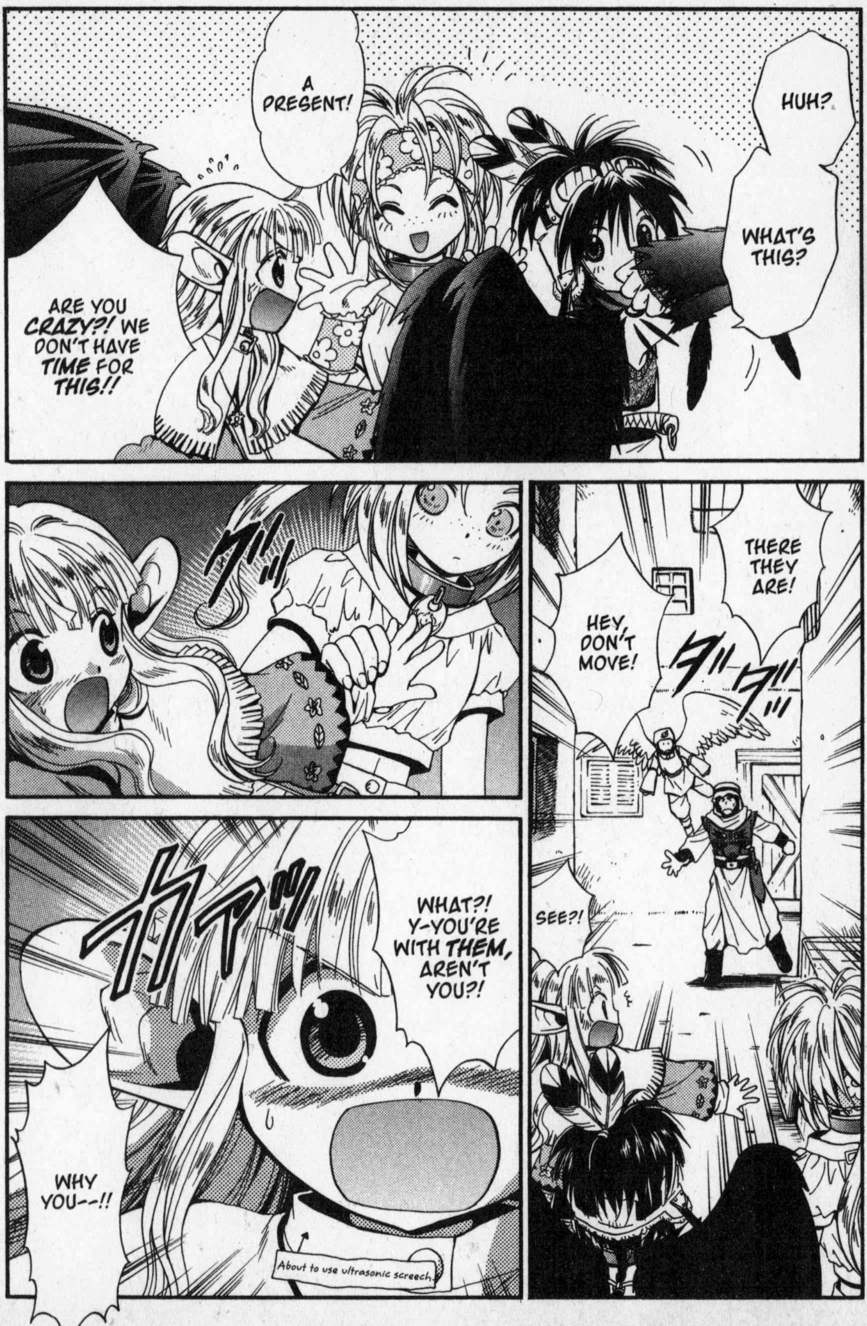
HUH?
WHAT'S THIS?
A PRESENT!
ARE YOU CRAZY?! WE DON'T HAVE TIME FOR THIS!!
THERE THEY ARE!
HEY, DON'T MOVE!
SEE?!
WHAT?! Y-YOU'RE WITH THEM, AREN'T YOU?!
WHY YOU--!!
About to use ultrasonic screech.

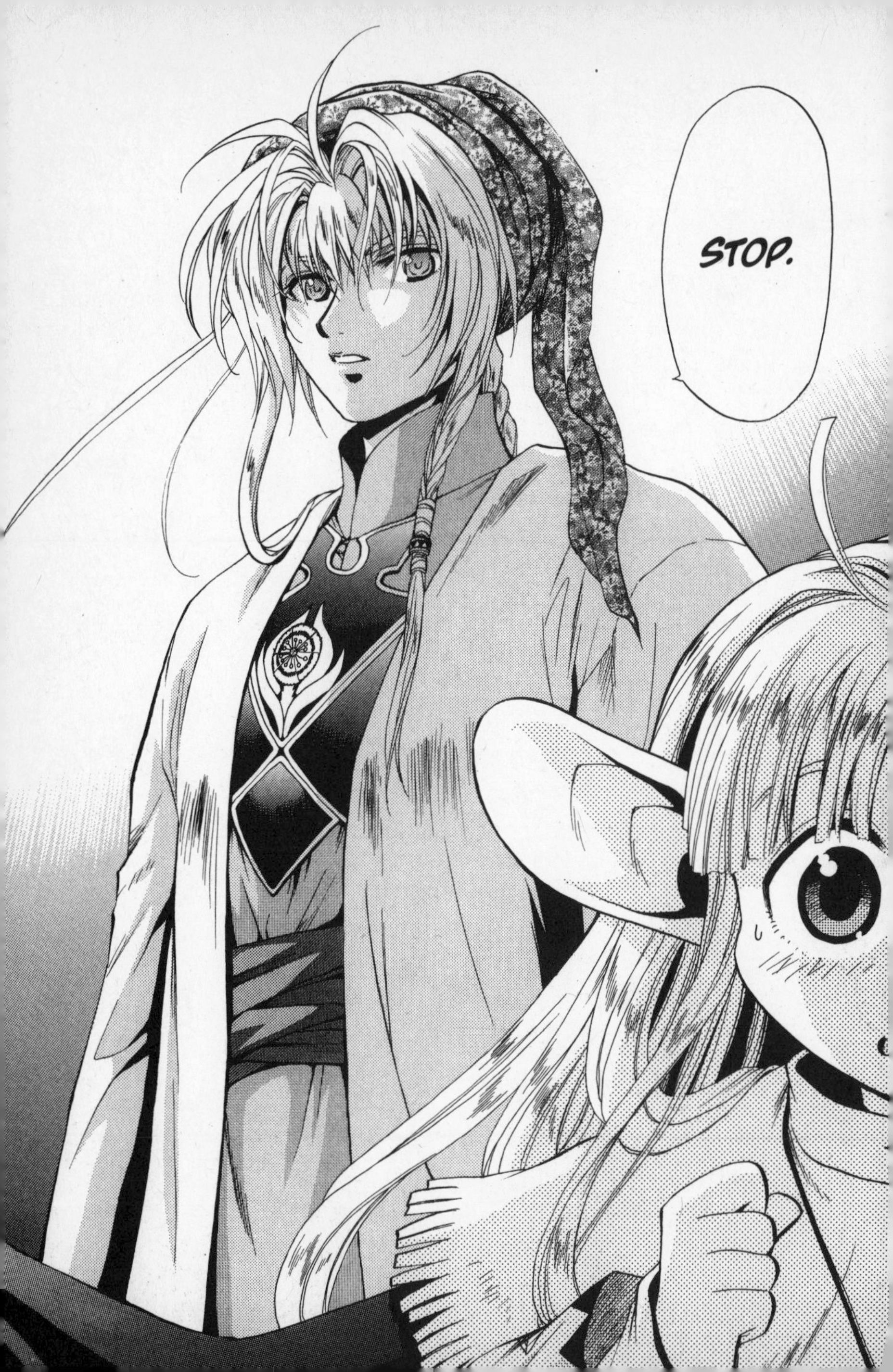
STOP.

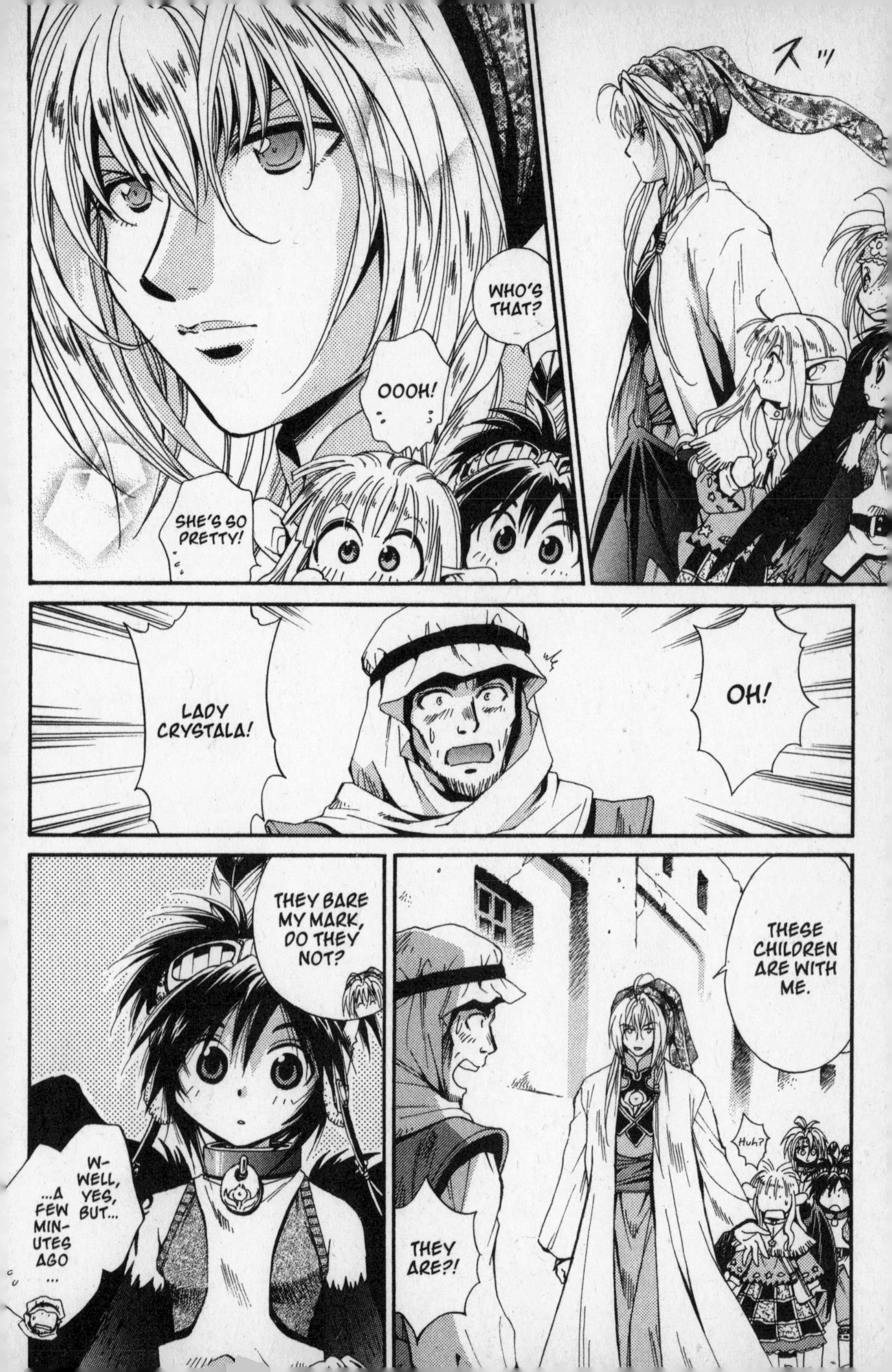
スッ
WHO'S THAT?
OOOH!
SHE'S SO PRETTY!
OH!
LADY CRYSTALA!
THESE CHILDREN ARE WITH ME.
Huh?
THEY ARE?!
THEY BARE MY MARK, DO THEY NOT?
W-WELL, YES, BUT...
...A FEW MIN-UTES AGO...

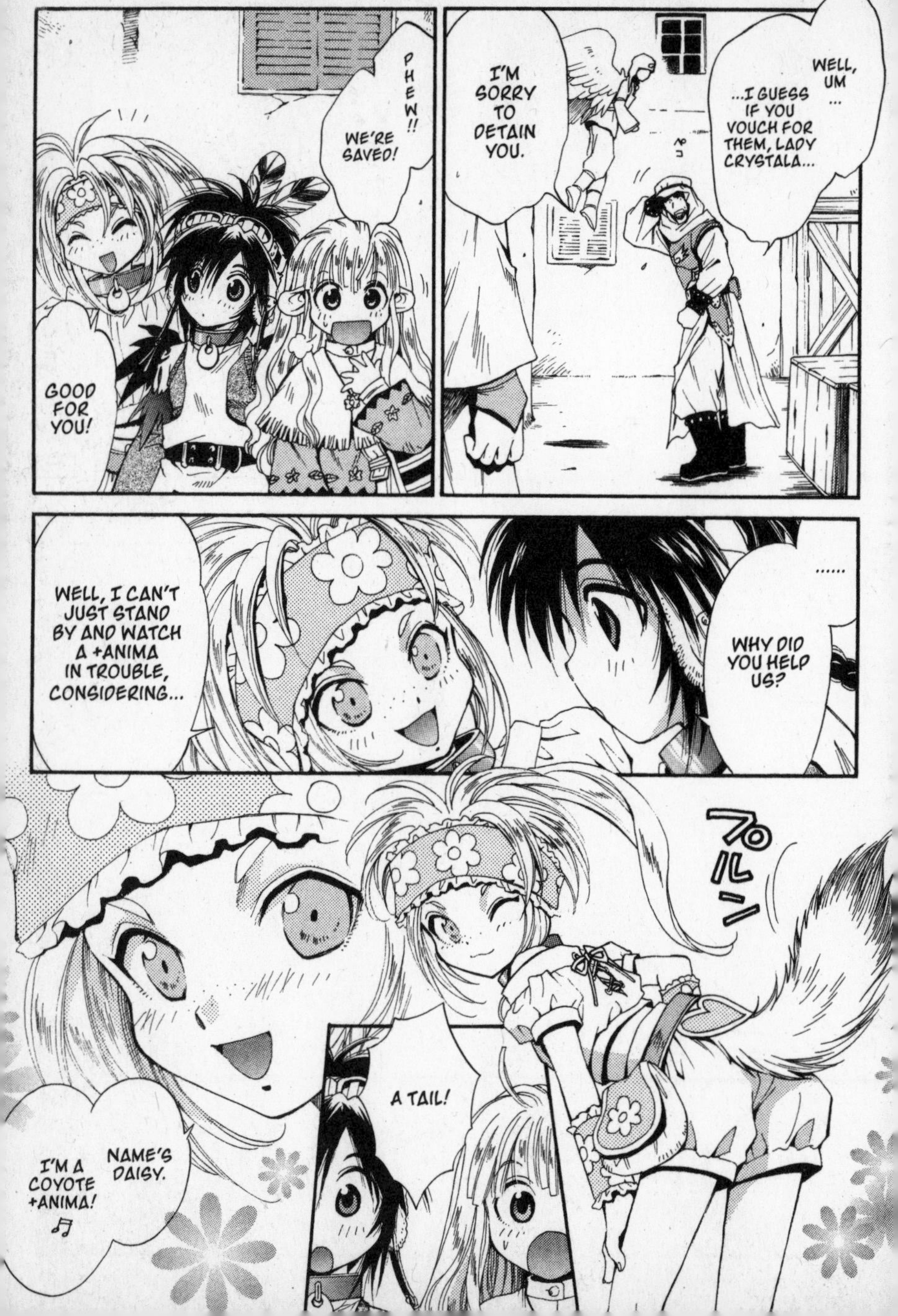
WELL, UM ...
...I GUESS IF YOU VOUCH FOR THEM, LADY CRYSTALA...
I'M SORRY TO DETAIN YOU.
PHEW!!
WE'RE SAVED!
GOOD FOR YOU!
......
WHY DID YOU HELP US?
WELL, I CAN'T JUST STAND BY AND WATCH A +ANIMA IN TROUBLE, CONSIDERING...
プルン
A TAIL!
NAME'S DAISY.
I'M A COYOTE +ANIMA! ♫

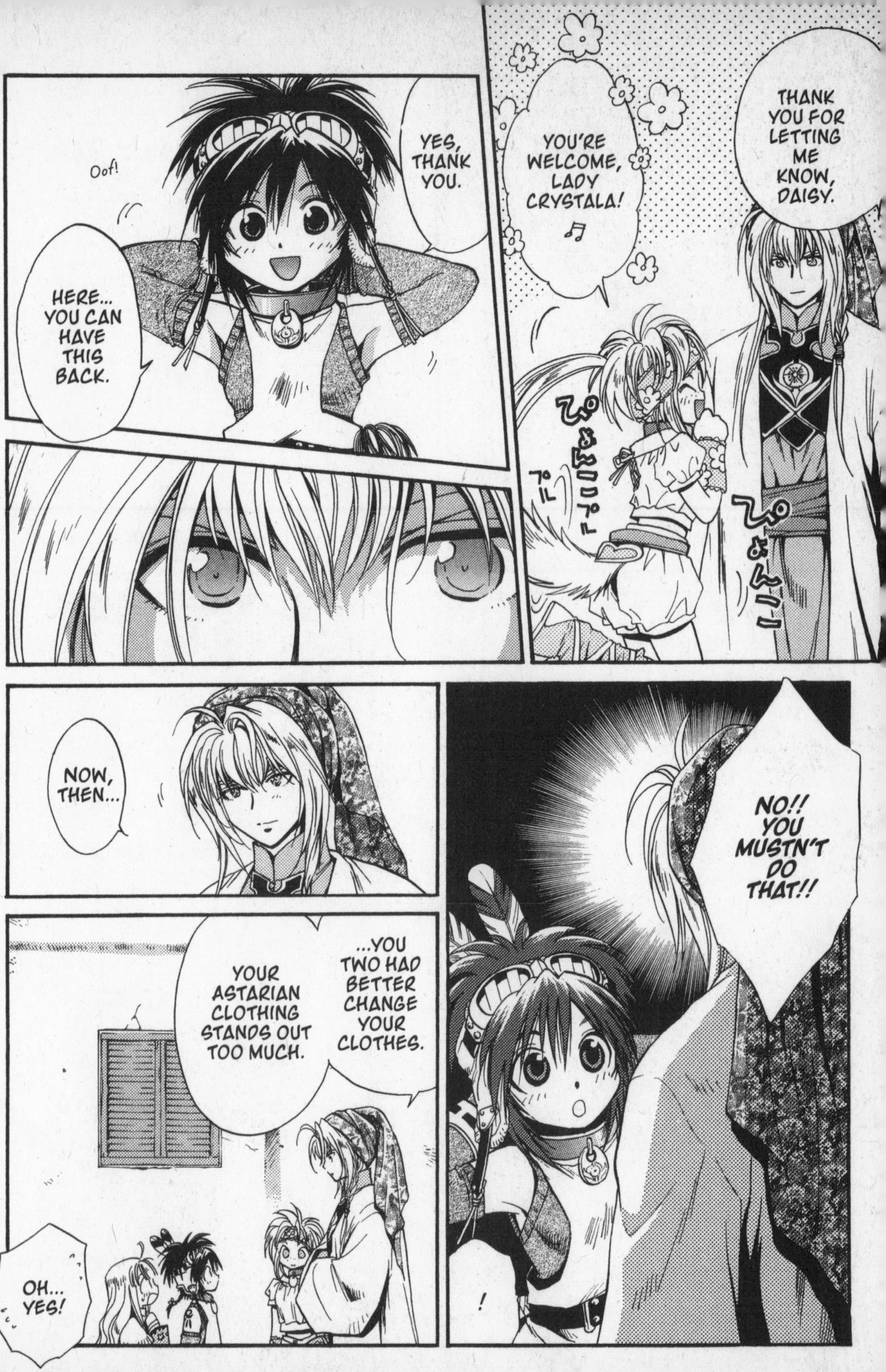
THANK YOU FOR LETTING ME KNOW, DAISY.
YOU'RE WELCOME, LADY CRYSTALA! ♪
ぴょんーー
ぴょんーーぷル
ぷル
YES, THANK YOU.
Oof!
HERE... YOU CAN HAVE THIS BACK.
NO!! YOU MUSTN'T DO THAT!!
!
NOW, THEN...
...YOU TWO HAD BETTER CHANGE YOUR CLOTHES.
YOUR ASTARIAN CLOTHING STANDS OUT TOO MUCH.
OH... YES!

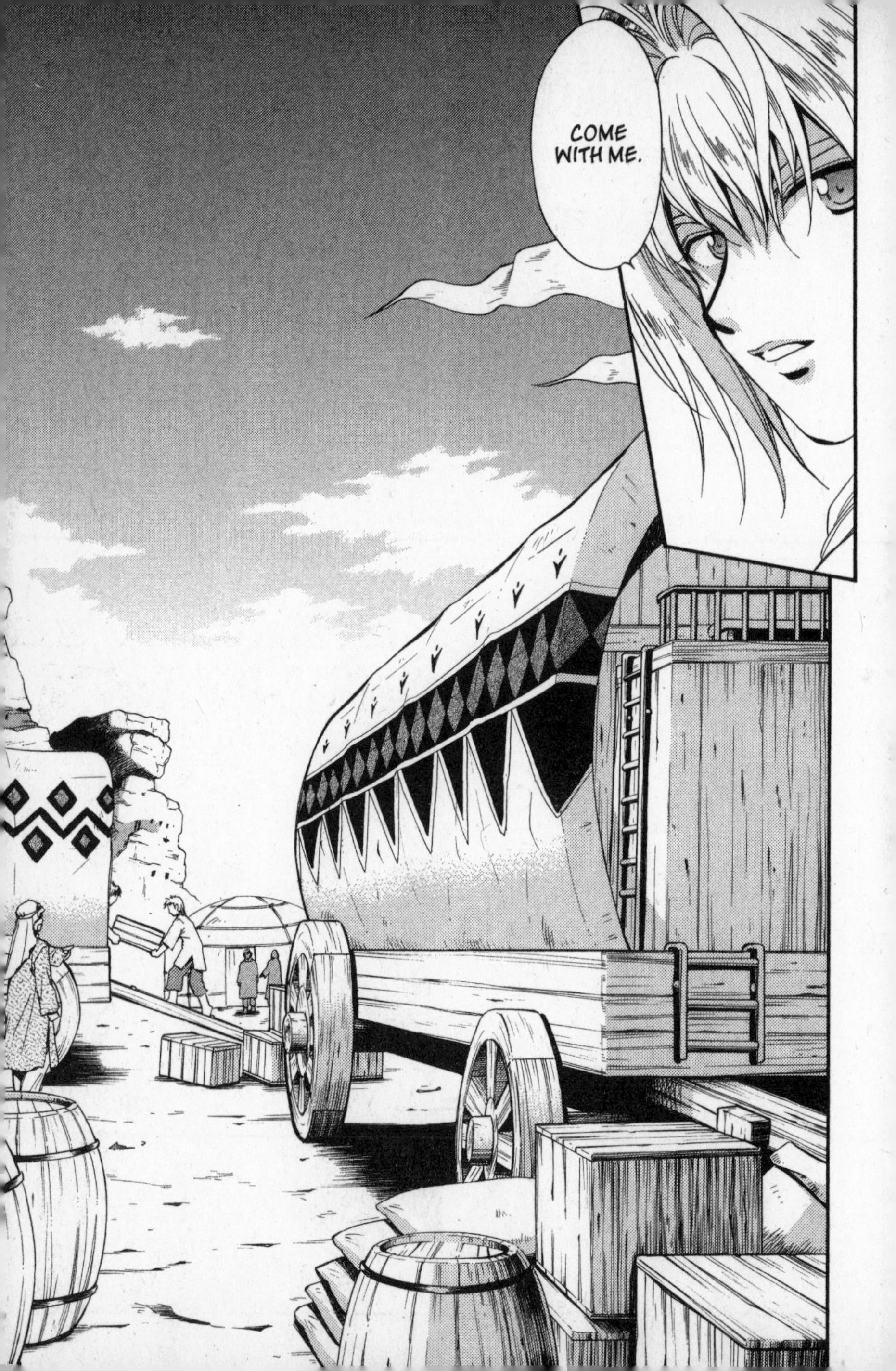
COME WITH ME.

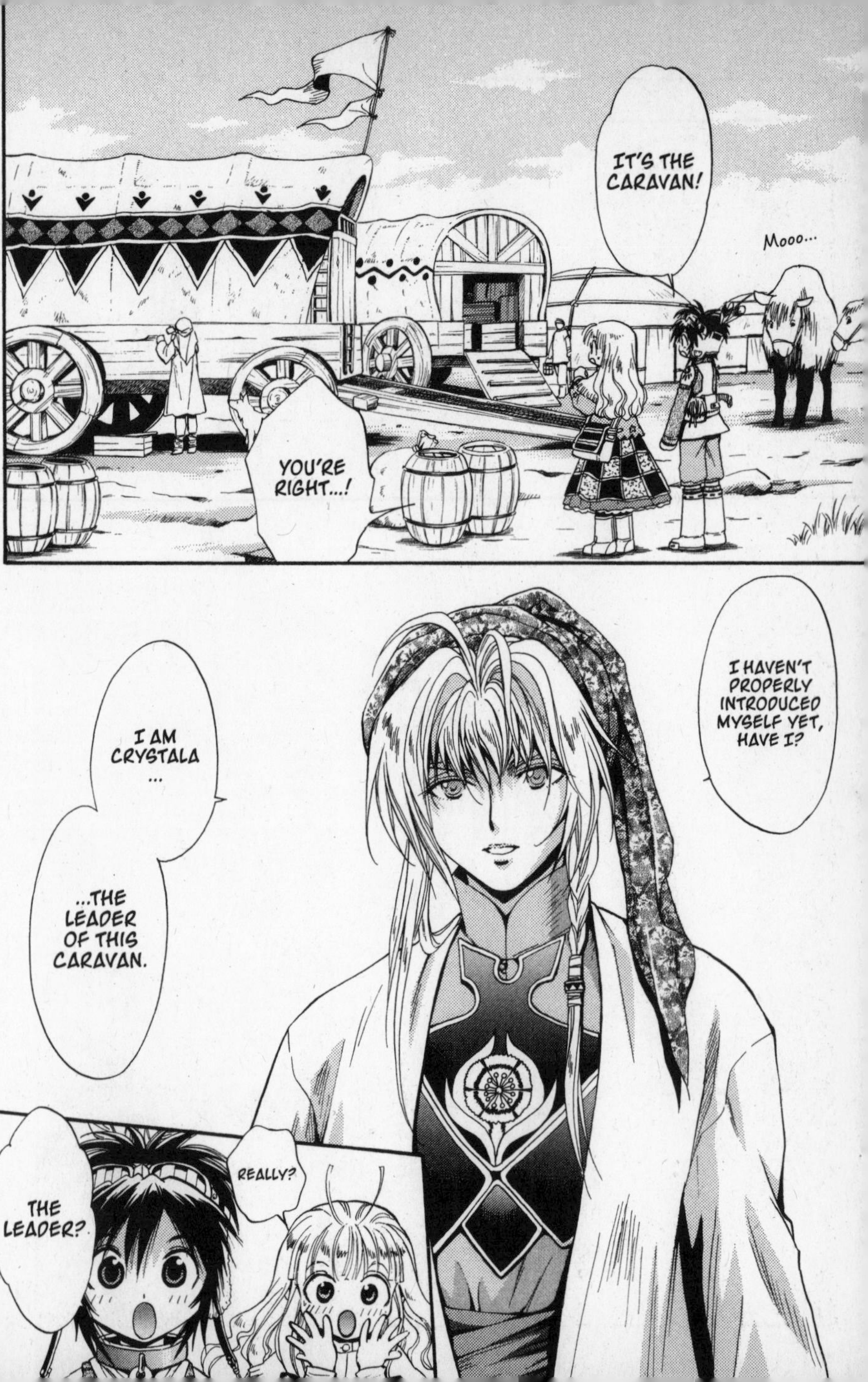
IT'S THE CARAVAN!
Mooo...
YOU'RE RIGHT...!
I HAVEN'T PROPERLY INTRODUCED MYSELF YET, HAVE I?
I AM CRYSTALA ...
...THE LEADER OF THIS CARAVAN.
REALLY?
THE LEADER?

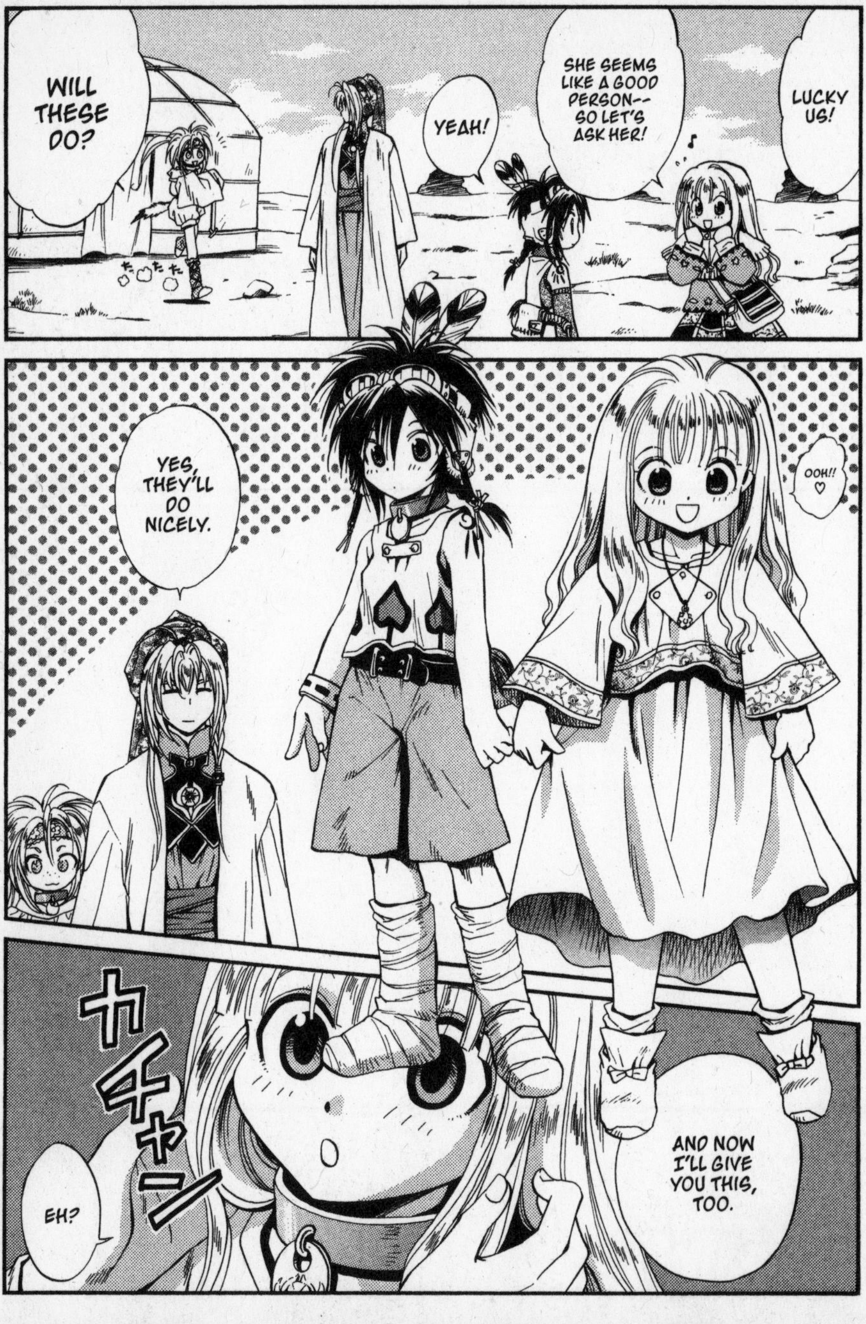
LUCKY US!
SHE SEEMS LIKE A GOOD PERSON-- SO LET'S ASK HER!
YEAH!
WILL THESE DO?
OOH!! ♡
YES, THEY'LL DO NICELY.
AND NOW I'LL GIVE YOU THIS, TOO.
カチャーン
EH?

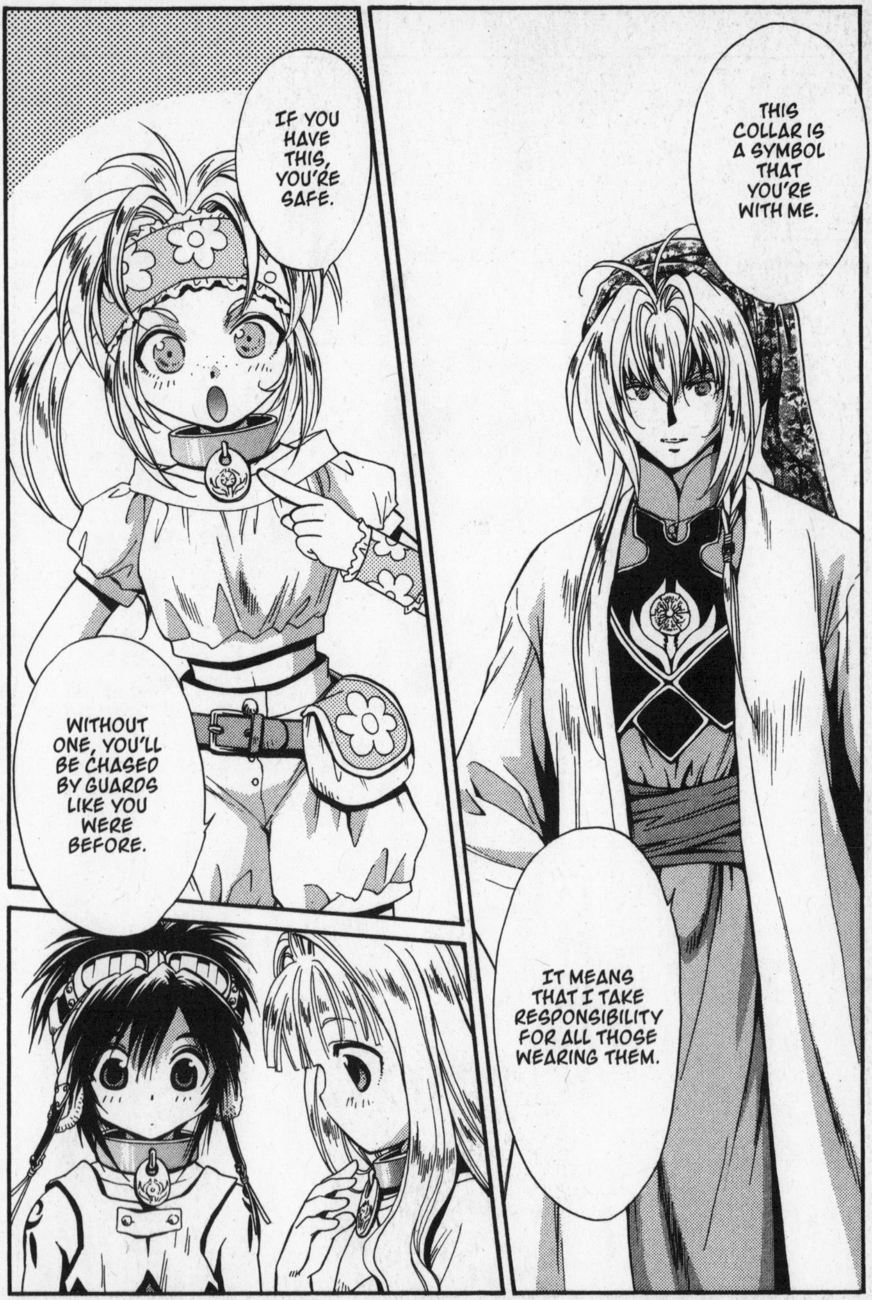
THIS COLLAR IS A SYMBOL THAT YOU'RE WITH ME.
IT MEANS THAT I TAKE RESPONSIBILITY FOR ALL THOSE WEARING THEM.
IF YOU HAVE THIS, YOU'RE SAFE.
WITHOUT ONE, YOU'LL BE CHASED BY GUARDS LIKE YOU WERE BEFORE.

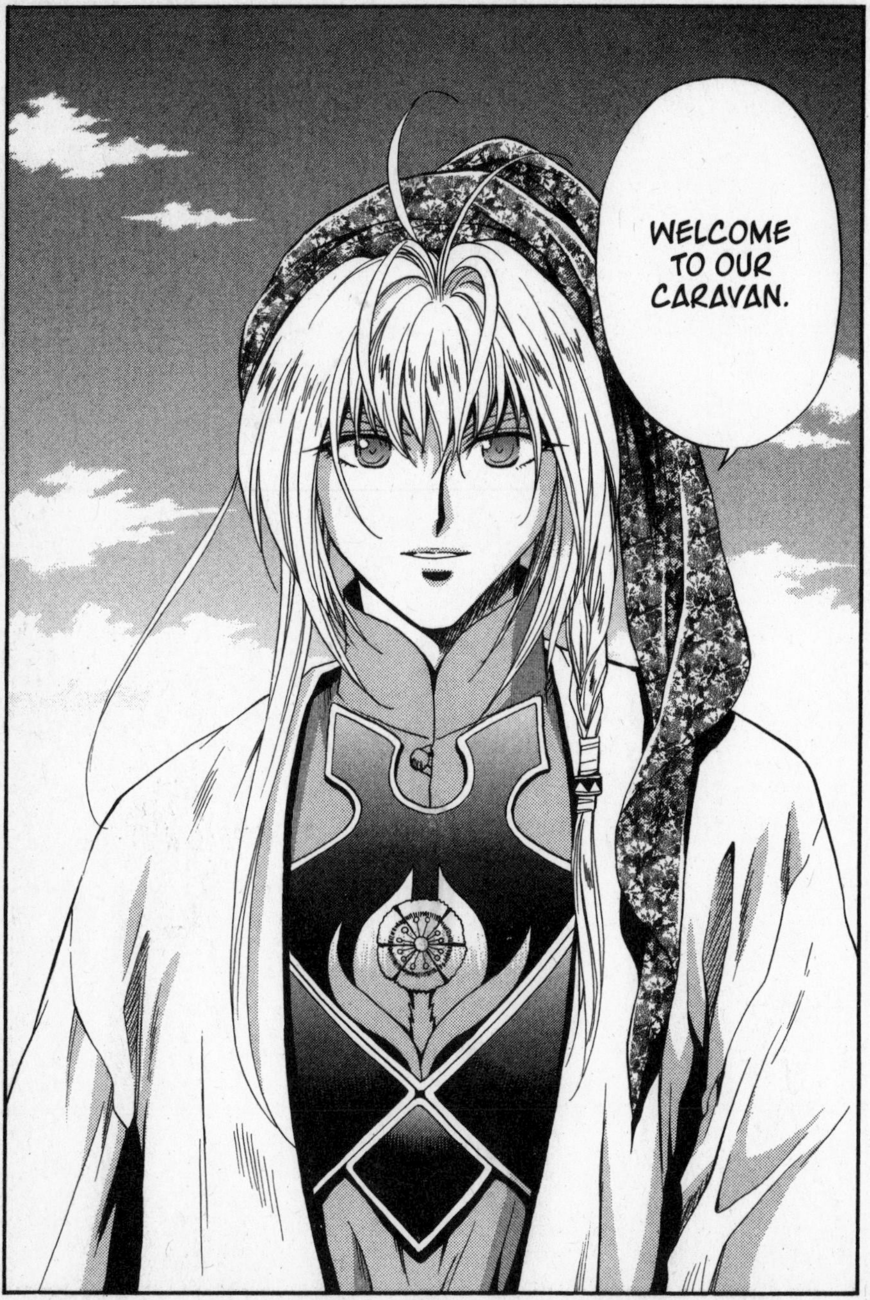
WELCOME TO OUR CARAVAN.

Her eyes are twinkling!

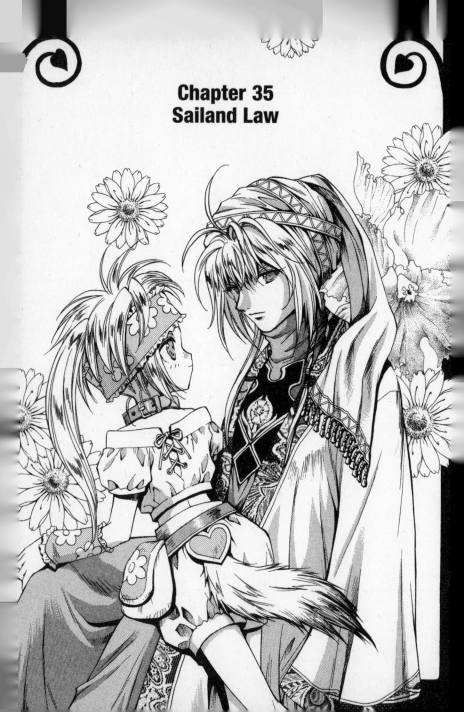

Chapter 35
Sailand Law

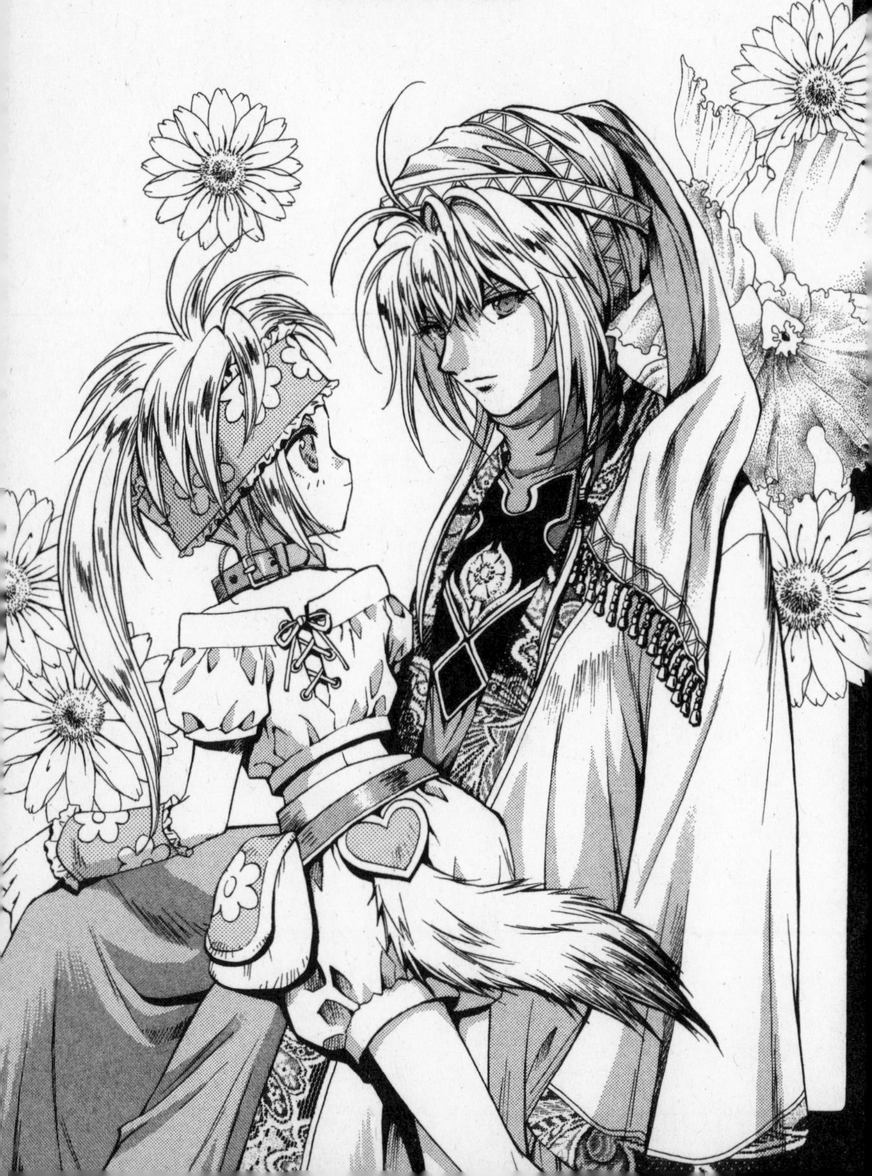

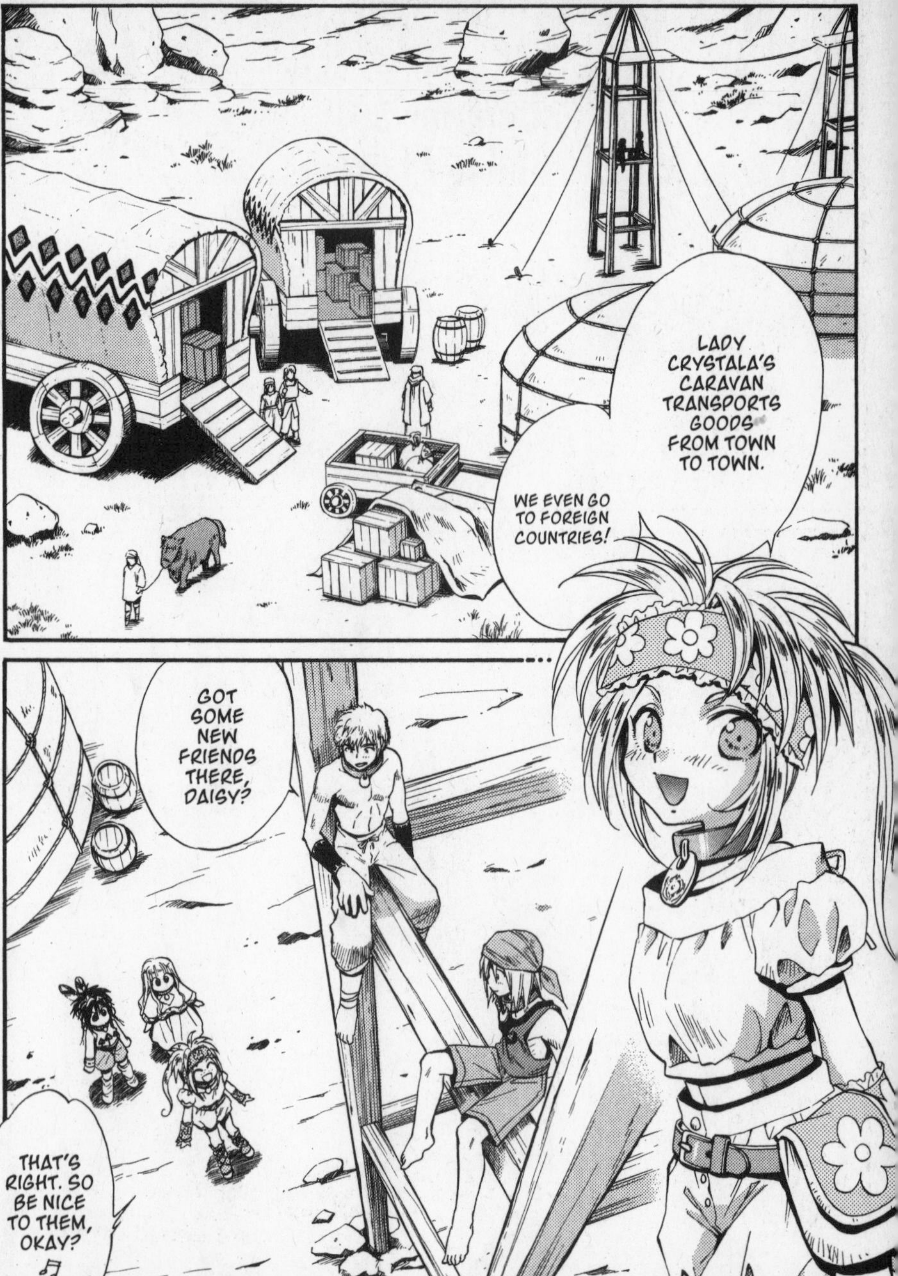
LADY CRYSTALA'S CARAVAN TRANSPORTS GOODS FROM TOWN TO TOWN.
WE EVEN GO TO FOREIGN COUNTRIES!
GOT SOME NEW FRIENDS THERE, DAISY?
THAT'S RIGHT. SO BE NICE TO THEM, OKAY? ♫

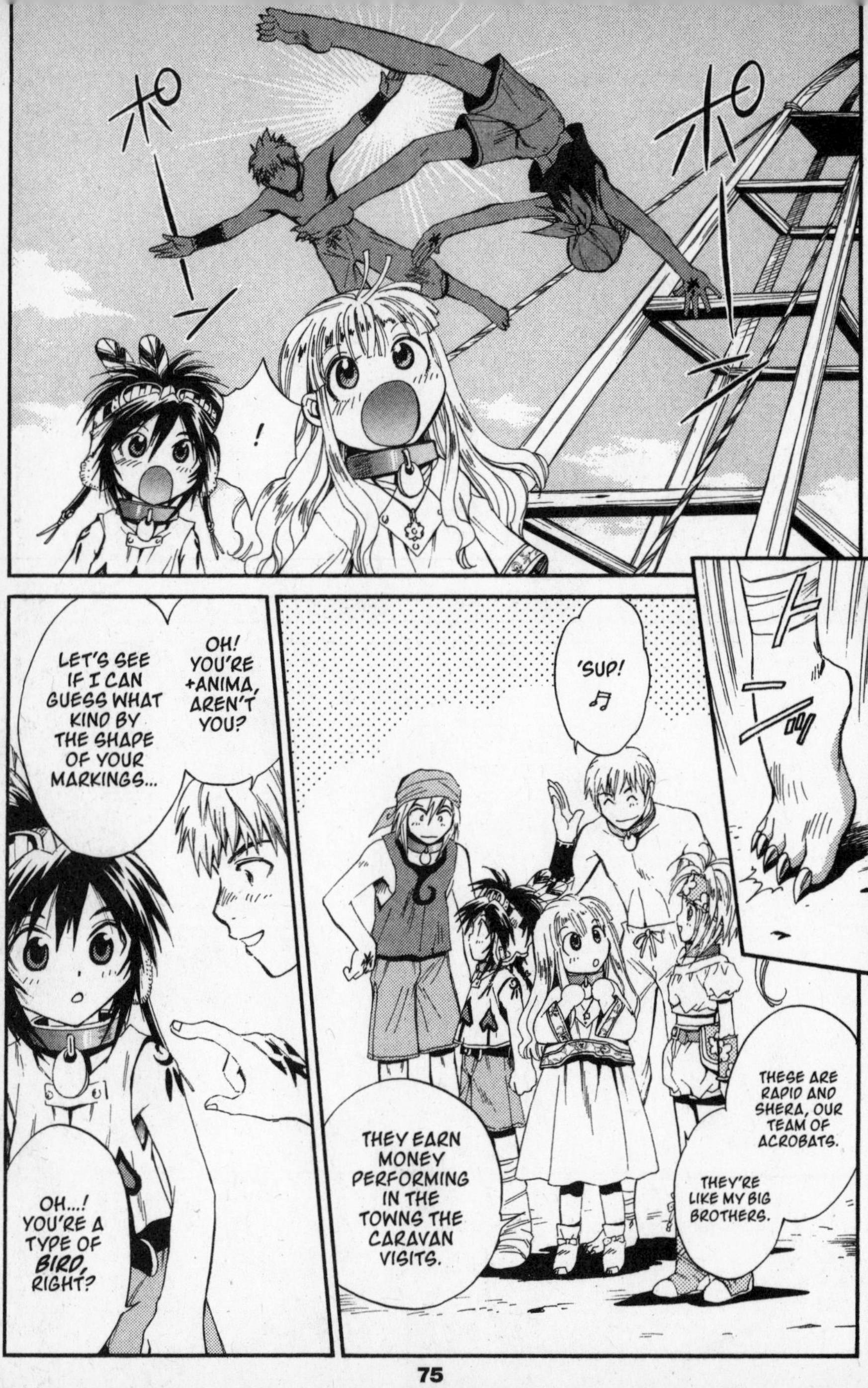
!
'SUP! ♪
THESE ARE RAPID AND SHERA, OUR TEAM OF ACROBATS.
THEY'RE LIKE MY BIG BROTHERS.
THEY EARN MONEY PERFORMING IN THE TOWNS THE CARAVAN VISITS.
OH! YOU'RE +ANIMA, AREN'T YOU?
LET'S SEE IF I CAN GUESS WHAT KIND BY THE SHAPE OF YOUR MARKINGS...
OH...! YOU'RE A TYPE OF *BIRD*, RIGHT?

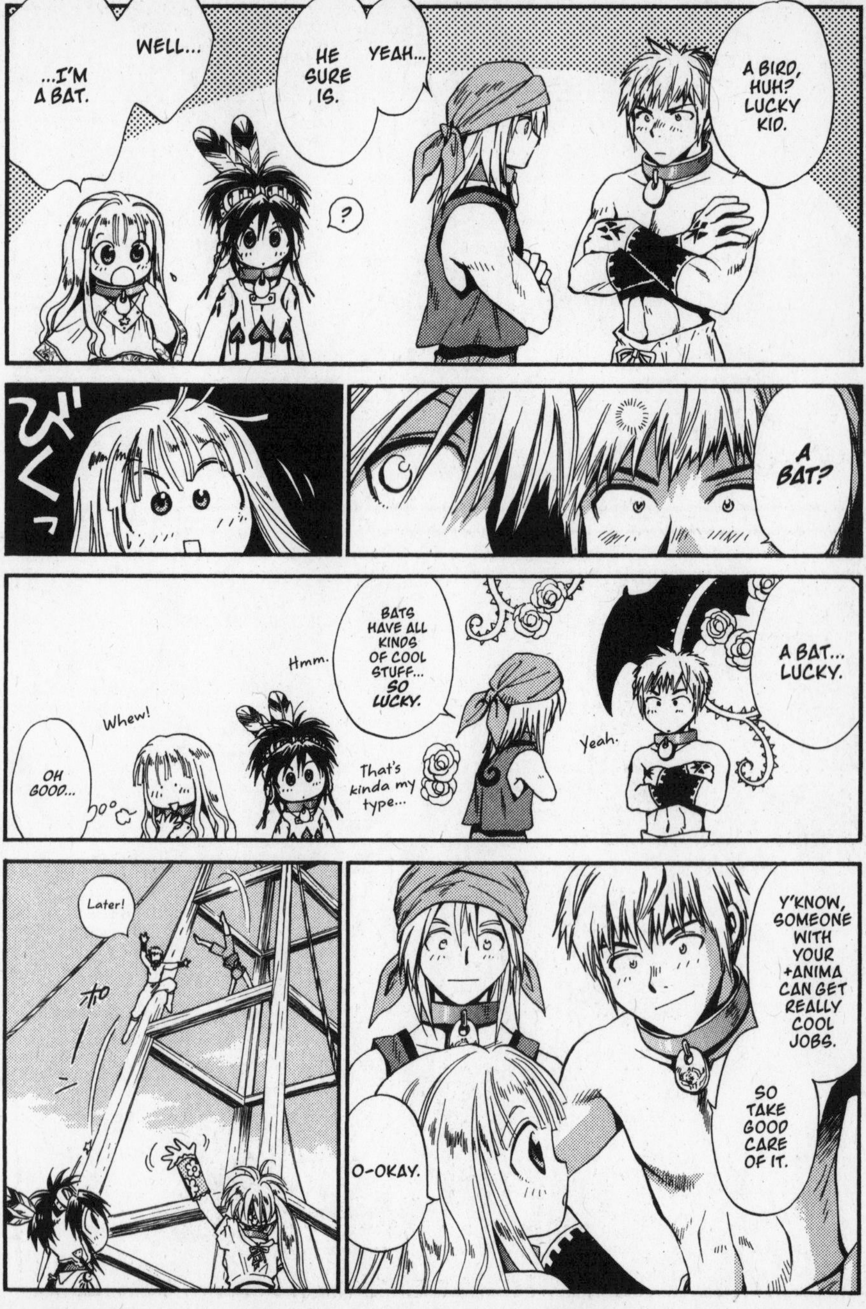
A BIRD, HUH? LUCKY KID.
YEAH...
HE SURE IS.
?
WELL...
...I'M A BAT.
A BAT?
びくっ
A BAT... LUCKY.
Yeah.
BATS HAVE ALL KINDS OF COOL STUFF... SO LUCKY.
Hmm.
That's kinda my type...
Whew!
OH GOOD...
Y'KNOW, SOMEONE WITH YOUR +ANIMA CAN GET REALLY COOL JOBS.
SO TAKE GOOD CARE OF IT.
O-OKAY.
Later!

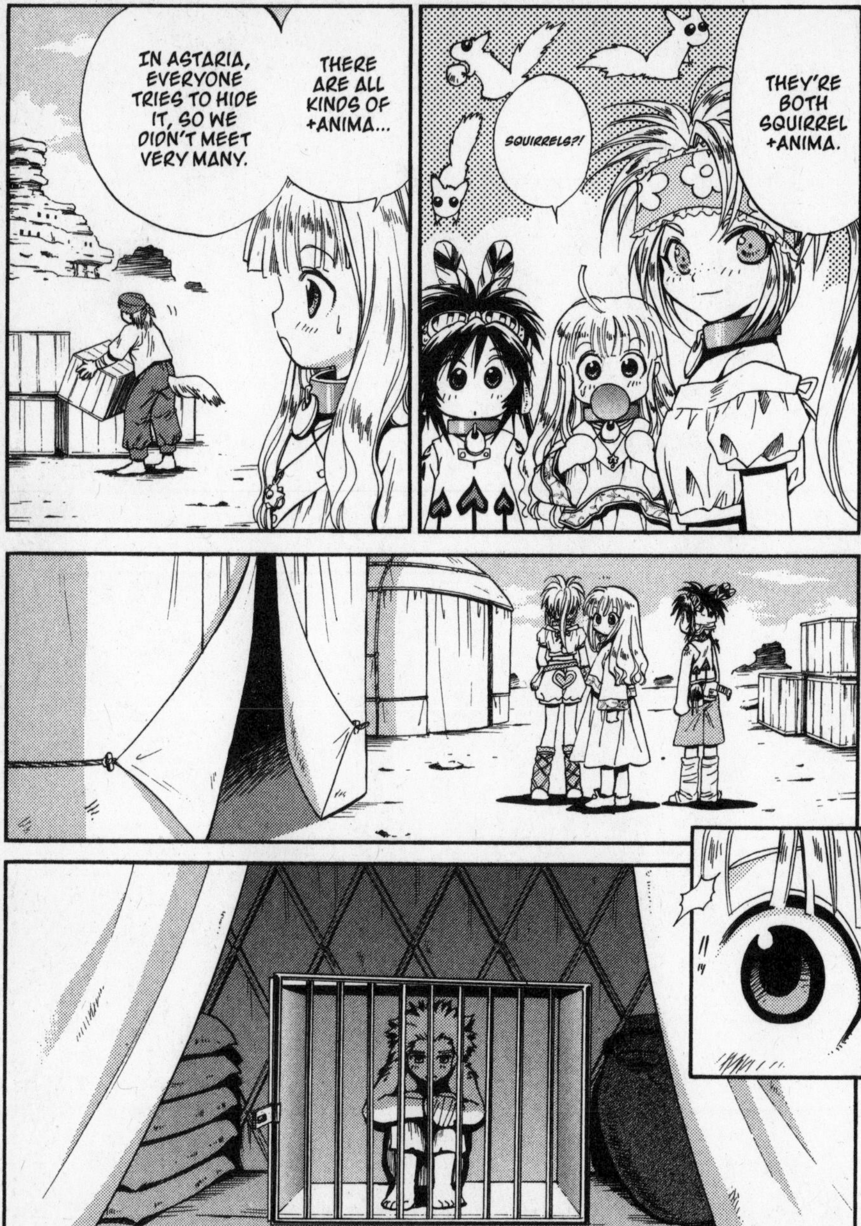
THEY'RE BOTH SQUIRREL +ANIMA.
SQUIRRELS?!
THERE ARE ALL KINDS OF +ANIMA...
IN ASTARIA, EVERYONE TRIES TO HIDE IT, SO WE DIDN'T MEET VERY MANY.

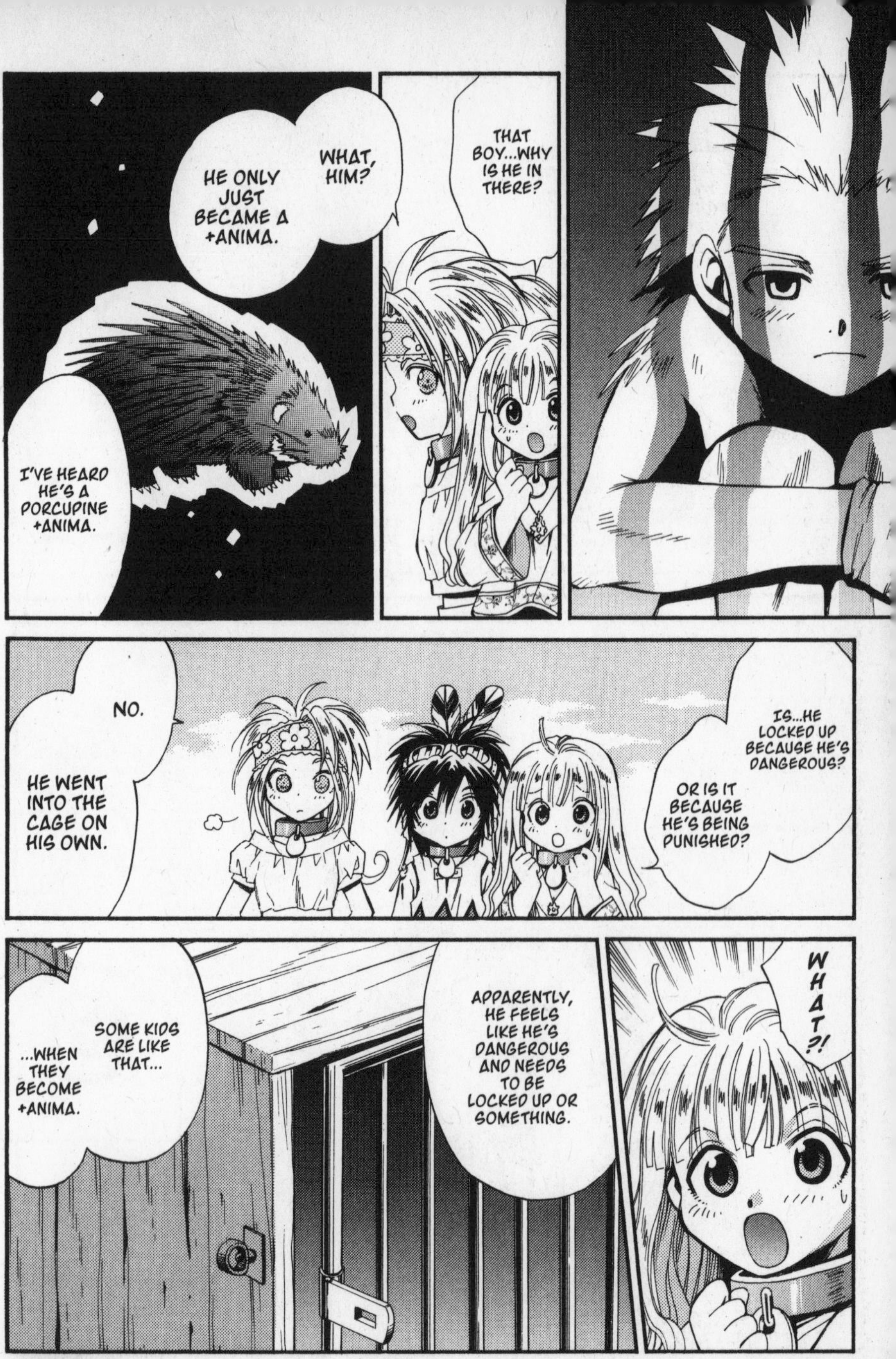
THAT BOY...WHY IS HE IN THERE?
WHAT, HIM?
HE ONLY JUST BECAME A +ANIMA.
I'VE HEARD HE'S A PORCUPINE +ANIMA.
IS...HE LOCKED UP BECAUSE HE'S DANGEROUS?
OR IS IT BECAUSE HE'S BEING PUNISHED?
NO.
HE WENT INTO THE CAGE ON HIS OWN.
WHAT?!
APPARENTLY, HE FEELS LIKE HE'S DANGEROUS AND NEEDS TO BE LOCKED UP OR SOMETHING.
SOME KIDS ARE LIKE THAT...
...WHEN THEY BECOME +ANIMA.

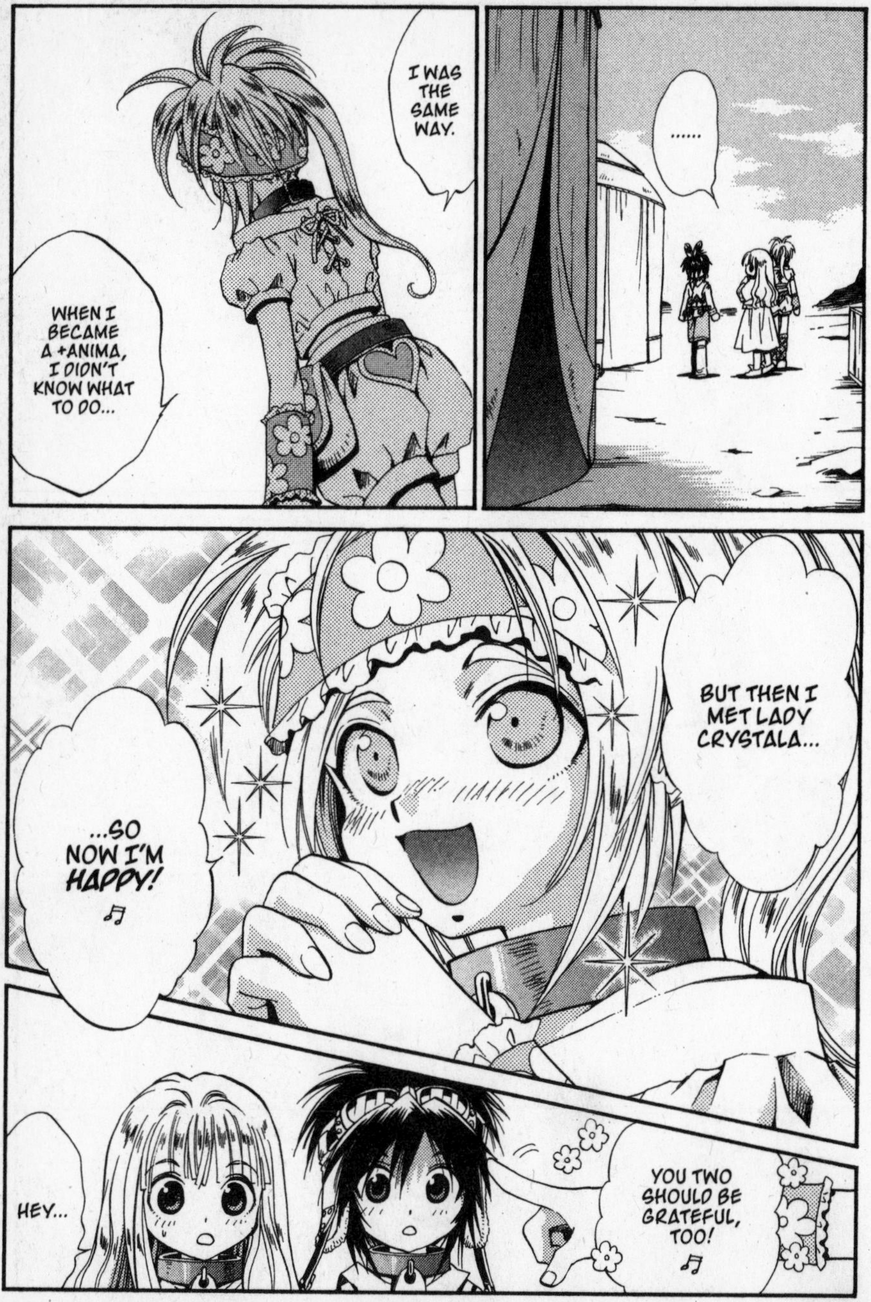
......
I WAS THE SAME WAY.
WHEN I BECAME A +ANIMA, I DIDN'T KNOW WHAT TO DO...
BUT THEN I MET LADY CRYSTALA...
...SO NOW I'M HAPPY! ♪
YOU TWO SHOULD BE GRATEFUL, TOO! ♪
HEY...

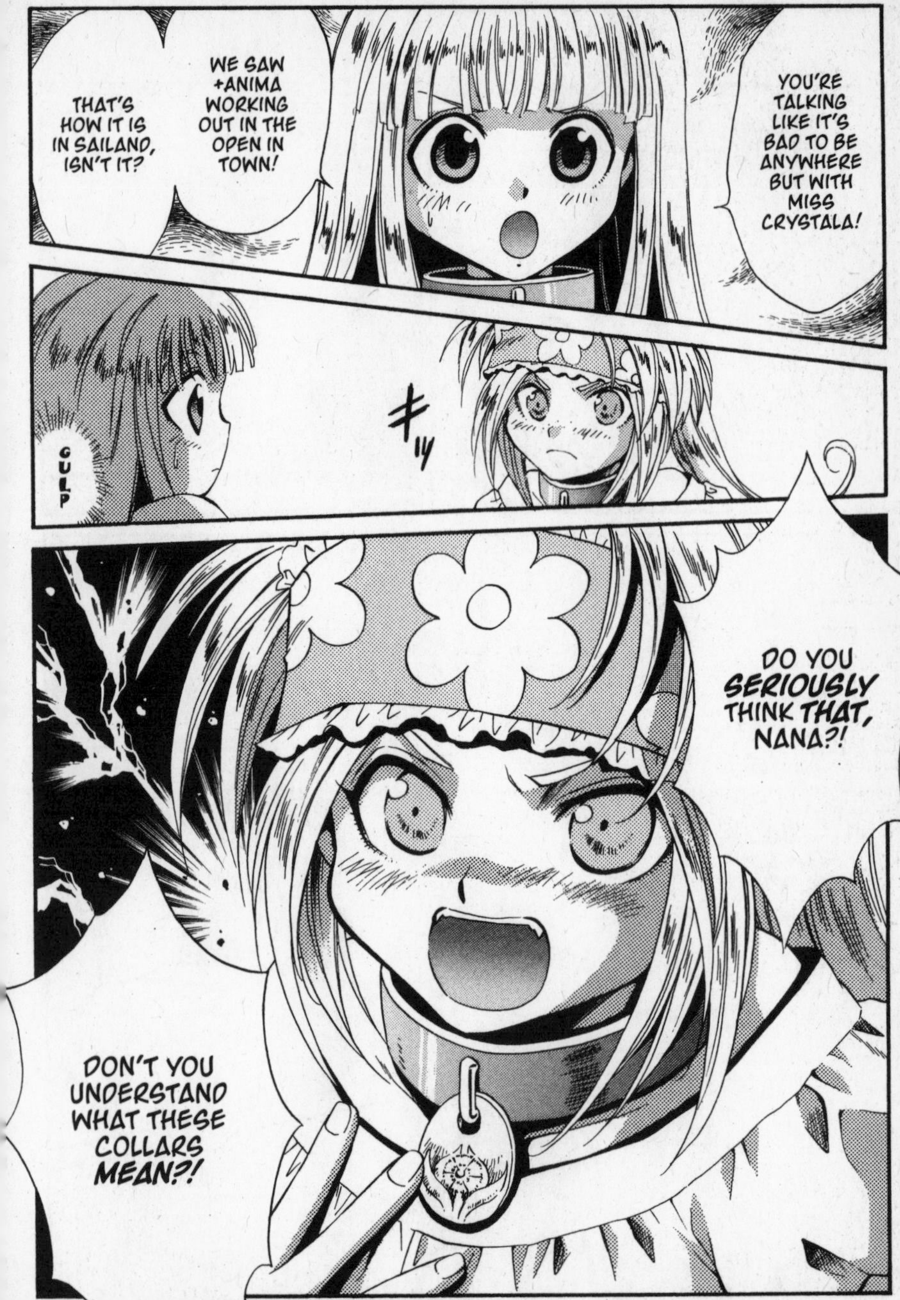
YOU'RE TALKING LIKE IT'S BAD TO BE ANYWHERE BUT WITH MISS CRYSTALA!
WE SAW +ANIMA WORKING OUT IN THE OPEN IN TOWN!
THAT'S HOW IT IS IN SAILAND, ISN'T IT?
キッ
GULP
DO YOU SERIOUSLY THINK THAT, NANA?!
DON'T YOU UNDERSTAND WHAT THESE COLLARS MEAN?!

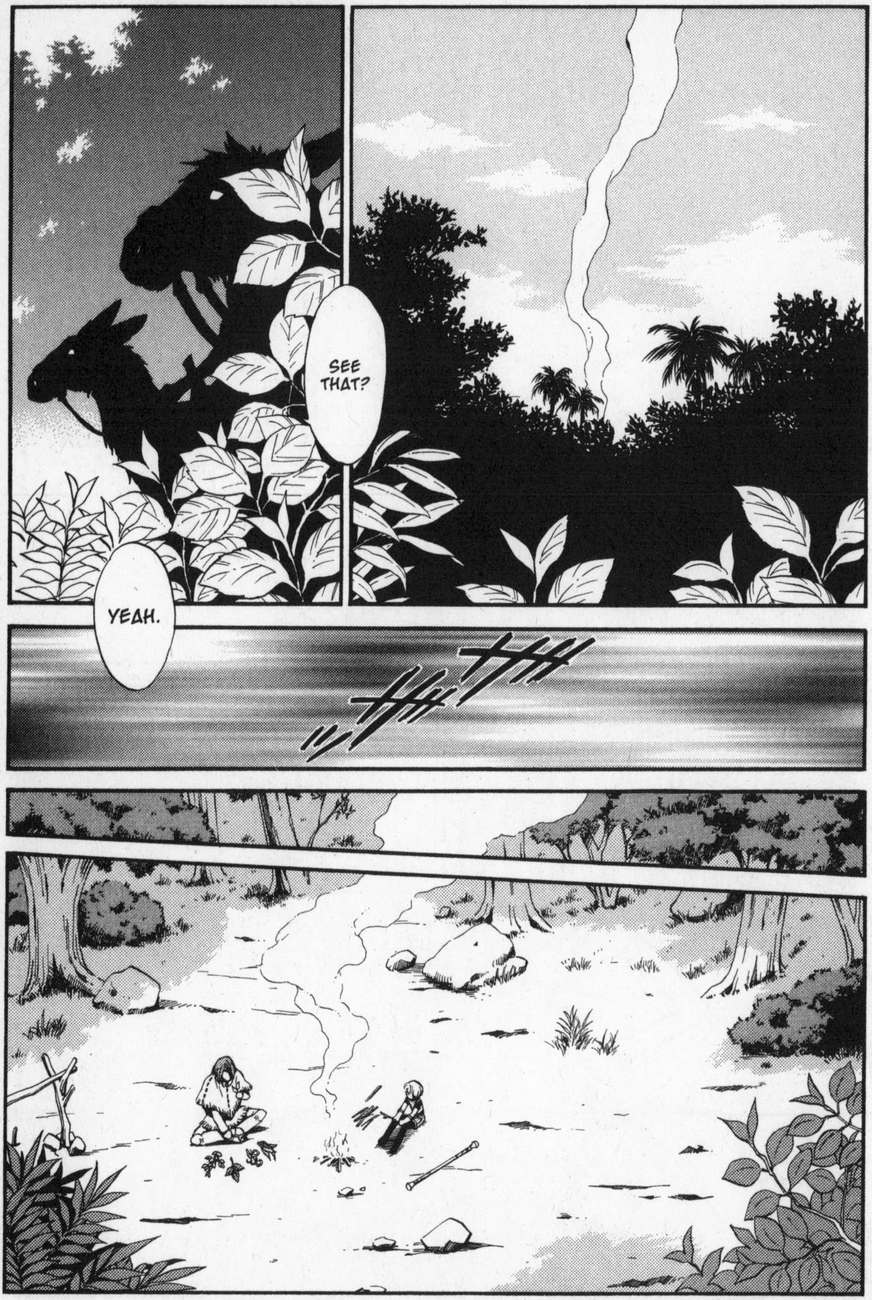
SEE THAT?
YEAH.

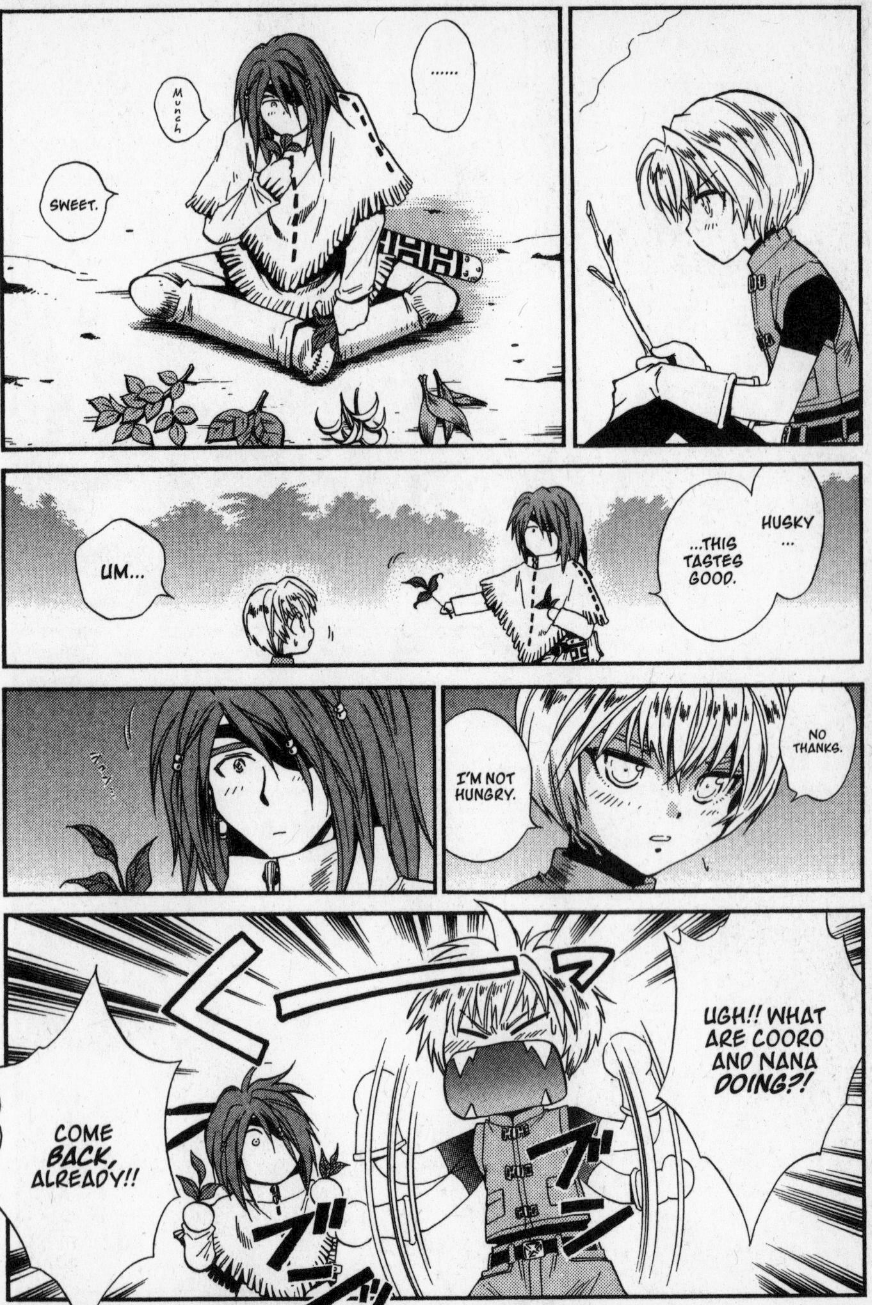

......
Munch
SWEET.
HUSKY ...
...THIS TASTES GOOD.
UM...
NO THANKS.
I'M NOT HUNGRY.
UGH!! WHAT ARE COORO AND NANA DOING?!
COME BACK, ALREADY!!

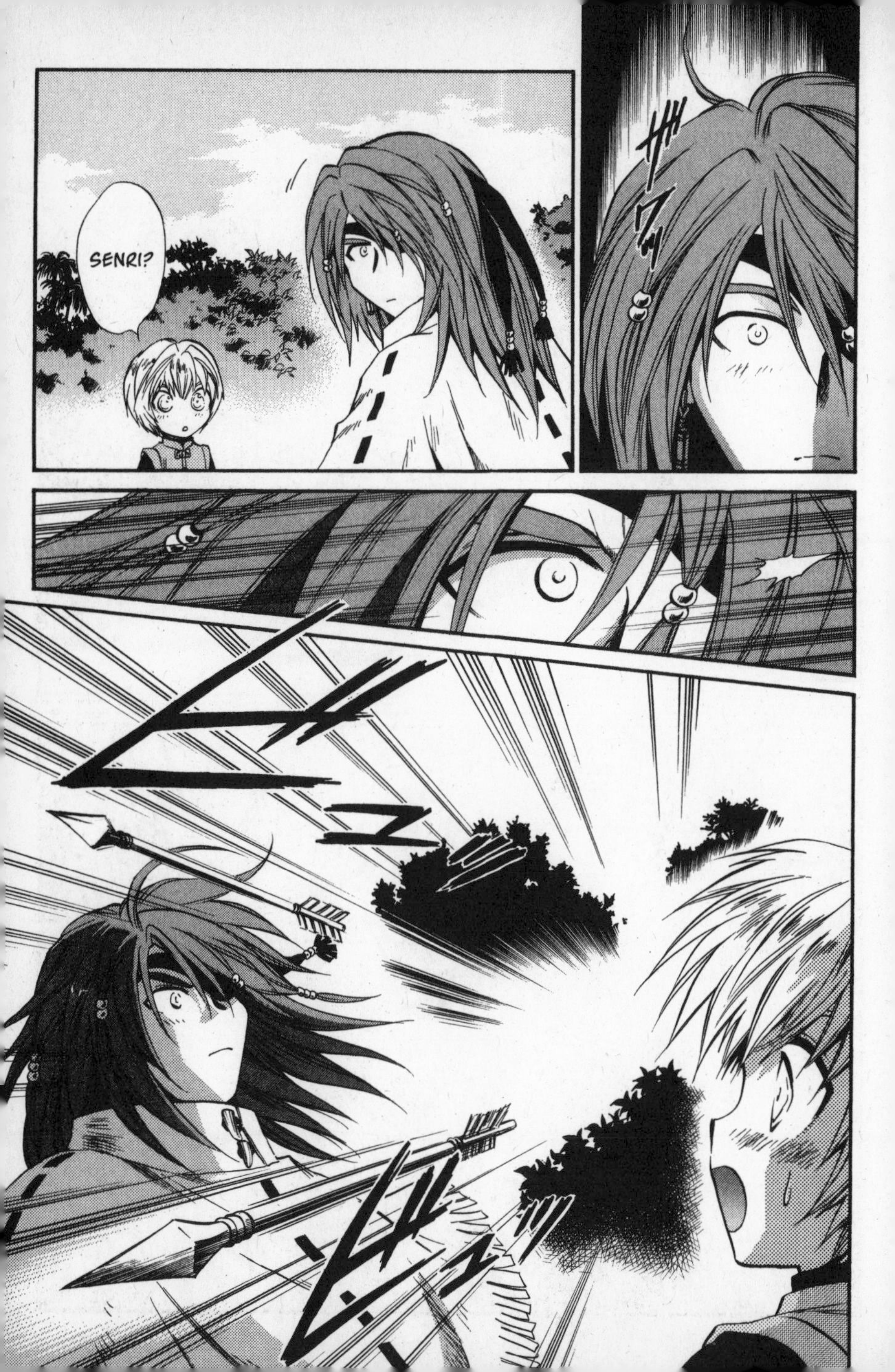
SENRI?

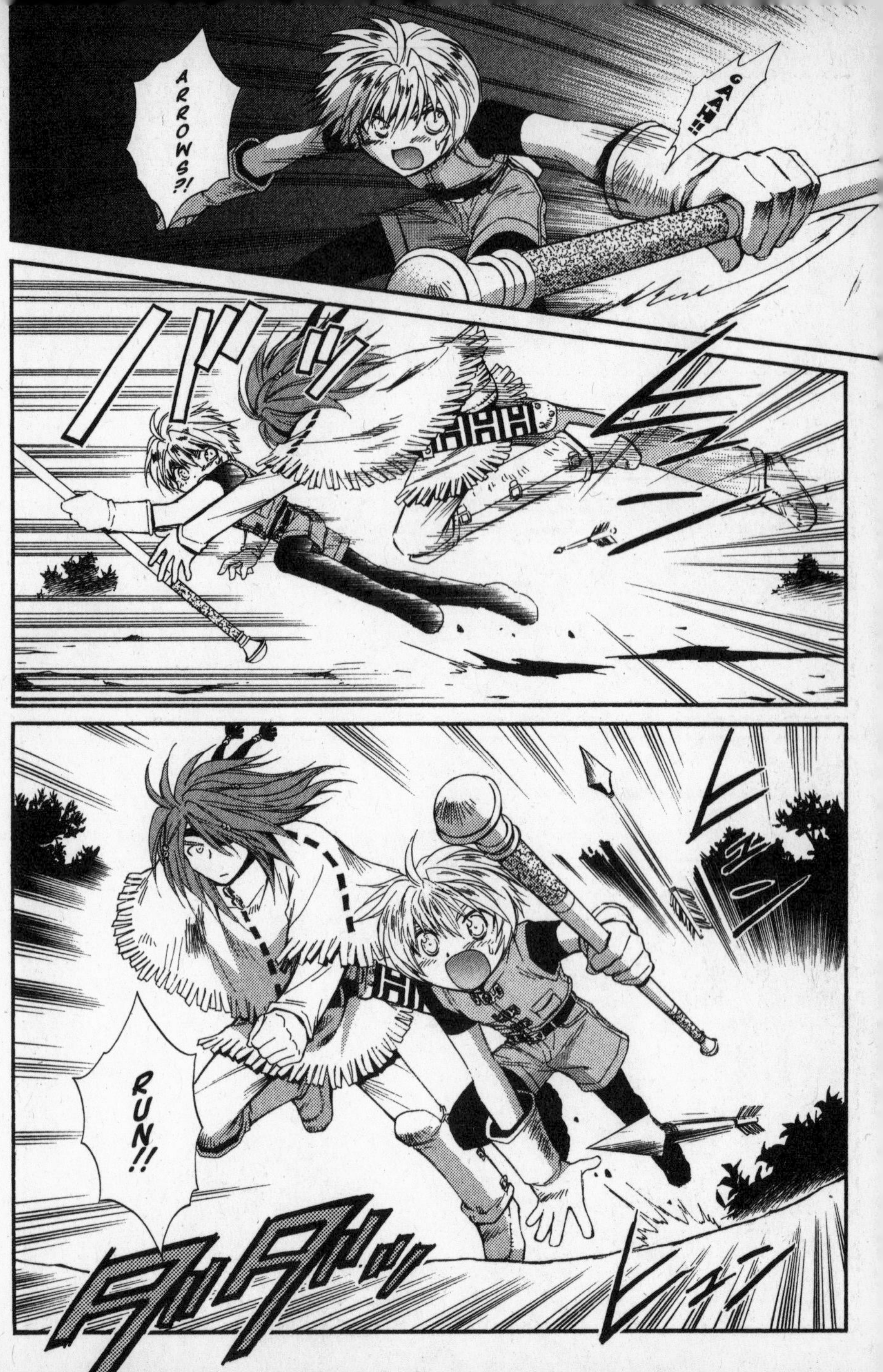
GAAH!!
ARROWS?!
RUN!!

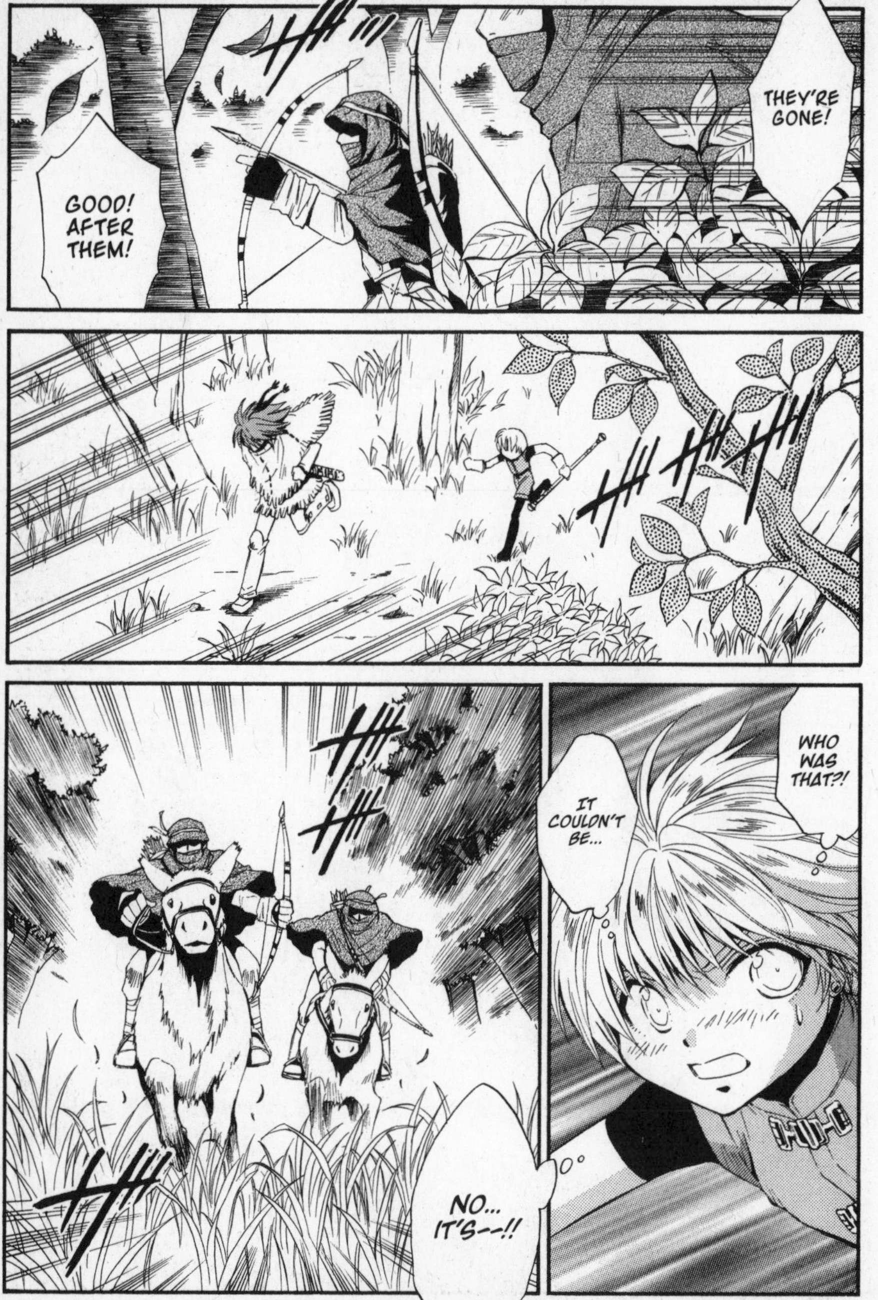

THEY'RE GONE!
GOOD! AFTER THEM!
WHO WAS THAT?!
IT COULDN'T BE...
NO... IT'S--!!

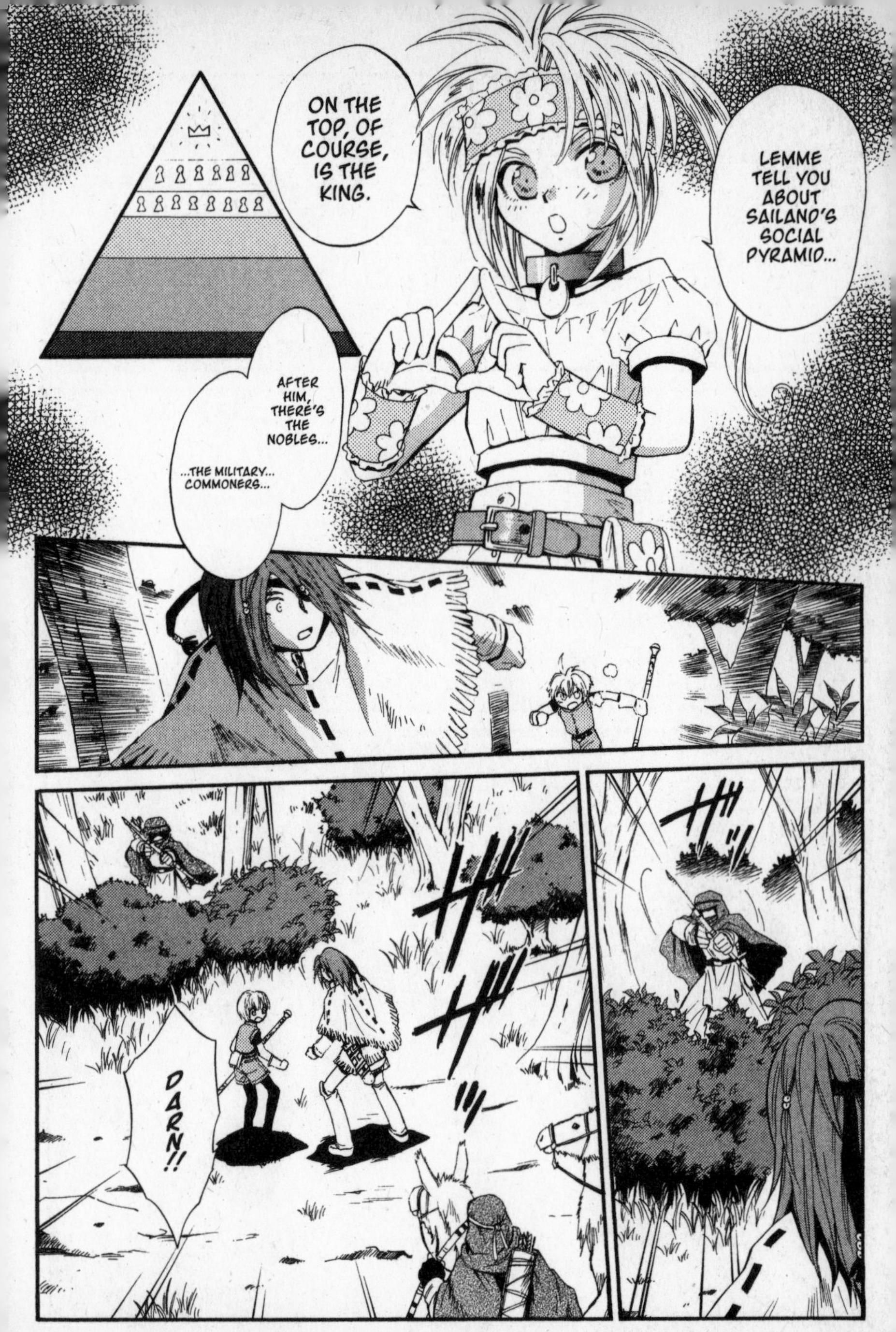
LEMME TELL YOU ABOUT SAILAND'S SOCIAL PYRAMID...
ON THE TOP, OF COURSE, IS THE KING.
AFTER HIM, THERE'S THE NOBLES...
...THE MILITARY... COMMONERS...
DARN!!

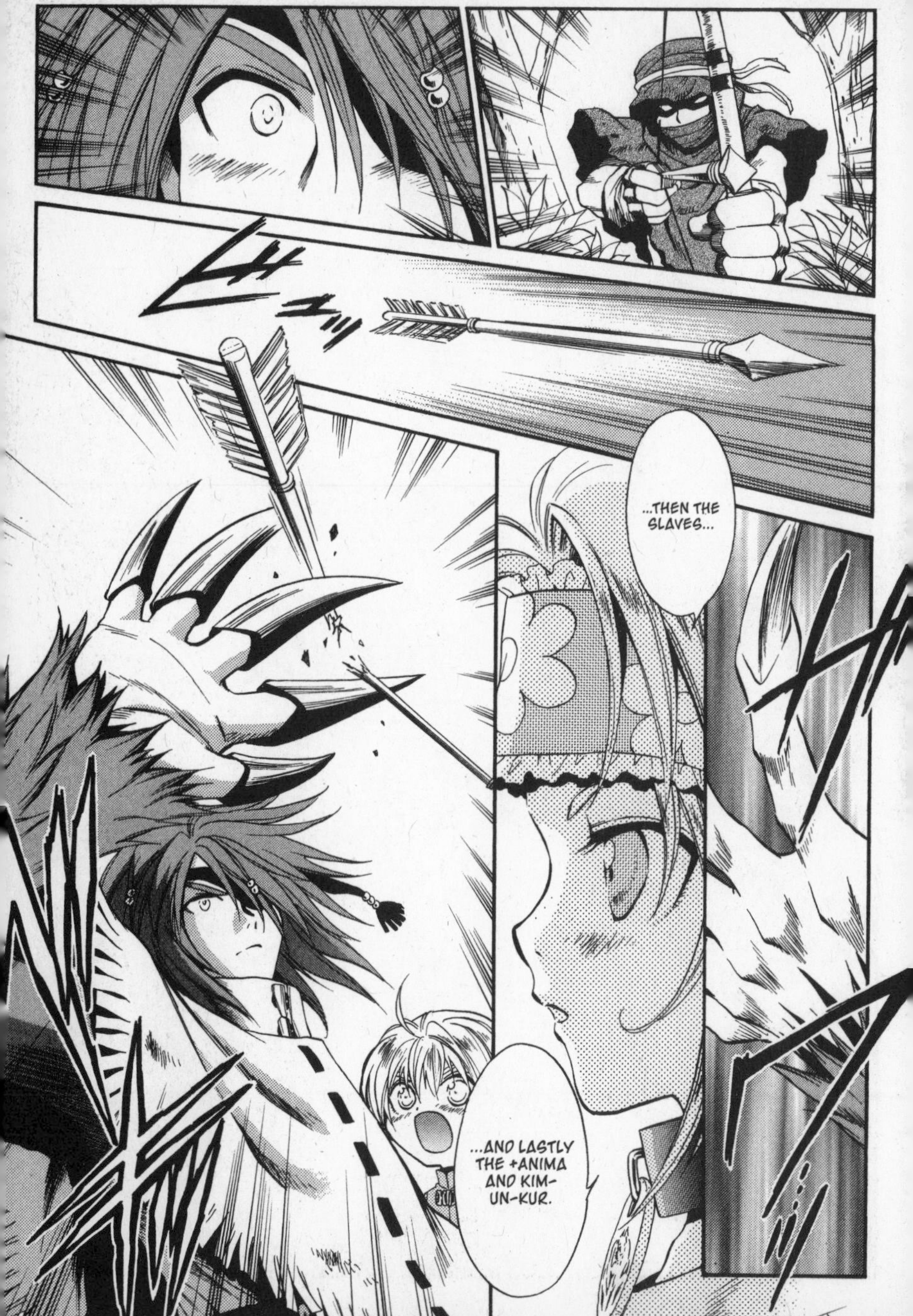
...THEN THE SLAVES...
...AND LASTLY THE +ANIMA AND KIM-UN-KUR.

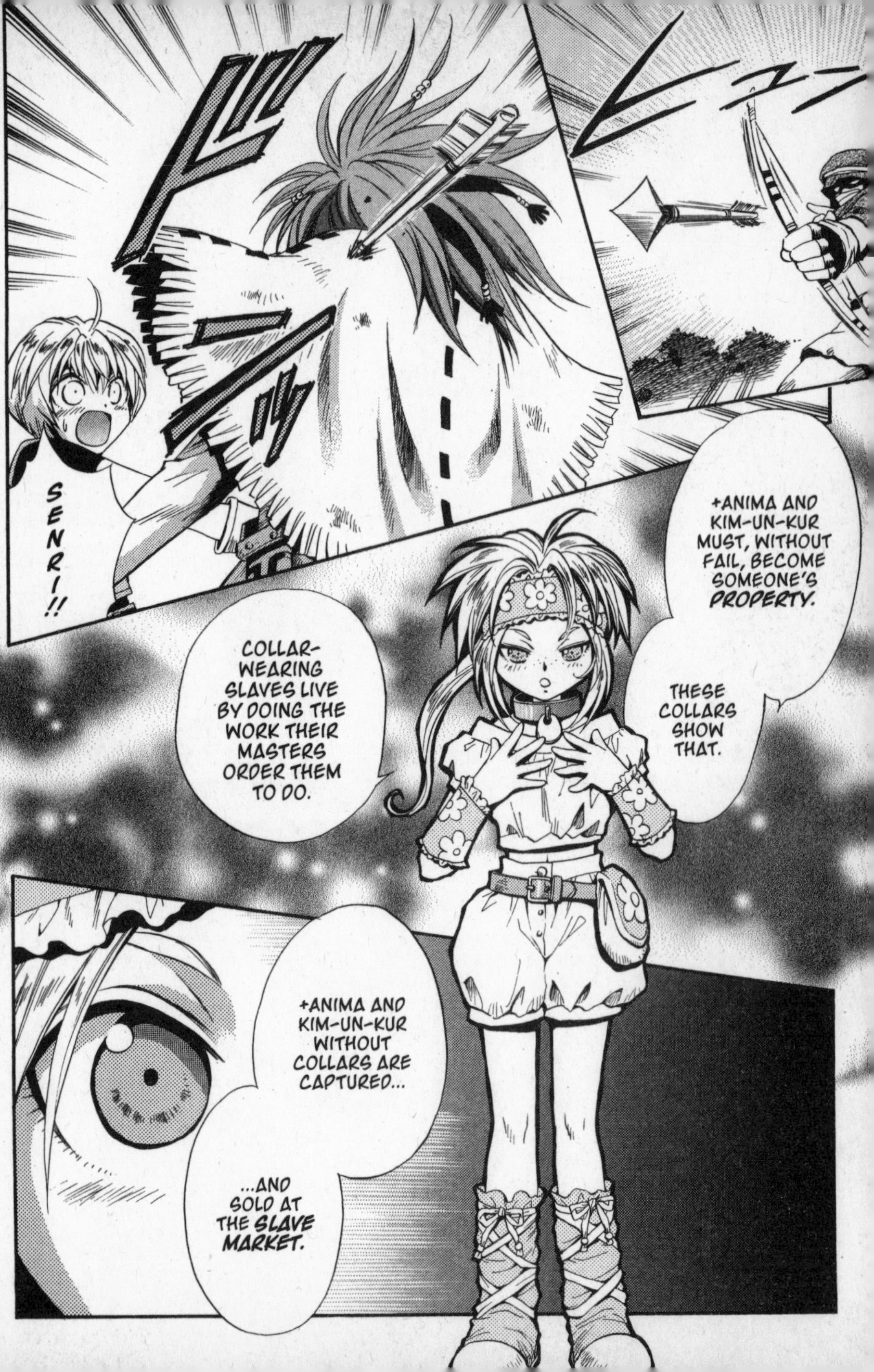
SENRI!!
+ANIMA AND KIM-UN-KUR MUST, WITHOUT FAIL, BECOME SOMEONE'S PROPERTY.
THESE COLLARS SHOW THAT.
COLLAR-WEARING SLAVES LIVE BY DOING THE WORK THEIR MASTERS ORDER THEM TO DO.
+ANIMA AND KIM-UN-KUR WITHOUT COLLARS ARE CAPTURED...
...AND SOLD AT THE SLAVE MARKET.

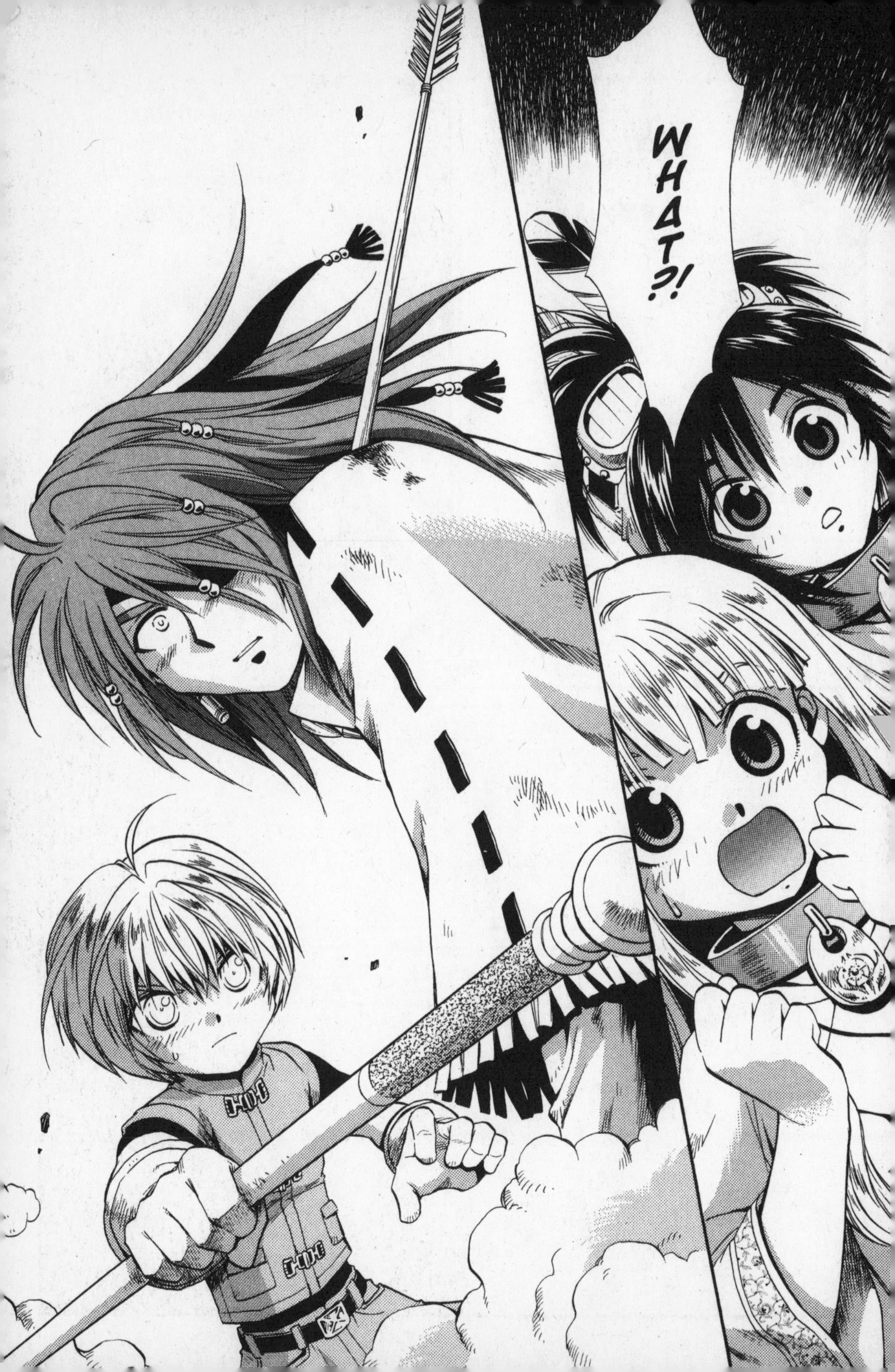
WHAT?!

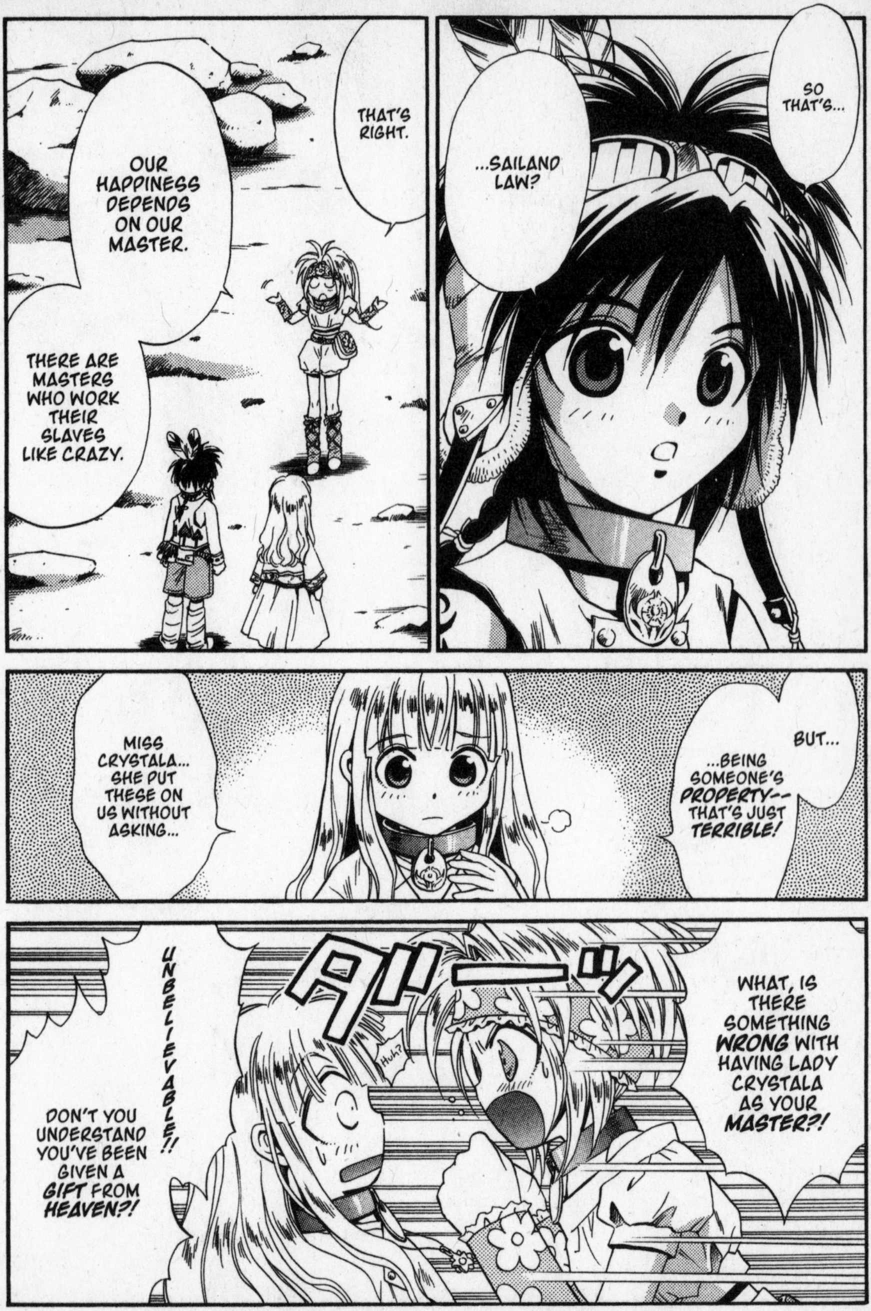
SO THAT'S...
...SAILAND LAW?
THAT'S RIGHT.
OUR HAPPINESS DEPENDS ON OUR MASTER.
THERE ARE MASTERS WHO WORK THEIR SLAVES LIKE CRAZY.
BUT...
...BEING SOMEONE'S PROPERTY--THAT'S JUST TERRIBLE!
MISS CRYSTALA... SHE PUT THESE ON US WITHOUT ASKING...
WHAT, IS THERE SOMETHING WRONG WITH HAVING LADY CRYSTALA AS YOUR MASTER?!
ダーッ
Huh?
UNBELIEVABLE!!
DON'T YOU UNDERSTAND YOU'VE BEEN GIVEN A GIFT FROM HEAVEN?!

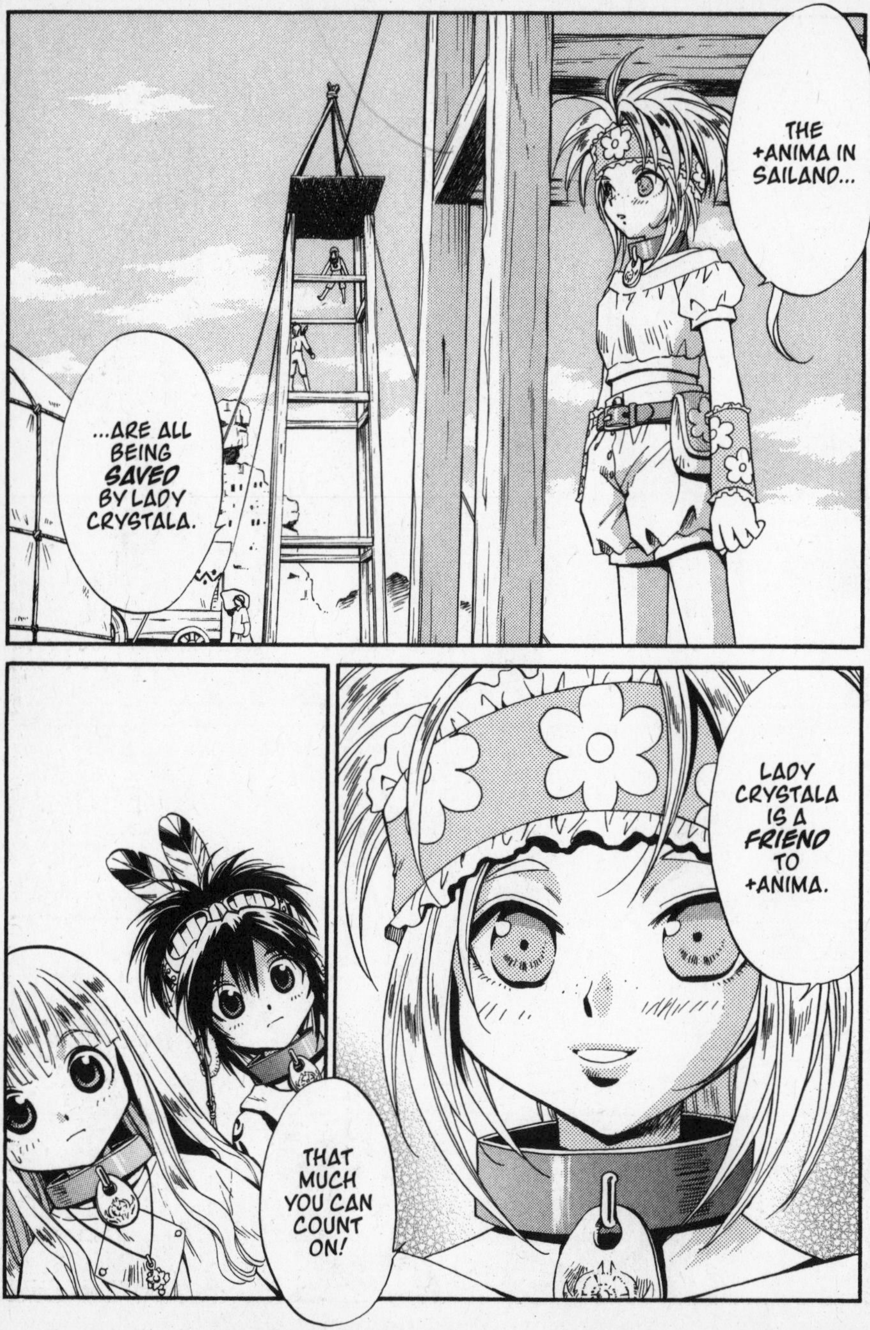
THE +ANIMA IN SAILAND...
...ARE ALL BEING SAVED BY LADY CRYSTALA.
LADY CRYSTALA IS A FRIEND TO +ANIMA.
THAT MUCH YOU CAN COUNT ON!

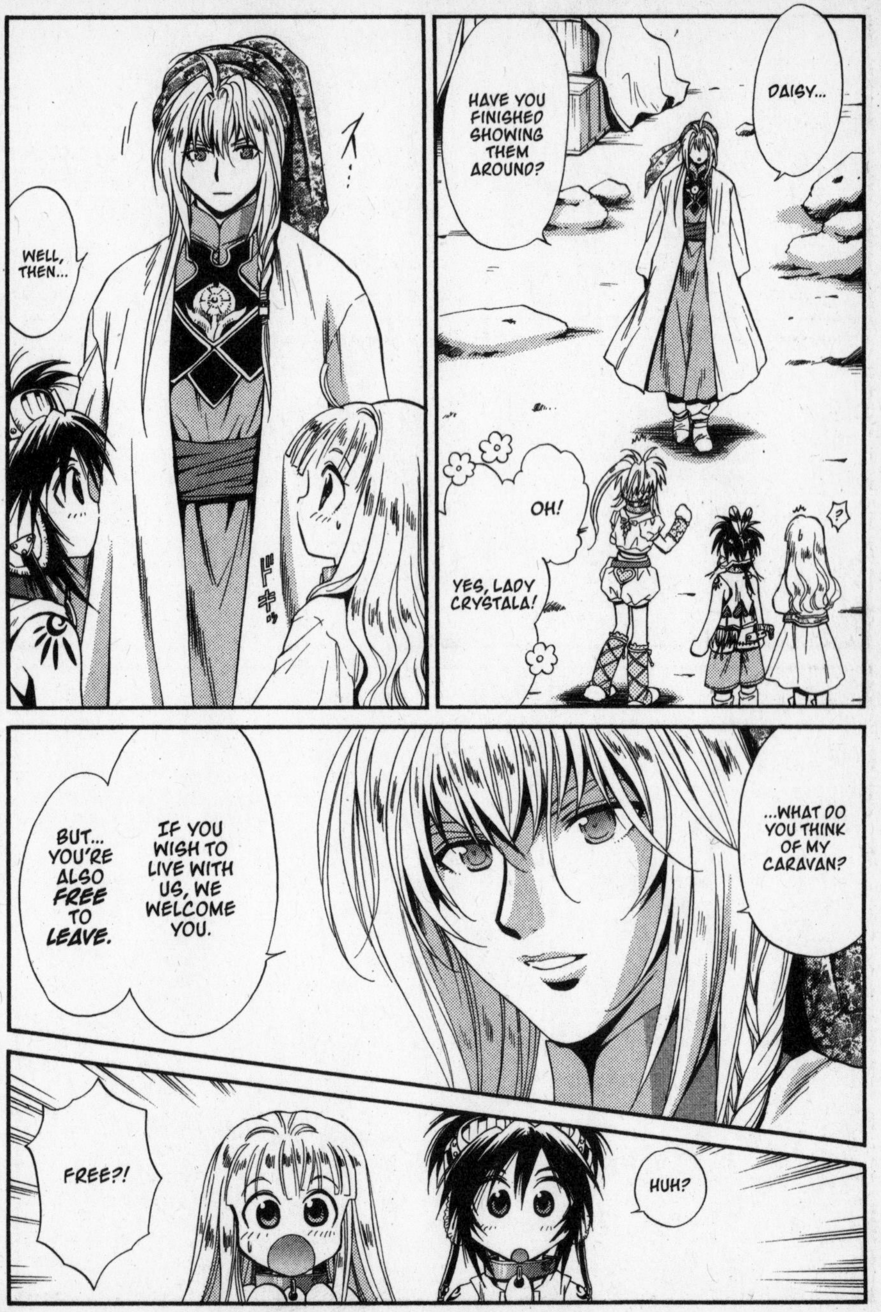
DAISY...
HAVE YOU FINISHED SHOWING THEM AROUND?
OH!
YES, LADY CRYSTALA!
?
WELL, THEN...
ドキッ
...WHAT DO YOU THINK OF MY CARAVAN?
IF YOU WISH TO LIVE WITH US, WE WELCOME YOU.
BUT... YOU'RE ALSO *FREE* TO *LEAVE*.
HUH?
FREE?!

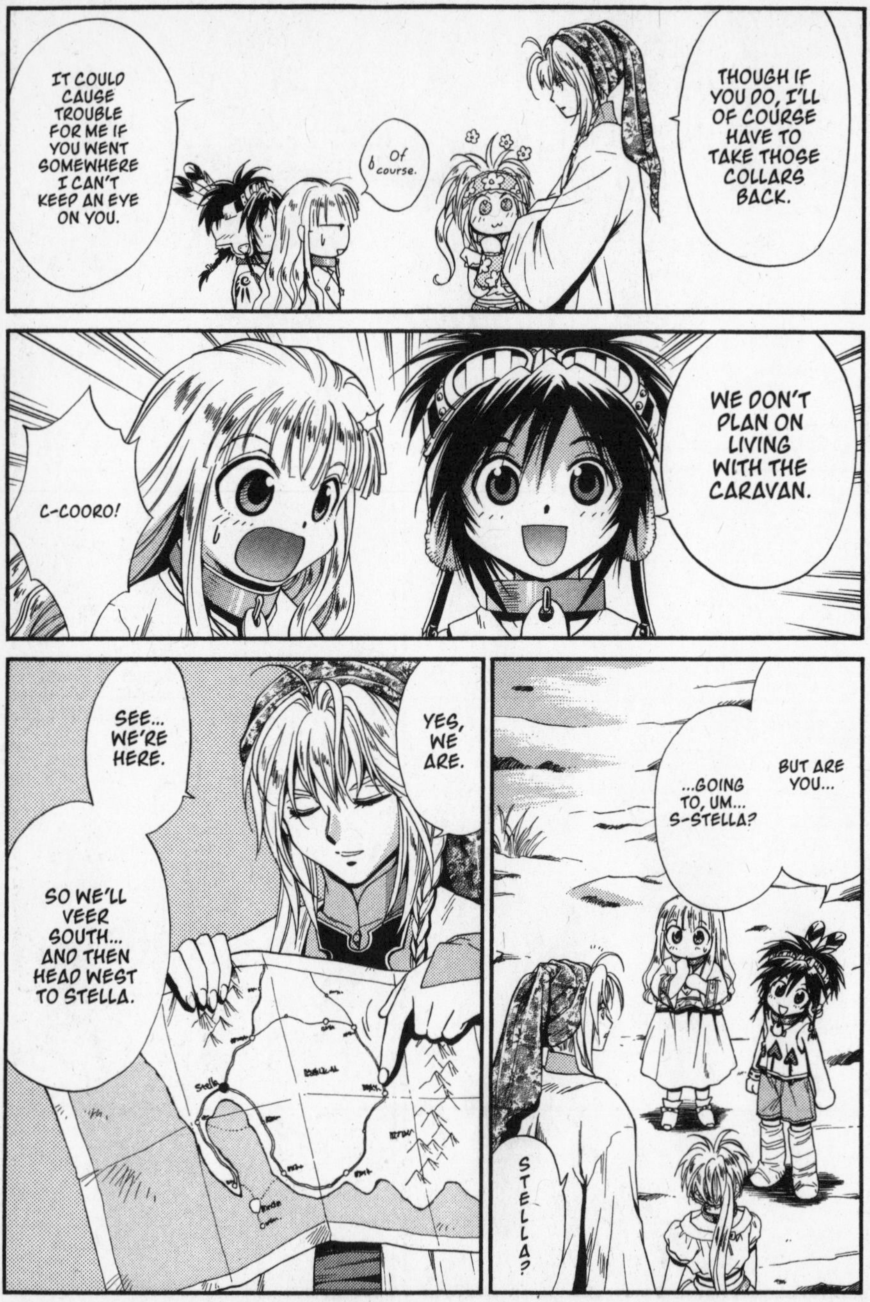
THOUGH IF YOU DO, I'LL OF COURSE HAVE TO TAKE THOSE COLLARS BACK.
Of course.
IT COULD CAUSE TROUBLE FOR ME IF YOU WENT SOMEWHERE I CAN'T KEEP AN EYE ON YOU.
WE DON'T PLAN ON LIVING WITH THE CARAVAN.
C-COORO!
BUT ARE YOU...
...GOING TO, UM... S-STELLA?
STELLA?
YES, WE ARE.
SEE... WE'RE HERE.
SO WE'LL VEER SOUTH... AND THEN HEAD WEST TO STELLA.
Stella

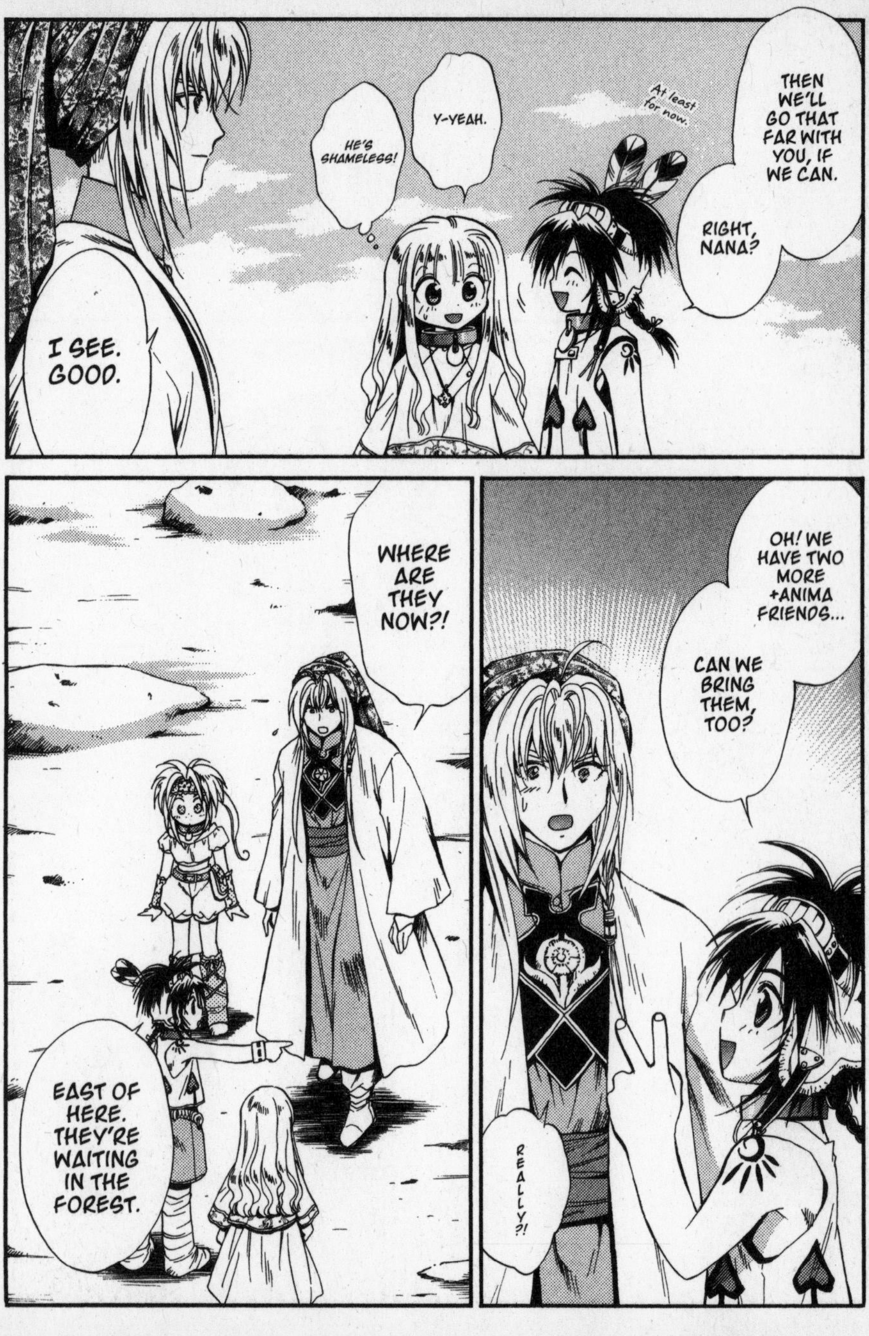
THEN WE'LL GO THAT FAR WITH YOU, IF WE CAN.
At least for now.
RIGHT, NANA?
Y-YEAH.
HE'S SHAMELESS!
I SEE. GOOD.
OH! WE HAVE TWO MORE +ANIMA FRIENDS...
CAN WE BRING THEM, TOO?
REALLY?!
WHERE ARE THEY NOW?!
EAST OF HERE. THEY'RE WAITING IN THE FOREST.

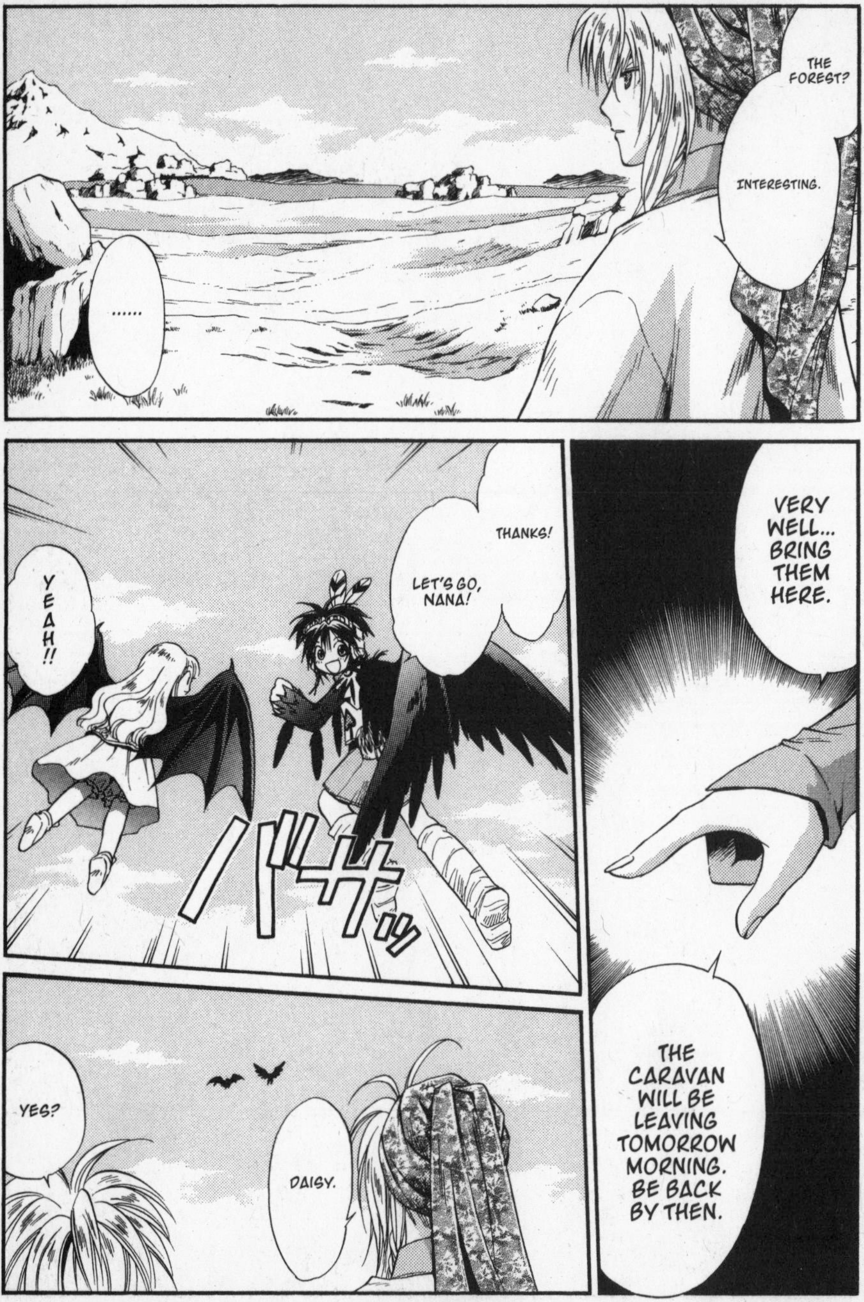
THE FOREST?
INTERESTING.
......
VERY WELL... BRING THEM HERE.
THE CARAVAN WILL BE LEAVING TOMORROW MORNING. BE BACK BY THEN.
THANKS!
LET'S GO, NANA!
YEAH!!
DAISY.
YES?

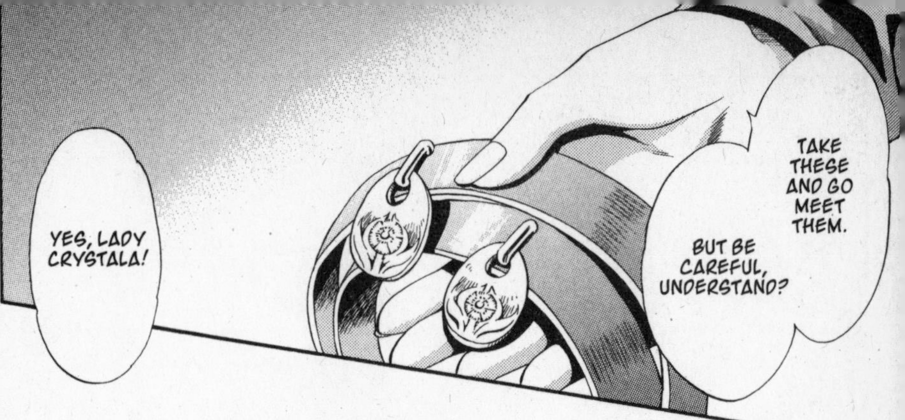
TAKE THESE AND GO MEET THEM.
BUT BE CAREFUL, UNDERSTAND?
YES, LADY CRYSTALA!

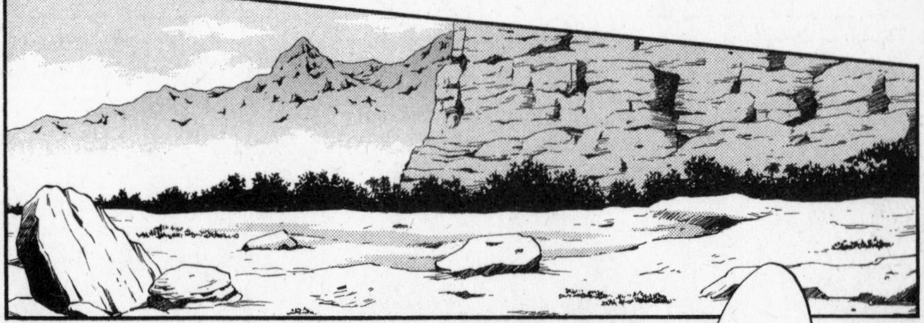

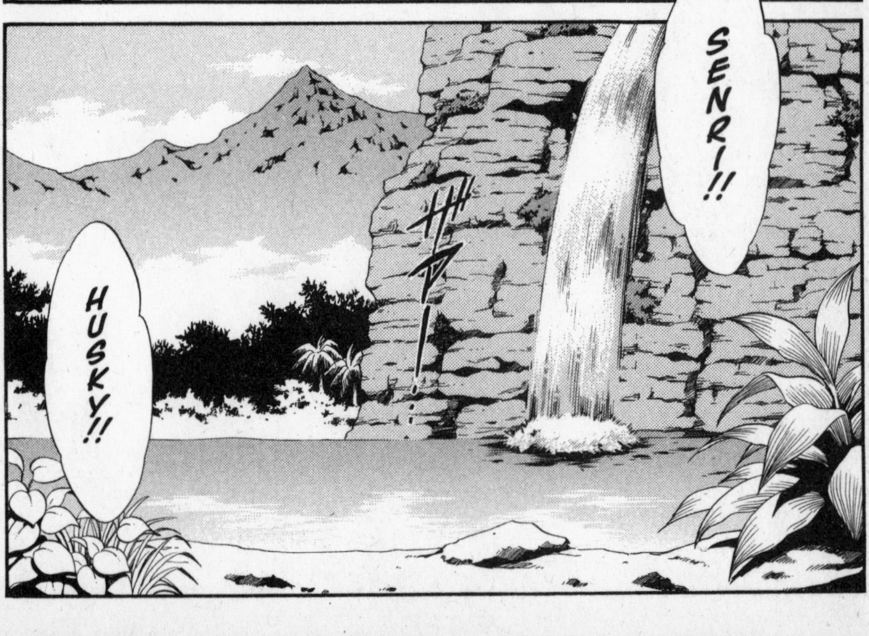
SENRI!!
HUSKY!!

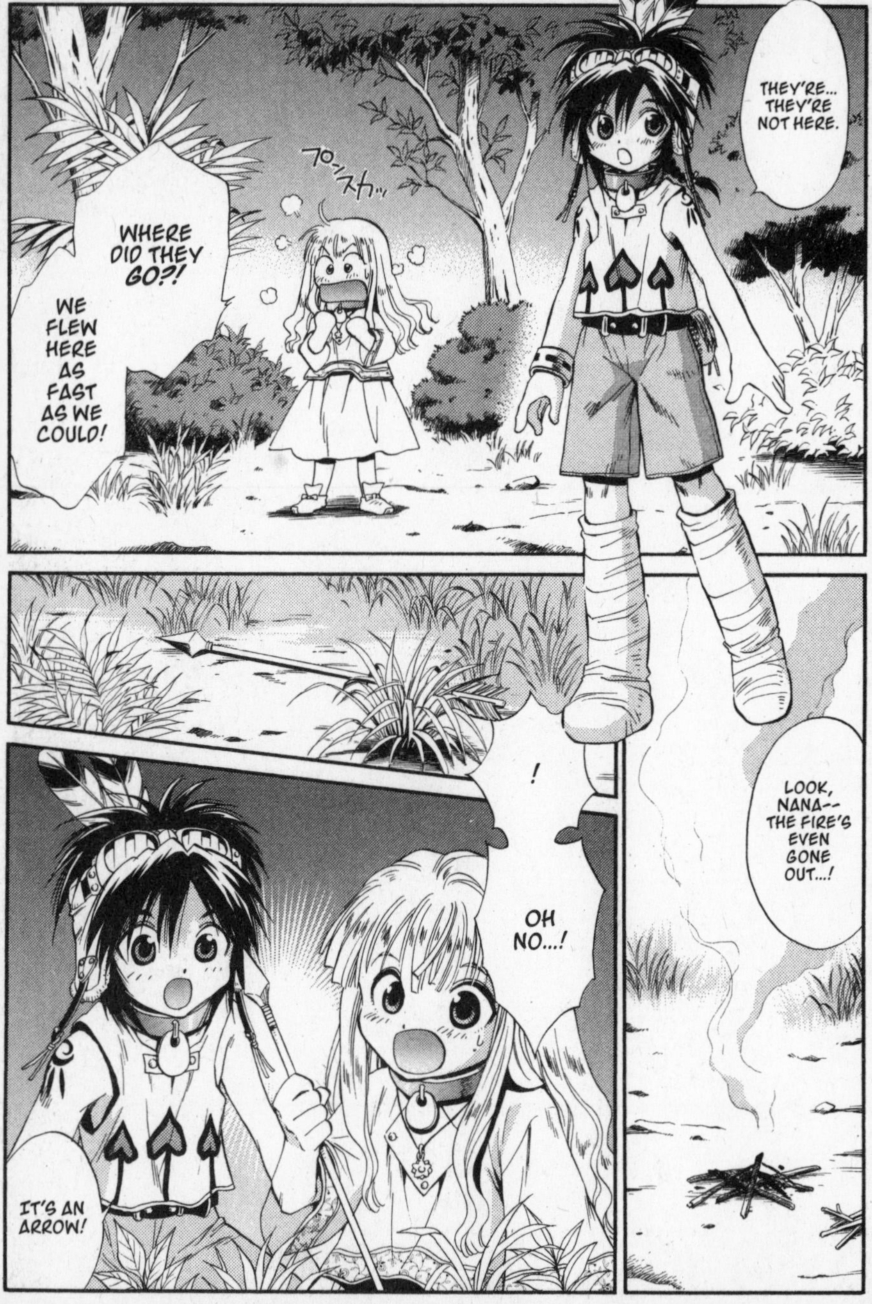
THEY'RE... THEY'RE NOT HERE.
フロ〜ンスカッ
WHERE DID THEY GO?!
WE FLEW HERE AS FAST AS WE COULD!
LOOK, NANA-- THE FIRE'S EVEN GONE OUT...!
!
OH NO...!
IT'S AN ARROW!

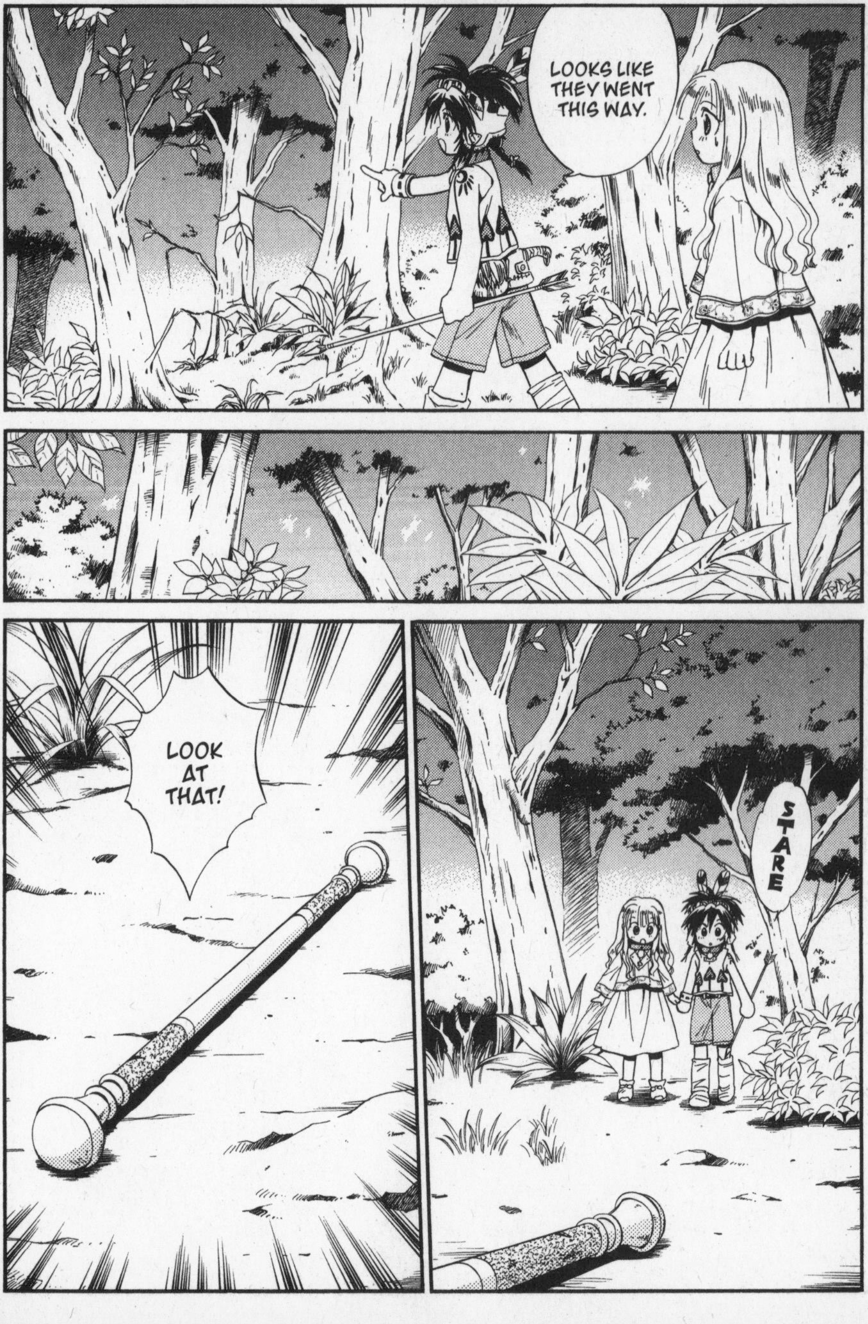
LOOKS LIKE THEY WENT THIS WAY.
STARE
LOOK AT THAT!

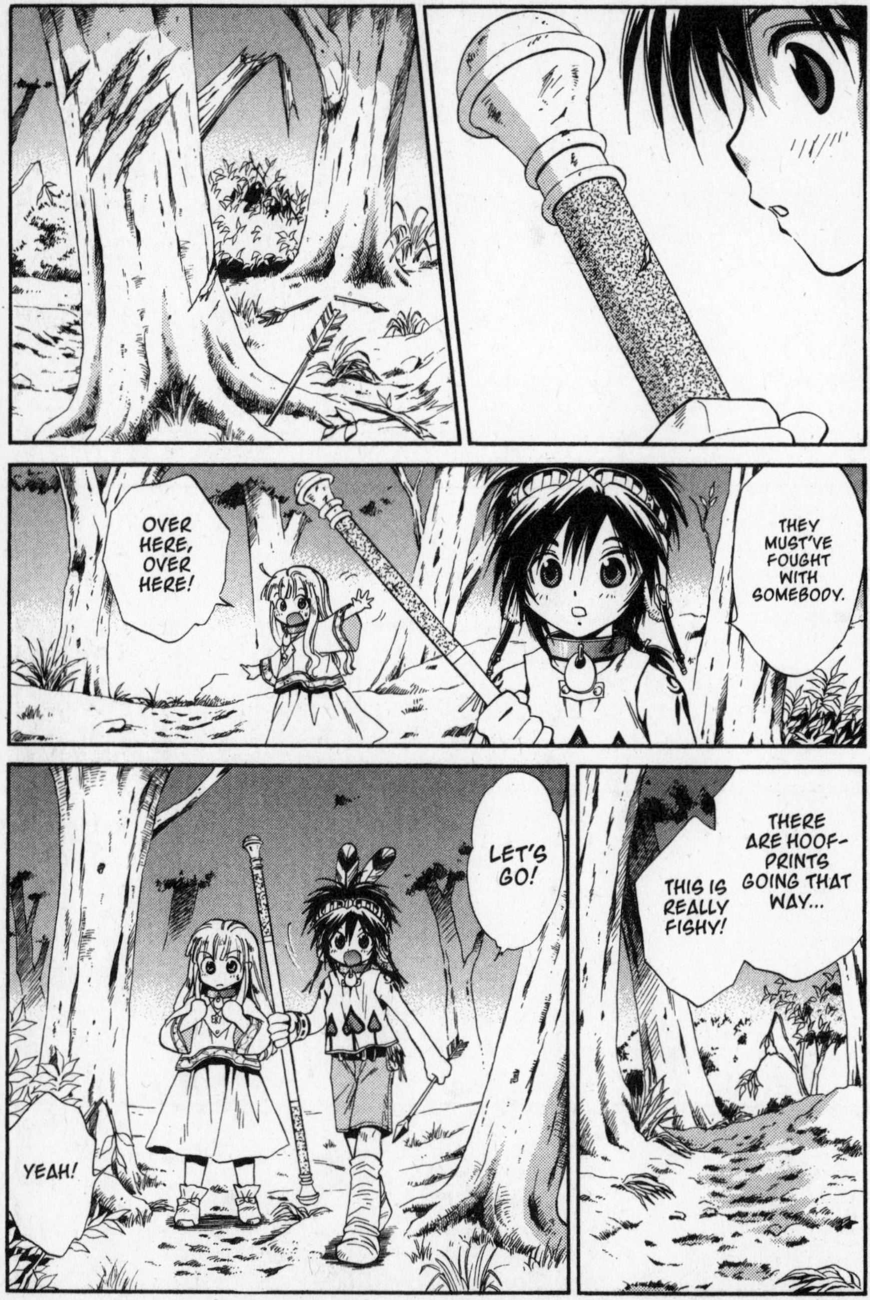
THEY MUST'VE FOUGHT WITH SOMEBODY.
OVER HERE, OVER HERE!
THERE ARE HOOF-PRINTS GOING THAT WAY...
THIS IS REALLY FISHY!
LET'S GO!
YEAH!

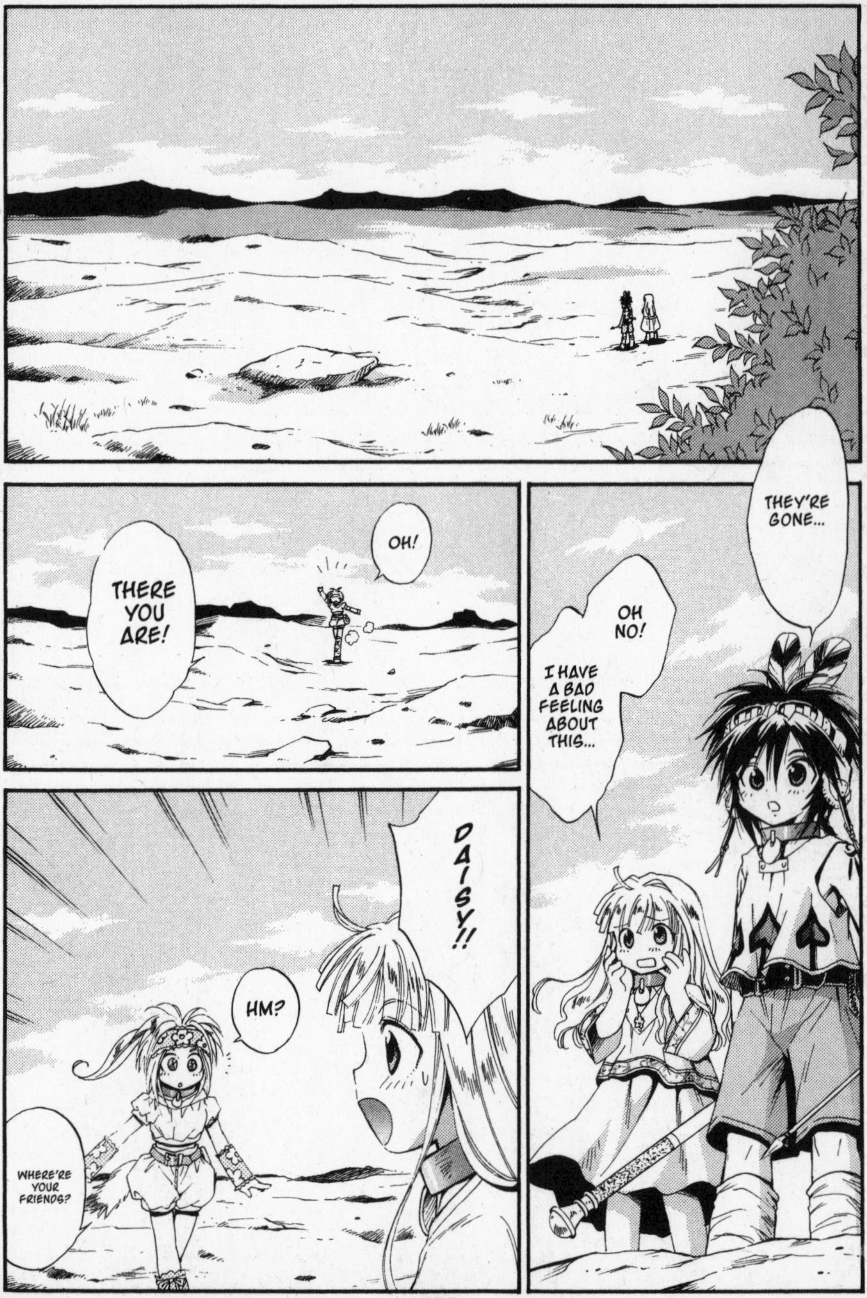
THEY'RE GONE...
OH NO!
I HAVE A BAD FEELING ABOUT THIS...
OH!
THERE YOU ARE!
DAISY!!
HM?
WHERE'RE YOUR FRIENDS?

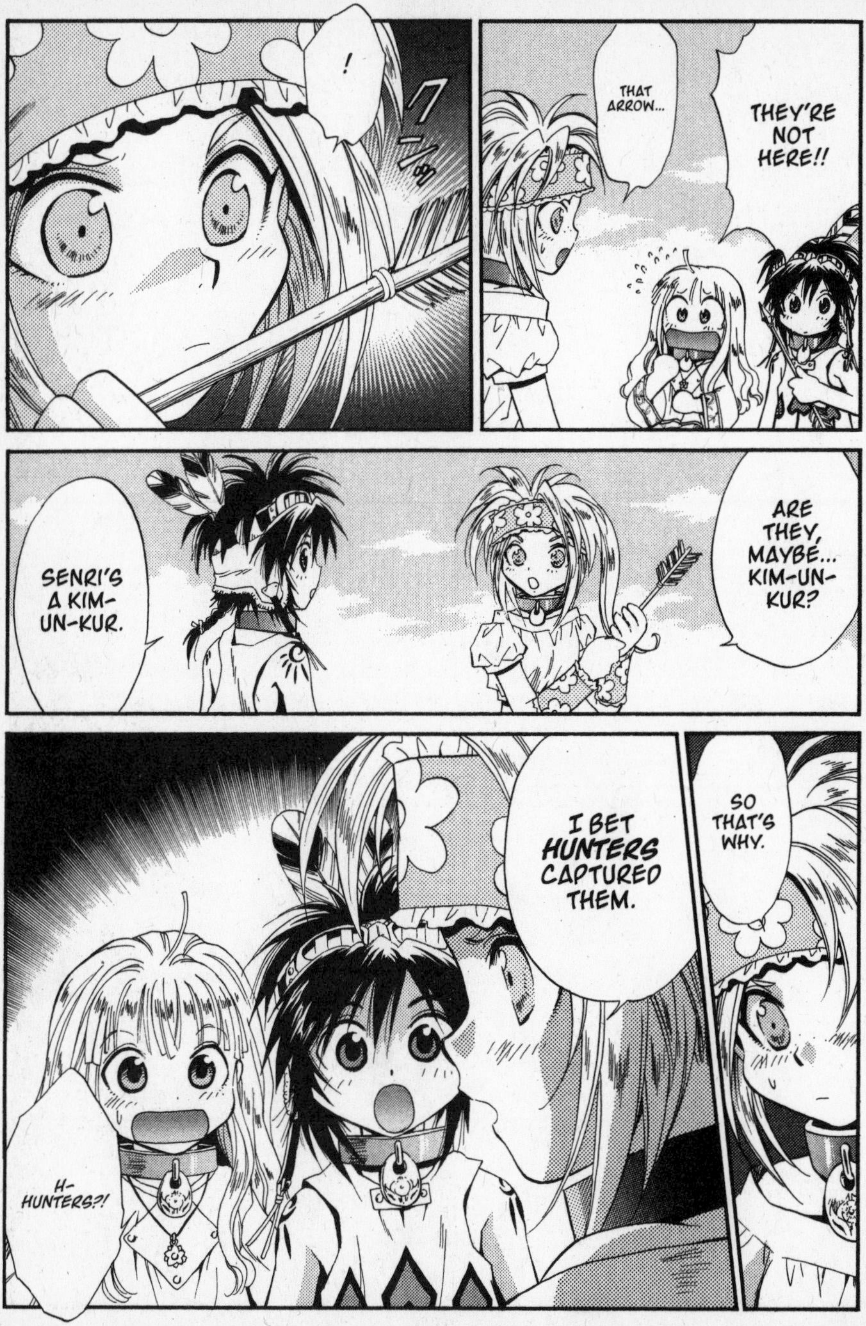
THEY'RE NOT HERE!!
THAT ARROW...
!
ARE THEY, MAYBE... KIM-UN-KUR?
SENRI'S A KIM-UN-KUR.
SO THAT'S WHY.
I BET **HUNTERS** CAPTURED THEM.
H-HUNTERS?!

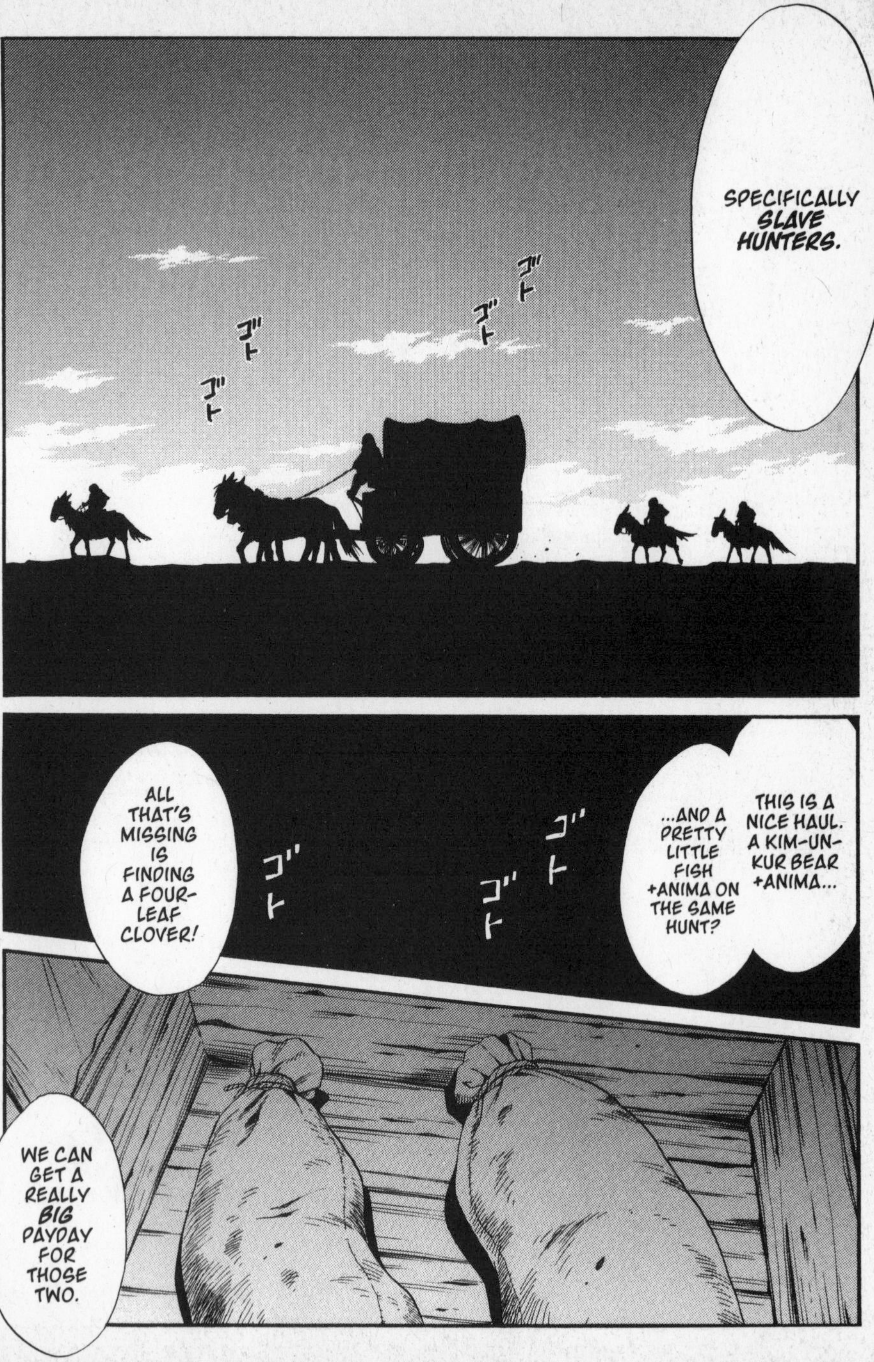
SPECIFICALLY *SLAVE HUNTERS.*
ゴト
ゴト
ゴト
ゴト
THIS IS A NICE HAUL. A KIM-UN-KUR BEAR +ANIMA...
...AND A PRETTY LITTLE FISH +ANIMA ON THE SAME HUNT?
ゴト
ゴト
ゴト
ALL THAT'S MISSING IS FINDING A FOUR-LEAF CLOVER!
WE CAN GET A REALLY *BIG* PAYDAY FOR THOSE TWO.

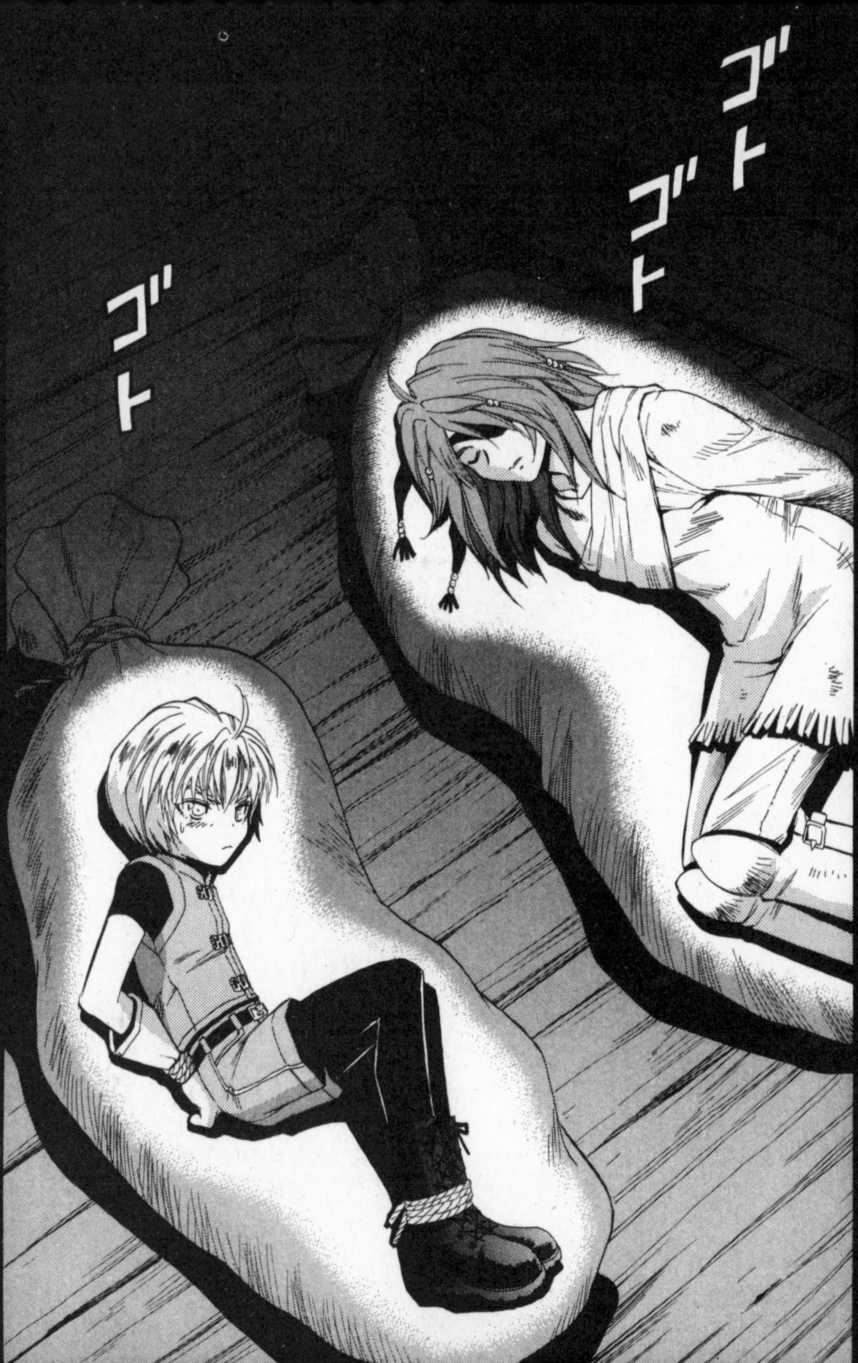
ゴト
ゴト
ゴト

I cannot sleep well!

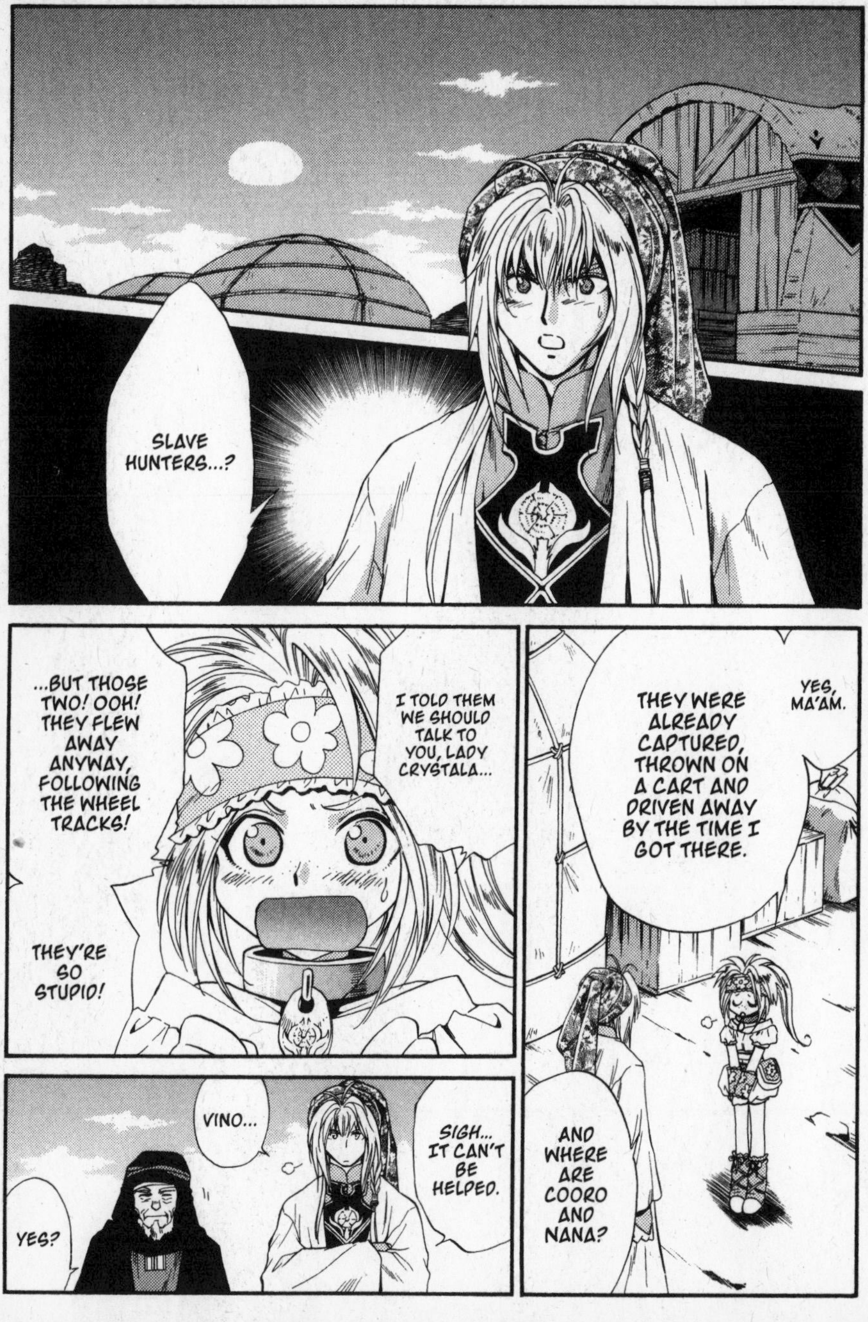
SLAVE HUNTERS...?
YES, MA'AM.
THEY WERE ALREADY CAPTURED, THROWN ON A CART AND DRIVEN AWAY BY THE TIME I GOT THERE.
AND WHERE ARE COORO AND NANA?
I TOLD THEM WE SHOULD TALK TO YOU, LADY CRYSTALA...
...BUT THOSE TWO! OOH! THEY FLEW AWAY ANYWAY, FOLLOWING THE WHEEL TRACKS!
THEY'RE SO STUPID!
SIGH... IT CAN'T BE HELPED.
VINO...
YES?

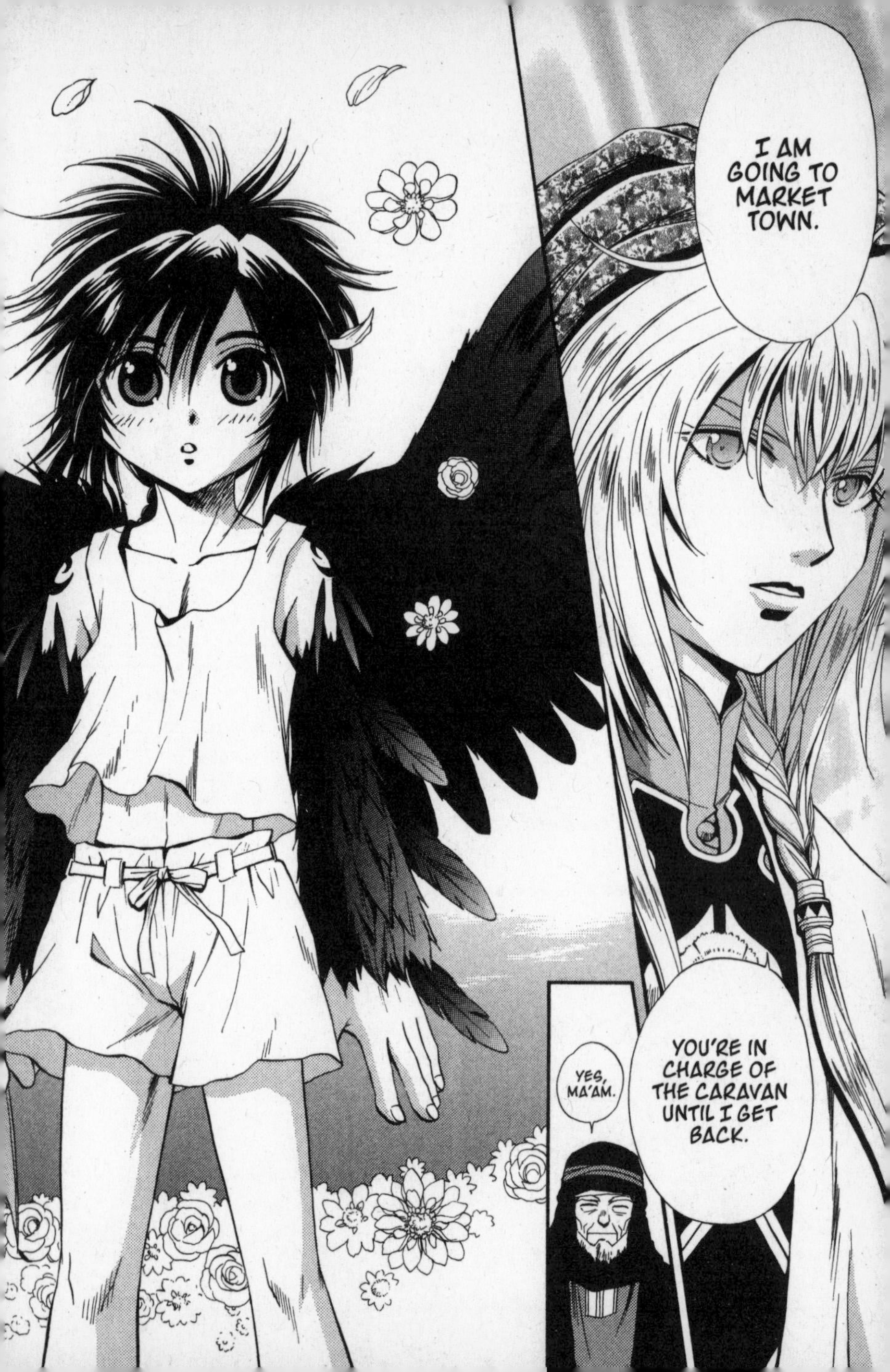
I AM GOING TO MARKET TOWN.
YOU'RE IN CHARGE OF THE CARAVAN UNTIL I GET BACK.
YES, MA'AM.

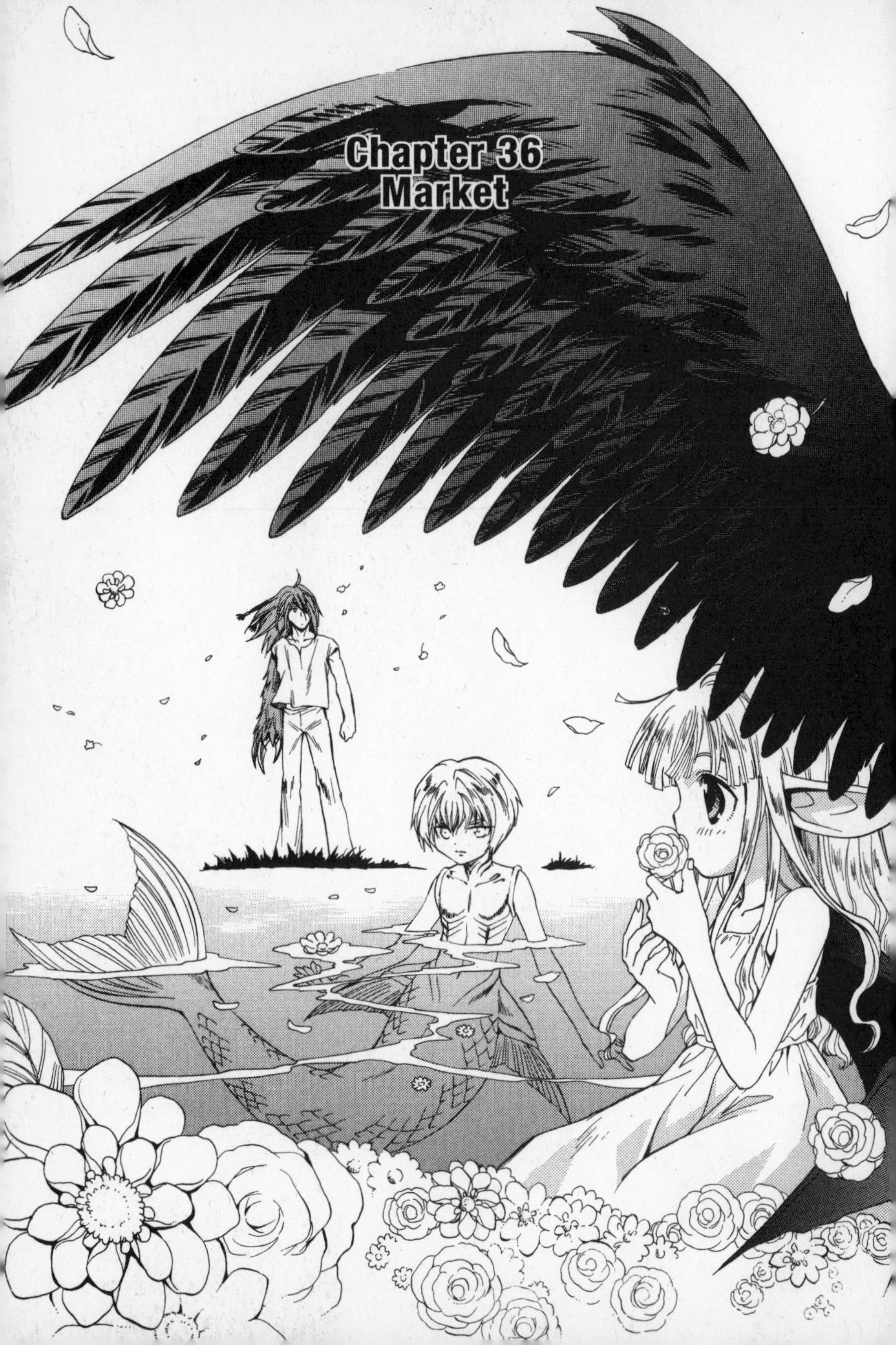
Chapter 36
Market

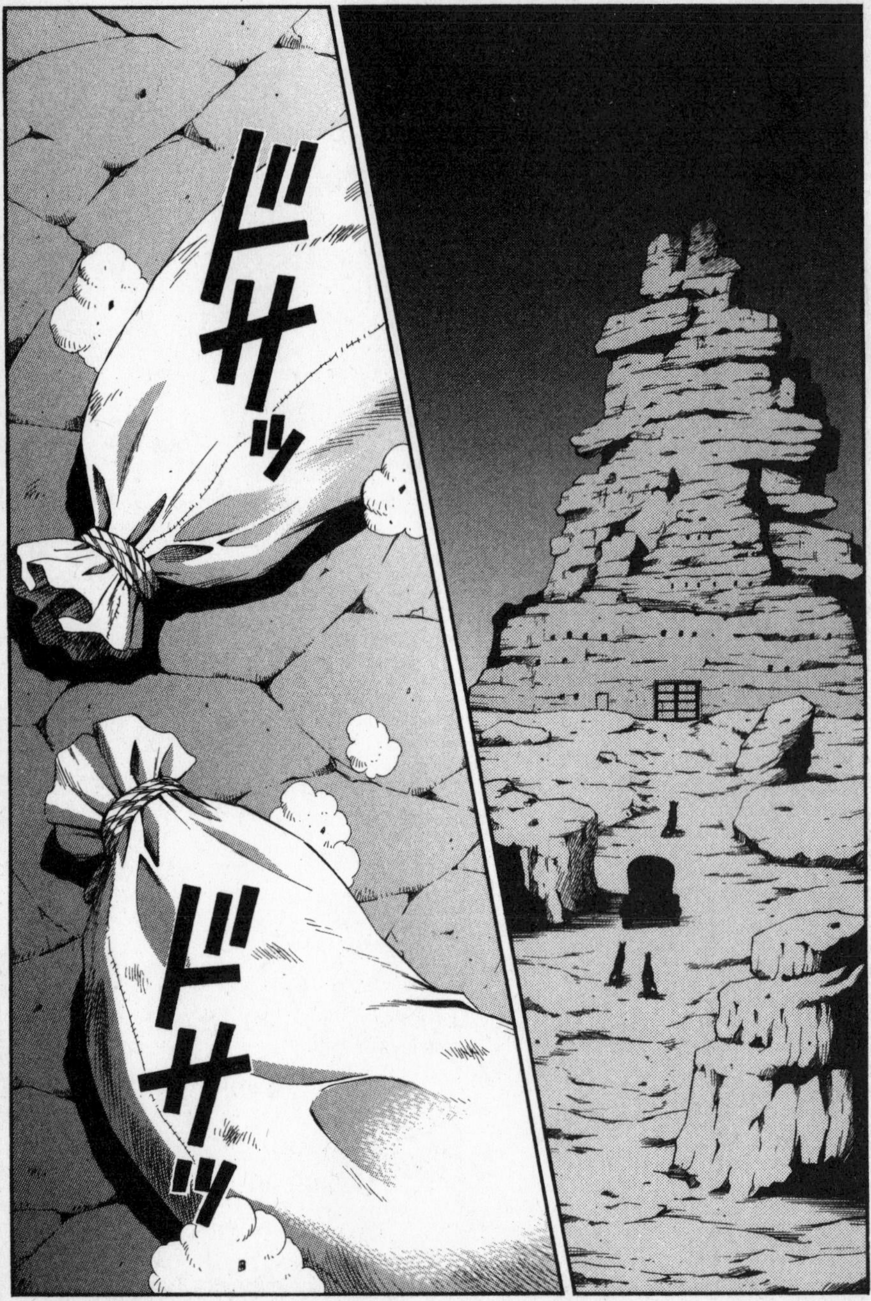
ドサッ
ドサッ

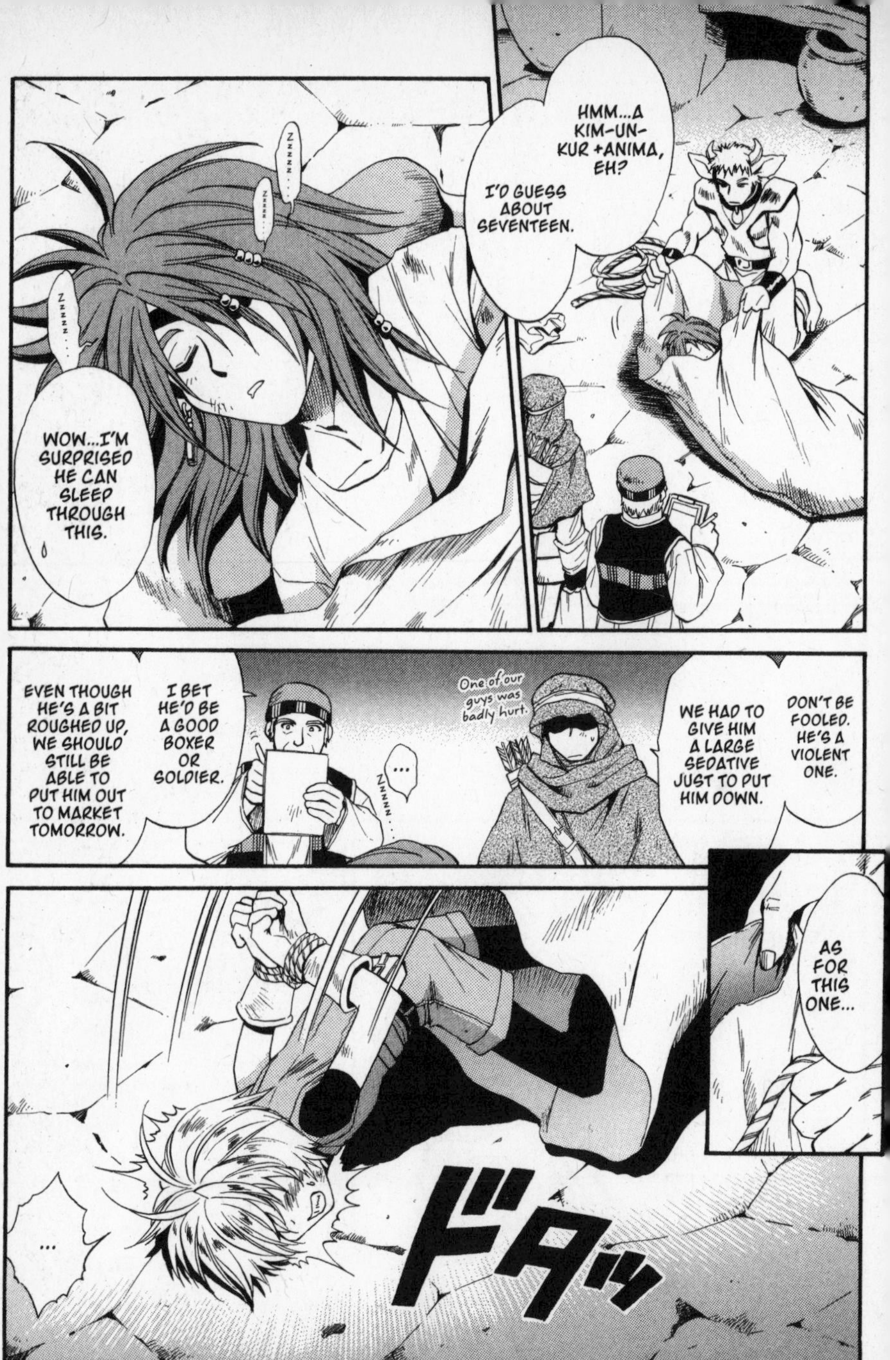
HMM...A KIM-UN-KUR +ANIMA, EH?
I'D GUESS ABOUT SEVENTEEN.
Zzzzz...
Zzzzz...
Zzzzz...
WOW...I'M SURPRISED HE CAN SLEEP THROUGH THIS.
DON'T BE FOOLED. HE'S A VIOLENT ONE.
WE HAD TO GIVE HIM A LARGE SEDATIVE JUST TO PUT HIM DOWN.
One of our guys was badly hurt.
...
Zzzzz...
I BET HE'D BE A GOOD BOXER OR SOLDIER.
EVEN THOUGH HE'S A BIT ROUGHED UP, WE SHOULD STILL BE ABLE TO PUT HIM OUT TO MARKET TOMORROW.
AS FOR THIS ONE...
!
ドタッ
...

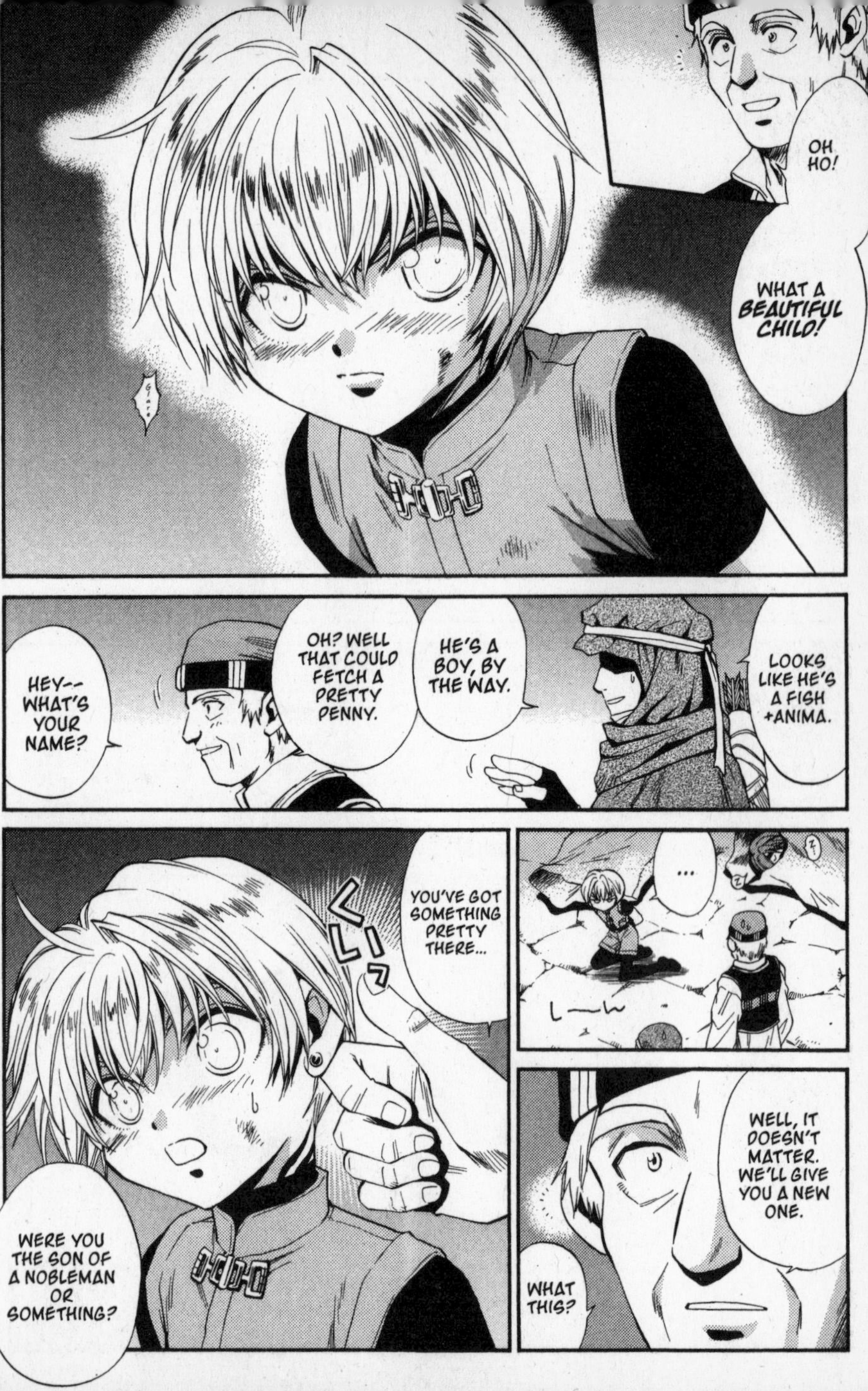
OH HO!
WHAT A BEAUTIFUL CHILD!
Glare
LOOKS LIKE HE'S A FISH +ANIMA.
HE'S A BOY, BY THE WAY.
OH? WELL THAT COULD FETCH A PRETTY PENNY.
HEY-- WHAT'S YOUR NAME?
...
WELL, IT DOESN'T MATTER. WE'LL GIVE YOU A NEW ONE.
WHAT THIS?
YOU'VE GOT SOMETHING PRETTY THERE...
WERE YOU THE SON OF A NOBLEMAN OR SOMETHING?

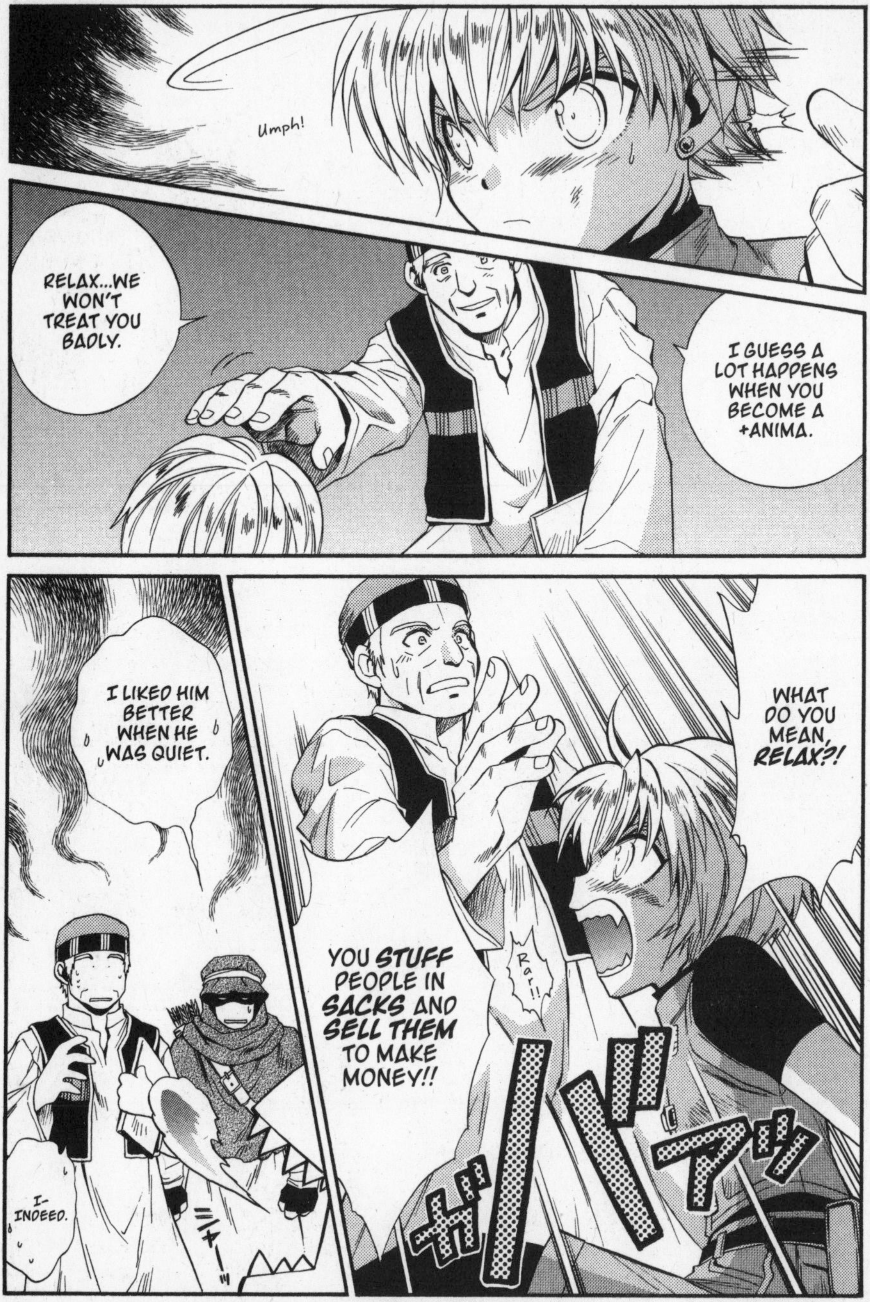
Umph!
I GUESS A LOT HAPPENS WHEN YOU BECOME A +ANIMA.
RELAX...WE WON'T TREAT YOU BADLY.
WHAT DO YOU MEAN, **RELAX**?!
YOU **STUFF** PEOPLE IN **SACKS** AND **SELL THEM** TO MAKE MONEY!!
Rar!!
I LIKED HIM BETTER WHEN HE WAS QUIET.
I-INDEED.

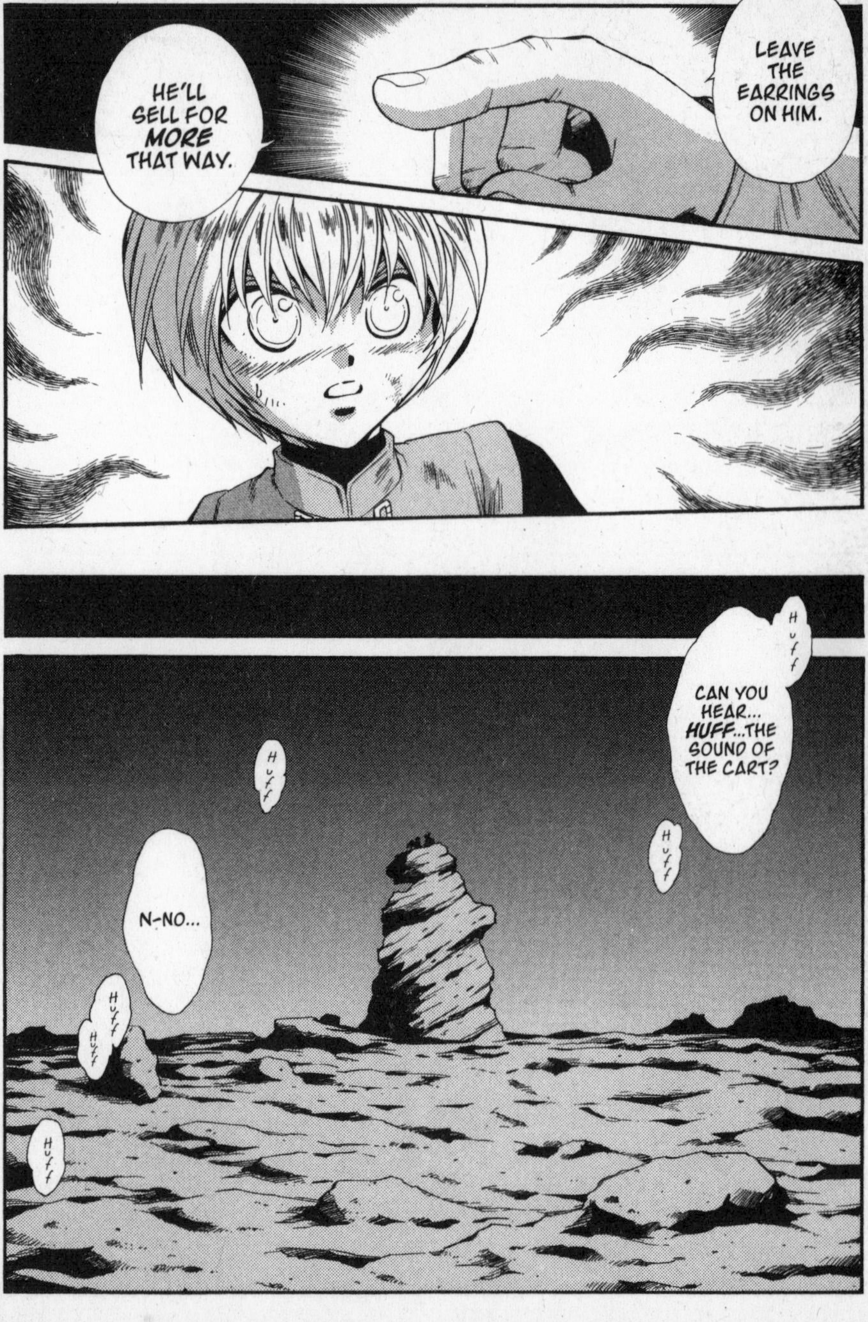
LEAVE THE EARRINGS ON HIM.
HE'LL SELL FOR MORE THAT WAY.
Huff
CAN YOU HEAR... HUFF...THE SOUND OF THE CART?
Huff
Huff
N-NO...
Huff
Huff
Huff

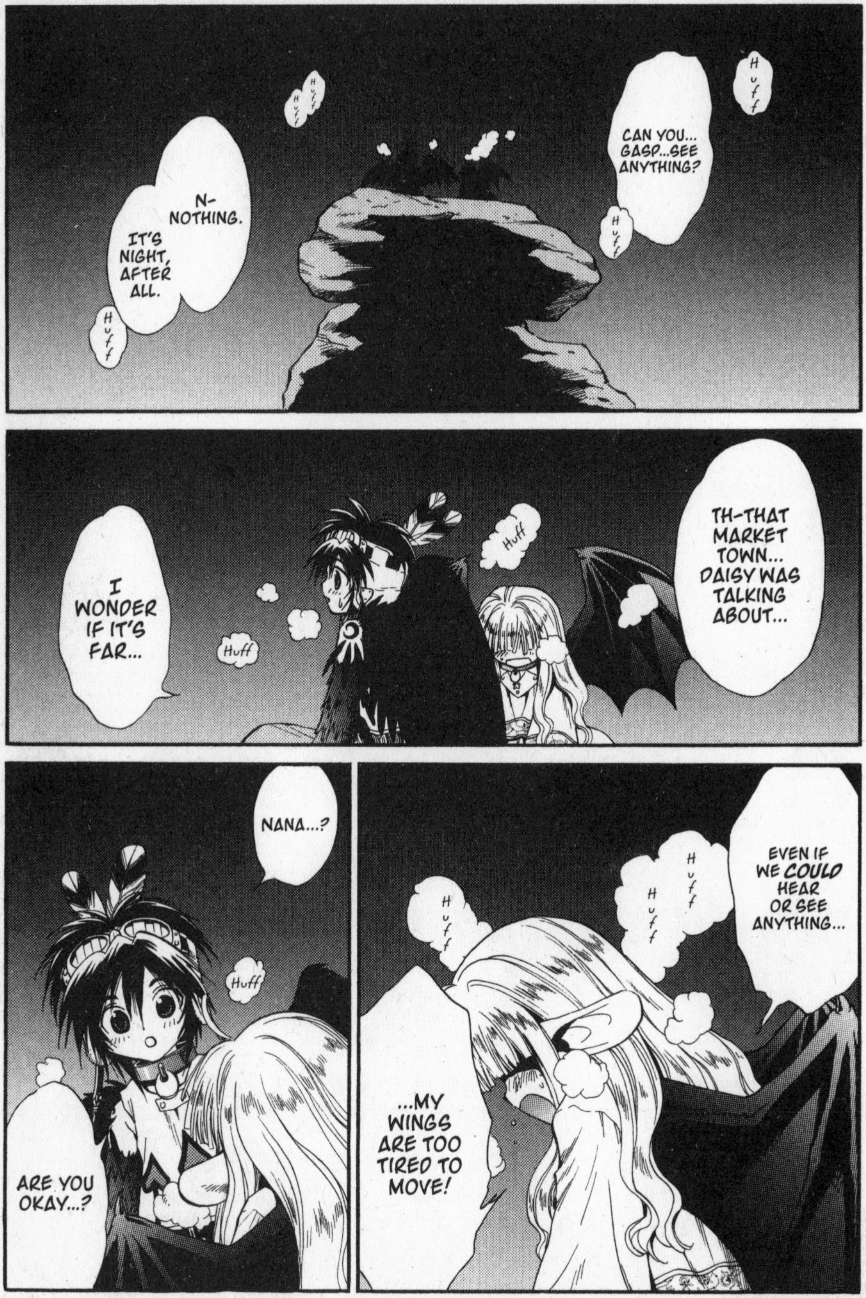
Huff
CAN YOU... GASP...SEE ANYTHING?
Huff
Huff Huff
N-NOTHING.
IT'S NIGHT, AFTER ALL.
Huff
TH-THAT MARKET TOWN... DAISY WAS TALKING ABOUT...
Huff
I WONDER IF IT'S FAR...
Huff
EVEN IF WE *COULD* HEAR OR SEE ANYTHING...
Huff
Huff
Huff
...MY WINGS ARE TOO TIRED TO MOVE!
NANA...?
Huff
ARE YOU OKAY...?

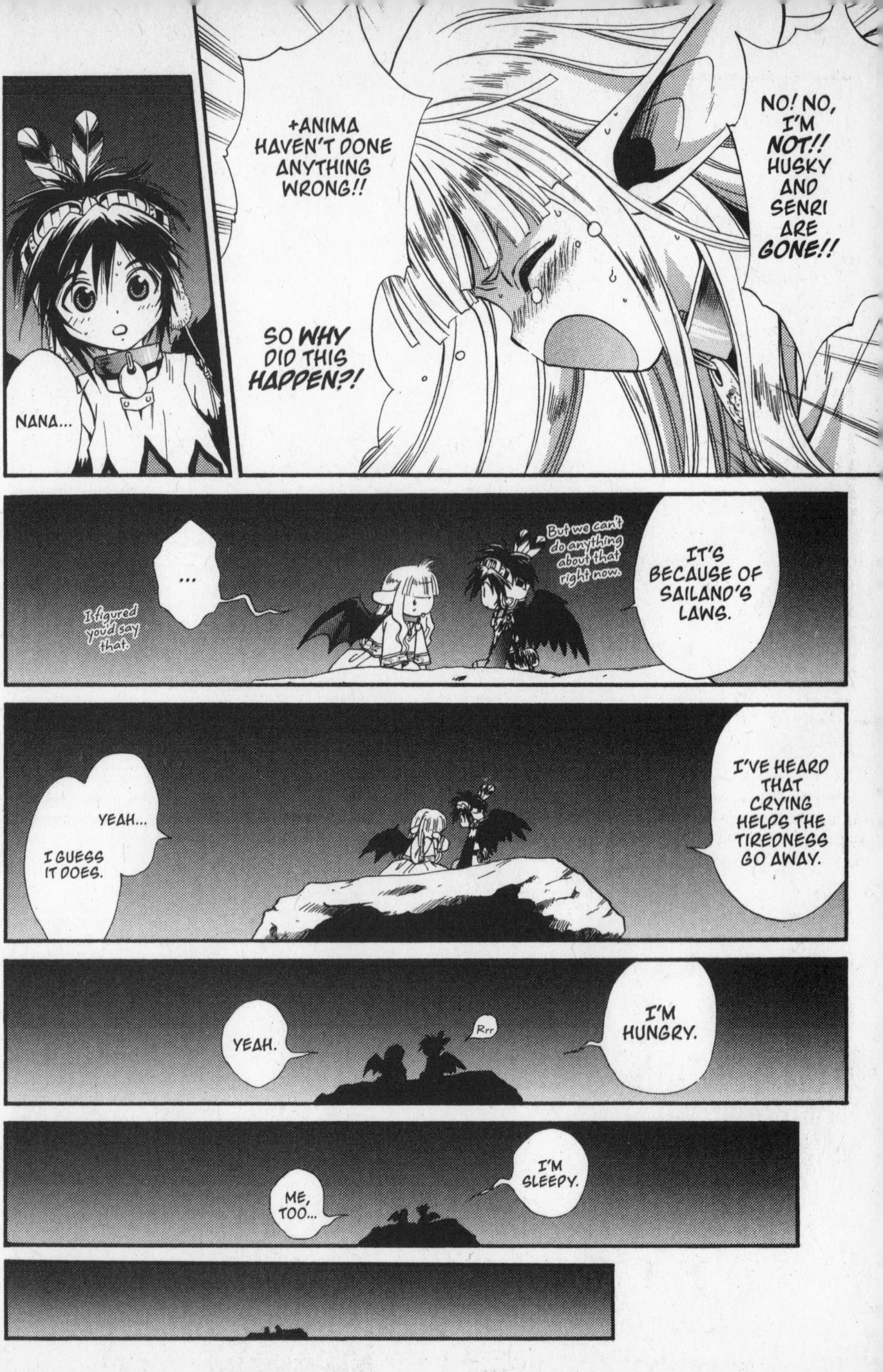
NO! NO, I'M NOT!! HUSKY AND SENRI ARE GONE!!
+ANIMA HAVEN'T DONE ANYTHING WRONG!!
SO WHY DID THIS HAPPEN?!
NANA...
IT'S BECAUSE OF SAILAND'S LAWS.
But we can't do anything about that right now.
...
I figured you'd say that.
I'VE HEARD THAT CRYING HELPS THE TIREDNESS GO AWAY.
YEAH... I GUESS IT DOES.
I'M HUNGRY.
Rrr
YEAH.
I'M SLEEPY.
ME, TOO...

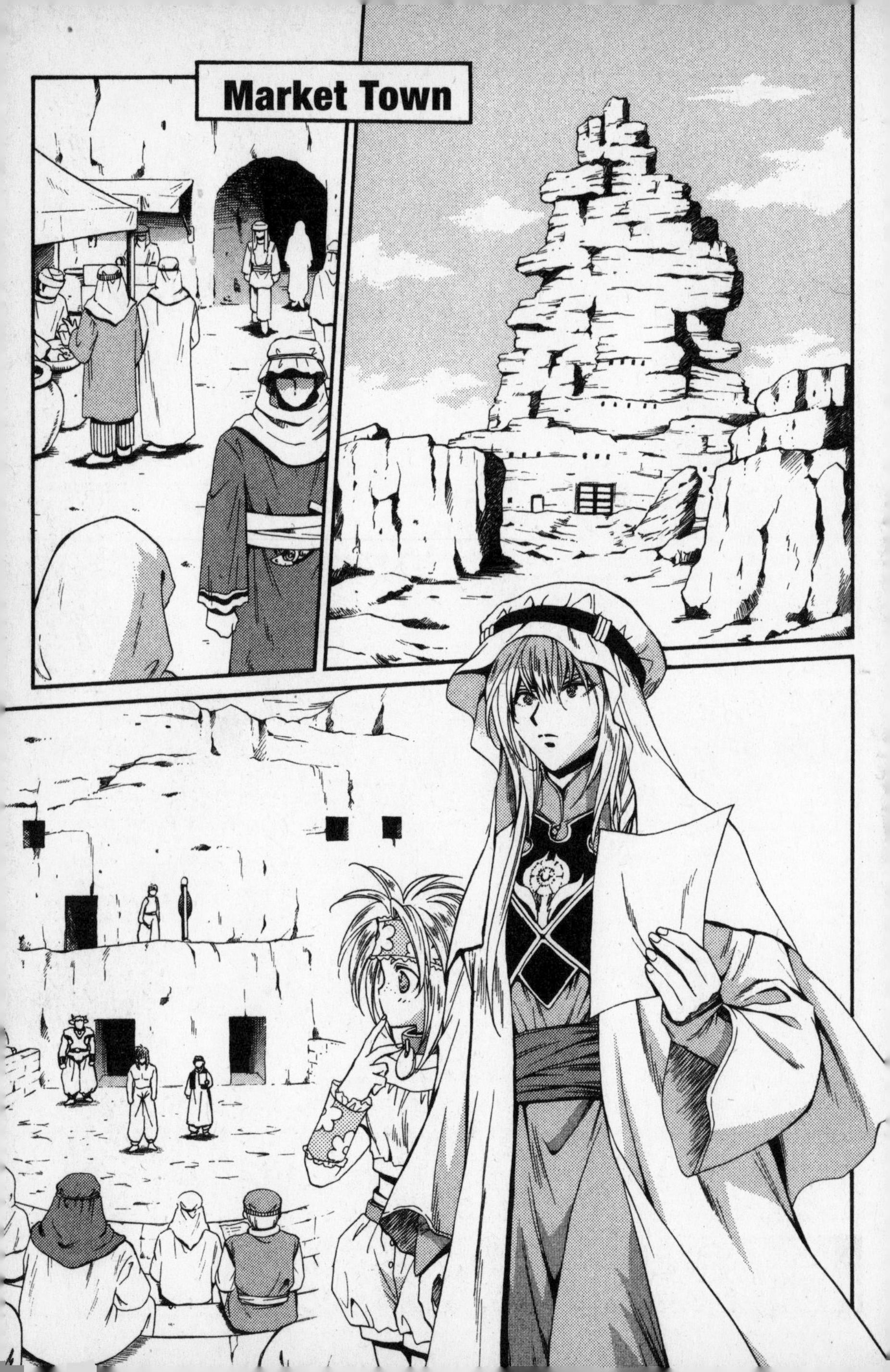
Market Town

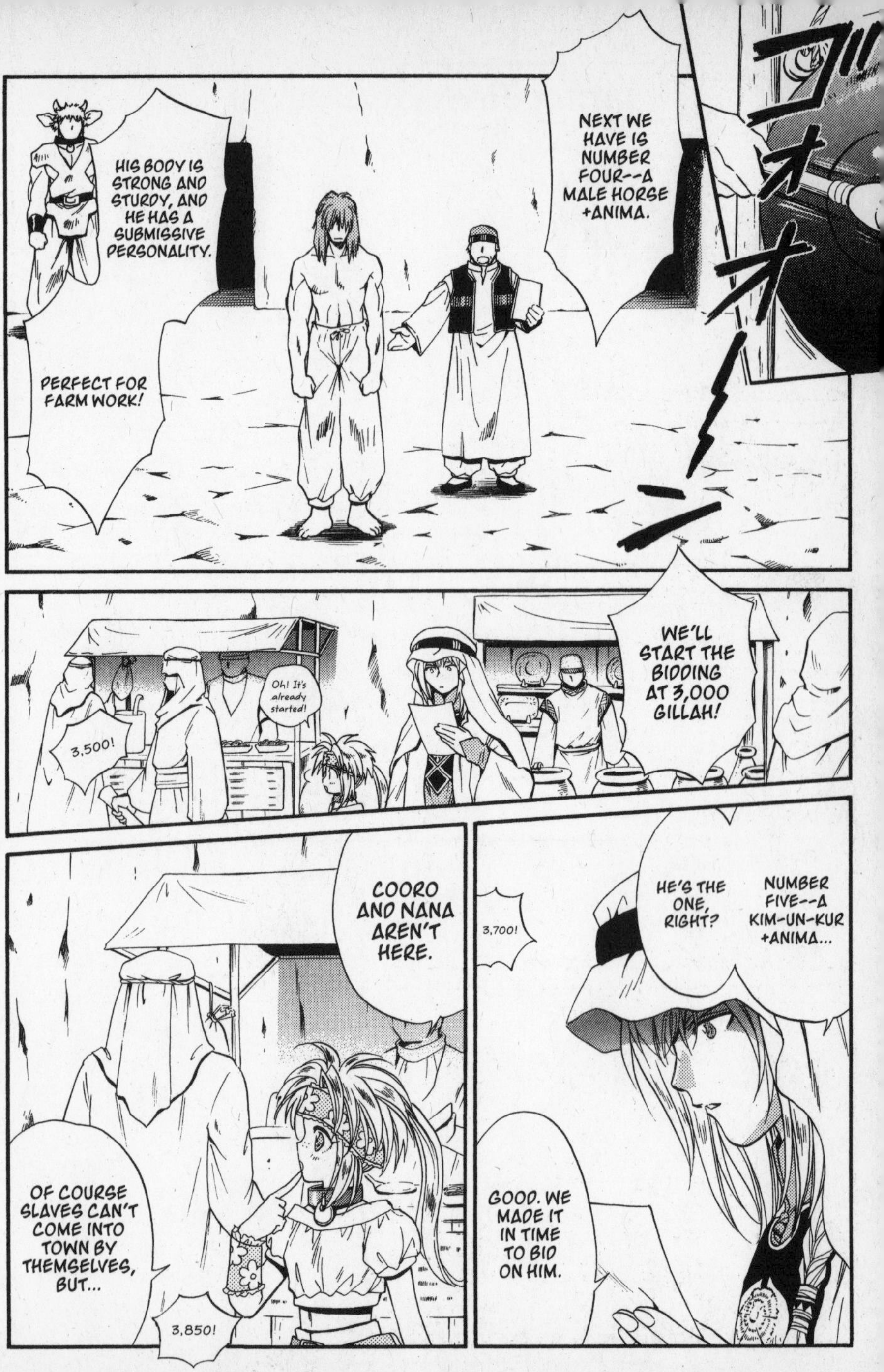
NEXT WE HAVE IS NUMBER FOUR--A MALE HORSE +ANIMA.
HIS BODY IS STRONG AND STURDY, AND HE HAS A SUBMISSIVE PERSONALITY.
PERFECT FOR FARM WORK!
WE'LL START THE BIDDING AT 3,000 GILLAH!
Oh! It's already started!
3,500!
NUMBER FIVE--A KIM-UN-KUR +ANIMA...
HE'S THE ONE, RIGHT?
3,700!
GOOD. WE MADE IT IN TIME TO BID ON HIM.
COORO AND NANA AREN'T HERE.
OF COURSE SLAVES CAN'T COME INTO TOWN BY THEMSELVES, BUT...
3,850!

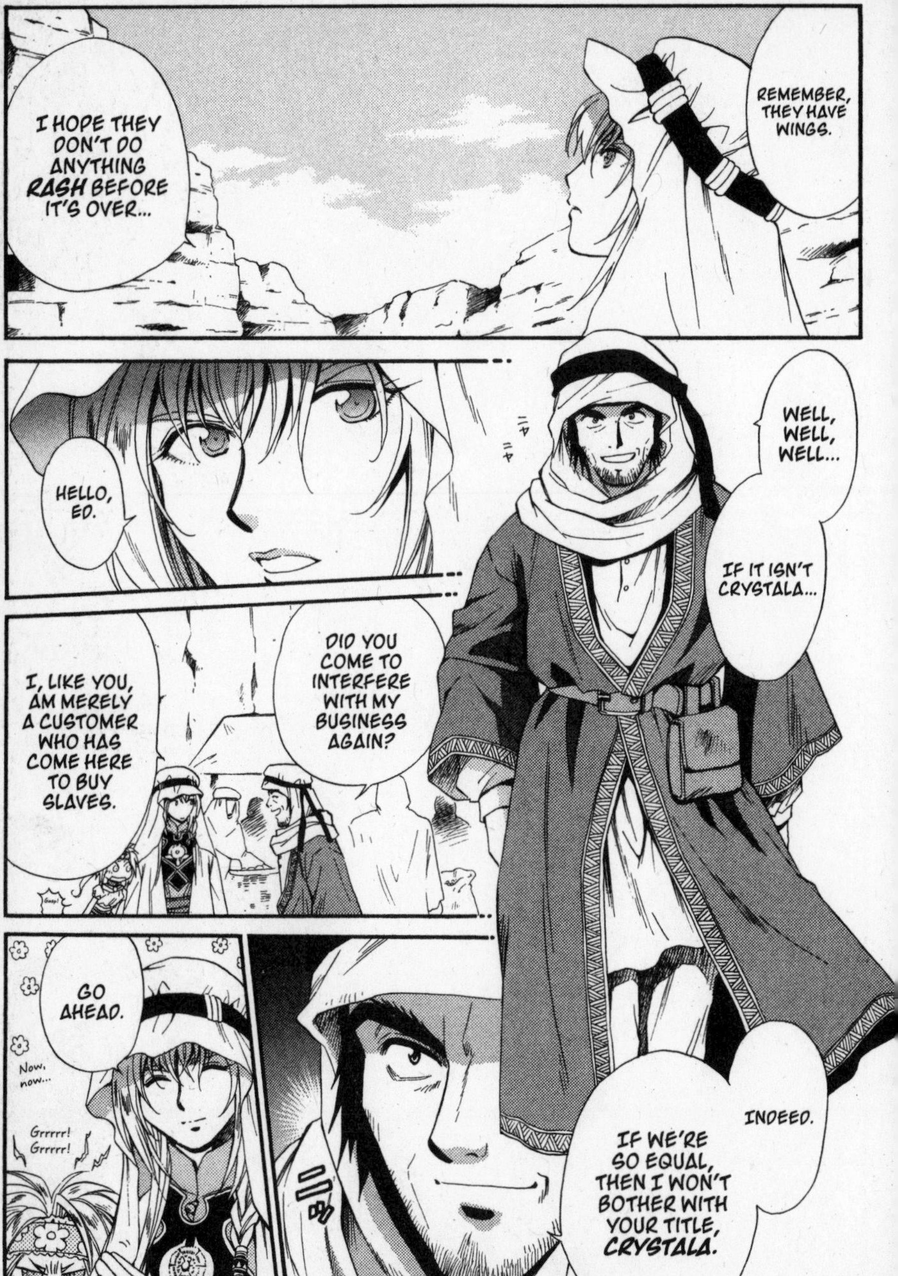
REMEMBER, THEY HAVE WINGS.
I HOPE THEY DON'T DO ANYTHING RASH BEFORE IT'S OVER...
ニヤ ニヤ
WELL, WELL, WELL...
IF IT ISN'T CRYSTALA...
HELLO, ED.
DID YOU COME TO INTERFERE WITH MY BUSINESS AGAIN?
I, LIKE YOU, AM MERELY A CUSTOMER WHO HAS COME HERE TO BUY SLAVES.
Gasp!
INDEED.
IF WE'RE SO EQUAL, THEN I WON'T BOTHER WITH YOUR TITLE, CRYSTALA.
GO AHEAD.
Now, now...
Grrrrr! Grrrrr!

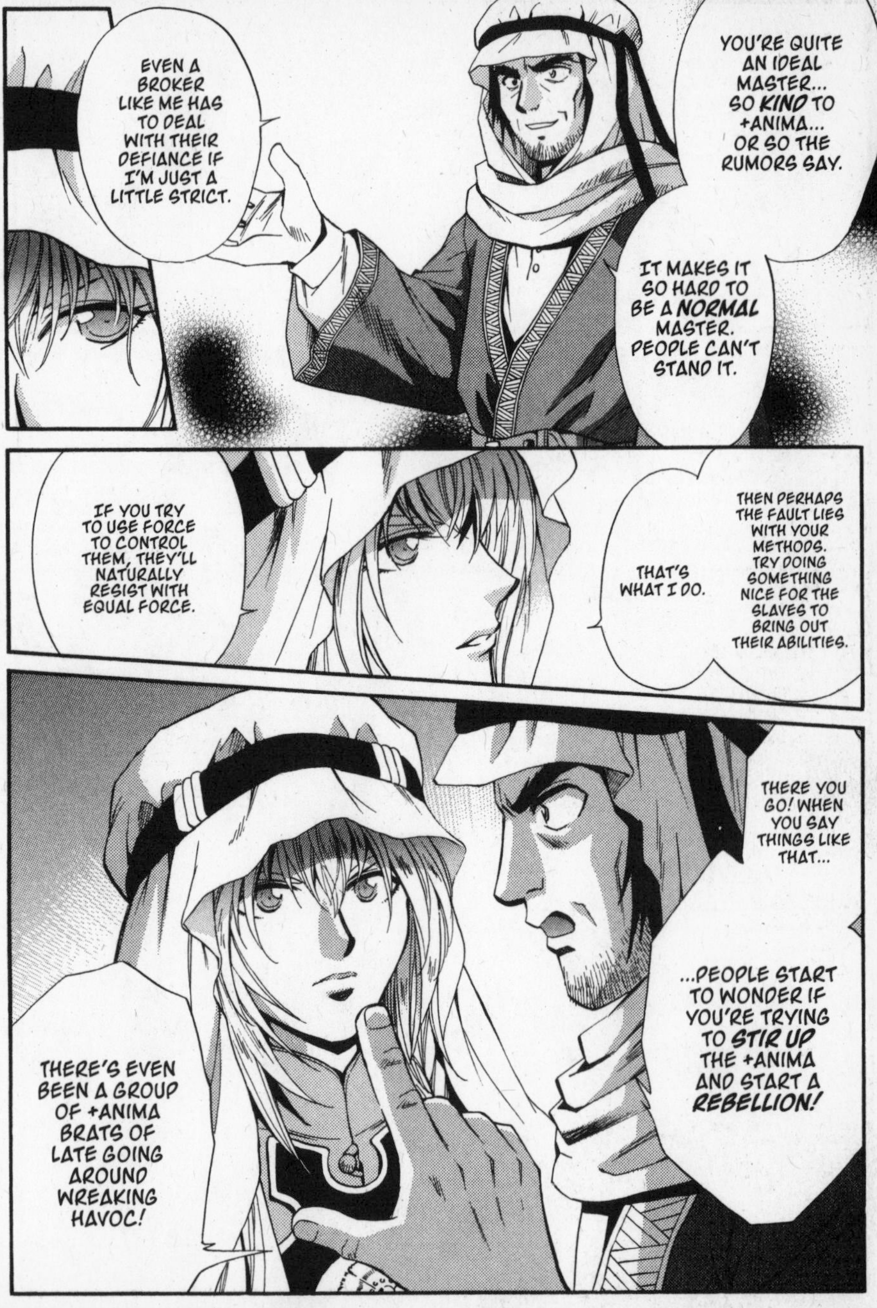
YOU'RE QUITE AN IDEAL MASTER... SO *KIND* TO +ANIMA... OR SO THE RUMORS SAY.
IT MAKES IT SO HARD TO BE A *NORMAL* MASTER. PEOPLE CAN'T STAND IT.
EVEN A BROKER LIKE ME HAS TO DEAL WITH THEIR DEFIANCE IF I'M JUST A LITTLE STRICT.
THEN PERHAPS THE FAULT LIES WITH YOUR METHODS. TRY DOING SOMETHING NICE FOR THE SLAVES TO BRING OUT THEIR ABILITIES.
THAT'S WHAT I DO.
IF YOU TRY TO USE FORCE TO CONTROL THEM, THEY'LL NATURALLY RESIST WITH EQUAL FORCE.
THERE YOU GO! WHEN YOU SAY THINGS LIKE THAT...
...PEOPLE START TO WONDER IF YOU'RE TRYING TO *STIR UP* THE +ANIMA AND START A *REBELLION!*
THERE'S EVEN BEEN A GROUP OF +ANIMA BRATS OF LATE GOING AROUND WREAKING HAVOC!

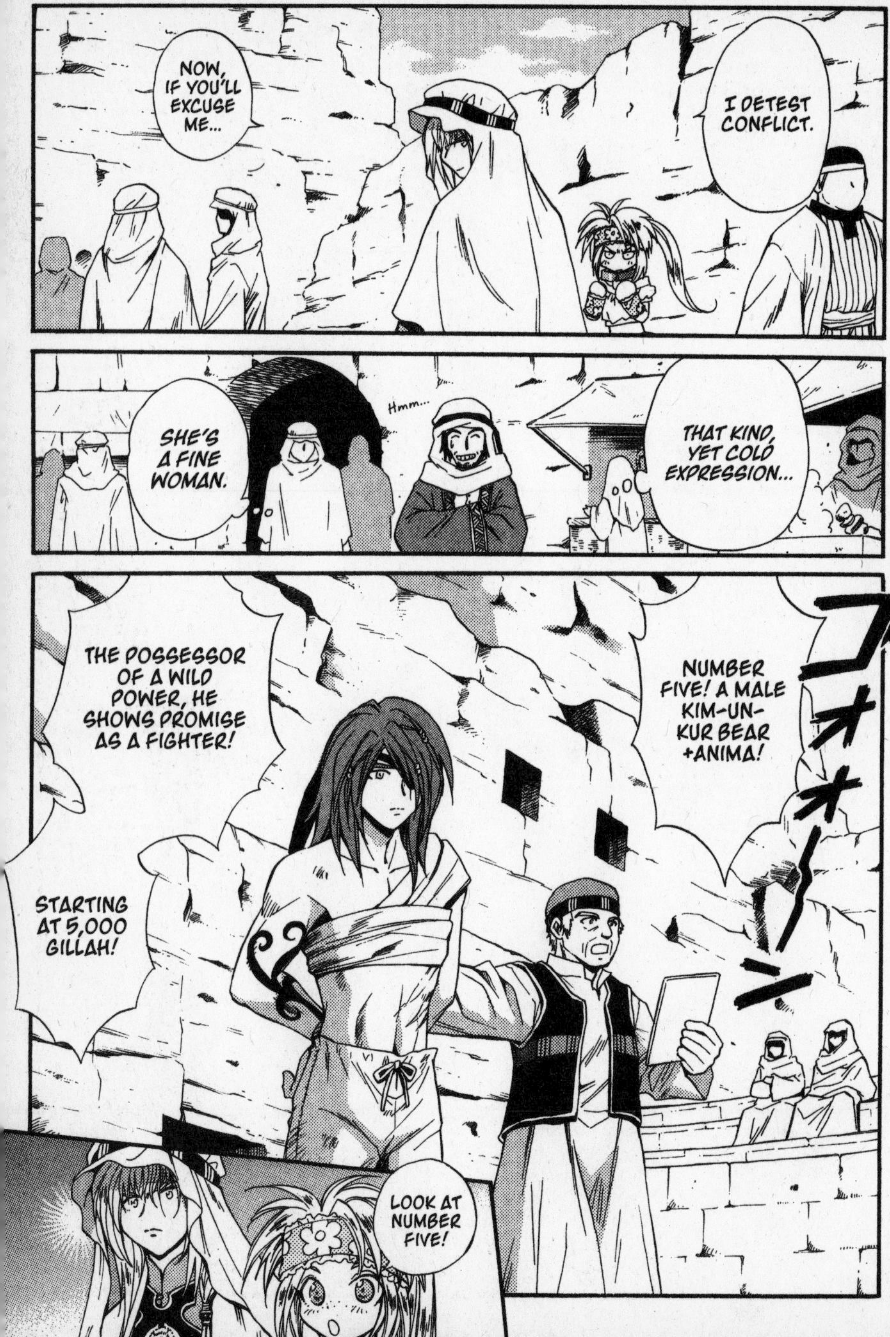
I DETEST CONFLICT.
NOW, IF YOU'LL EXCUSE ME...
THAT KIND, YET COLD EXPRESSION...
Hmm...
SHE'S A FINE WOMAN.
NUMBER FIVE! A MALE KIM-UN-KUR BEAR +ANIMA!
THE POSSESSOR OF A WILD POWER, HE SHOWS PROMISE AS A FIGHTER!
STARTING AT 5,000 GILLAH!
LOOK AT NUMBER FIVE!

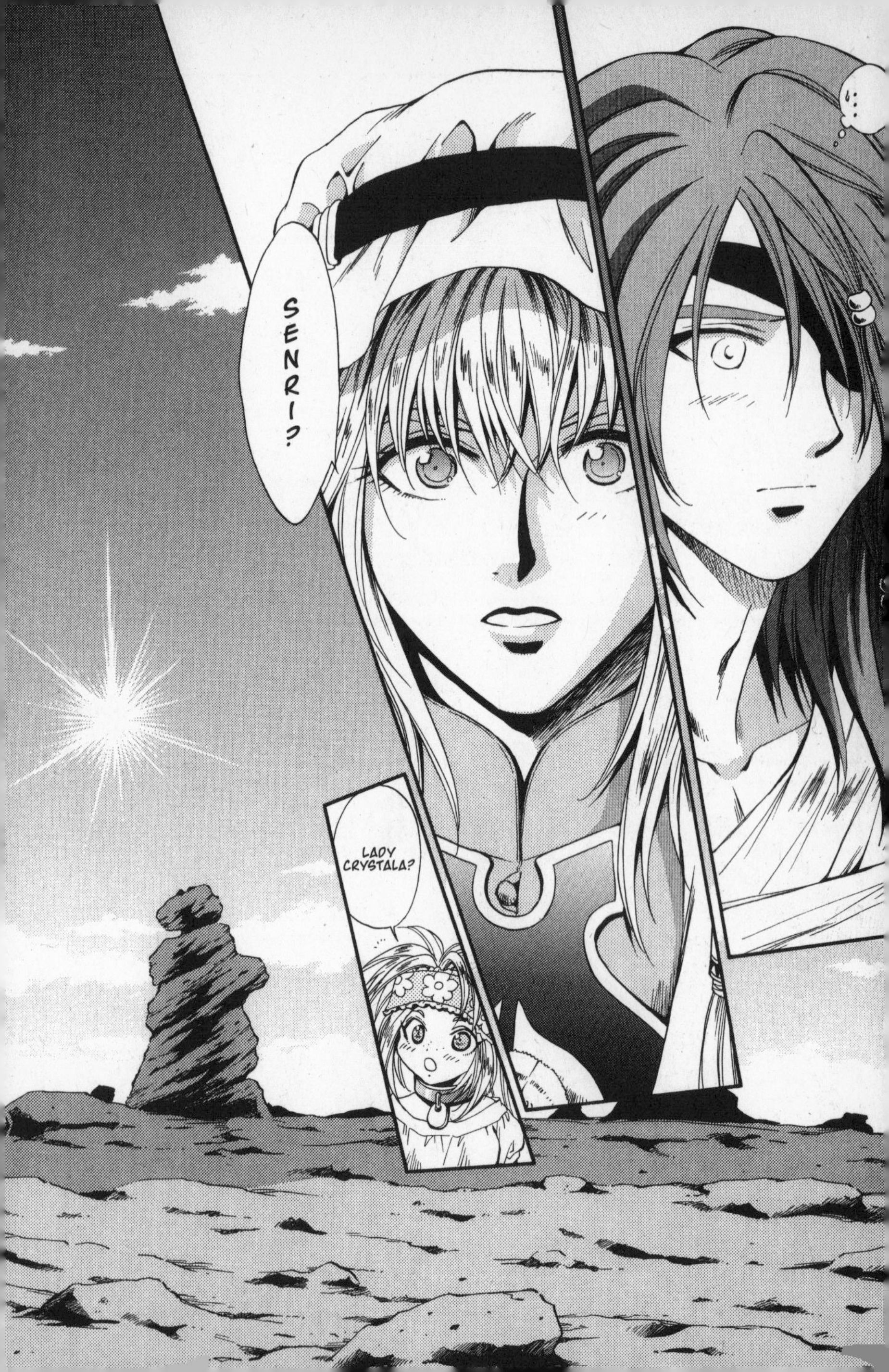
SENRI?
LADY CRYSTALA?

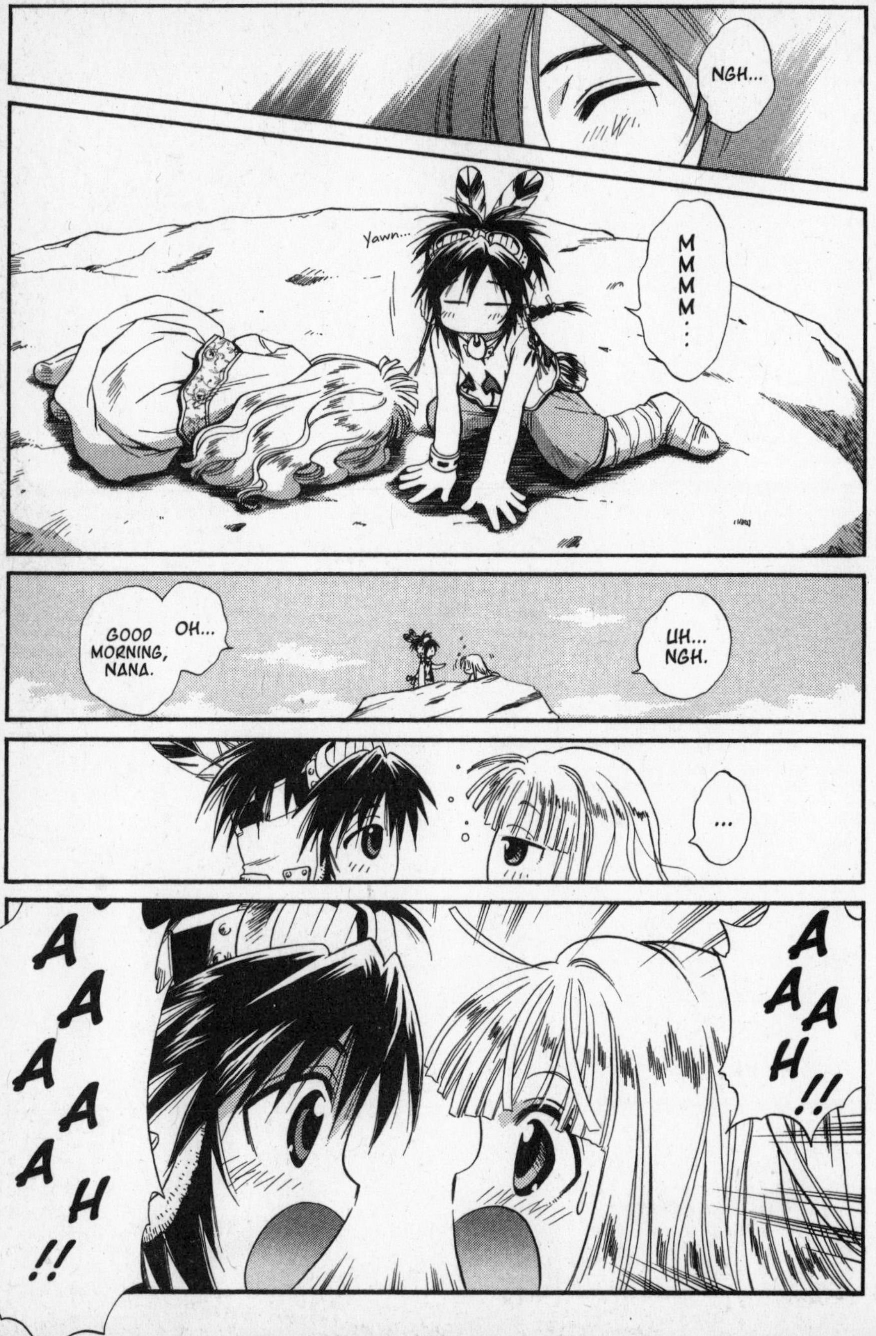
NGH...
MMMM...
Yawn...
UH... NGH.
OH... GOOD MORNING, NANA.
...
AAAH!!
AAAAAAH!!

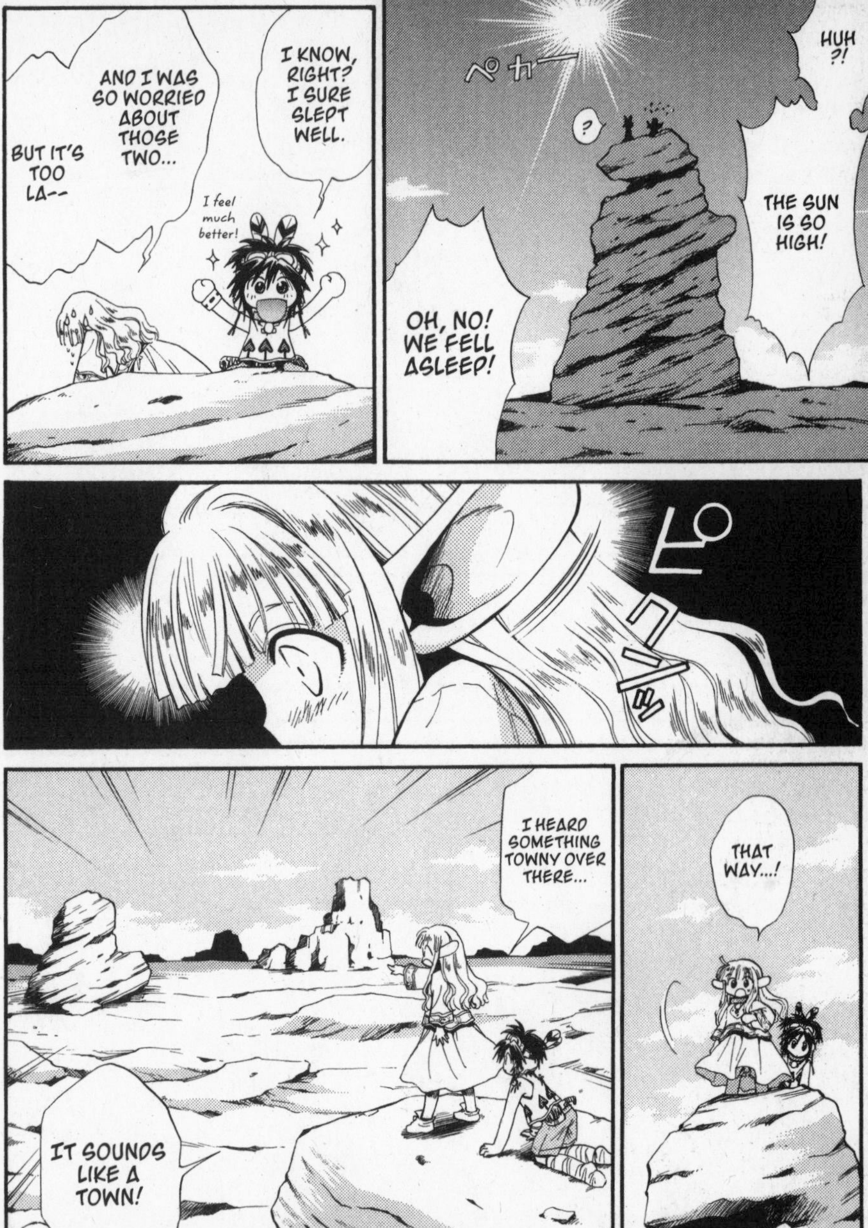
ペカー
?
HUH?!
THE SUN IS SO HIGH!
OH, NO! WE FELL ASLEEP!
I KNOW, RIGHT? I SURE SLEPT WELL.
I feel much better!
AND I WAS SO WORRIED ABOUT THOSE TWO...
BUT IT'S TOO LA--
THAT WAY...!
I HEARD SOMETHING TOWNY OVER THERE...
IT SOUNDS LIKE A TOWN!
Towny...?

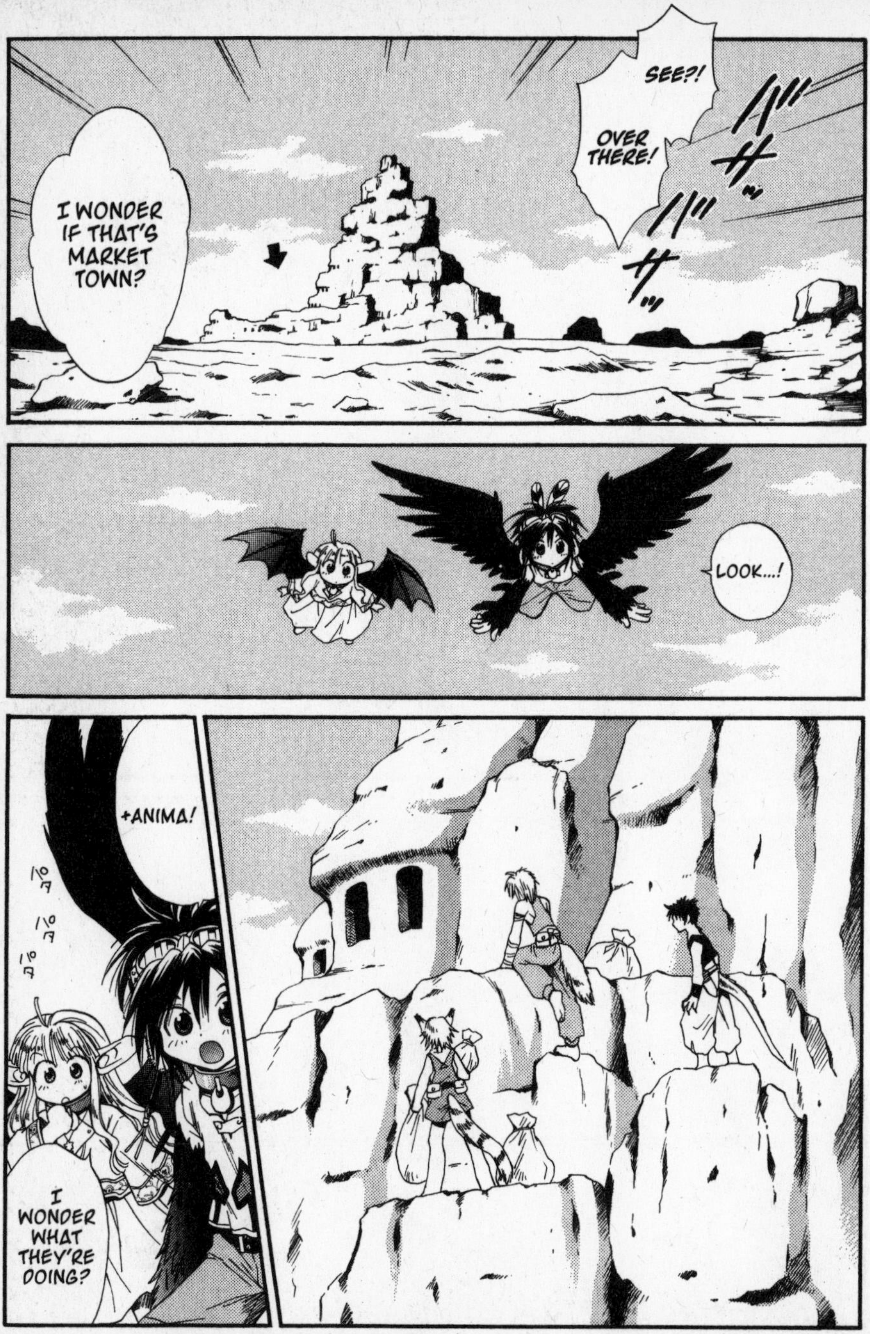
SEE?! OVER THERE!
バサッ
バサッ
I WONDER IF THAT'S MARKET TOWN?
LOOK...!
+ANIMA!
パタ
パタ
パタ
I WONDER WHAT THEY'RE DOING?

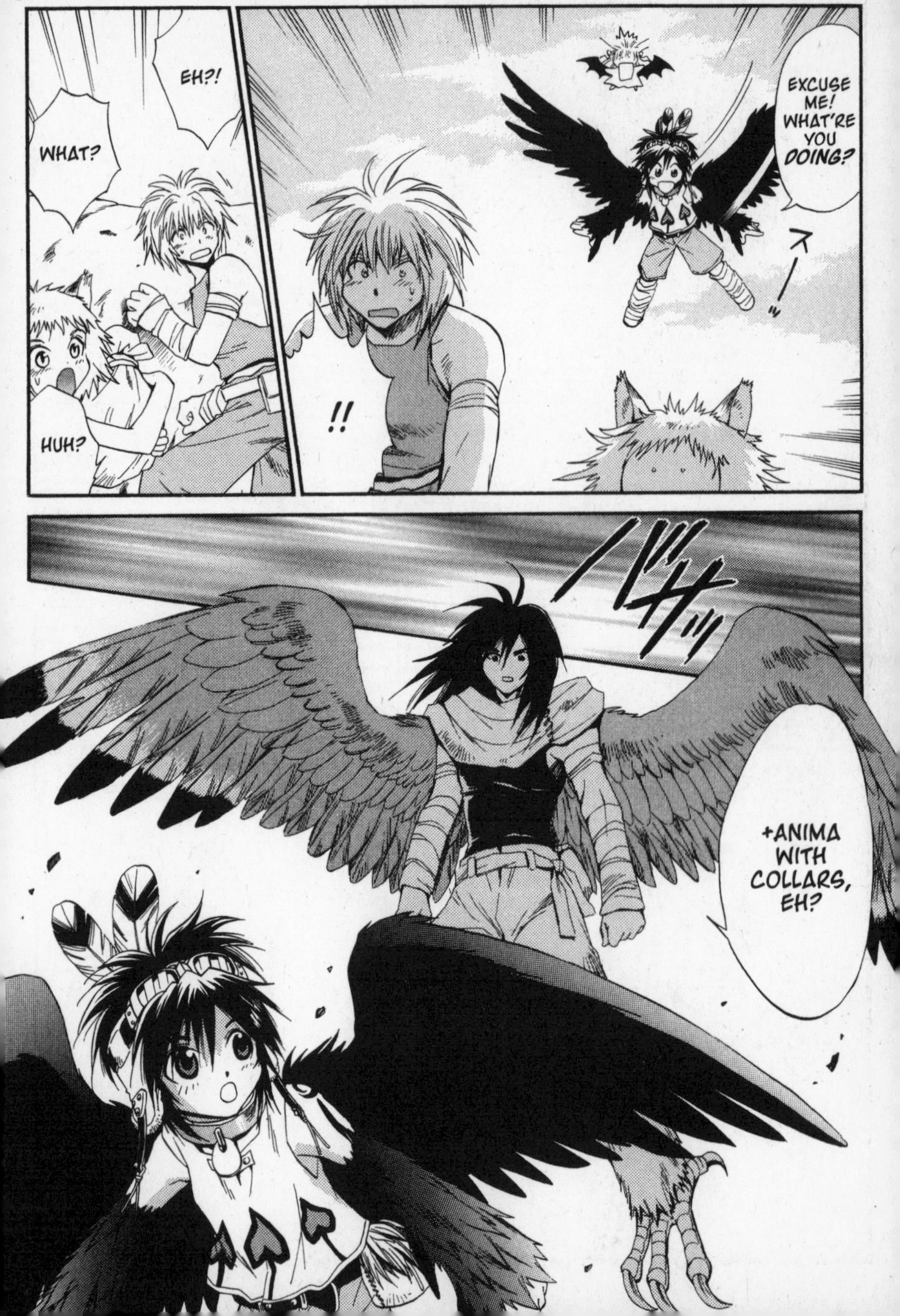
EXCUSE ME! WHAT'RE YOU DOING?
!!
EH?!
WHAT?
HUH?
バサッ
+ANIMA WITH COLLARS, EH?

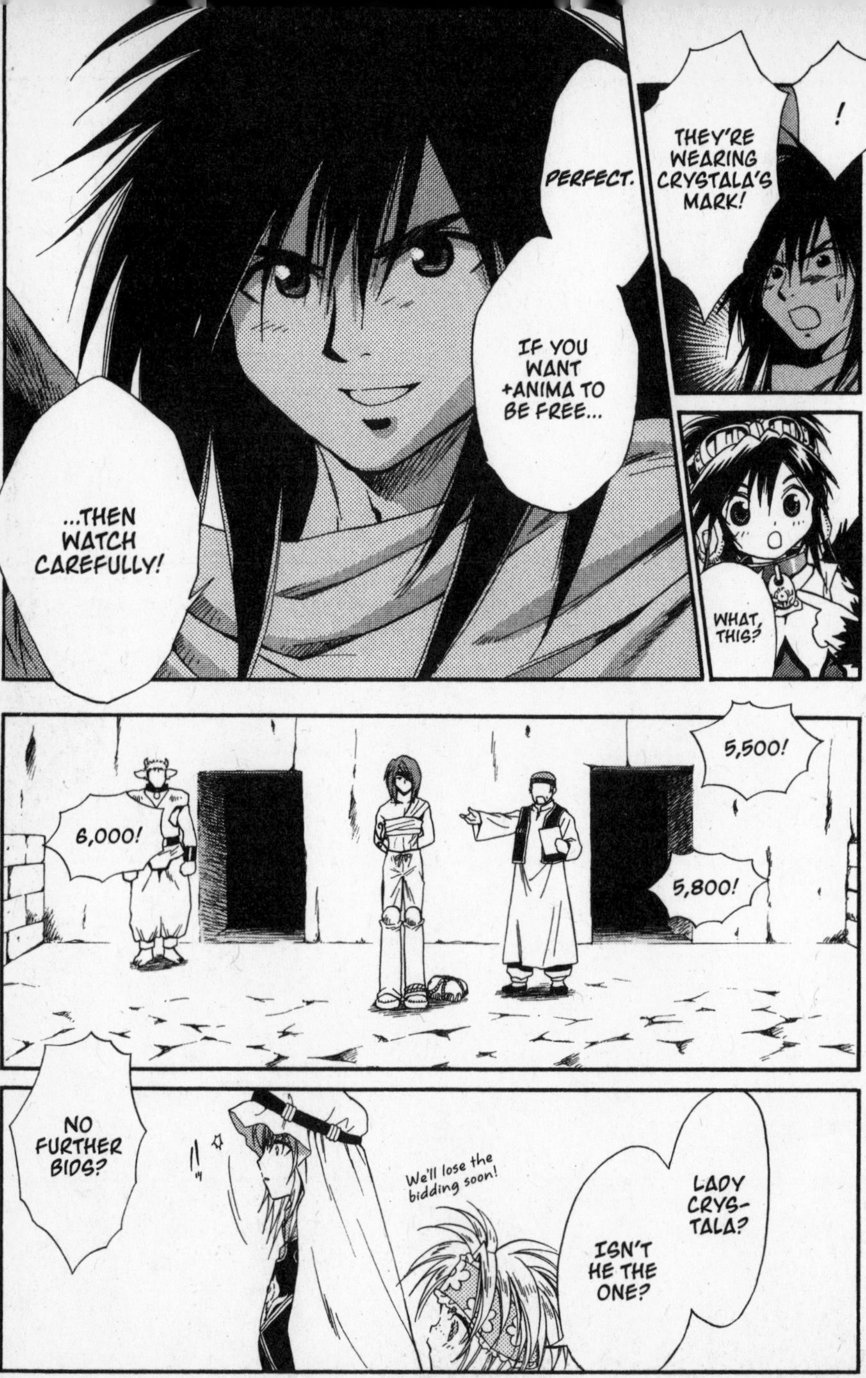
!
THEY'RE WEARING CRYSTALA'S MARK!
WHAT, THIS?
PERFECT.
IF YOU WANT +ANIMA TO BE FREE...
...THEN WATCH CAREFULLY!
5,500!
5,800!
6,000!
LADY CRYS-TALA?
ISN'T HE THE ONE?
We'll lose the bidding soon!
NO FURTHER BIDS?

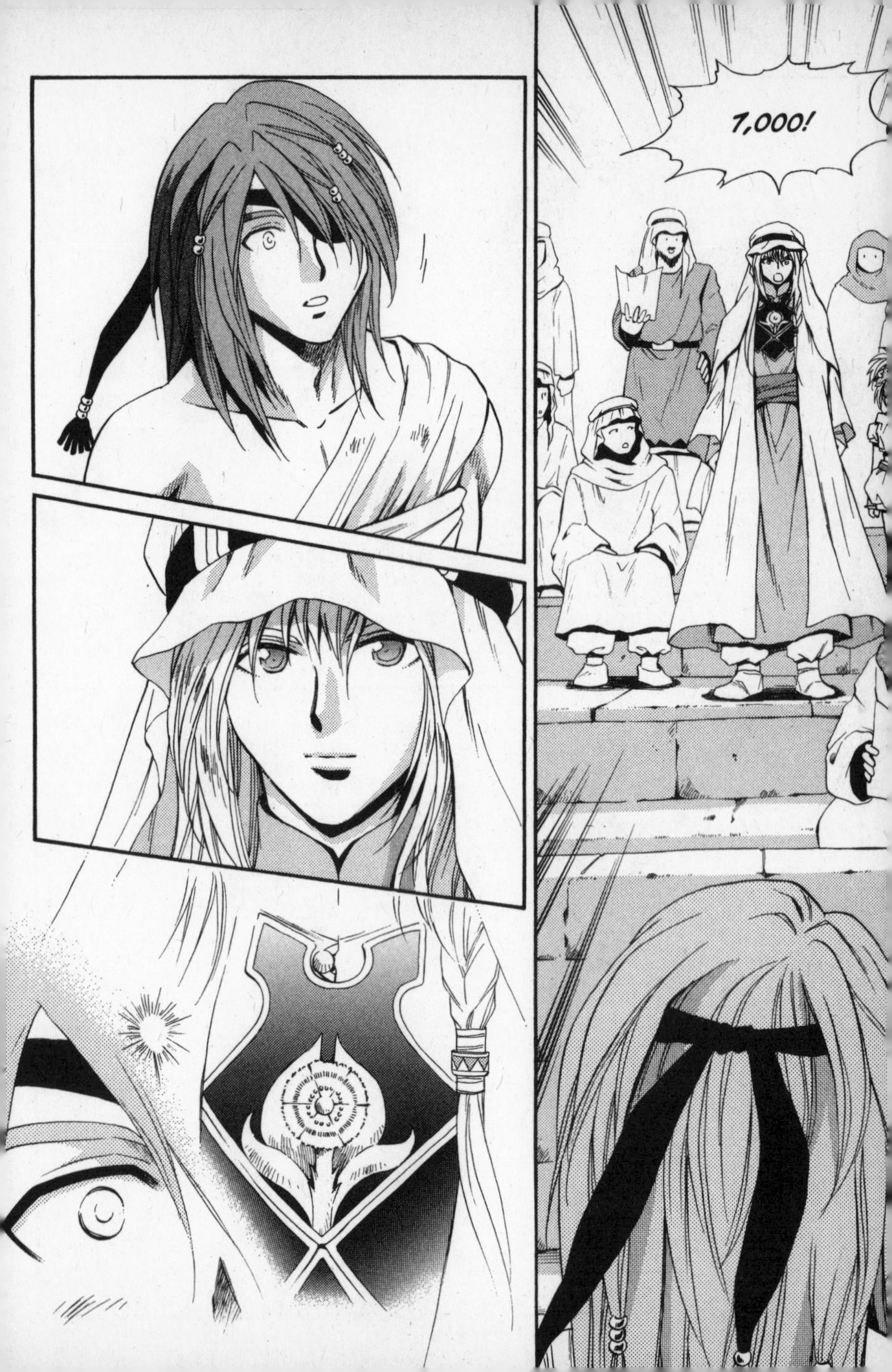
7,000!

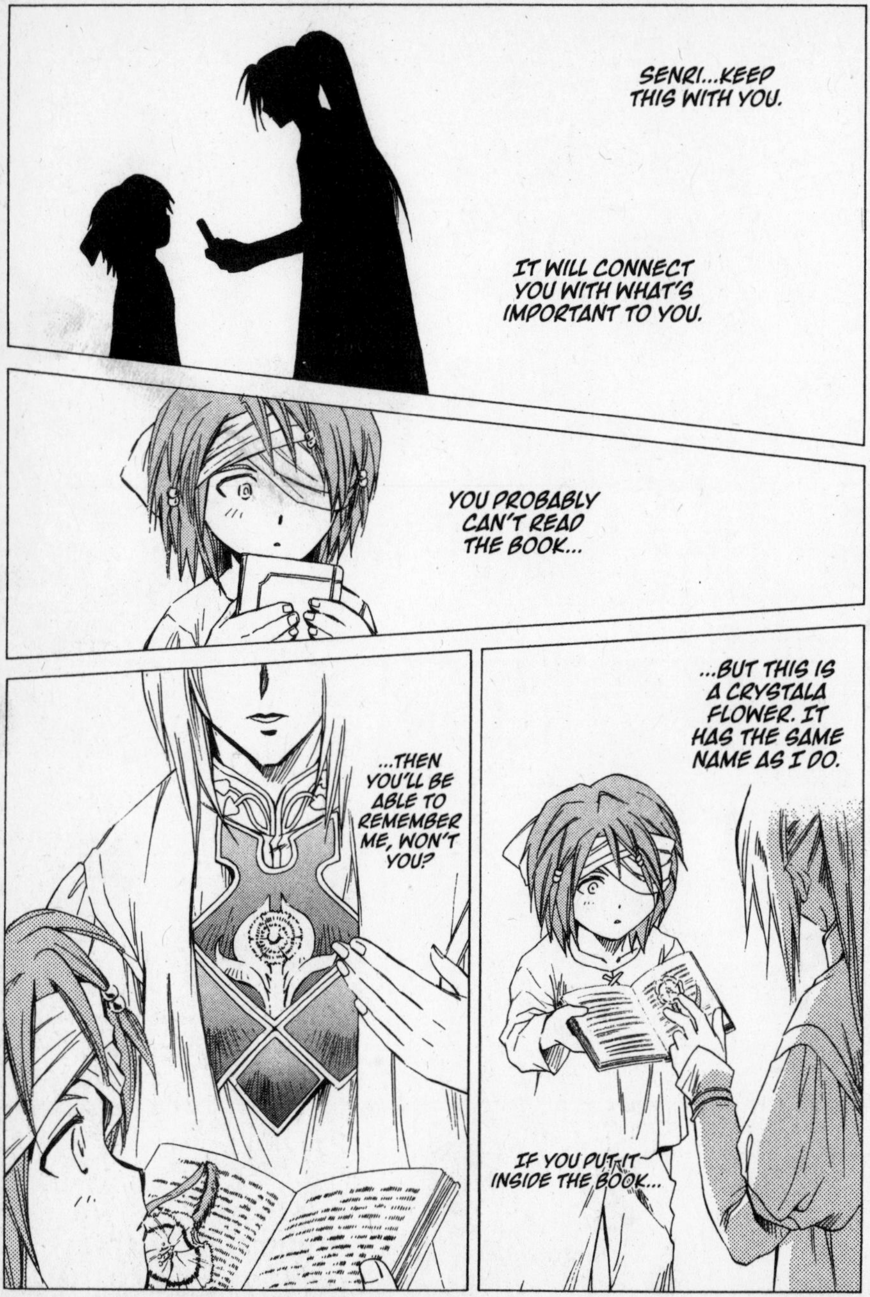
SENRI...KEEP THIS WITH YOU.
IT WILL CONNECT YOU WITH WHAT'S IMPORTANT TO YOU.
YOU PROBABLY CAN'T READ THE BOOK...
...BUT THIS IS A CRYSTALA FLOWER. IT HAS THE SAME NAME AS I DO.
IF YOU PUT IT INSIDE THE BOOK...
...THEN YOU'LL BE ABLE TO REMEMBER ME, WON'T YOU?

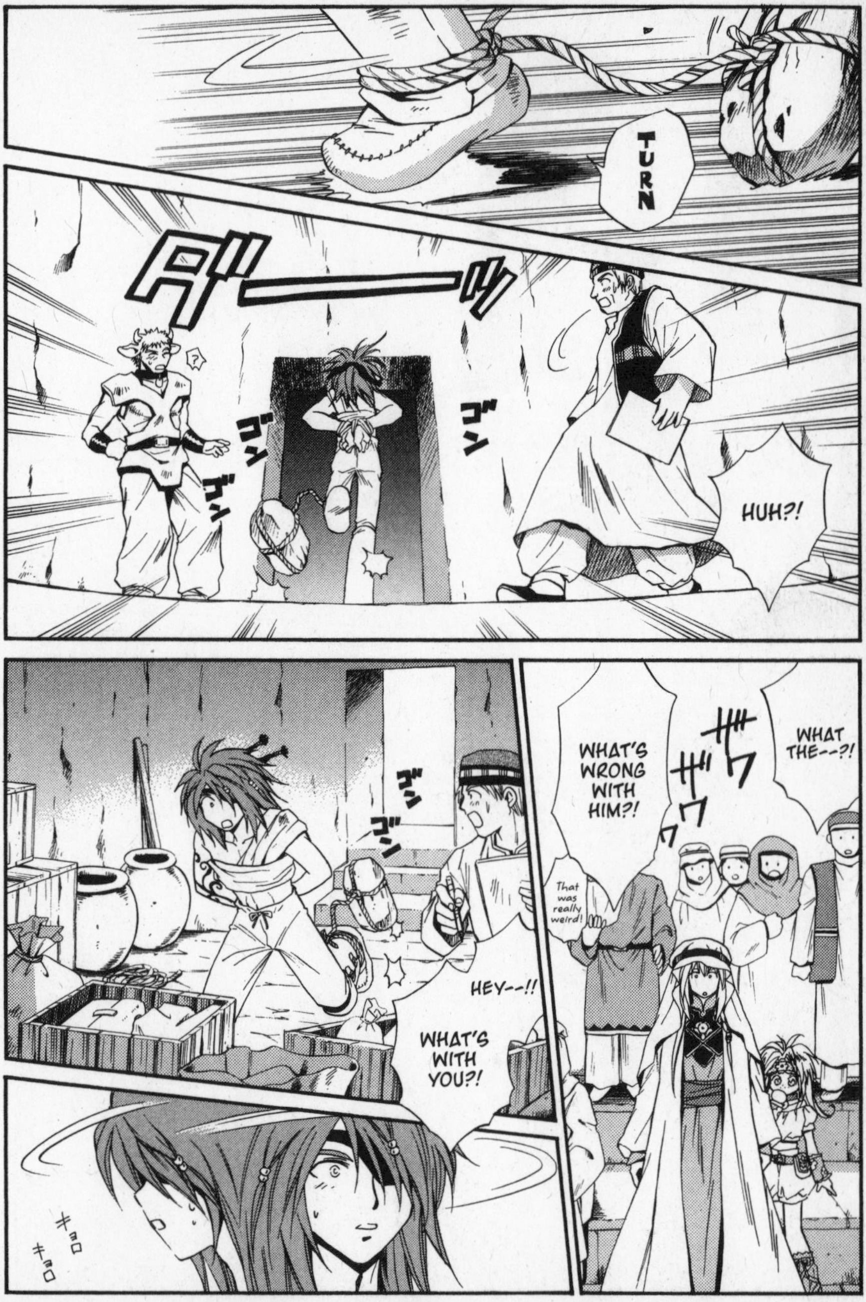
TURN
ダーーッ
HUH?!
?
ゴン
ゴン
ゴン
WHAT THE--?!
ザワ
ザワ
ワ
WHAT'S WRONG WITH HIM?!
That was really weird!
ゴン
ゴン
HEY--!!
WHAT'S WITH YOU?!
キョロ
キョロ

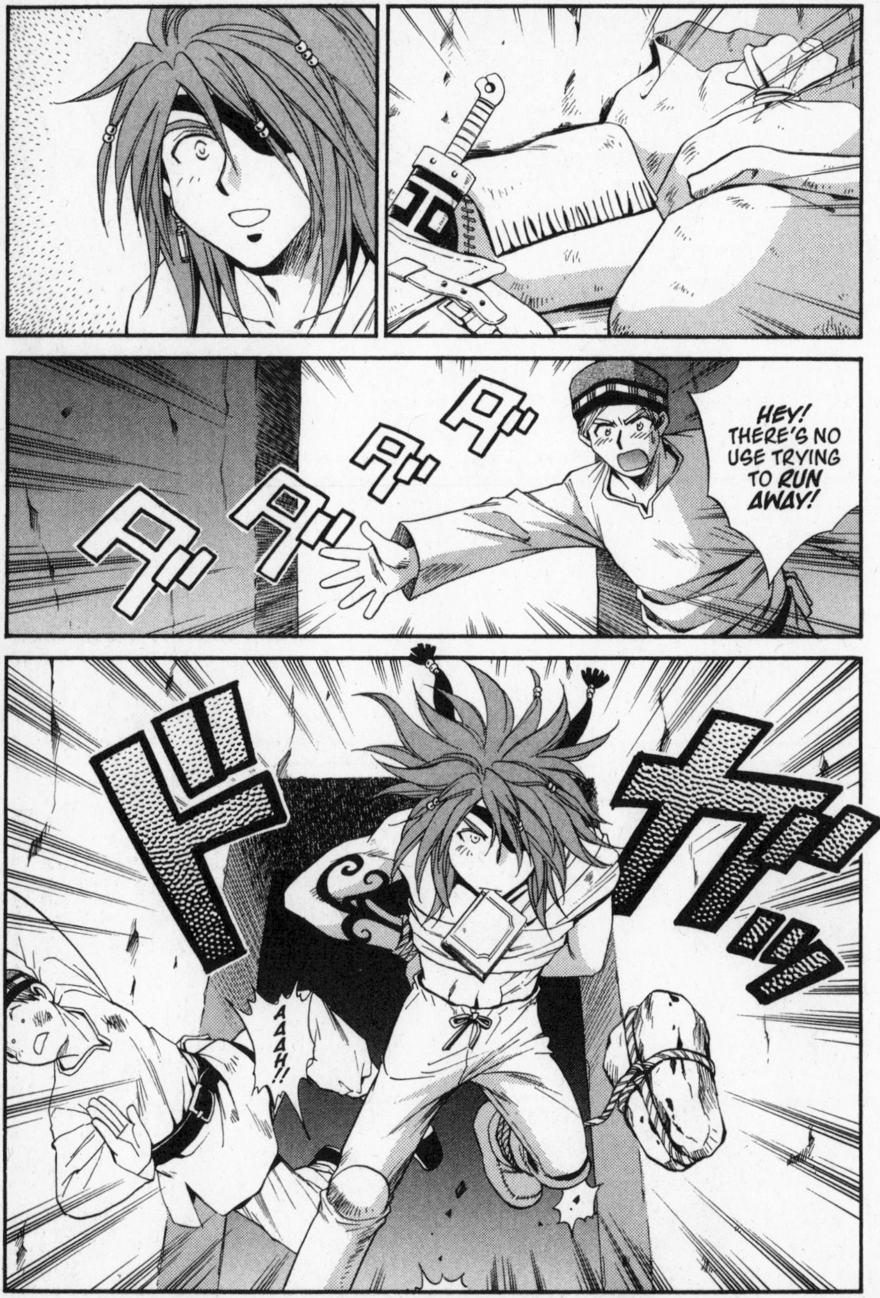
HEY! THERE'S NO USE TRYING TO RUN AWAY!
ダッ ダッ ダッ
ドガッ
AAAH!!

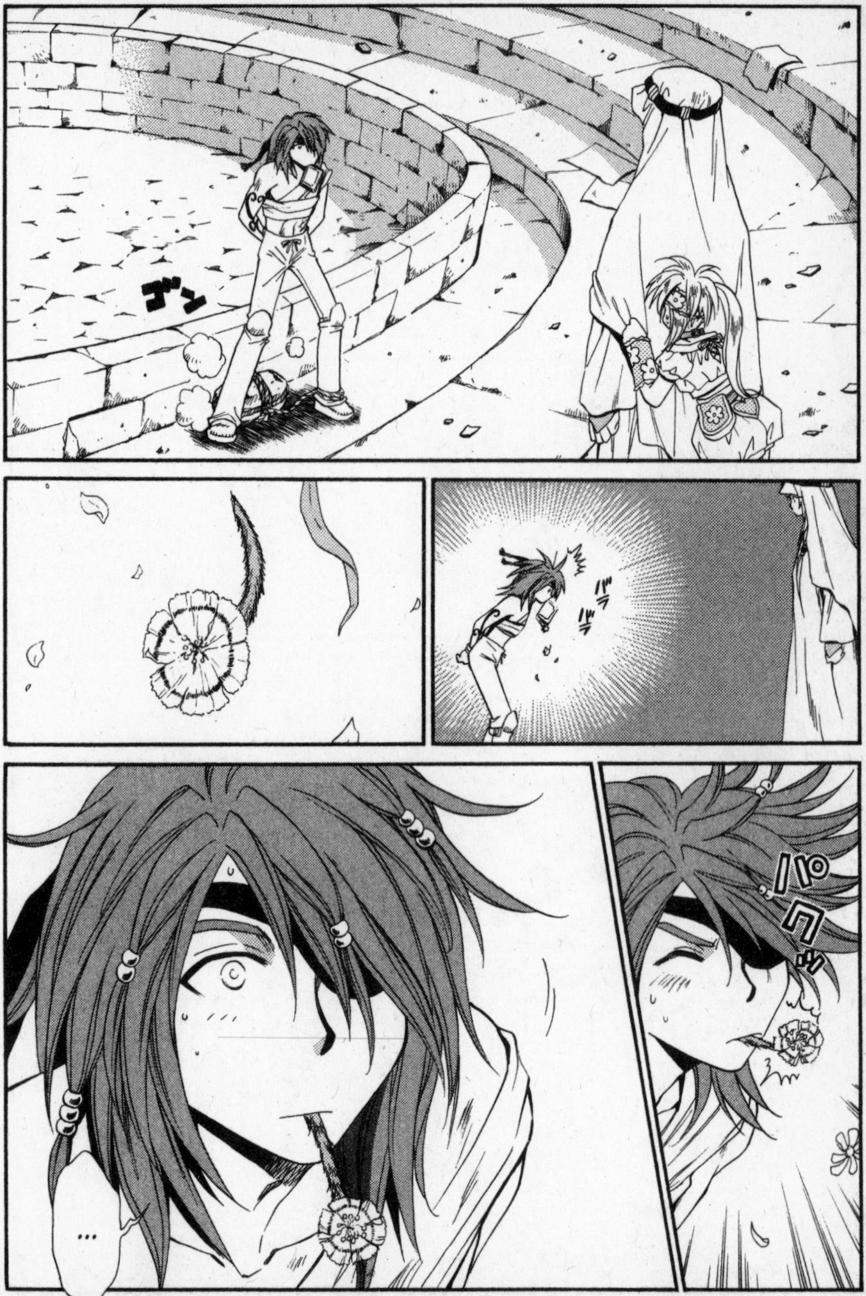
ゴン
バラ
バラ
パクッ
...

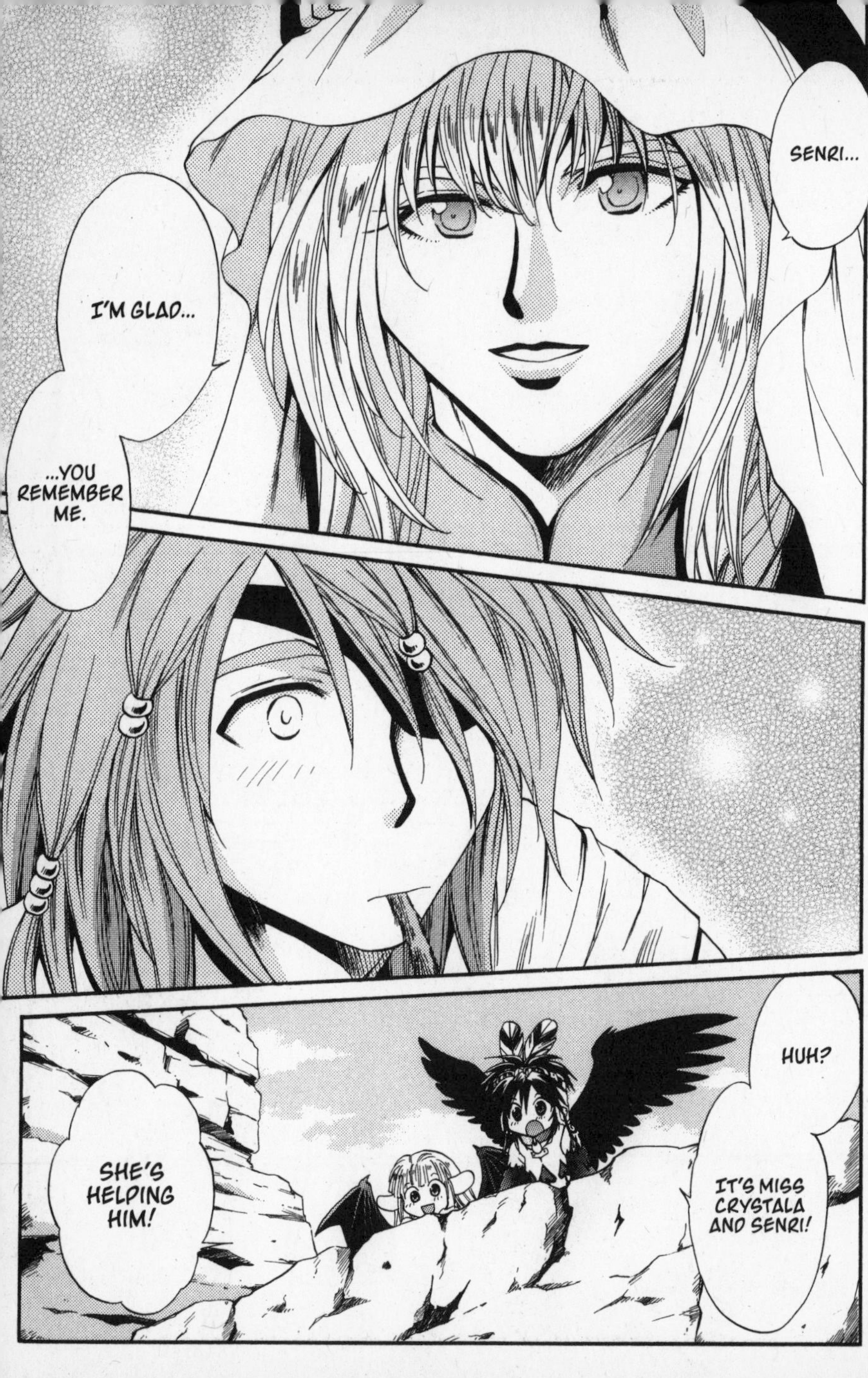
SENRI...
I'M GLAD...
...YOU REMEMBER ME.
HUH?
IT'S MISS CRYSTALA AND SENRI!
SHE'S HELPING HIM!

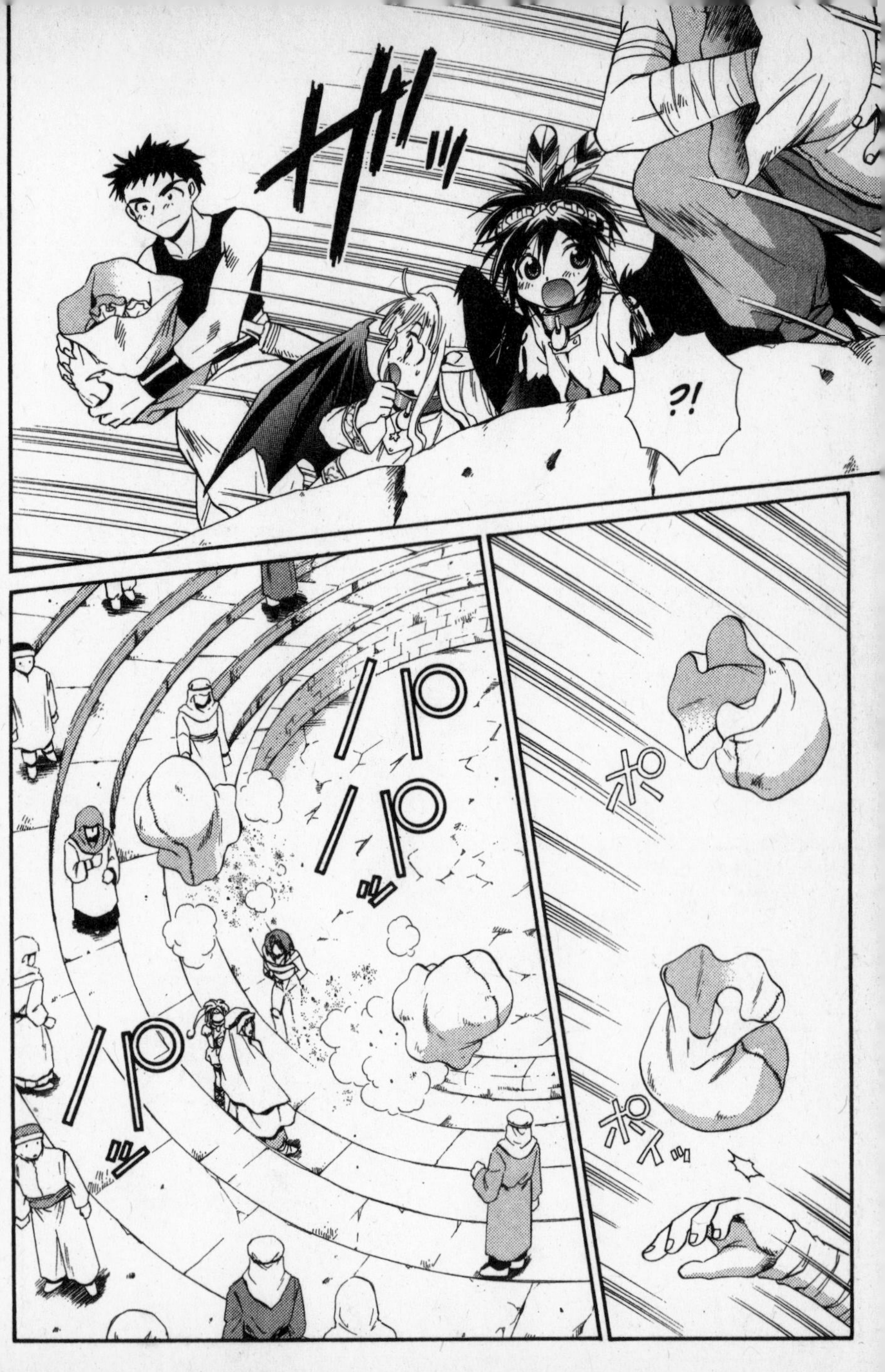
?!
ポイ
ポイッ

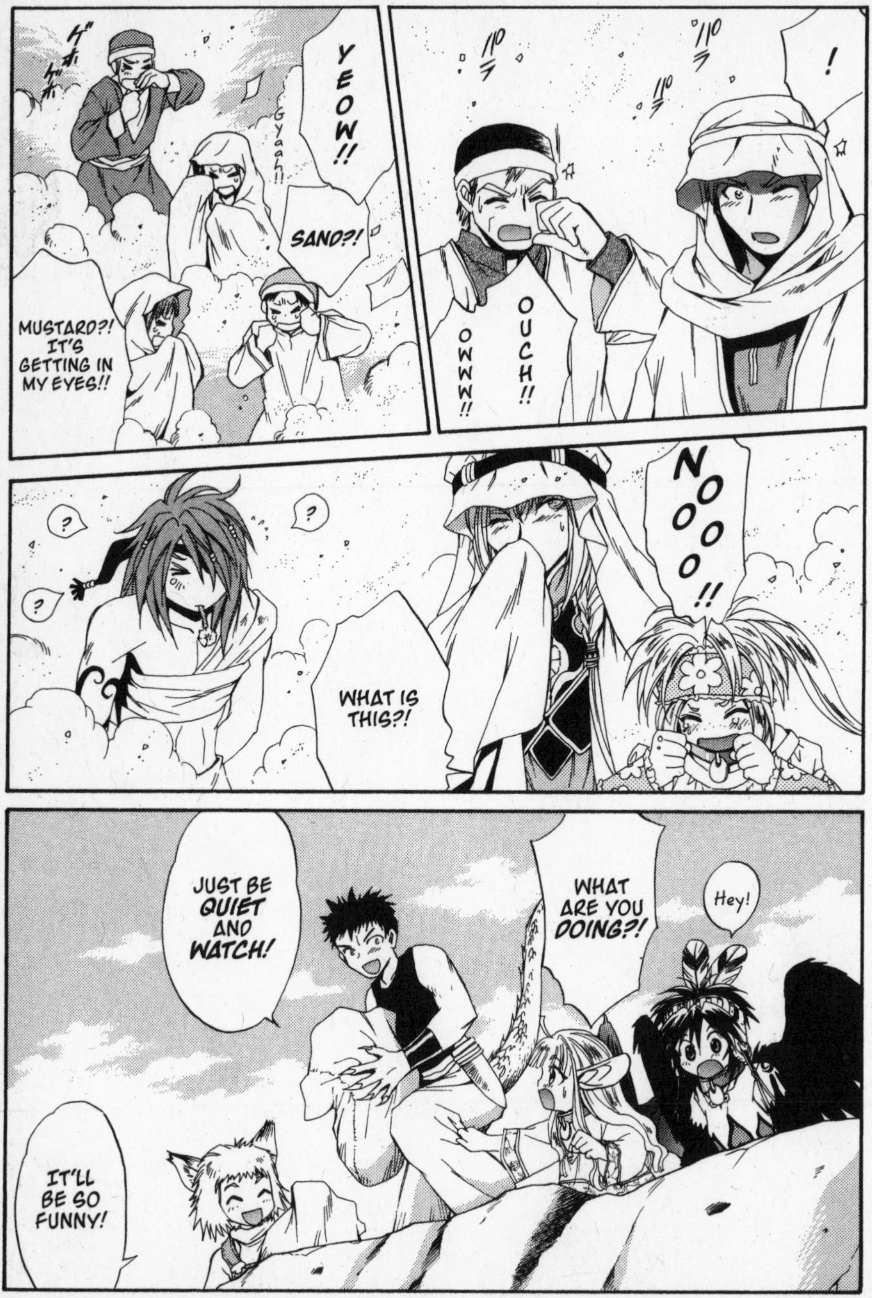
!
OUCH!!
OWWW!!
YEOW!!
Gyaah!!
SAND?!
MUSTARD?! IT'S GETTING IN MY EYES!!
NOOOOO!!
WHAT IS THIS?!
?
?
?
Hey!
WHAT ARE YOU DOING?!
JUST BE QUIET AND WATCH!
IT'LL BE SO FUNNY!

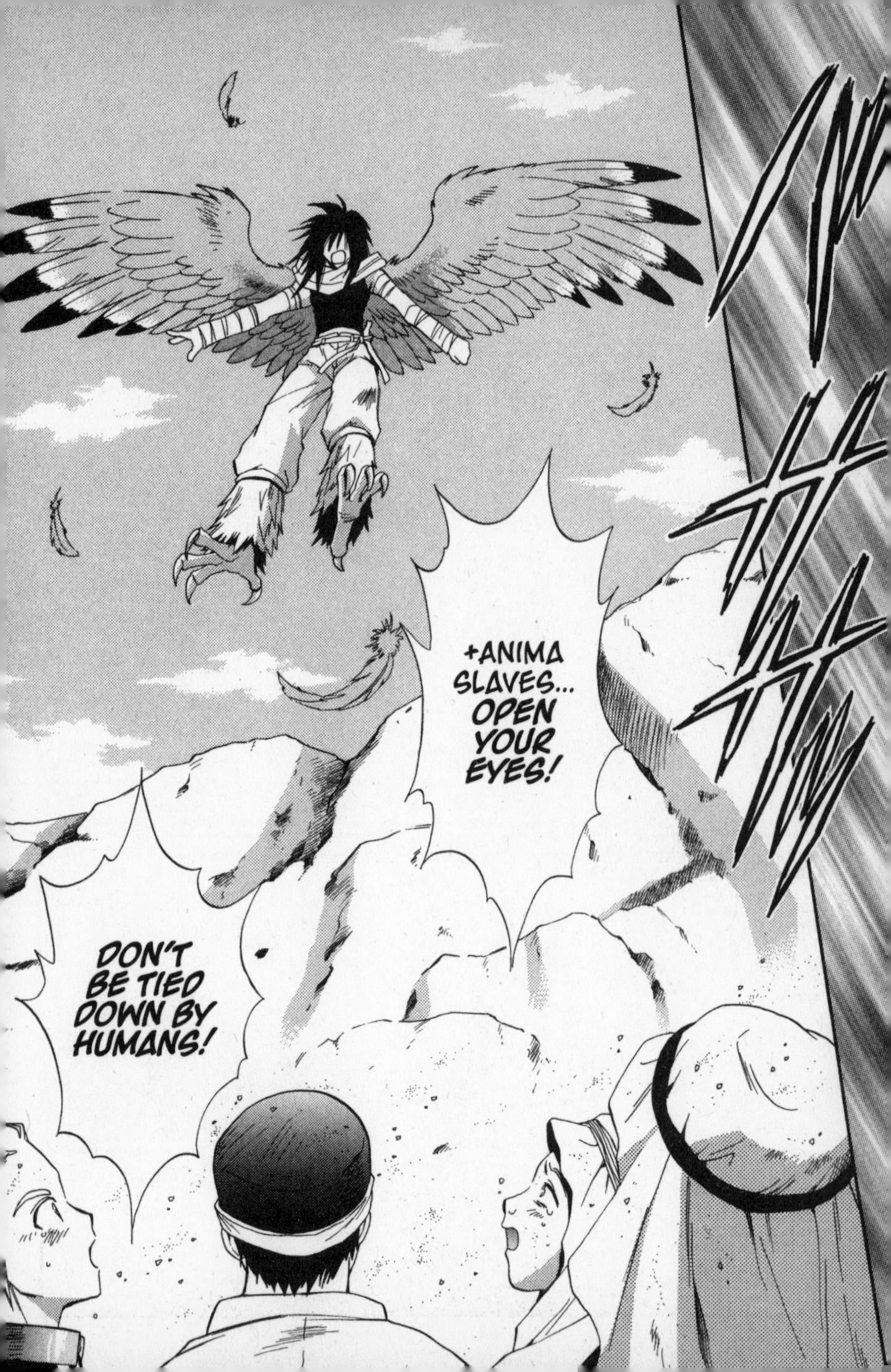
+ANIMA SLAVES... OPEN YOUR EYES!
DON'T BE TIED DOWN BY HUMANS!

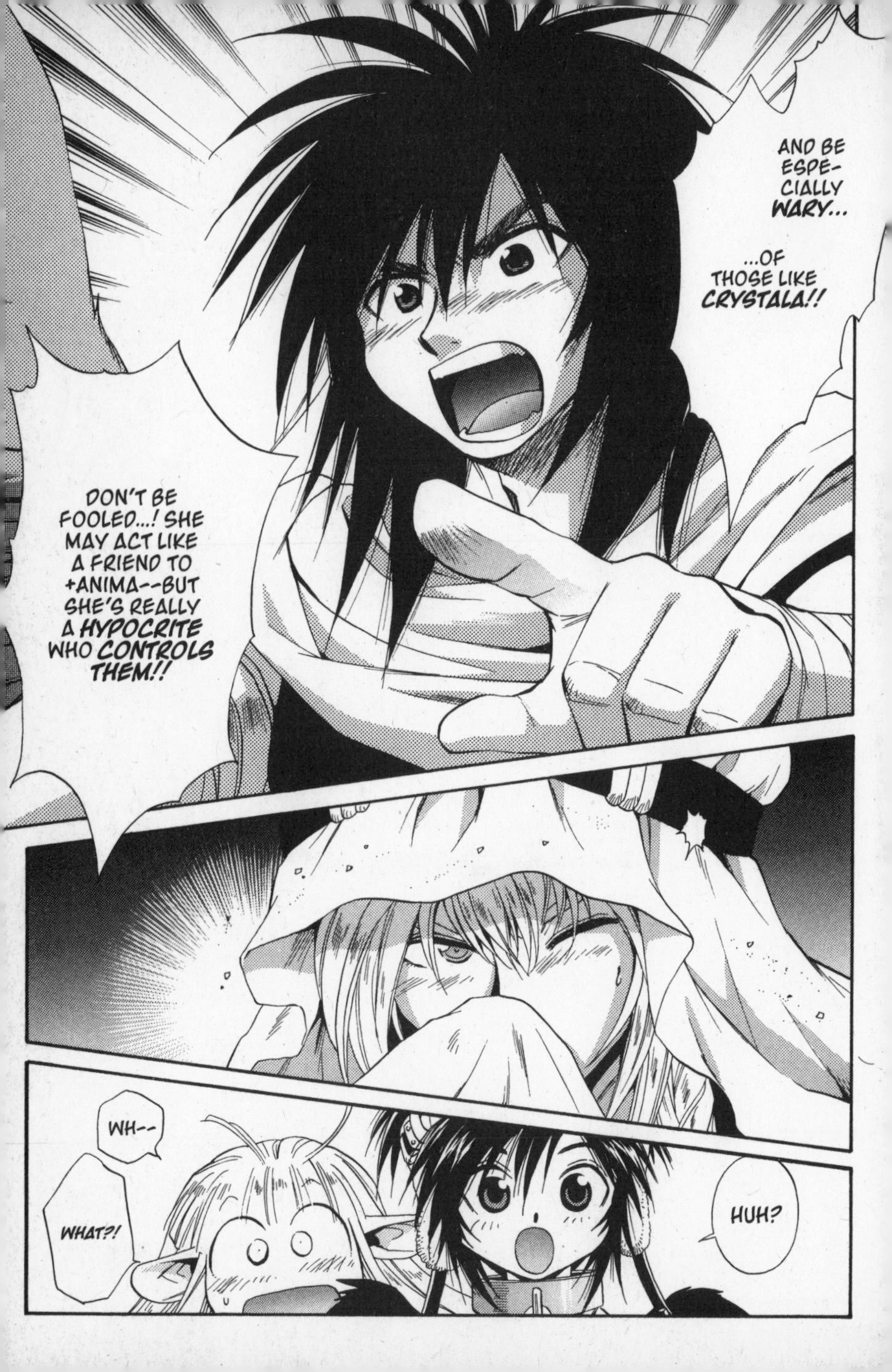
AND BE ESPE-CIALLY WARY...
...OF THOSE LIKE CRYSTALA!!
DON'T BE FOOLED...! SHE MAY ACT LIKE A FRIEND TO +ANIMA--BUT SHE'S REALLY A HYPOCRITE WHO CONTROLS THEM!!
HUH?
WH--
WHAT?!

Wherever you go, we'll follow you!

Chapter 37
Wish

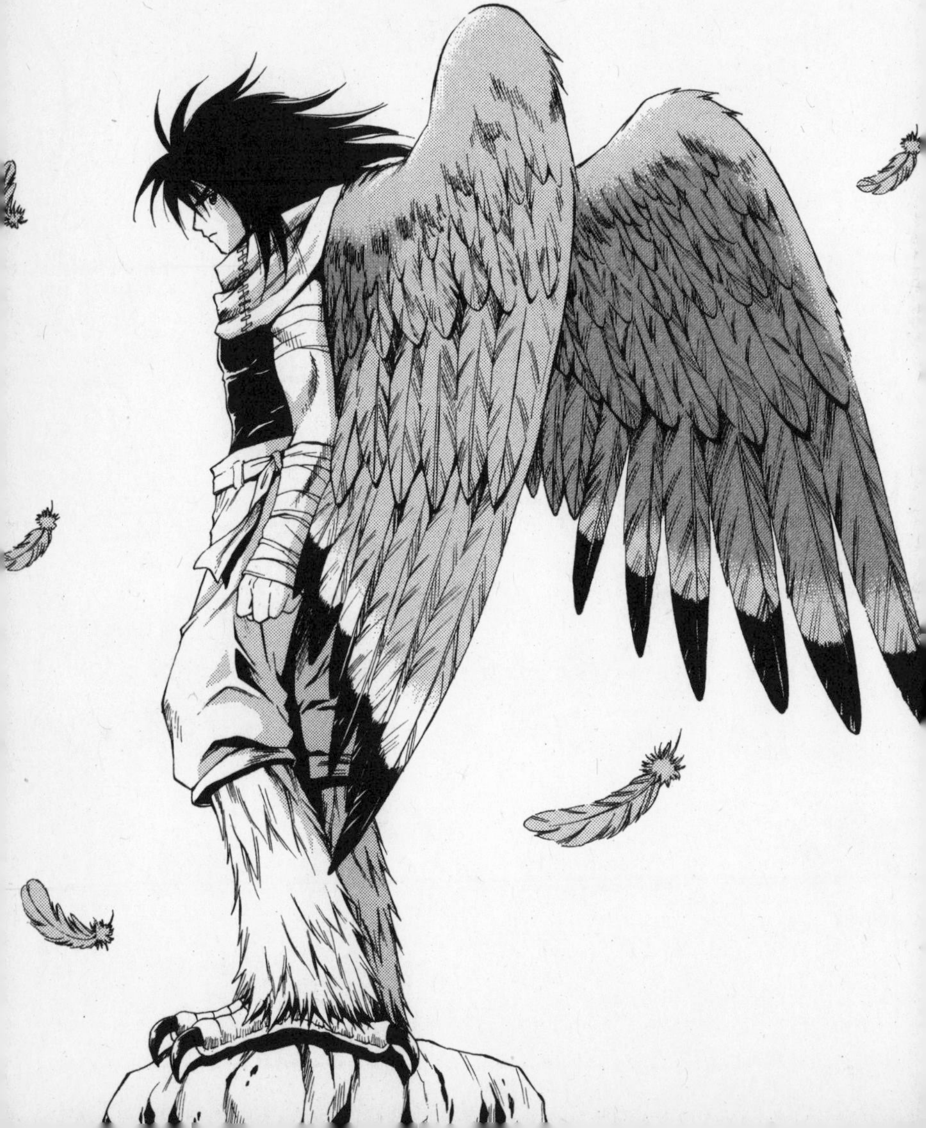

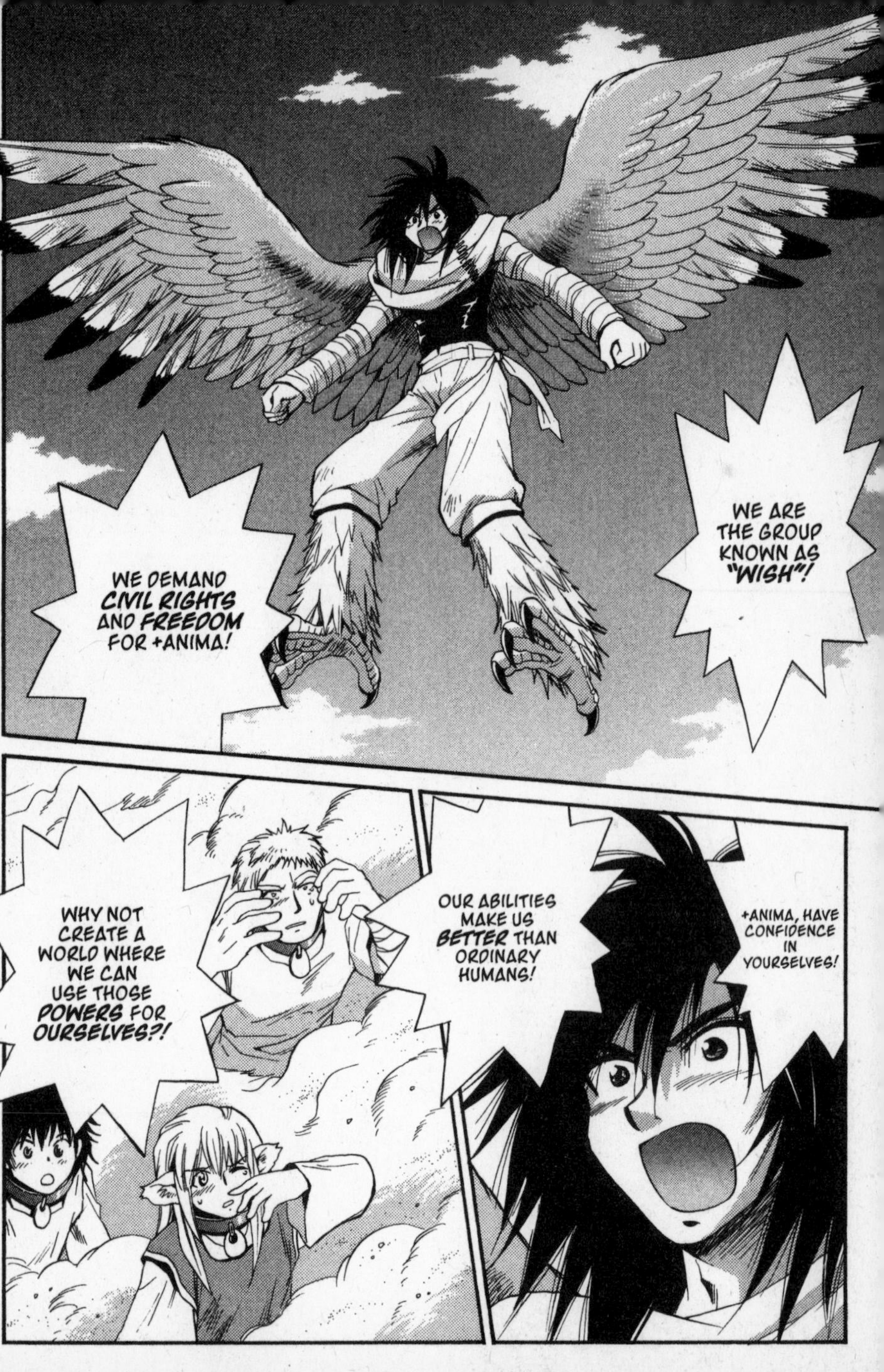
WE ARE THE GROUP KNOWN AS "WISH"!
WE DEMAND CIVIL RIGHTS AND FREEDOM FOR +ANIMA!
+ANIMA, HAVE CONFIDENCE IN YOURSELVES!
OUR ABILITIES MAKE US BETTER THAN ORDINARY HUMANS!
WHY NOT CREATE A WORLD WHERE WE CAN USE THOSE POWERS FOR OURSELVES?!

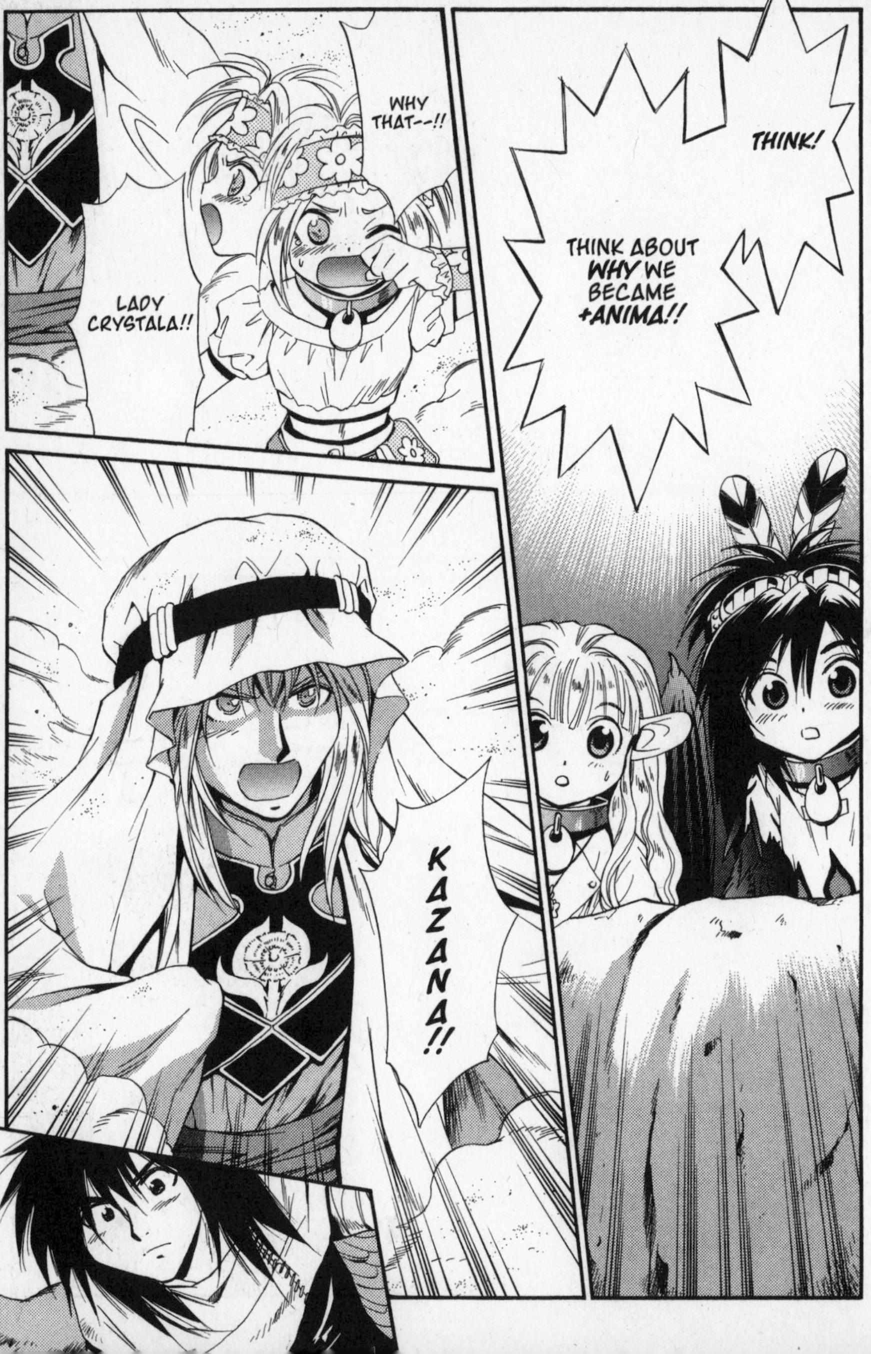
THINK!
THINK ABOUT WHY WE BECAME +ANIMA!!
WHY THAT--!!
LADY CRYSTALA!!
KAZANA!!

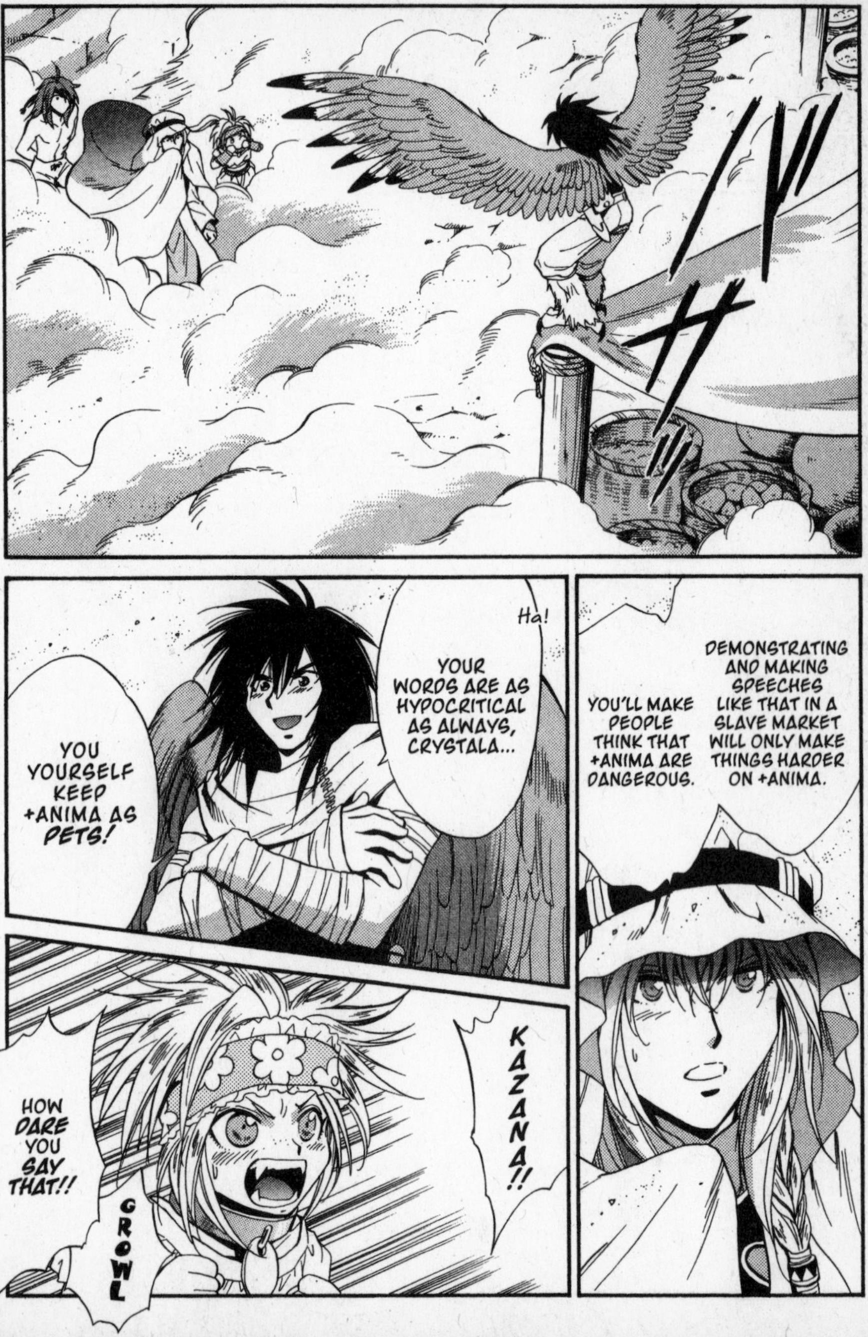
DEMONSTRATING AND MAKING SPEECHES LIKE THAT IN A SLAVE MARKET WILL ONLY MAKE THINGS HARDER ON +ANIMA.
YOU'LL MAKE PEOPLE THINK THAT +ANIMA ARE DANGEROUS.
Ha!
YOUR WORDS ARE AS HYPOCRITICAL AS ALWAYS, CRYSTALA...
YOU YOURSELF KEEP +ANIMA AS PETS!
KAZANA!!
GROWL
HOW DARE YOU SAY THAT!!

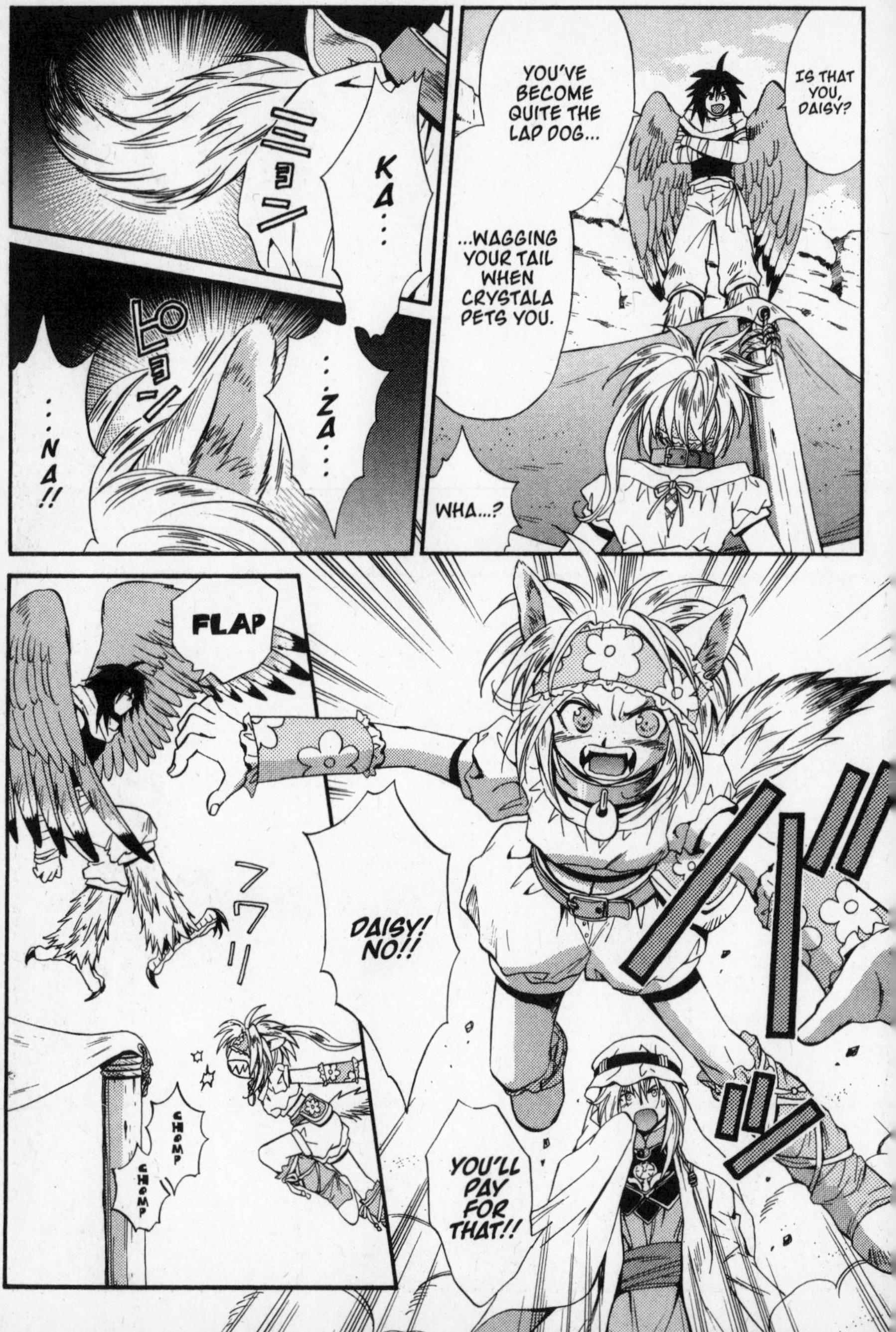
IS THAT YOU, DAISY?
YOU'VE BECOME QUITE THE LAP DOG...
...WAGGING YOUR TAIL WHEN CRYSTALA PETS YOU.
WHA...?
KA...
...ZA...
...NA!!
DAISY! NO!!
YOU'LL PAY FOR THAT!!
FLAP
CHOMP
CHOMP

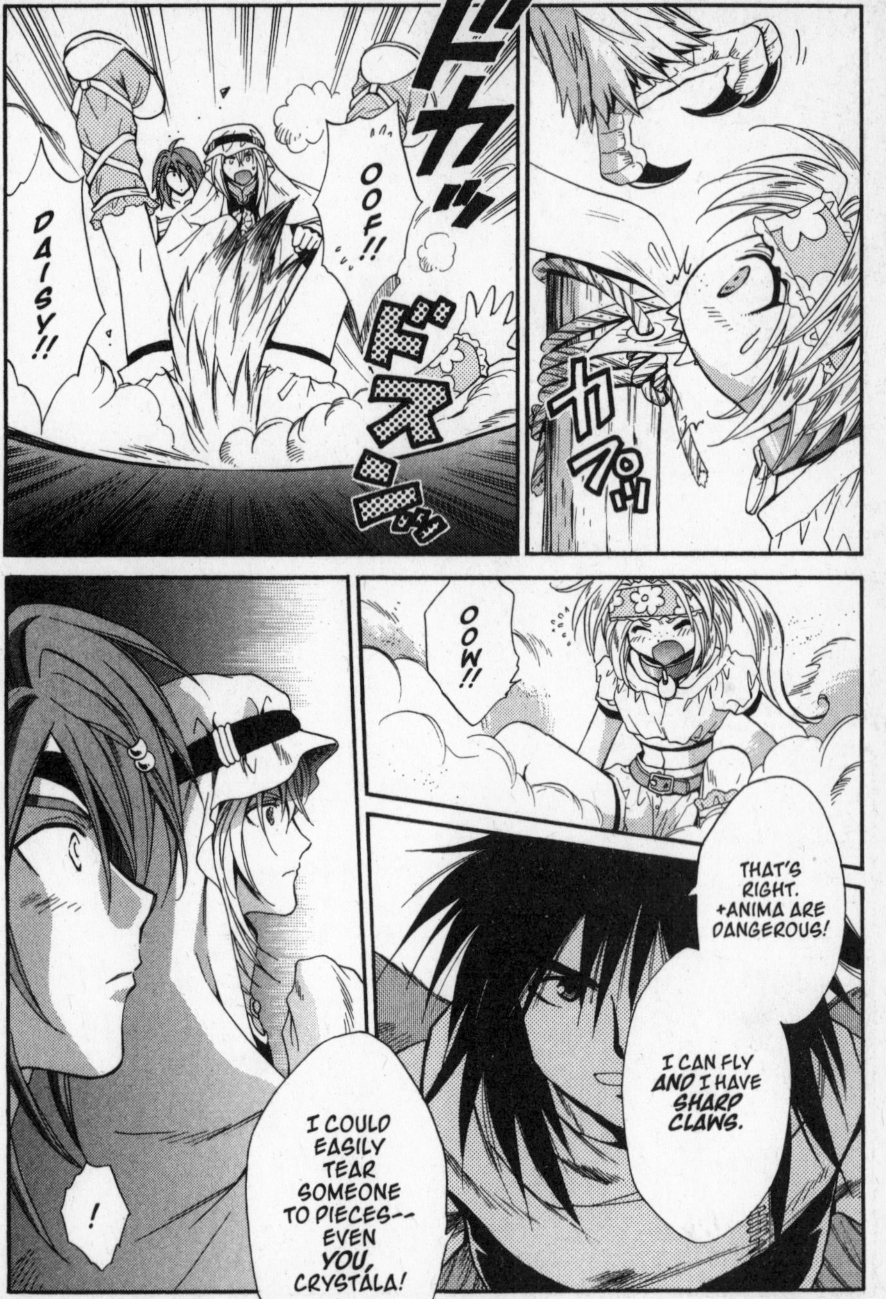

OOF!!
DAISY!!
OOW!!
THAT'S RIGHT. +ANIMA ARE DANGEROUS!
I CAN FLY AND I HAVE SHARP CLAWS.
I COULD EASILY TEAR SOMEONE TO PIECES--EVEN YOU, CRYSTALA!
!

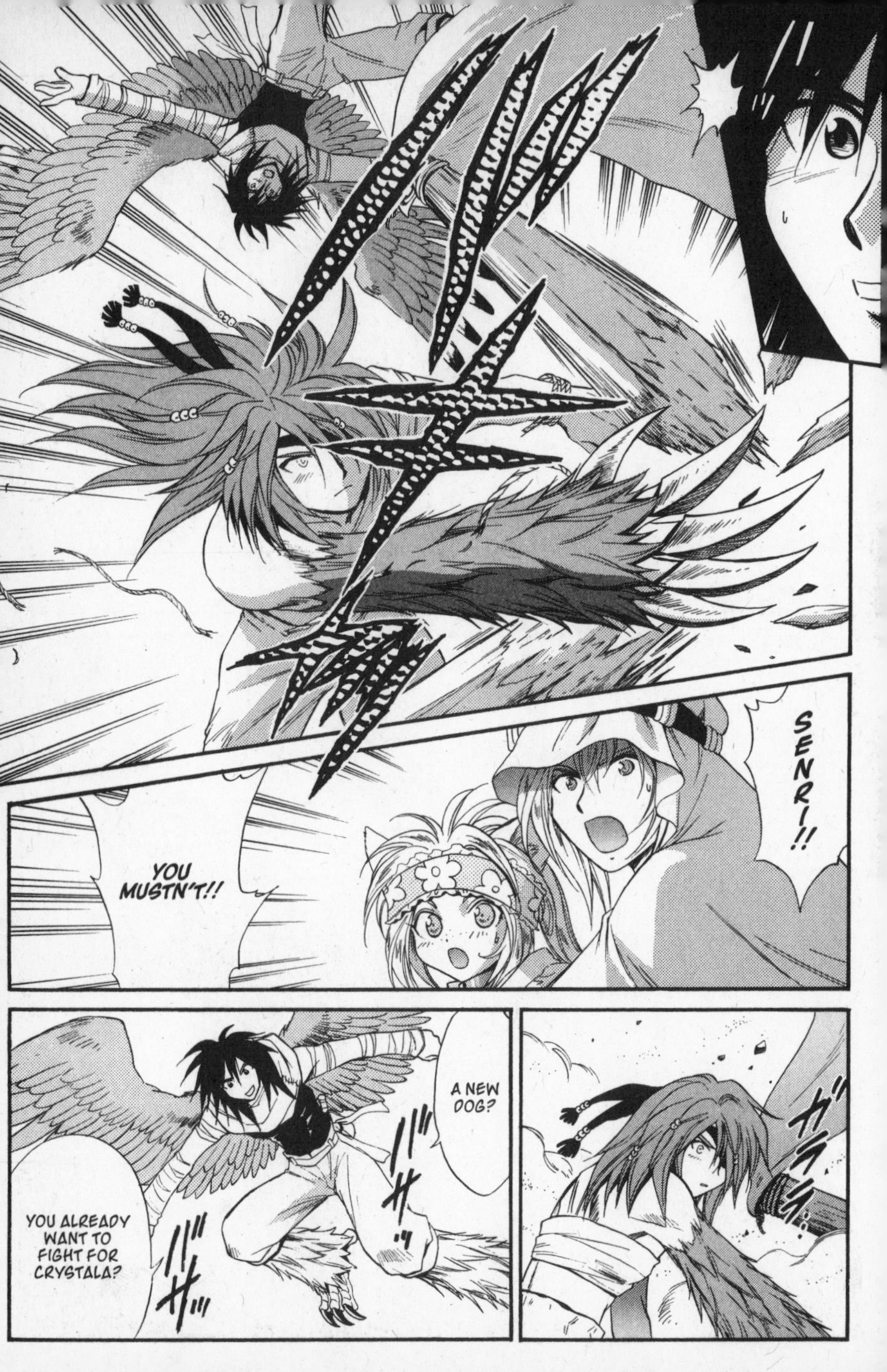
SENRI!!
YOU MUSTN'T!!
A NEW DOG?
YOU ALREADY WANT TO FIGHT FOR CRYSTALA?

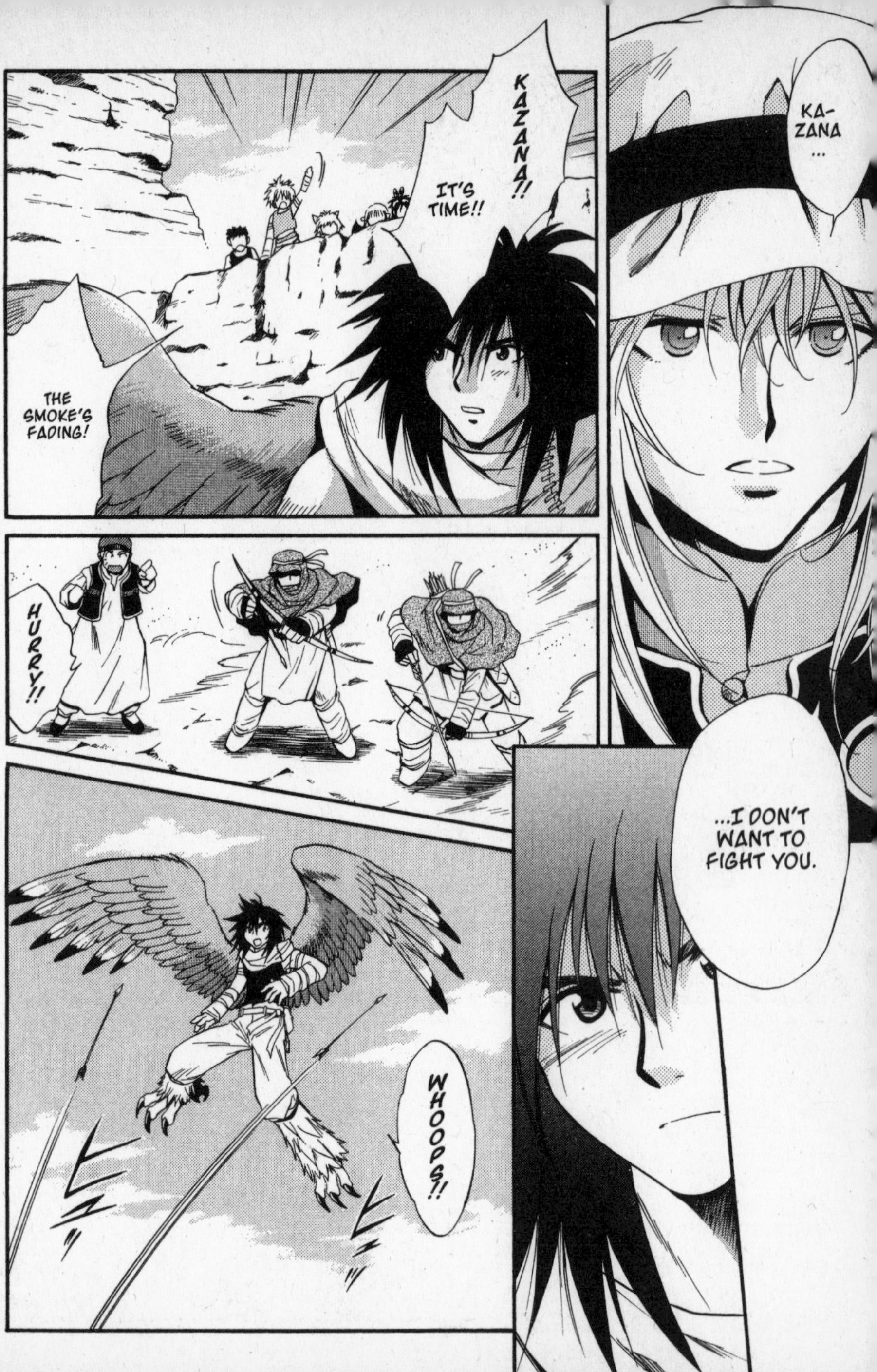

KA-ZANA...
KAZANA!!
IT'S TIME!!
THE SMOKE'S FADING!
HURRY!!
...I DON'T WANT TO FIGHT YOU.
WHOOPS!!

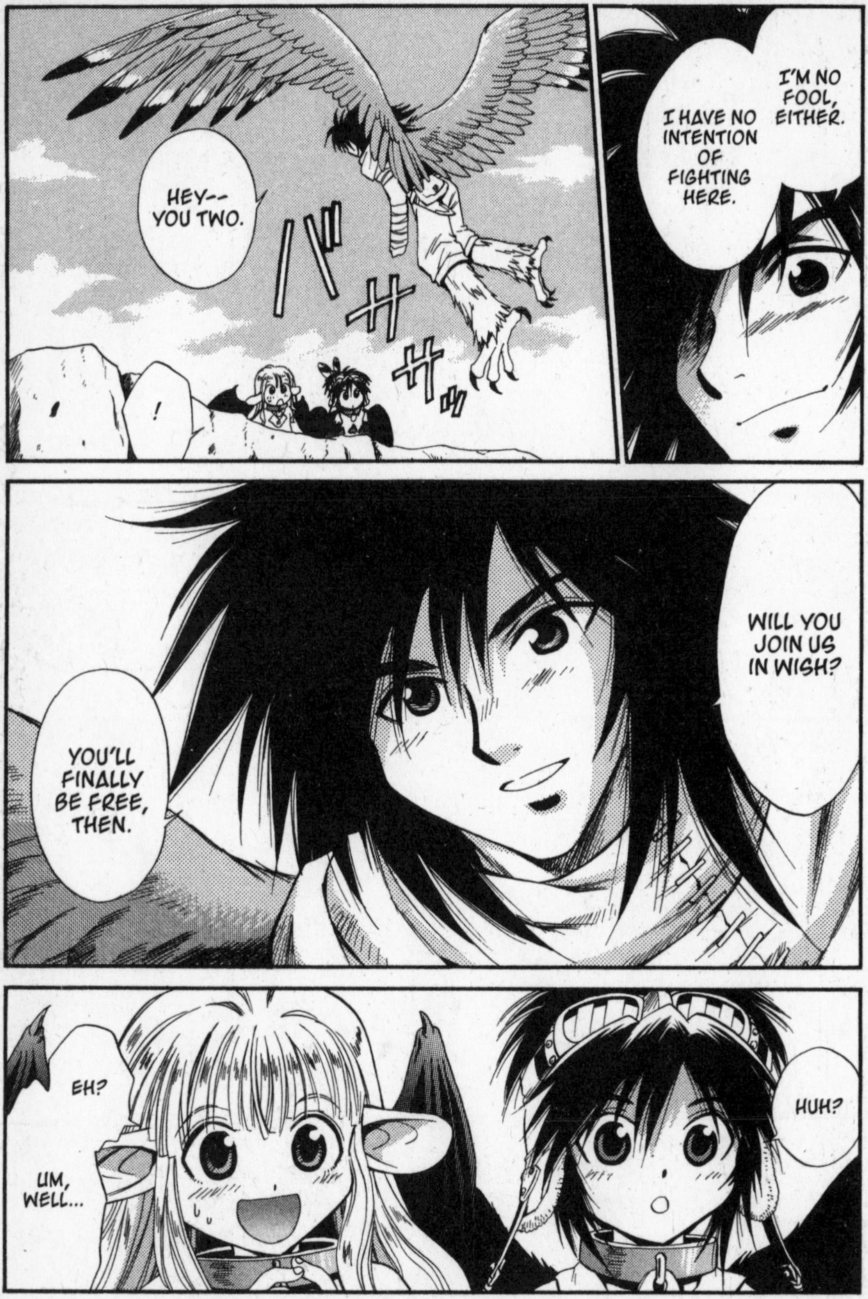
I'M NO FOOL, EITHER.
I HAVE NO INTENTION OF FIGHTING HERE.
HEY-- YOU TWO.
バササッ
!
WILL YOU JOIN US IN WISH?
YOU'LL FINALLY BE FREE, THEN.
HUH?
EH?
UM, WELL...

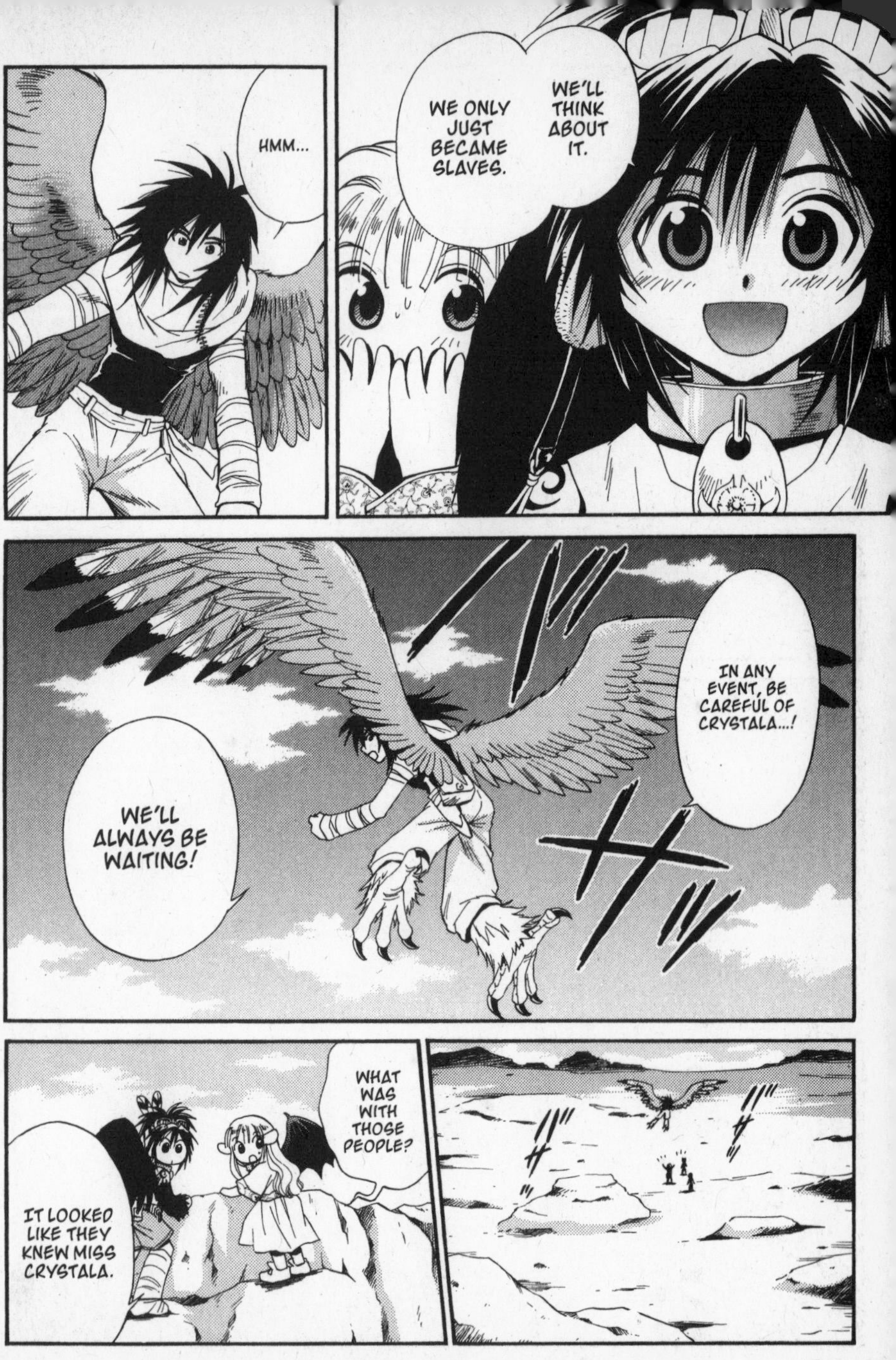
WE'LL THINK ABOUT IT.
WE ONLY JUST BECAME SLAVES.
HMM...
IN ANY EVENT, BE CAREFUL OF CRYSTALA...!
WE'LL ALWAYS BE WAITING!
WHAT WAS WITH THOSE PEOPLE?
IT LOOKED LIKE THEY KNEW MISS CRYSTALA.

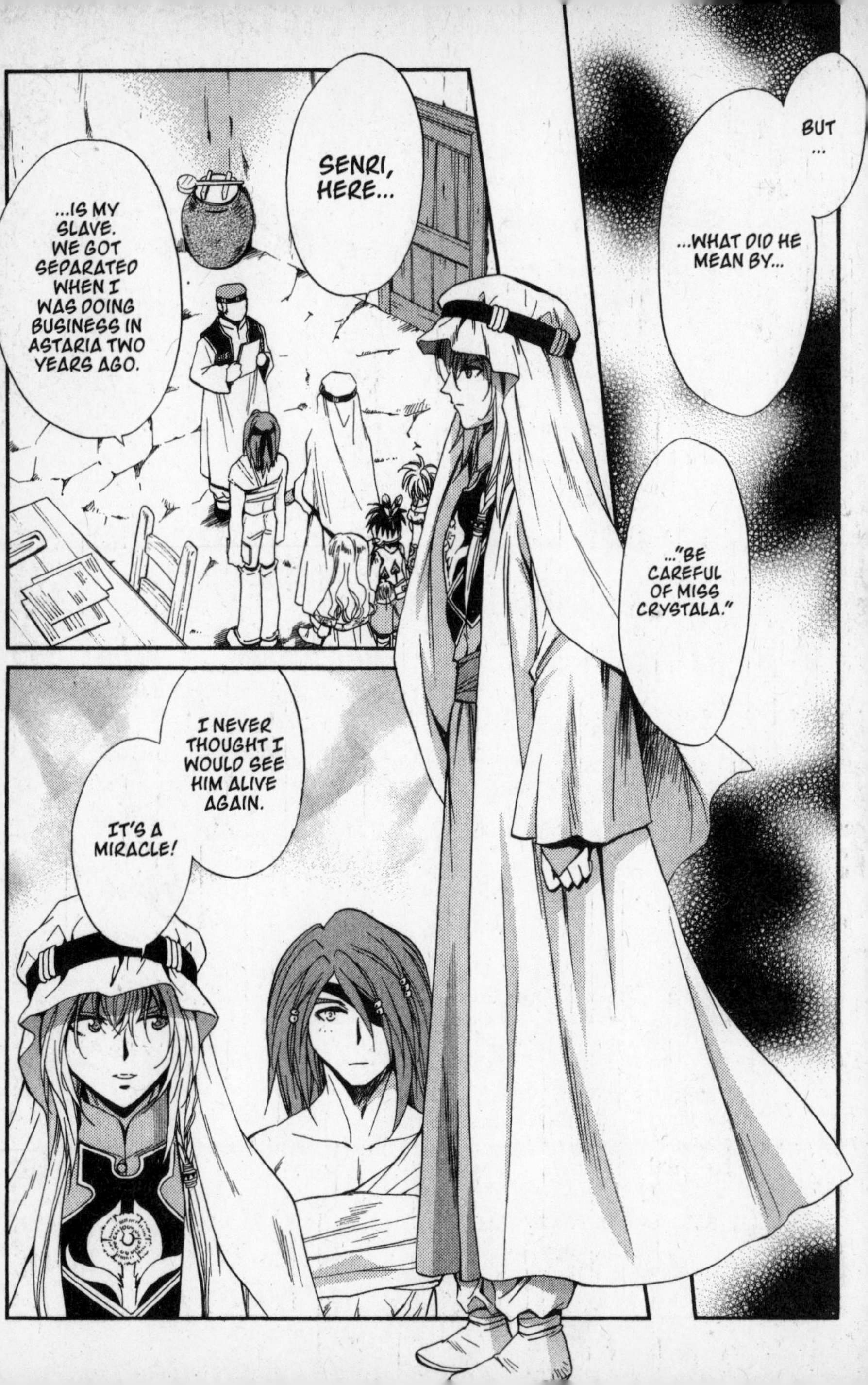
BUT ...
...WHAT DID HE MEAN BY...
..."BE CAREFUL OF MISS CRYSTALA."
SENRI, HERE...
...IS MY SLAVE. WE GOT SEPARATED WHEN I WAS DOING BUSINESS IN ASTARIA TWO YEARS AGO.
I NEVER THOUGHT I WOULD SEE HIM ALIVE AGAIN.
IT'S A MIRACLE!

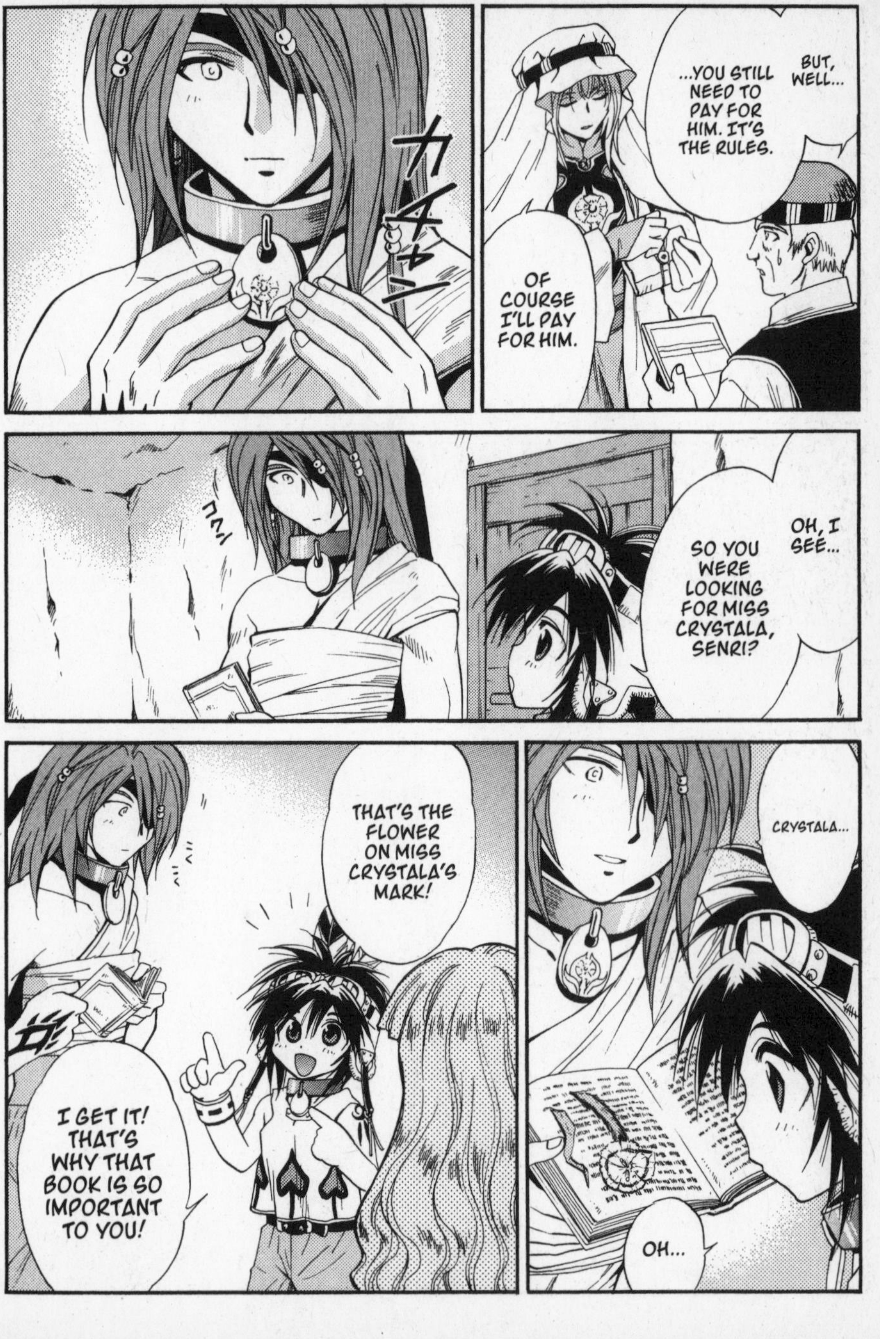
BUT, WELL...
...YOU STILL NEED TO PAY FOR HIM. IT'S THE RULES.
OF COURSE I'LL PAY FOR HIM.
OH, I SEE...
SO YOU WERE LOOKING FOR MISS CRYSTALA, SENRI?
CRYSTALA...
OH...
THAT'S THE FLOWER ON MISS CRYSTALA'S MARK!
I GET IT! THAT'S WHY THAT BOOK IS SO IMPORTANT TO YOU!

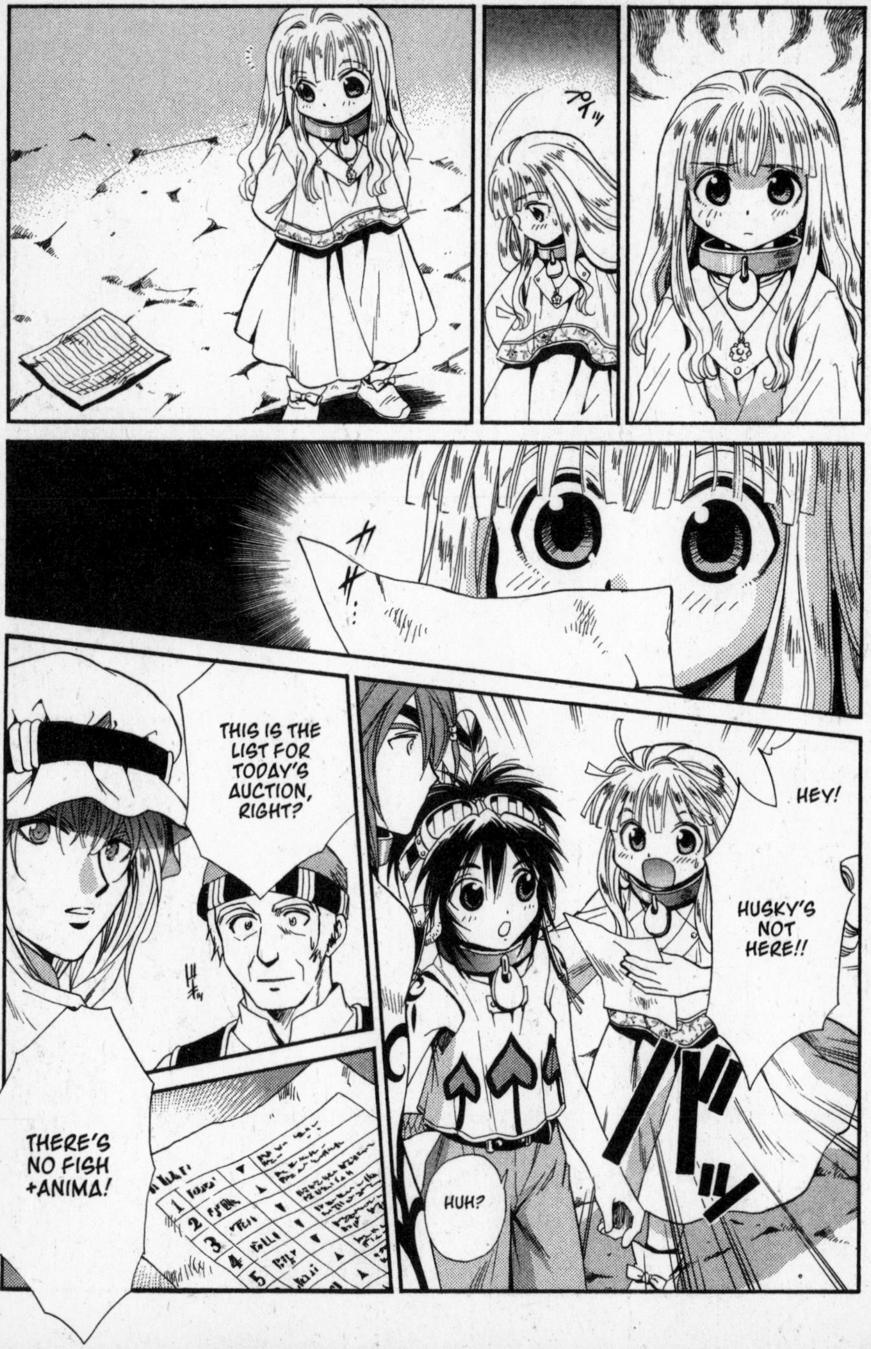
HEY!
HUSKY'S NOT HERE!!
HUH?
THIS IS THE LIST FOR TODAY'S AUCTION, RIGHT?
THERE'S NO FISH +ANIMA!

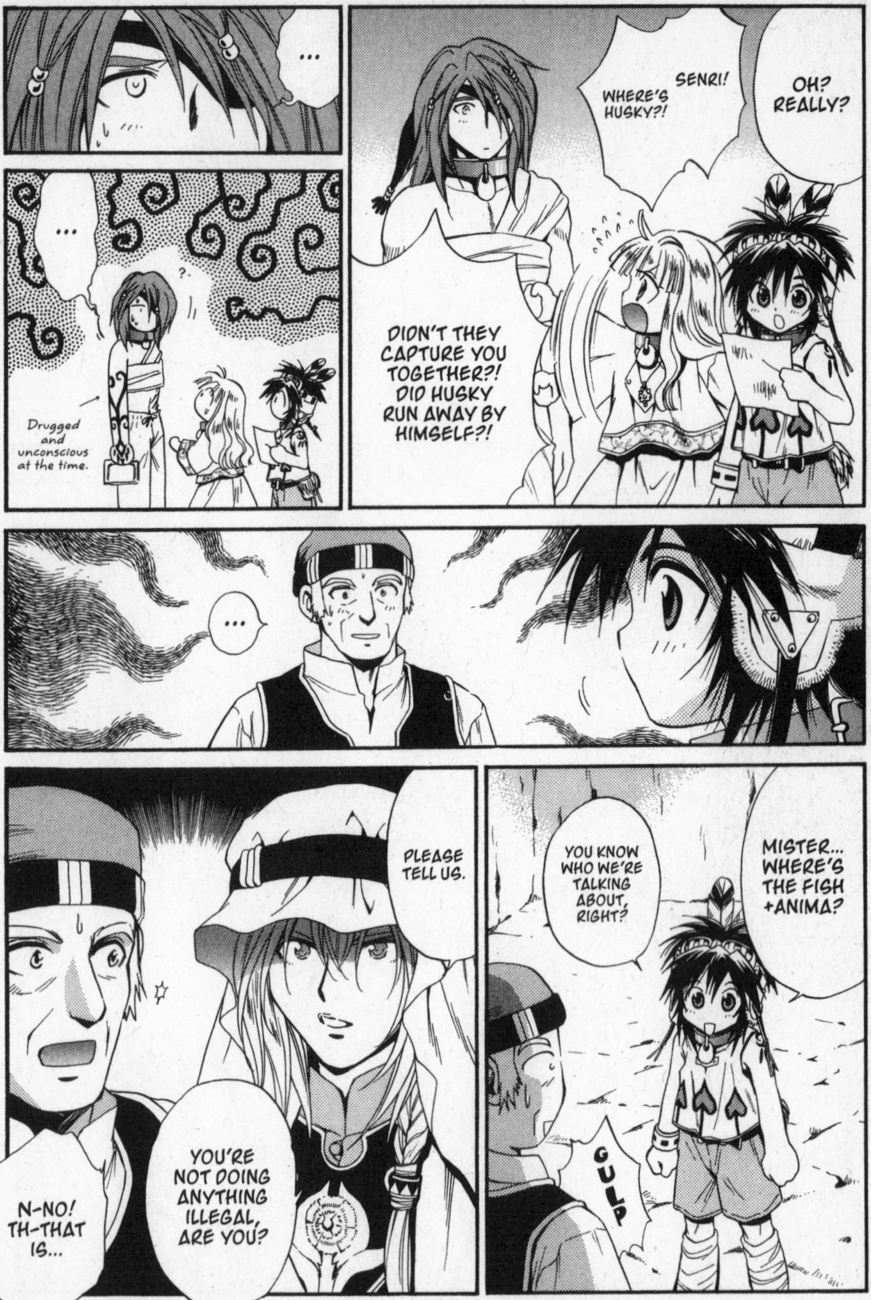
OH? REALLY?
SENRI!
WHERE'S HUSKY?!
DIDN'T THEY CAPTURE YOU TOGETHER?! DID HUSKY RUN AWAY BY HIMSELF?!
...
...
?
Drugged and unconscious at the time.
...
MISTER... WHERE'S THE FISH +ANIMA?
YOU KNOW WHO WE'RE TALKING ABOUT, RIGHT?
GULP
PLEASE TELL US.
YOU'RE NOT DOING ANYTHING ILLEGAL, ARE YOU?
N-NO! TH-THAT IS...

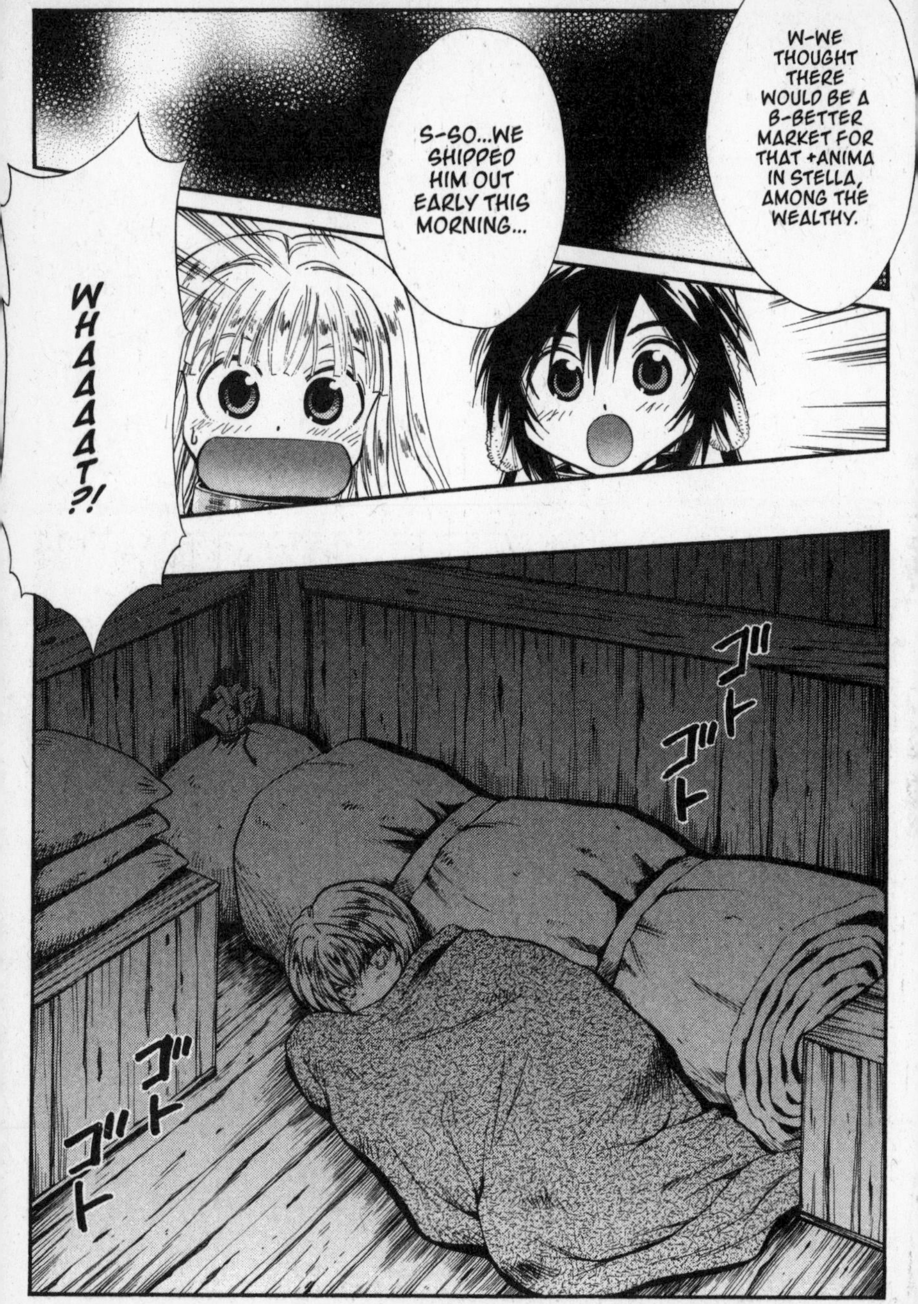
W-WE THOUGHT THERE WOULD BE A B-BETTER MARKET FOR THAT +ANIMA IN STELLA, AMONG THE WEALTHY.
S-SO...WE SHIPPED HIM OUT EARLY THIS MORNING...
WHAAAAAT?!
ゴト ゴト
ゴト ゴト

ARE WE HEADING WEST?

IT'S PROBABLY AFTERNOON BY NOW.

......

I WONDER IF THEY SOLD SENRI IN THAT LAST TOWN...

...OR IF HE WENT CRAZY AND THEY DID SOMETHING TERRIBLE TO HIM.

WERE COORO AND NANA CAPTURED BY SLAVE HUNTERS, TOO?

NO, THEY HAVE WINGS. THEY WOULDN'T GET CAPTURED SO EASILY.

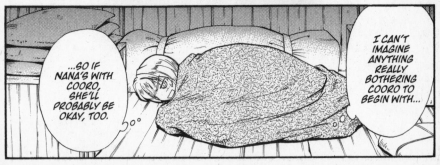

I CAN'T IMAGINE ANYTHING REALLY BOTHERING COORO TO BEGIN WITH...

...SO IF NANA'S WITH COORO, SHE'LL PROBABLY BE OKAY, TOO.

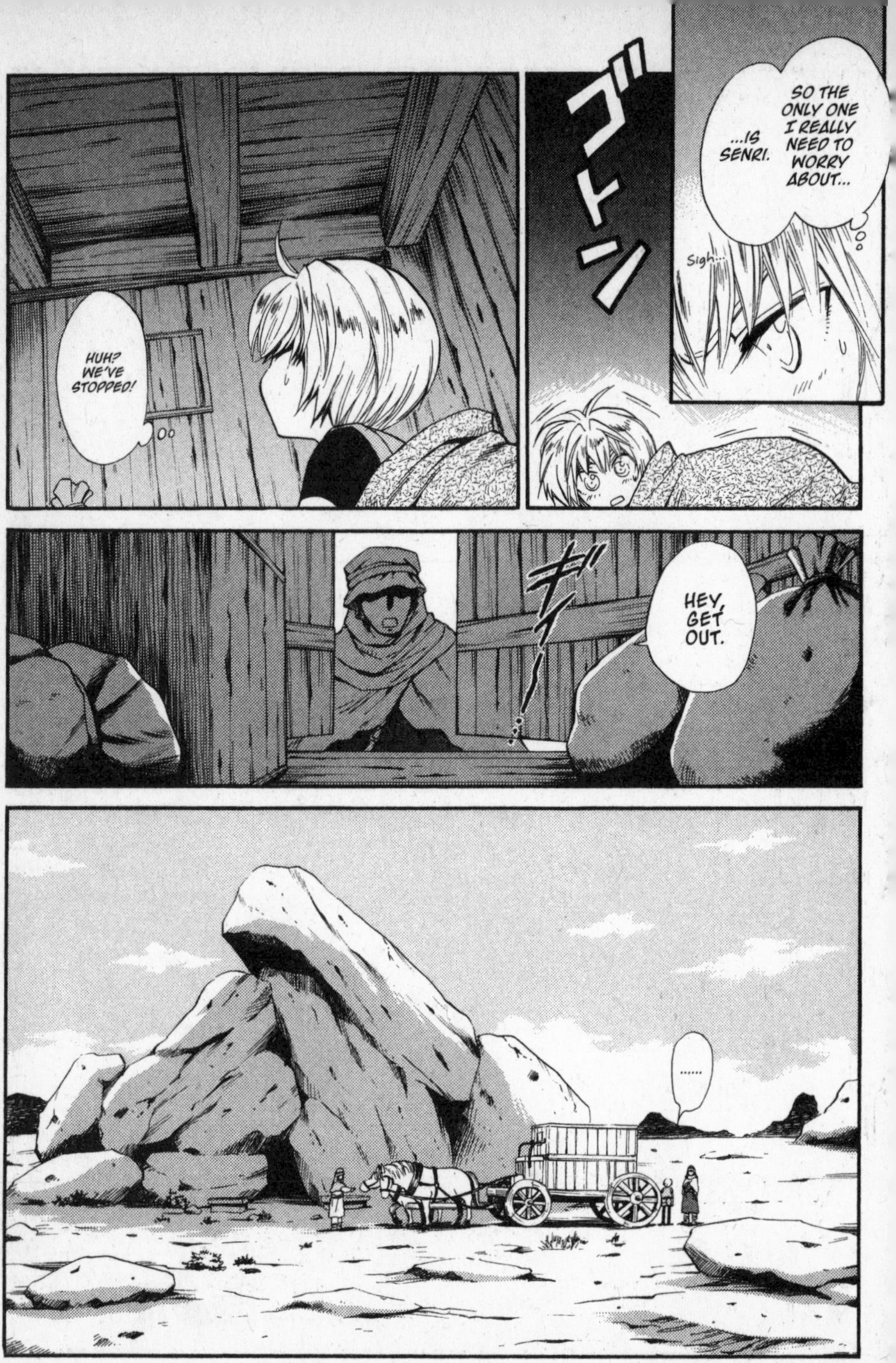

Sigh...
So the only one I really need to worry about...
...is Senri.
ゴトン
Huh? We've stopped!
ギイー
Hey, get out.
......

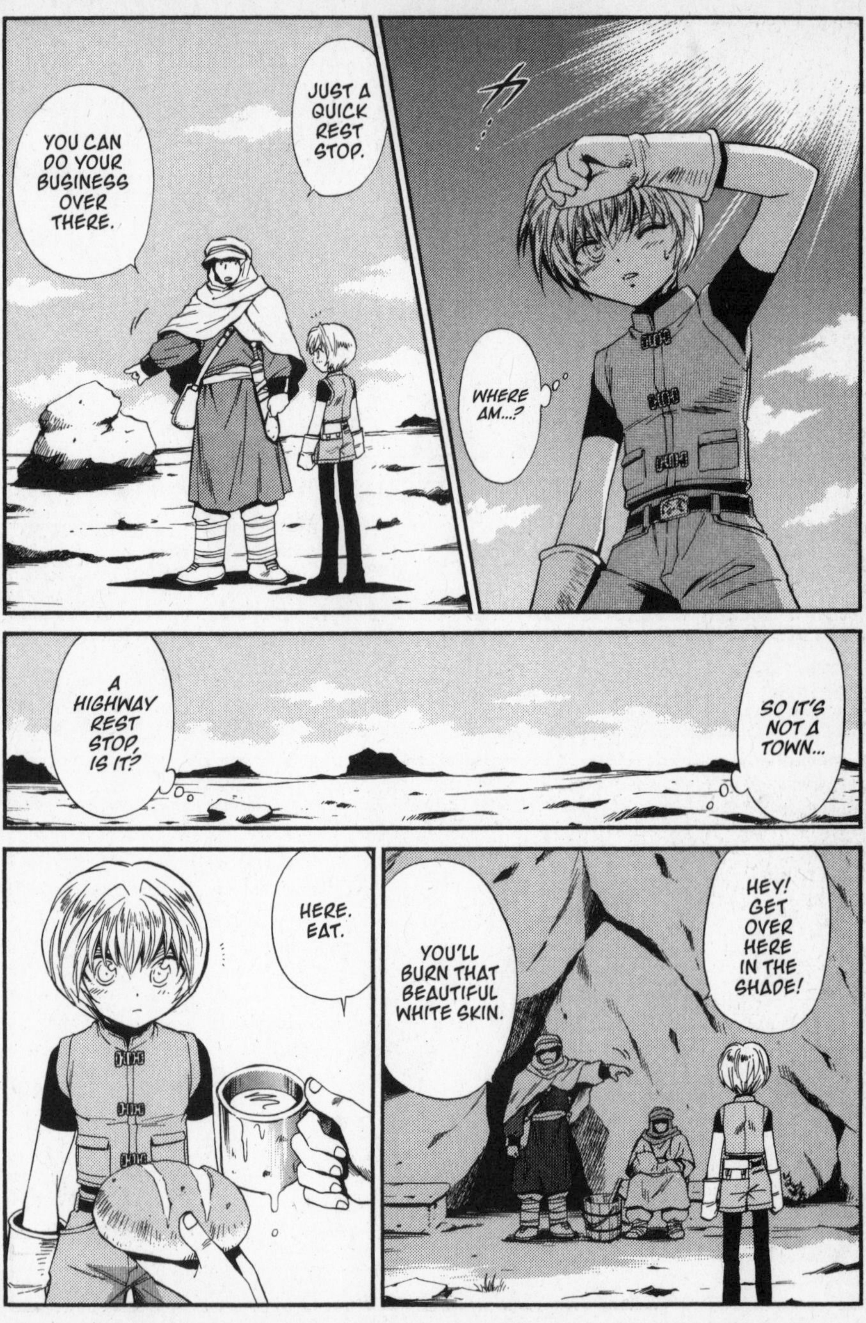
WHERE AM...?
JUST A QUICK REST STOP.
YOU CAN DO YOUR BUSINESS OVER THERE.
SO IT'S NOT A TOWN...
A HIGHWAY REST STOP, IS IT?
HEY! GET OVER HERE IN THE SHADE!
YOU'LL BURN THAT BEAUTIFUL WHITE SKIN.
HERE. EAT.

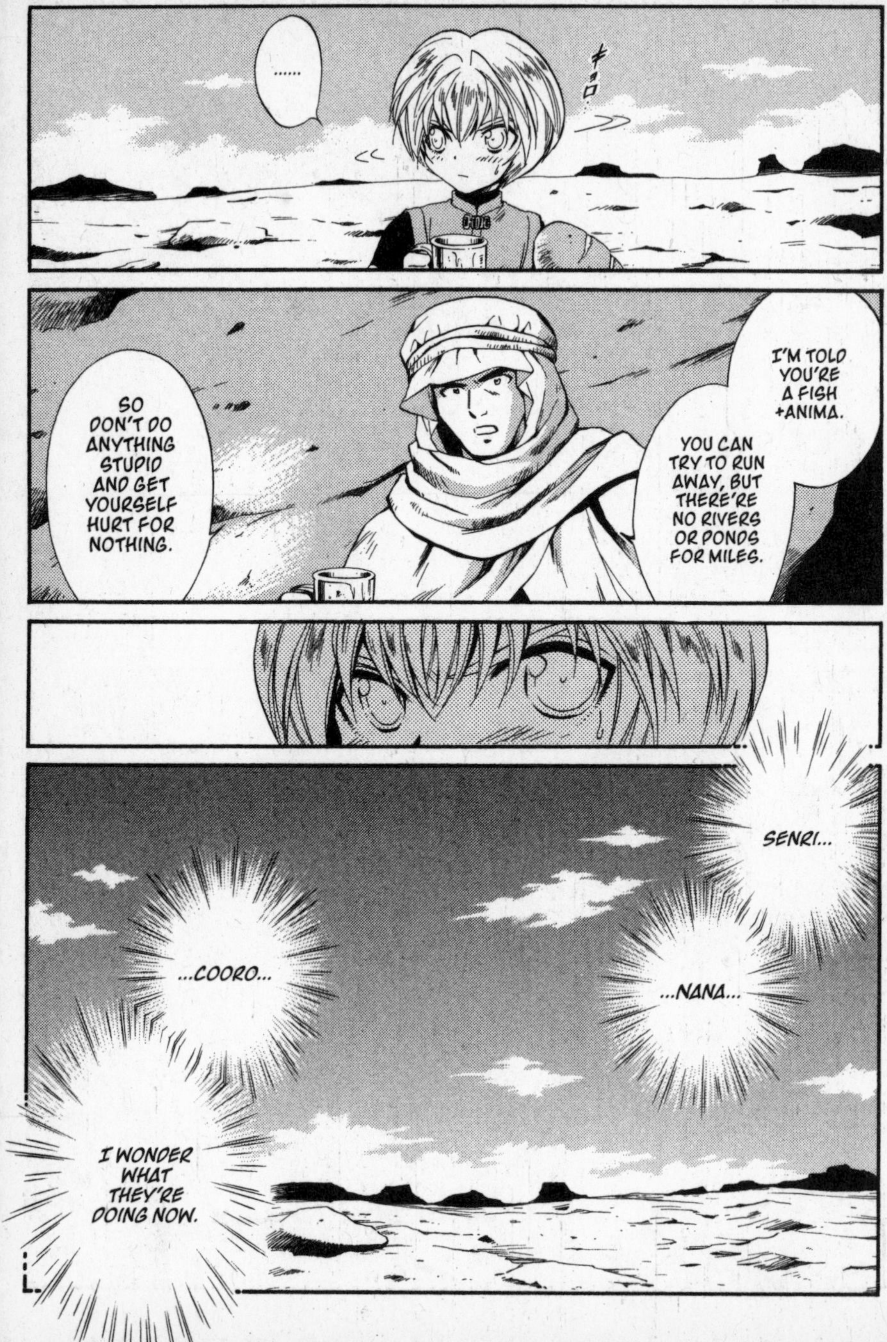
......
キョロ
I'M TOLD YOU'RE A FISH +ANIMA.
YOU CAN TRY TO RUN AWAY, BUT THERE'RE NO RIVERS OR PONDS FOR MILES.
SO DON'T DO ANYTHING STUPID AND GET YOURSELF HURT FOR NOTHING.
SENRI...
...NANA...
...COORO...
I WONDER WHAT THEY'RE DOING NOW.

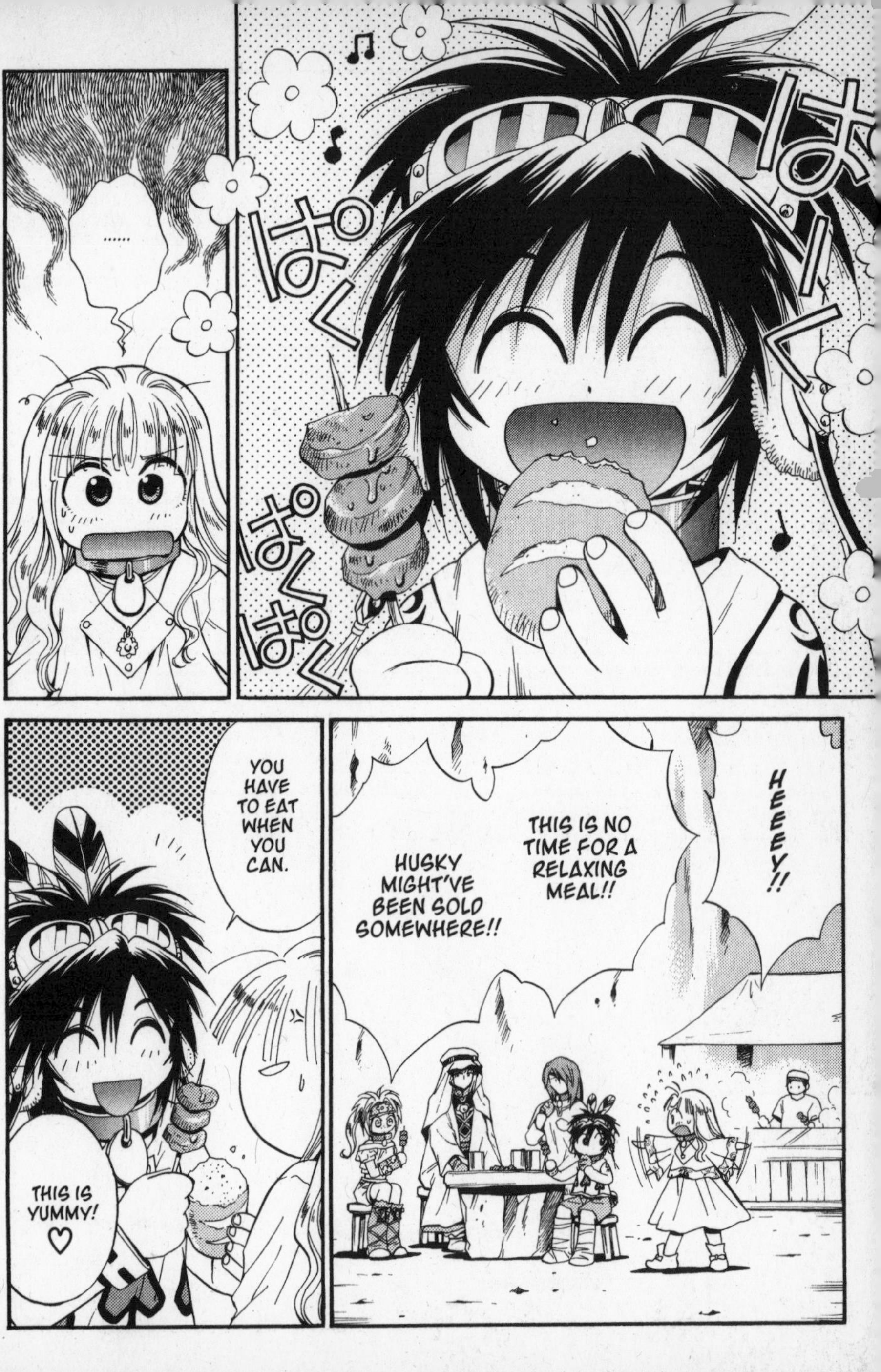

ぱく
ぱくぱく
......
HEEEY!!
THIS IS NO TIME FOR A RELAXING MEAL!!
HUSKY MIGHT'VE BEEN SOLD SOMEWHERE!!
YOU HAVE TO EAT WHEN YOU CAN.
THIS IS YUMMY! ♡

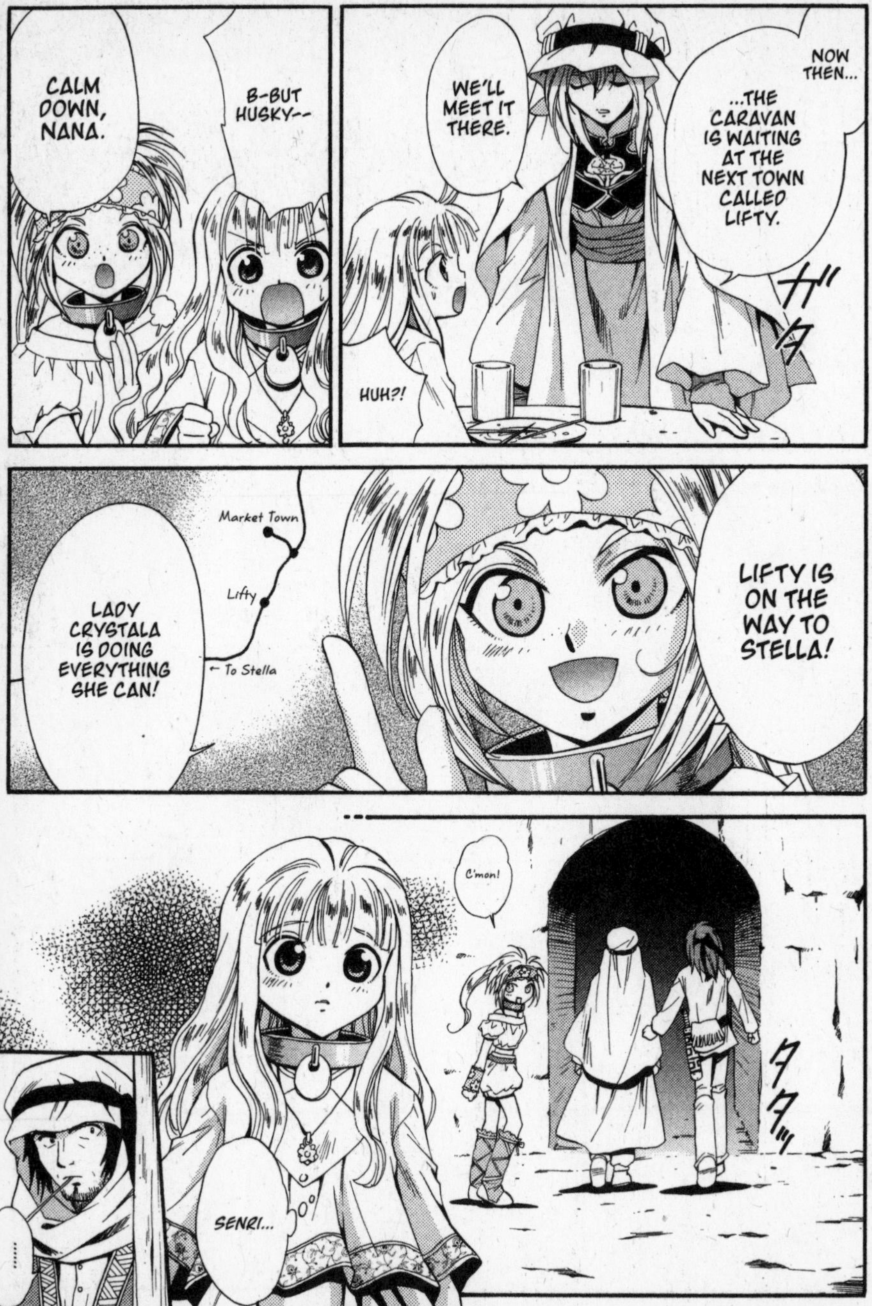
NOW THEN...
...THE CARAVAN IS WAITING AT THE NEXT TOWN CALLED LIFTY.
WE'LL MEET IT THERE.
HUH?!
B-BUT HUSKY--
CALM DOWN, NANA.
LIFTY IS ON THE WAY TO STELLA!
Market Town
Lifty
← To Stella
LADY CRYSTALA IS DOING EVERYTHING SHE CAN!
C'mon!
SENRI...
......

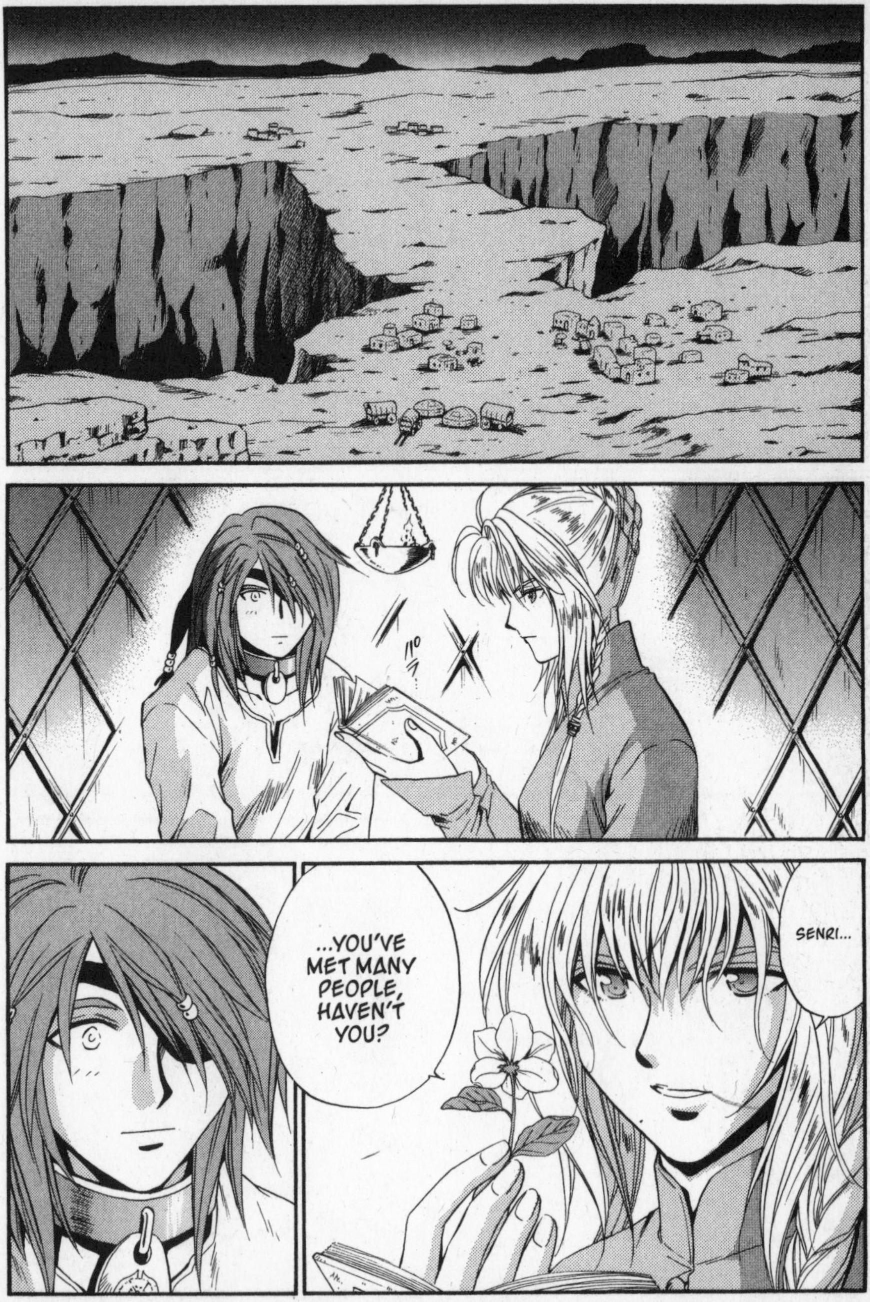
SENRI...
...YOU'VE MET MANY PEOPLE, HAVEN'T YOU?

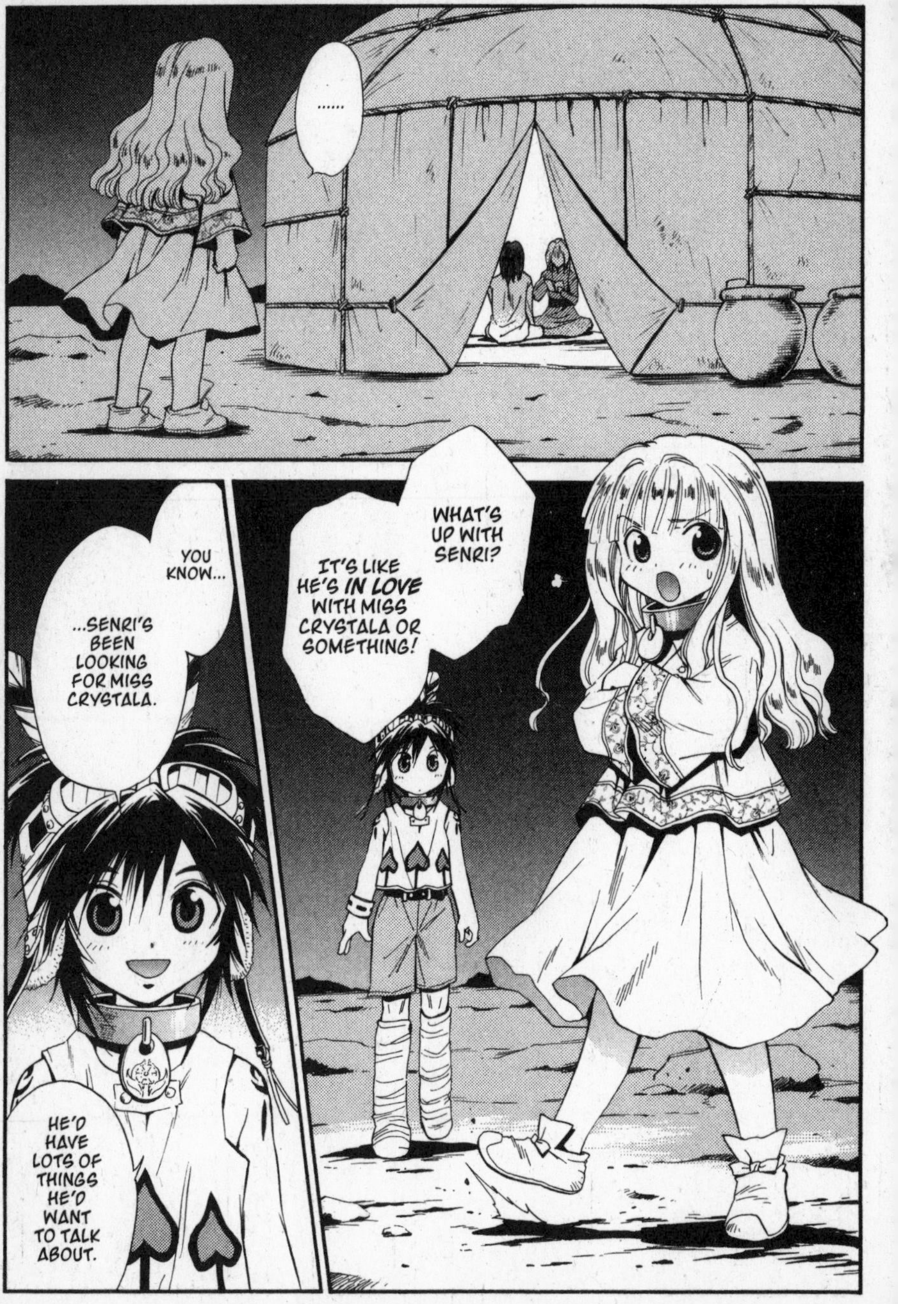
......
WHAT'S UP WITH SENRI?
IT'S LIKE HE'S IN LOVE WITH MISS CRYSTALA OR SOMETHING!
YOU KNOW...
...SENRI'S BEEN LOOKING FOR MISS CRYSTALA.
HE'D HAVE LOTS OF THINGS HE'D WANT TO TALK ABOUT.

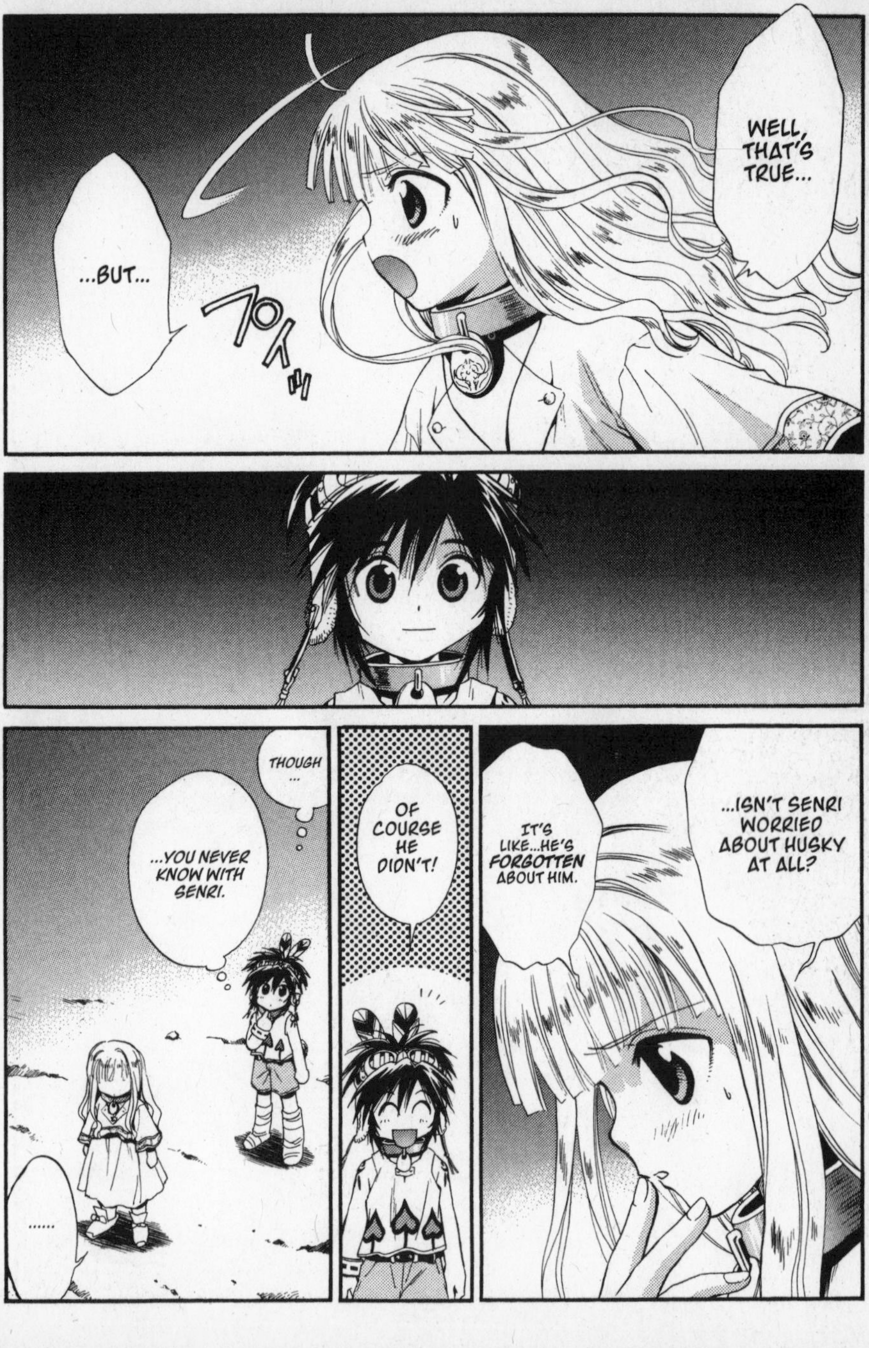
WELL, THAT'S TRUE...
...BUT...
プイッ
...ISN'T SENRI WORRIED ABOUT HUSKY AT ALL?
IT'S LIKE...HE'S FORGOTTEN ABOUT HIM.
OF COURSE HE DIDN'T!
THOUGH ...
...YOU NEVER KNOW WITH SENRI.
......

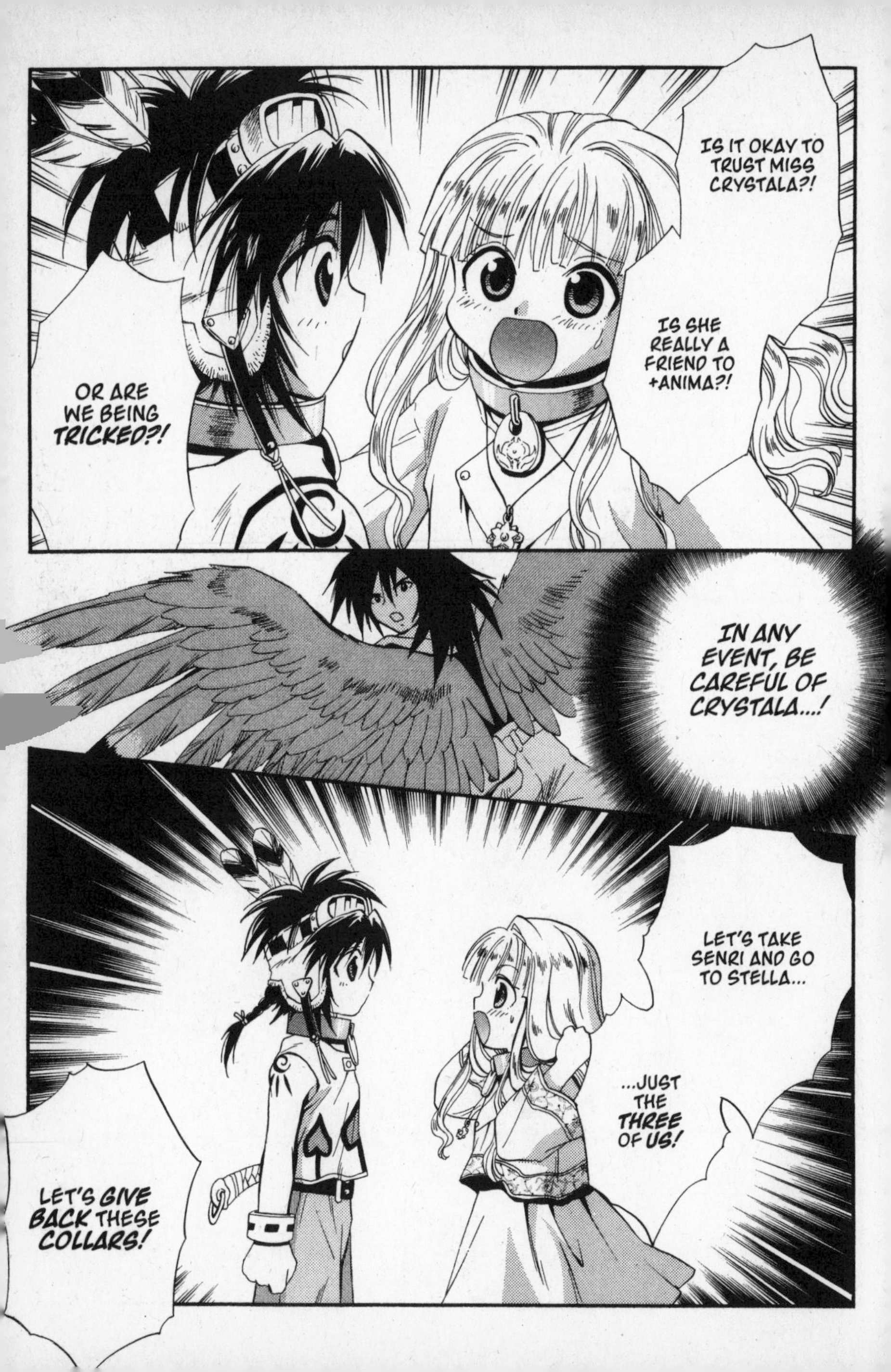
IS IT OKAY TO TRUST MISS CRYSTALA?!
IS SHE REALLY A FRIEND TO +ANIMA?!
OR ARE WE BEING TRICKED?!
IN ANY EVENT, BE CAREFUL OF CRYSTALA...!
LET'S TAKE SENRI AND GO TO STELLA...
...JUST THE THREE OF US!
LET'S GIVE BACK THESE COLLARS!

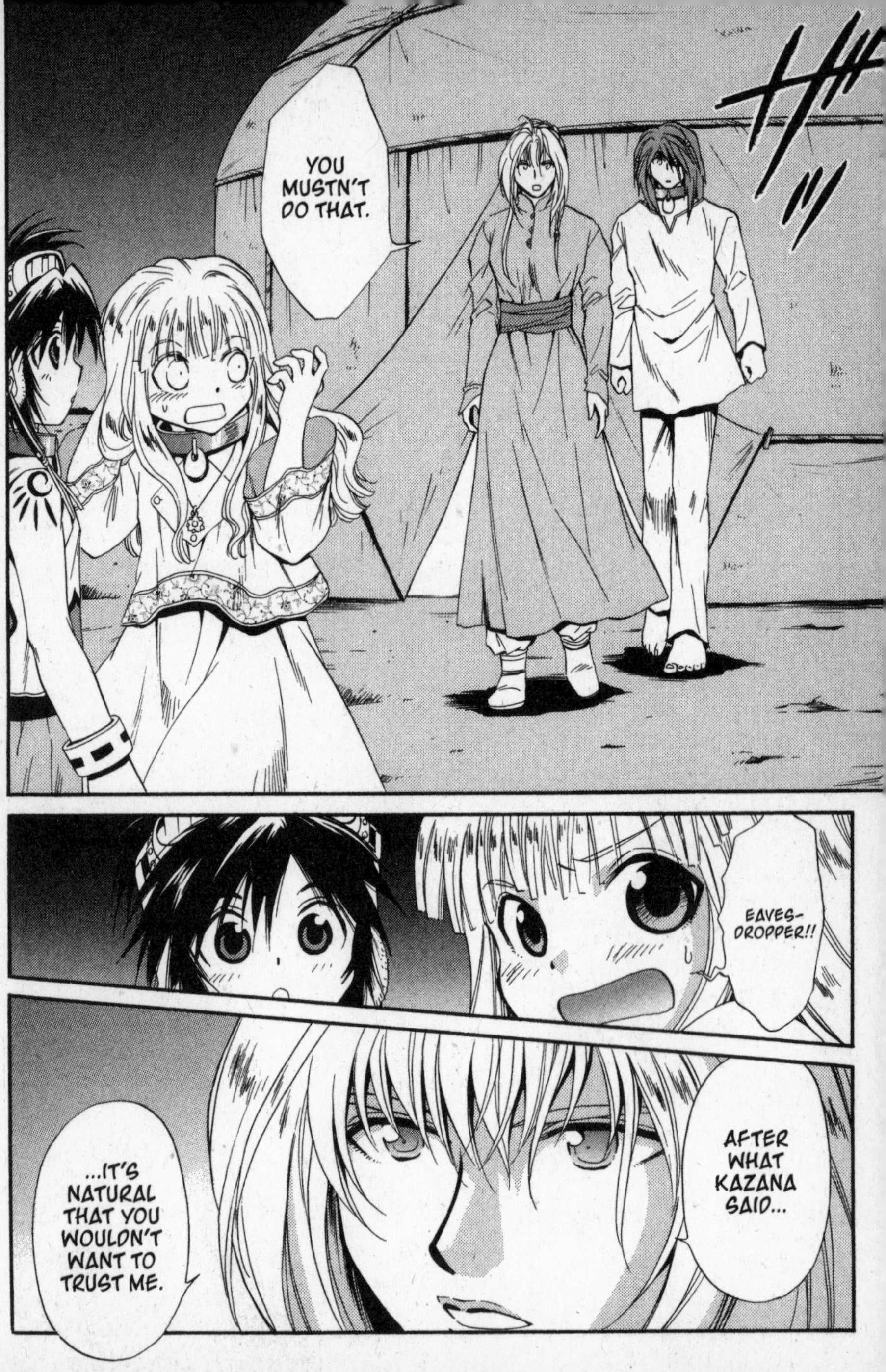
YOU MUSTN'T DO THAT.
EAVES-DROPPER!!
AFTER WHAT KAZANA SAID...
...IT'S NATURAL THAT YOU WOULDN'T WANT TO TRUST ME.

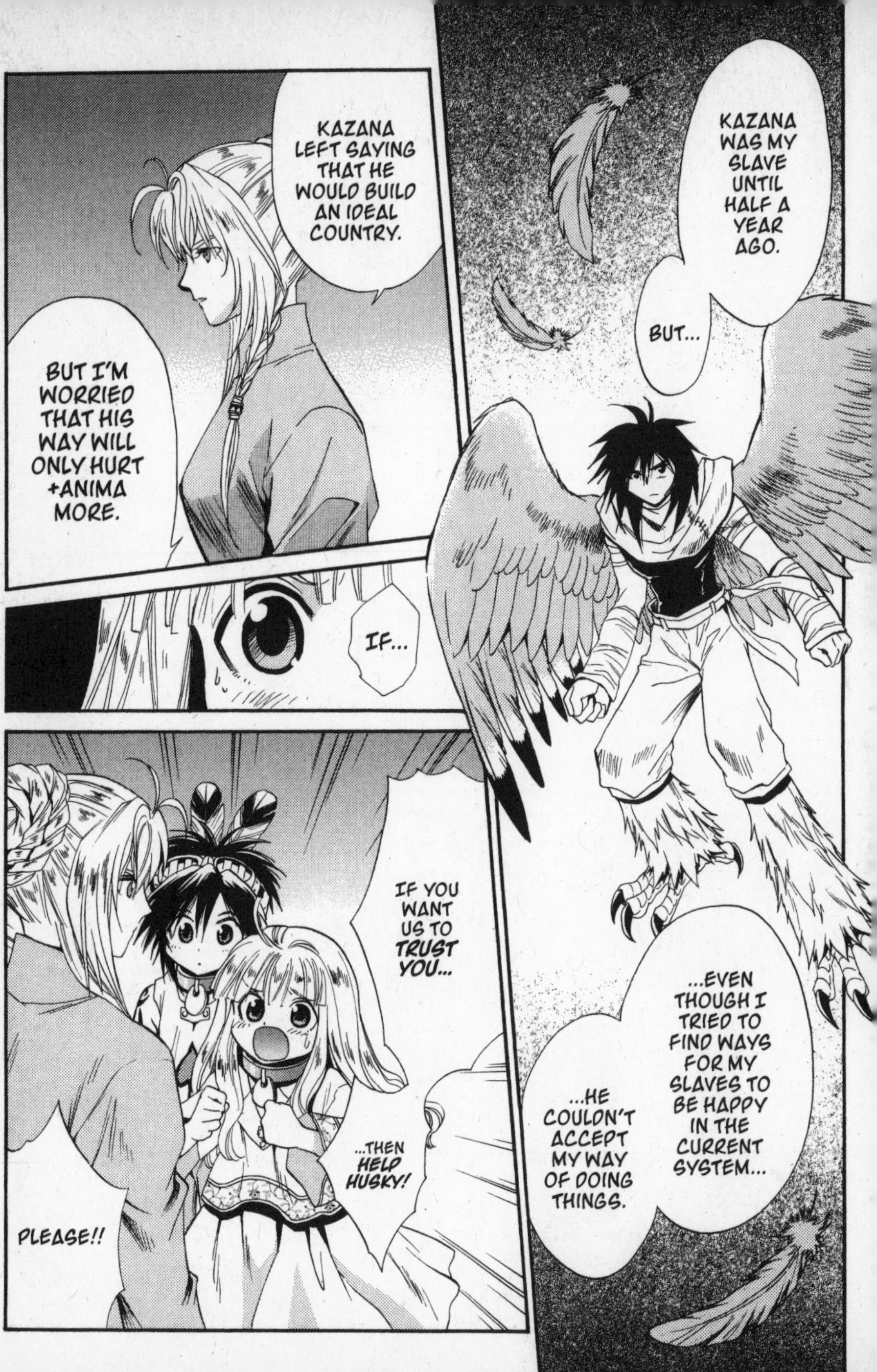
KAZANA WAS MY SLAVE UNTIL HALF A YEAR AGO.
BUT...
...EVEN THOUGH I TRIED TO FIND WAYS FOR MY SLAVES TO BE HAPPY IN THE CURRENT SYSTEM...
...HE COULDN'T ACCEPT MY WAY OF DOING THINGS.
KAZANA LEFT SAYING THAT HE WOULD BUILD AN IDEAL COUNTRY.
BUT I'M WORRIED THAT HIS WAY WILL ONLY HURT +ANIMA MORE.
IF...
IF YOU WANT US TO TRUST YOU...
...THEN HELP HUSKY!
PLEASE!!

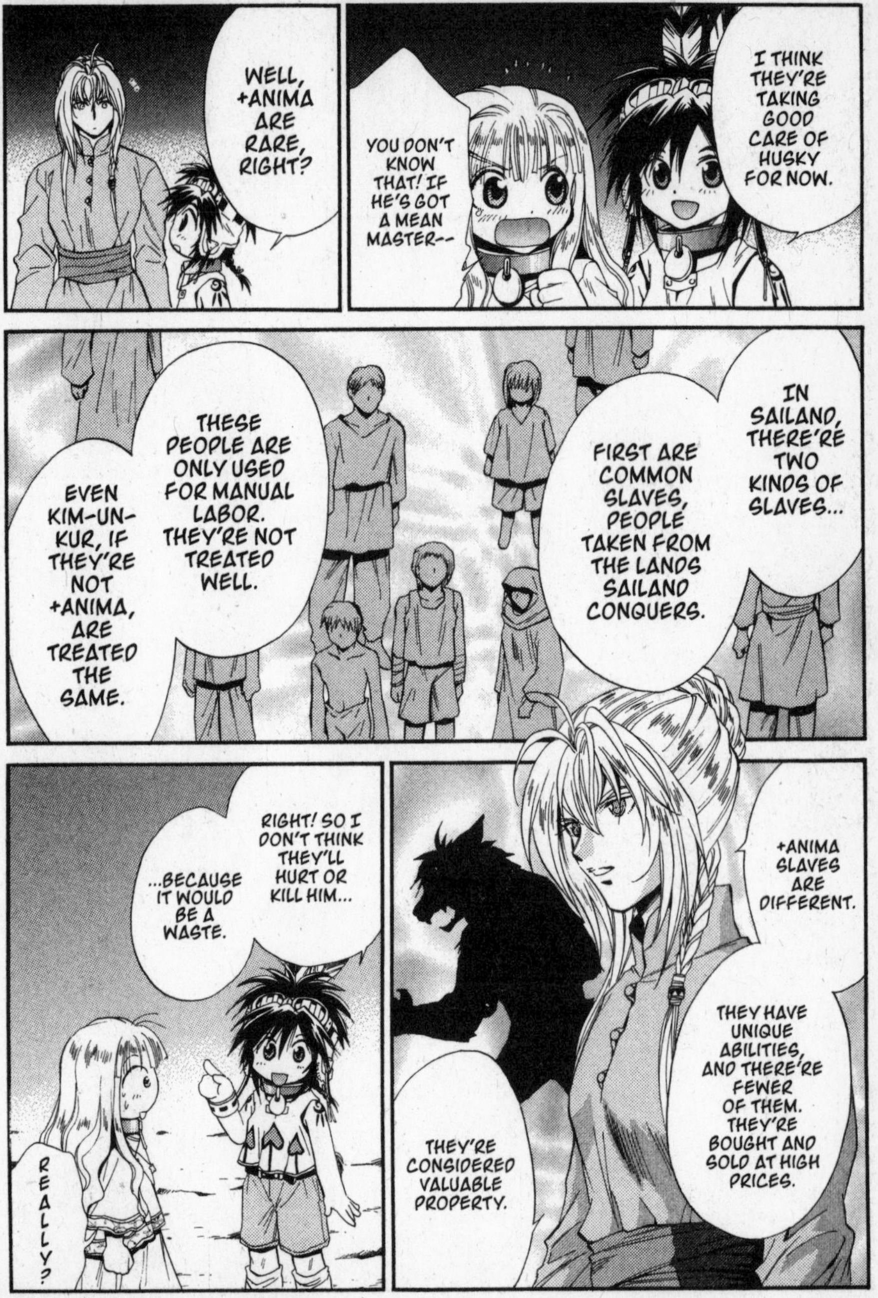

I THINK THEY'RE TAKING GOOD CARE OF HUSKY FOR NOW.
YOU DON'T KNOW THAT! IF HE'S GOT A MEAN MASTER--
WELL, +ANIMA ARE RARE, RIGHT?
IN SAILAND, THERE'RE TWO KINDS OF SLAVES...
FIRST ARE COMMON SLAVES, PEOPLE TAKEN FROM THE LANDS SAILAND CONQUERS.
THESE PEOPLE ARE ONLY USED FOR MANUAL LABOR. THEY'RE NOT TREATED WELL.
EVEN KIM-UN-KUR, IF THEY'RE NOT +ANIMA, ARE TREATED THE SAME.
+ANIMA SLAVES ARE DIFFERENT.
THEY HAVE UNIQUE ABILITIES, AND THERE'RE FEWER OF THEM. THEY'RE BOUGHT AND SOLD AT HIGH PRICES.
THEY'RE CONSIDERED VALUABLE PROPERTY.
RIGHT! SO I DON'T THINK THEY'LL HURT OR KILL HIM...
...BECAUSE IT WOULD BE A WASTE.
REALLY?

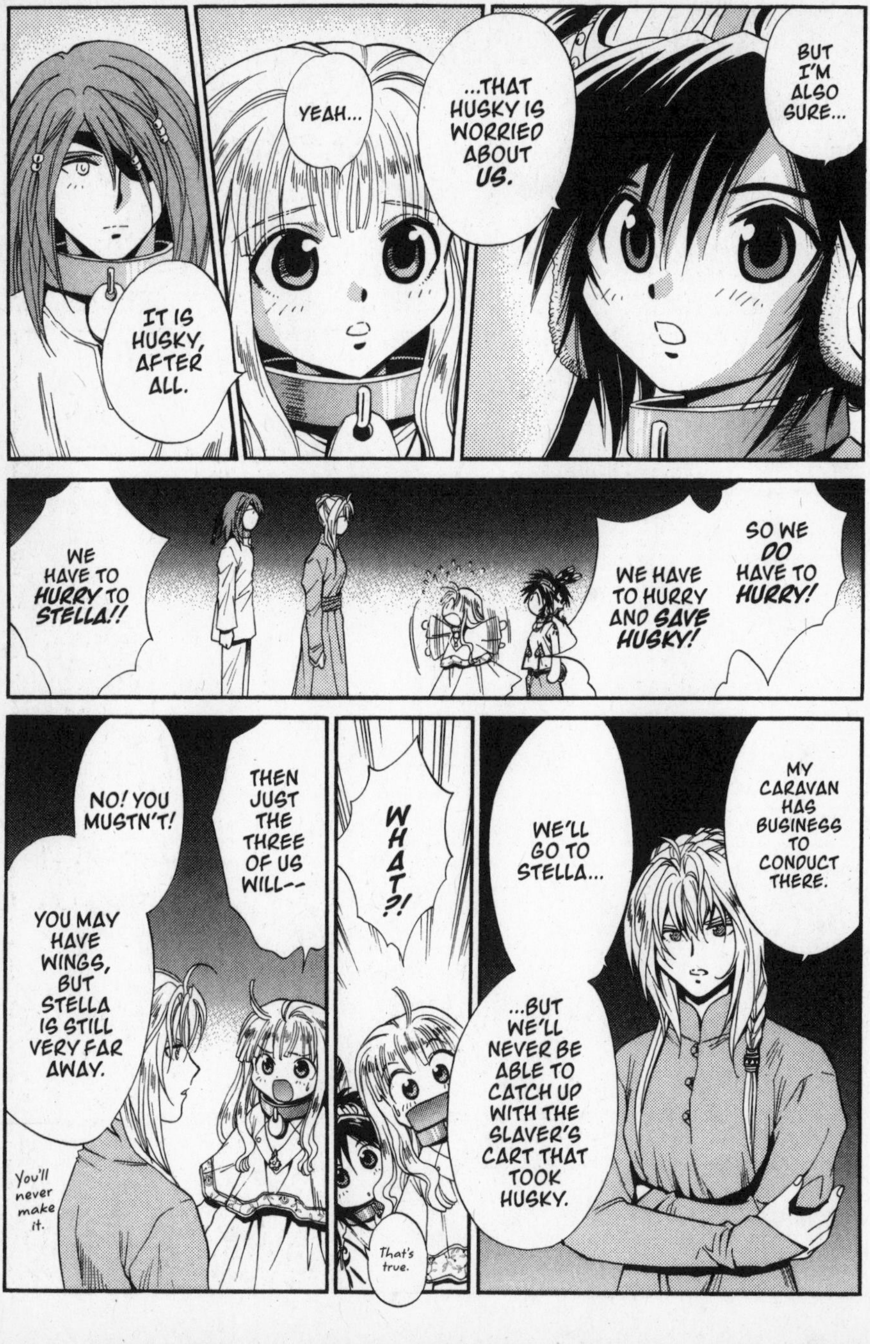
BUT I'M ALSO SURE...
...THAT HUSKY IS WORRIED ABOUT US.
YEAH...
IT IS HUSKY, AFTER ALL.
SO WE DO HAVE TO HURRY!
WE HAVE TO HURRY AND SAVE HUSKY!
WE HAVE TO HURRY TO STELLA!!
MY CARAVAN HAS BUSINESS TO CONDUCT THERE.
WE'LL GO TO STELLA...
...BUT WE'LL NEVER BE ABLE TO CATCH UP WITH THE SLAVER'S CART THAT TOOK HUSKY.
WHAT?!
THEN JUST THE THREE OF US WILL--
NO! YOU MUSTN'T!
YOU MAY HAVE WINGS, BUT STELLA IS STILL VERY FAR AWAY.
You'll never make it.
That's true.

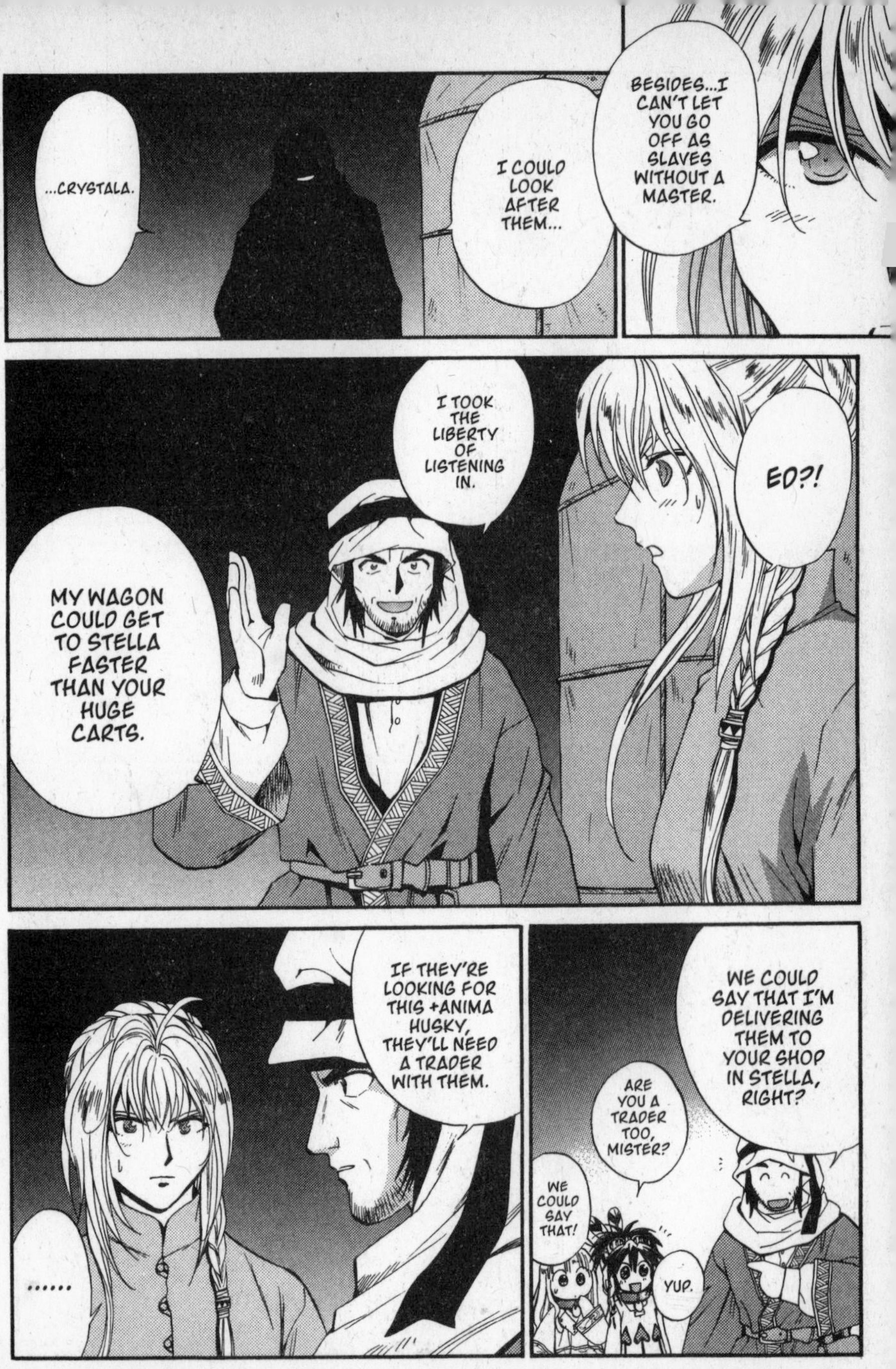
BESIDES...I CAN'T LET YOU GO OFF AS SLAVES WITHOUT A MASTER.
I COULD LOOK AFTER THEM...
...CRYSTALA.
ED?!
I TOOK THE LIBERTY OF LISTENING IN.
MY WAGON COULD GET TO STELLA FASTER THAN YOUR HUGE CARTS.
WE COULD SAY THAT I'M DELIVERING THEM TO YOUR SHOP IN STELLA, RIGHT?
ARE YOU A TRADER TOO, MISTER?
YUP.
WE COULD SAY THAT!
IF THEY'RE LOOKING FOR THIS +ANIMA HUSKY, THEY'LL NEED A TRADER WITH THEM.
......

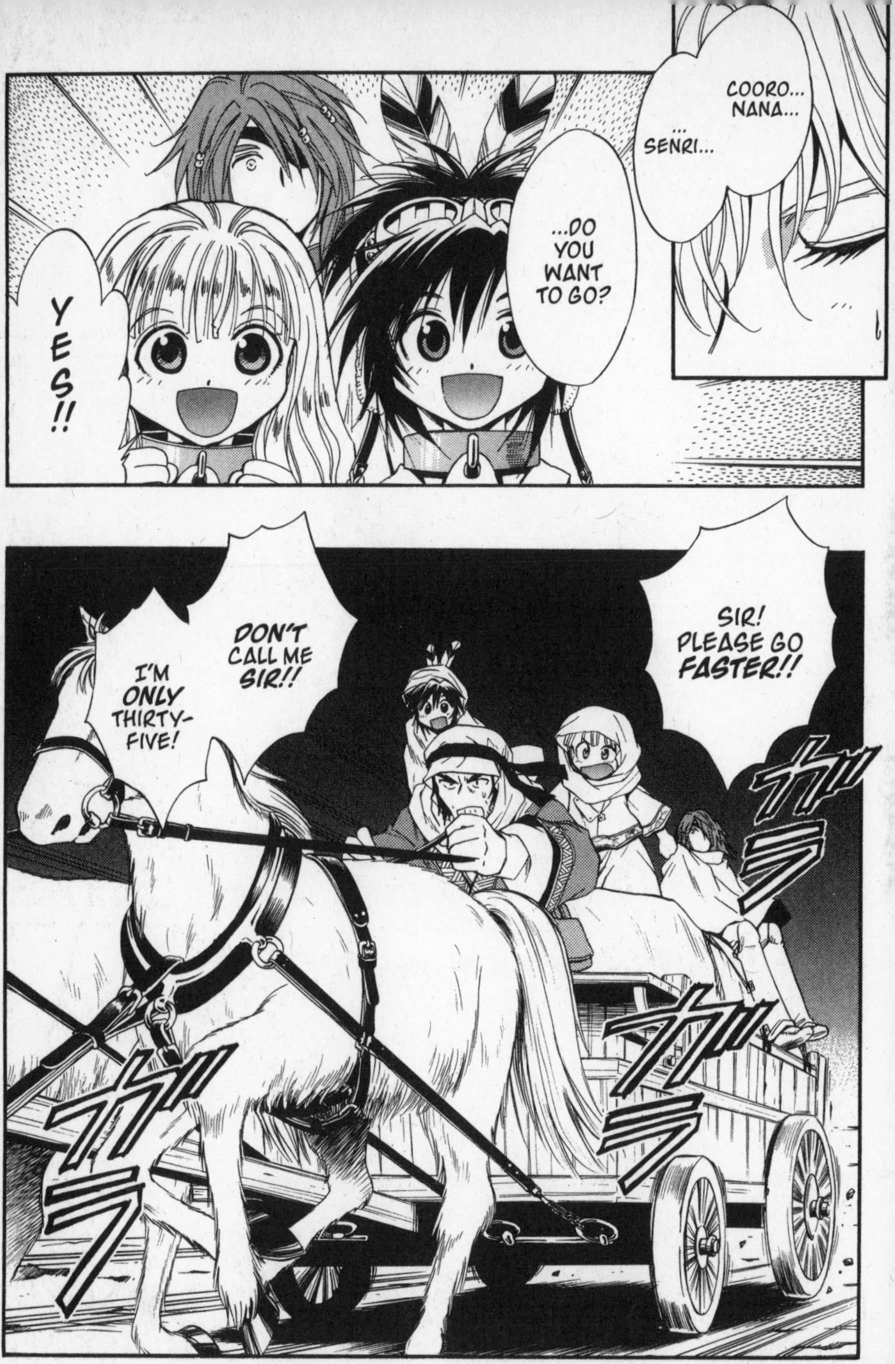
COORO... NANA...
... SENRI...
...
...DO YOU WANT TO GO?
YES!!
SIR! PLEASE GO FASTER!!
DON'T CALL ME SIR!!
I'M ONLY THIRTY-FIVE!
ガラ
ガラ
ガラ

You have big claws!

Chapter 38
Six Years Ago

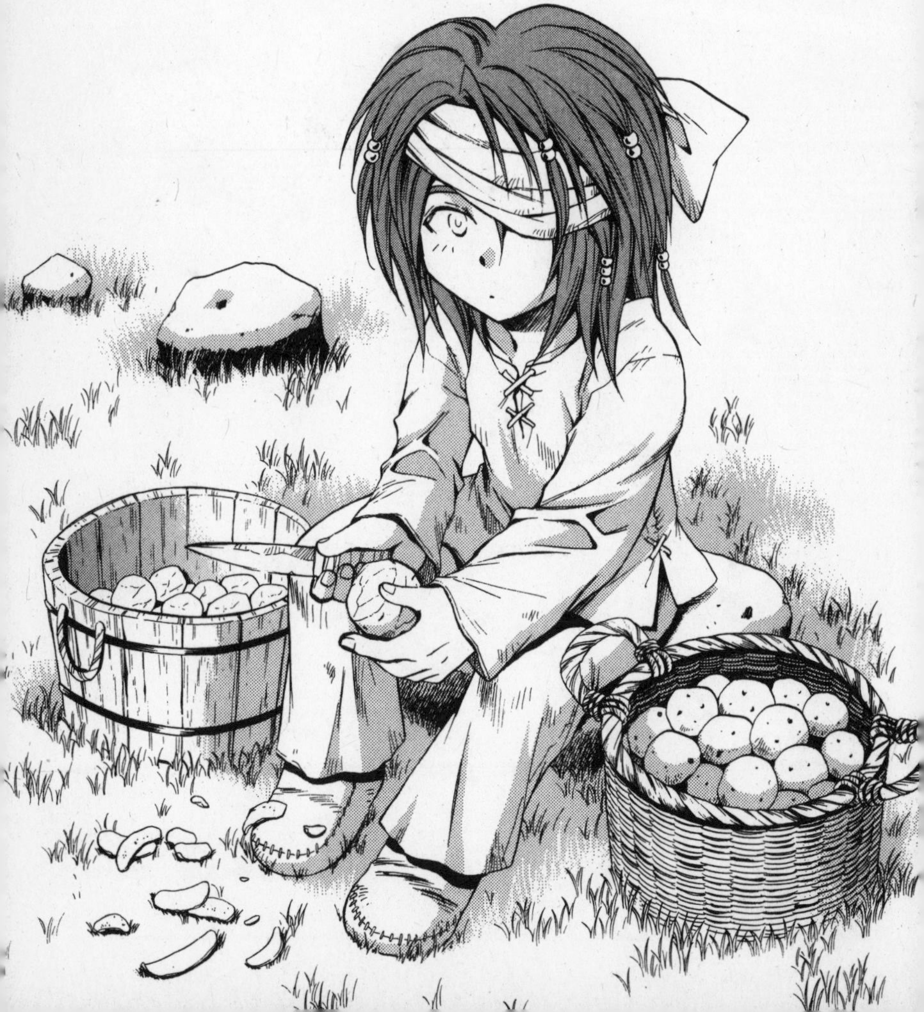

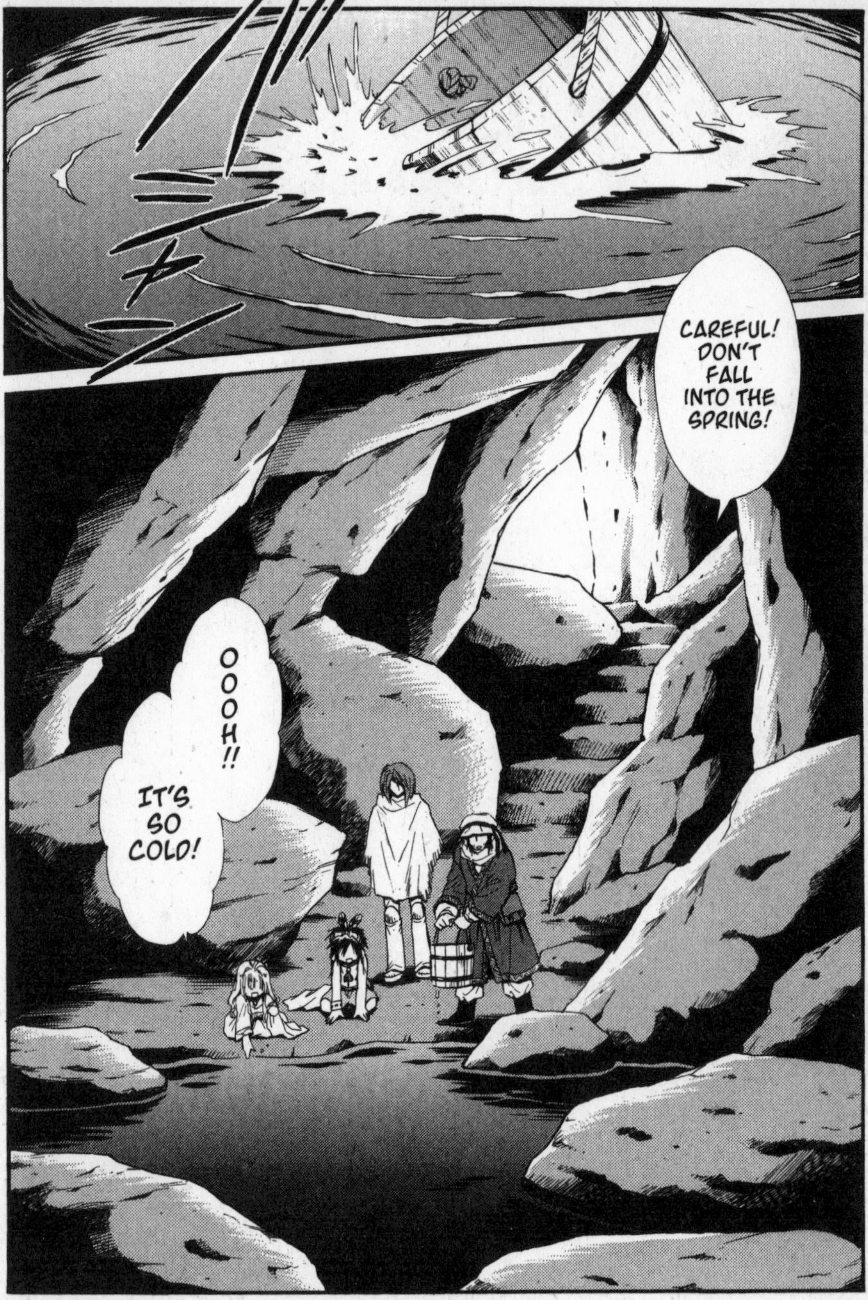
CAREFUL! DON'T FALL INTO THE SPRING!
OOOOH!!
IT'S SO COLD!

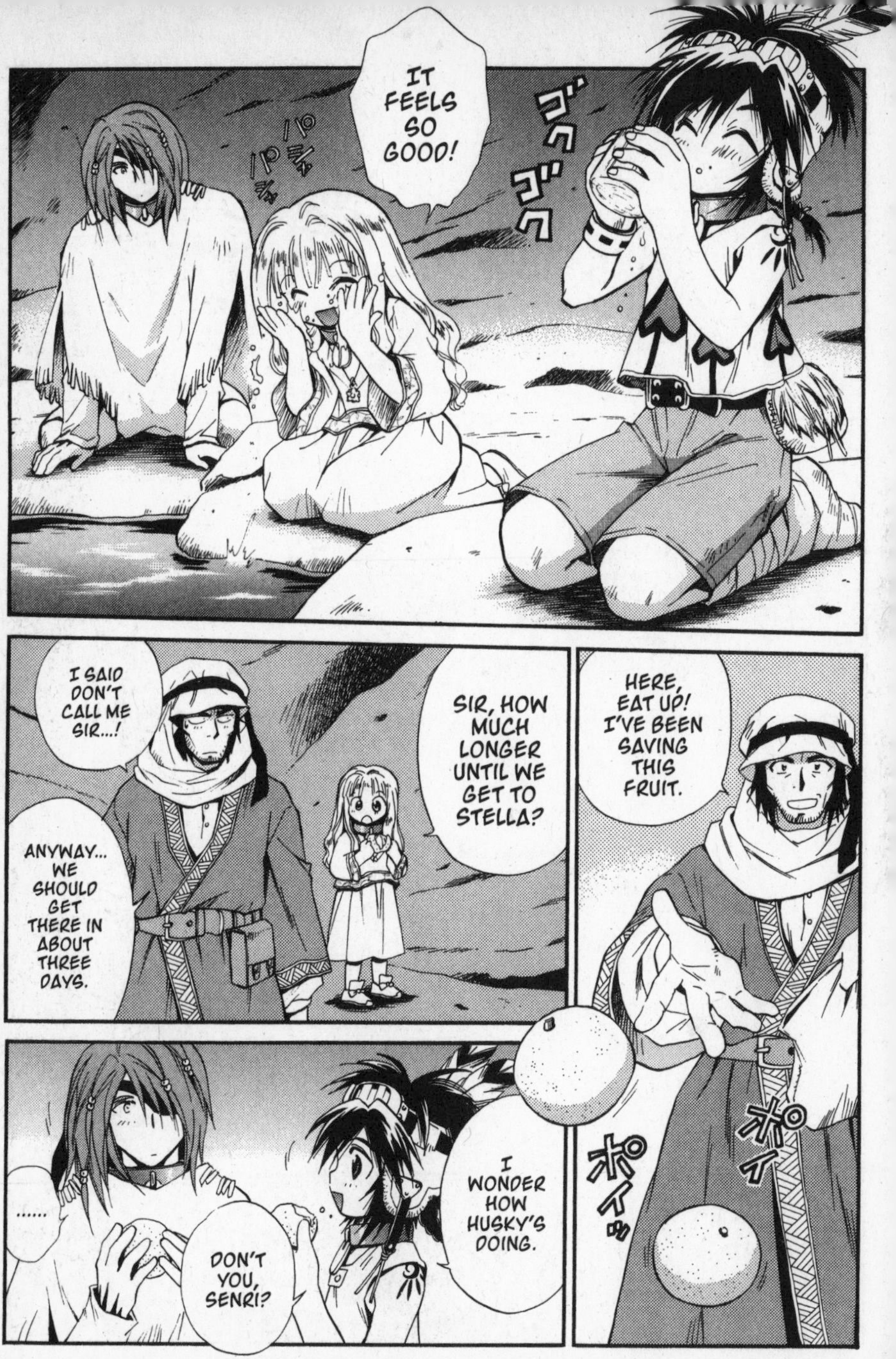
ゴクゴク
IT FEELS SO GOOD!
パシャパシャ
HERE, EAT UP! I'VE BEEN SAVING THIS FRUIT.
SIR, HOW MUCH LONGER UNTIL WE GET TO STELLA?
I SAID DON'T CALL ME SIR...!
ANYWAY... WE SHOULD GET THERE IN ABOUT THREE DAYS.
ポイポイッ
I WONDER HOW HUSKY'S DOING.
DON'T YOU, SENRI?
......

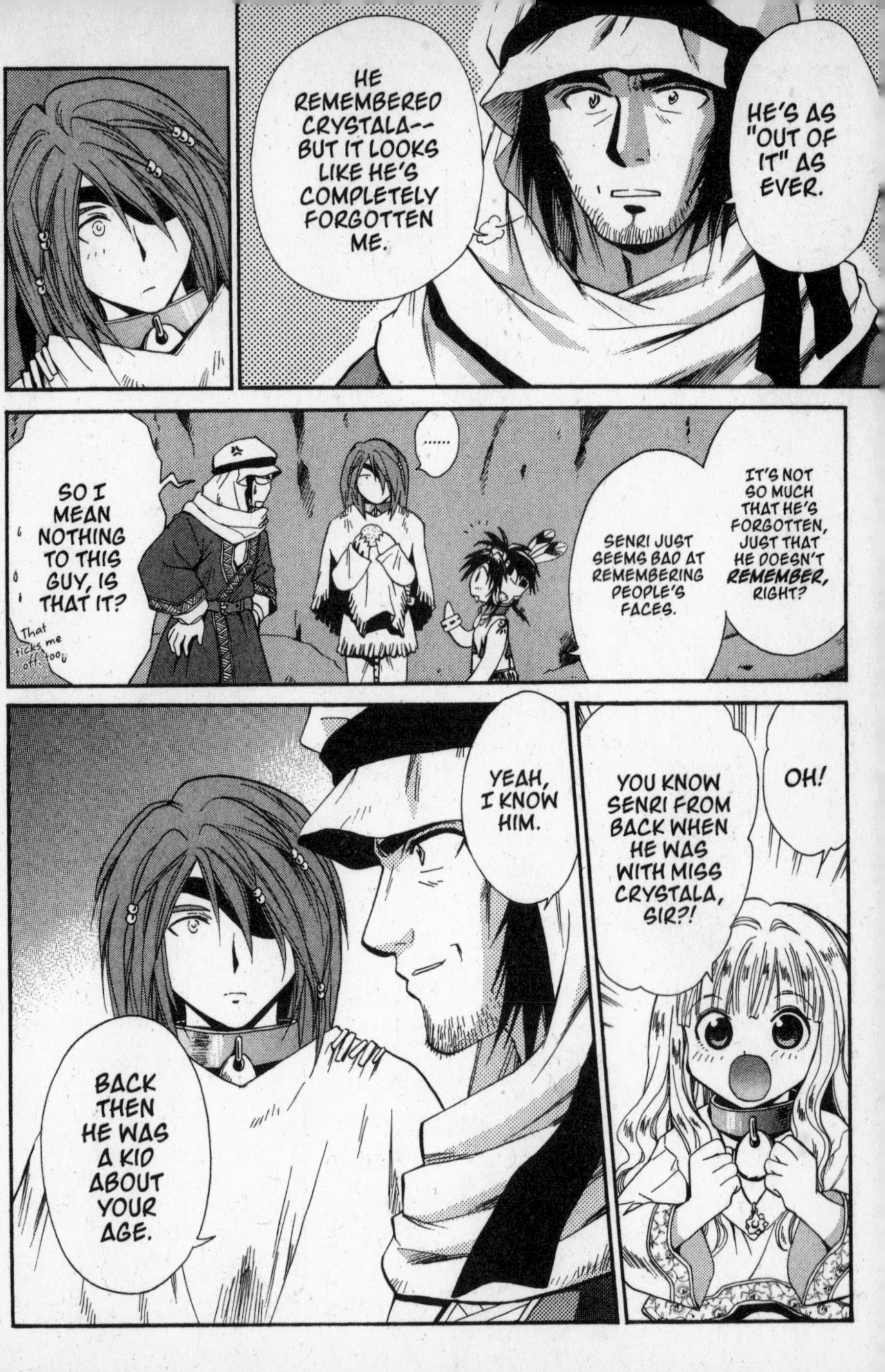
HE'S AS "OUT OF IT" AS EVER.
HE REMEMBERED CRYSTALA-- BUT IT LOOKS LIKE HE'S COMPLETELY FORGOTTEN ME.
IT'S NOT SO MUCH THAT HE'S FORGOTTEN, JUST THAT HE DOESN'T **REMEMBER**, RIGHT?
SENRI JUST SEEMS BAD AT REMEMBERING PEOPLE'S FACES.
......
SO I MEAN NOTHING TO THIS GUY, IS THAT IT?
That ticks me off, too.
OH!
YOU KNOW SENRI FROM BACK WHEN HE WAS WITH MISS CRYSTALA, SIR?!
YEAH, I KNOW HIM.
BACK THEN HE WAS A KID ABOUT YOUR AGE.

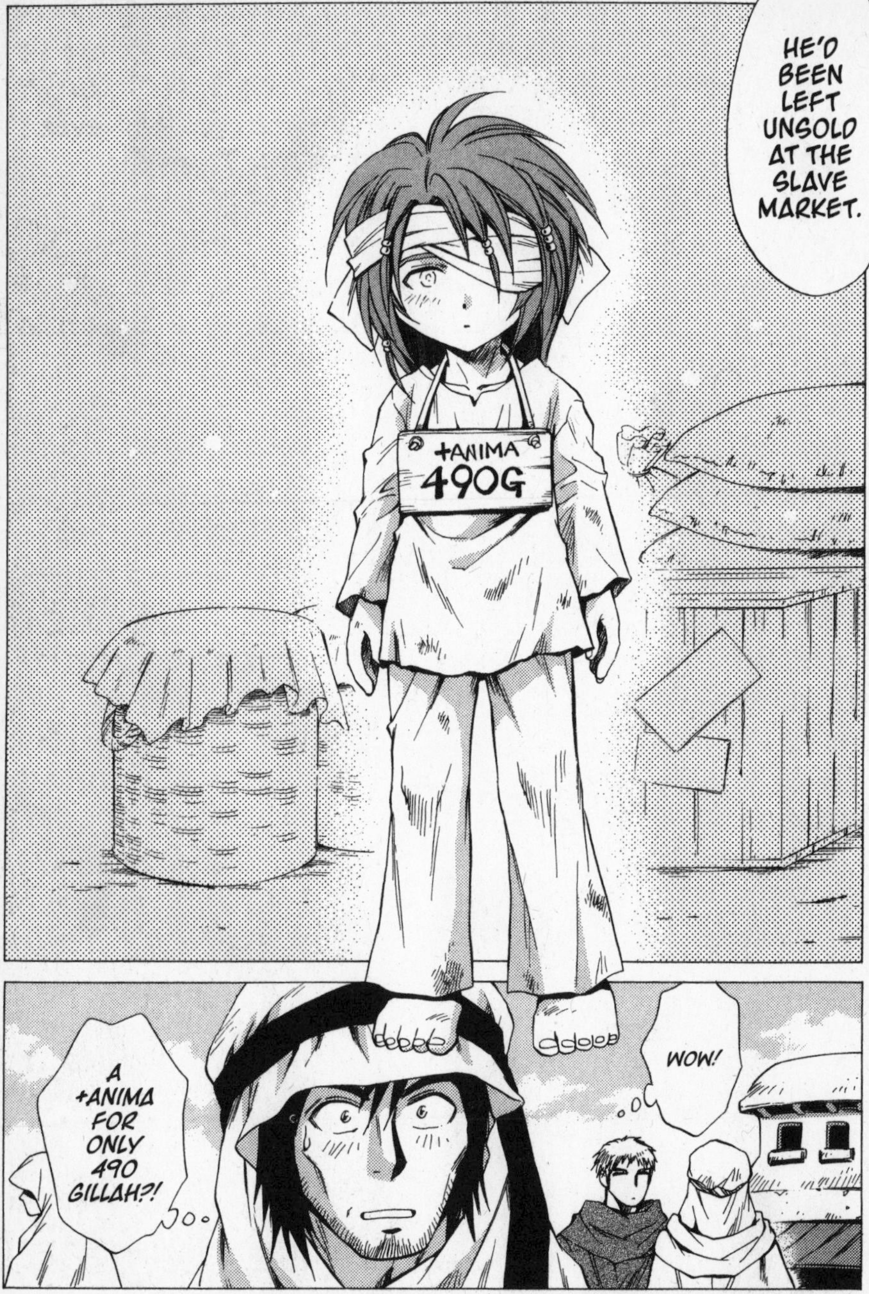
HE'D BEEN LEFT UNSOLD AT THE SLAVE MARKET.
+ANIMA 490G
WOW!
A +ANIMA FOR ONLY 490 GILLAH?!

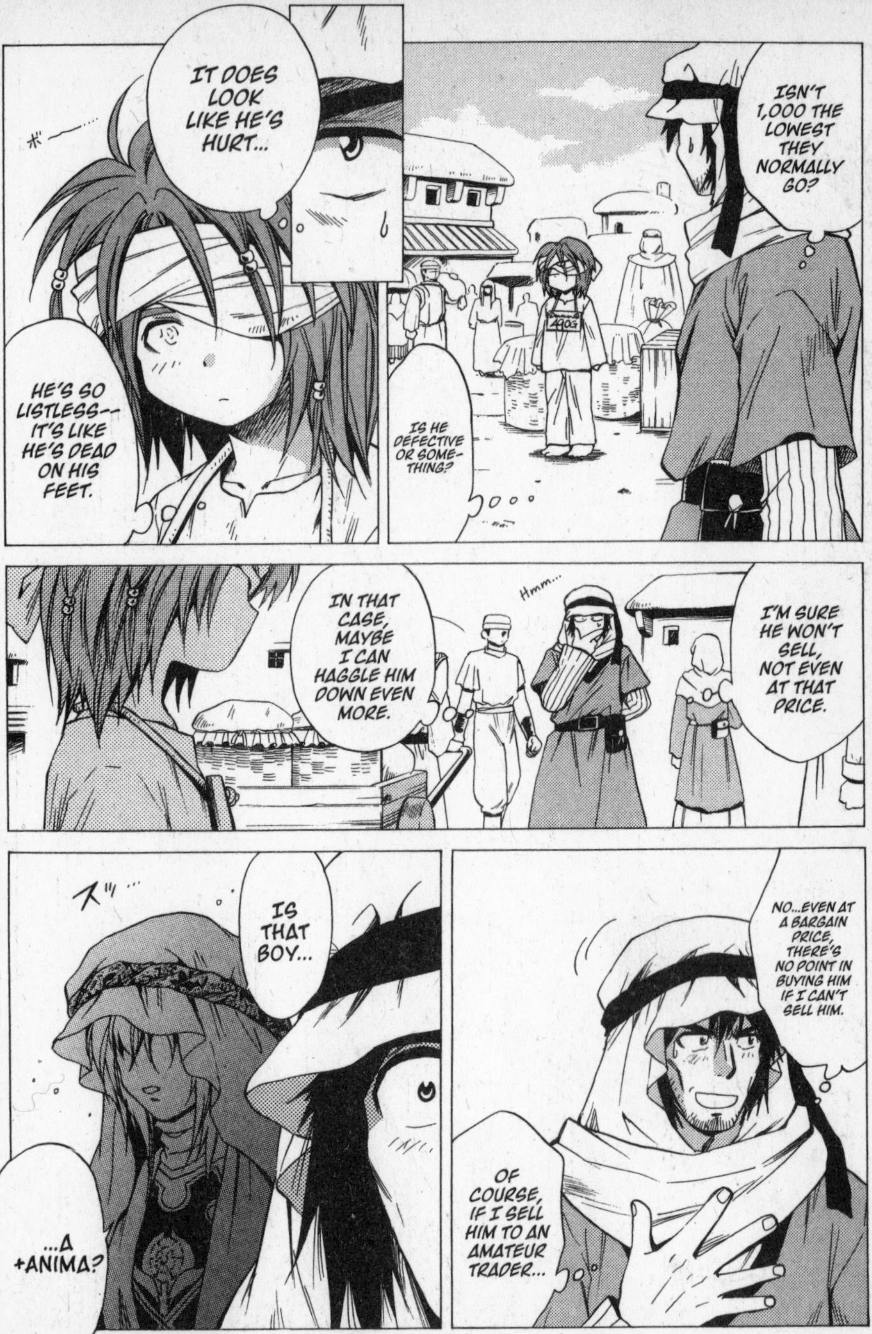
ISN'T 1,000 THE LOWEST THEY NORMALLY GO?
490G
IS HE DEFECTIVE OR SOMETHING?
IT DOES LOOK LIKE HE'S HURT...
ボー……
HE'S SO LISTLESS-- IT'S LIKE HE'S DEAD ON HIS FEET.
I'M SURE HE WON'T SELL, NOT EVEN AT THAT PRICE.
Hmm...
IN THAT CASE, MAYBE I CAN HAGGLE HIM DOWN EVEN MORE.
NO...EVEN AT A BARGAIN PRICE, THERE'S NO POINT IN BUYING HIM IF I CAN'T SELL HIM.
OF COURSE, IF I SELL HIM TO AN AMATEUR TRADER...
スッ…
IS THAT BOY...
...A +ANIMA?

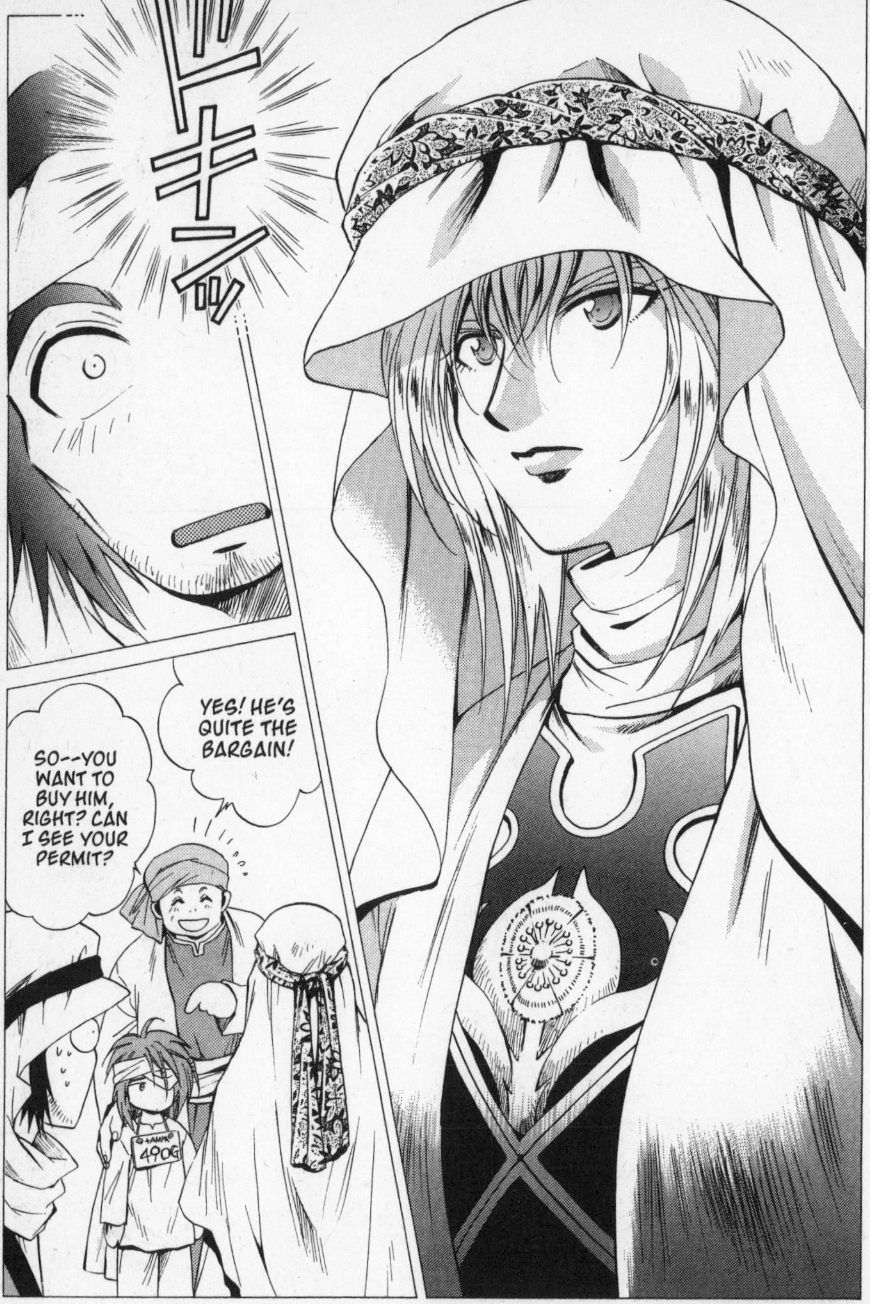
ドキーンッ
YES! HE'S QUITE THE BARGAIN!
SO--YOU WANT TO BUY HIM, RIGHT? CAN I SEE YOUR PERMIT?
490G

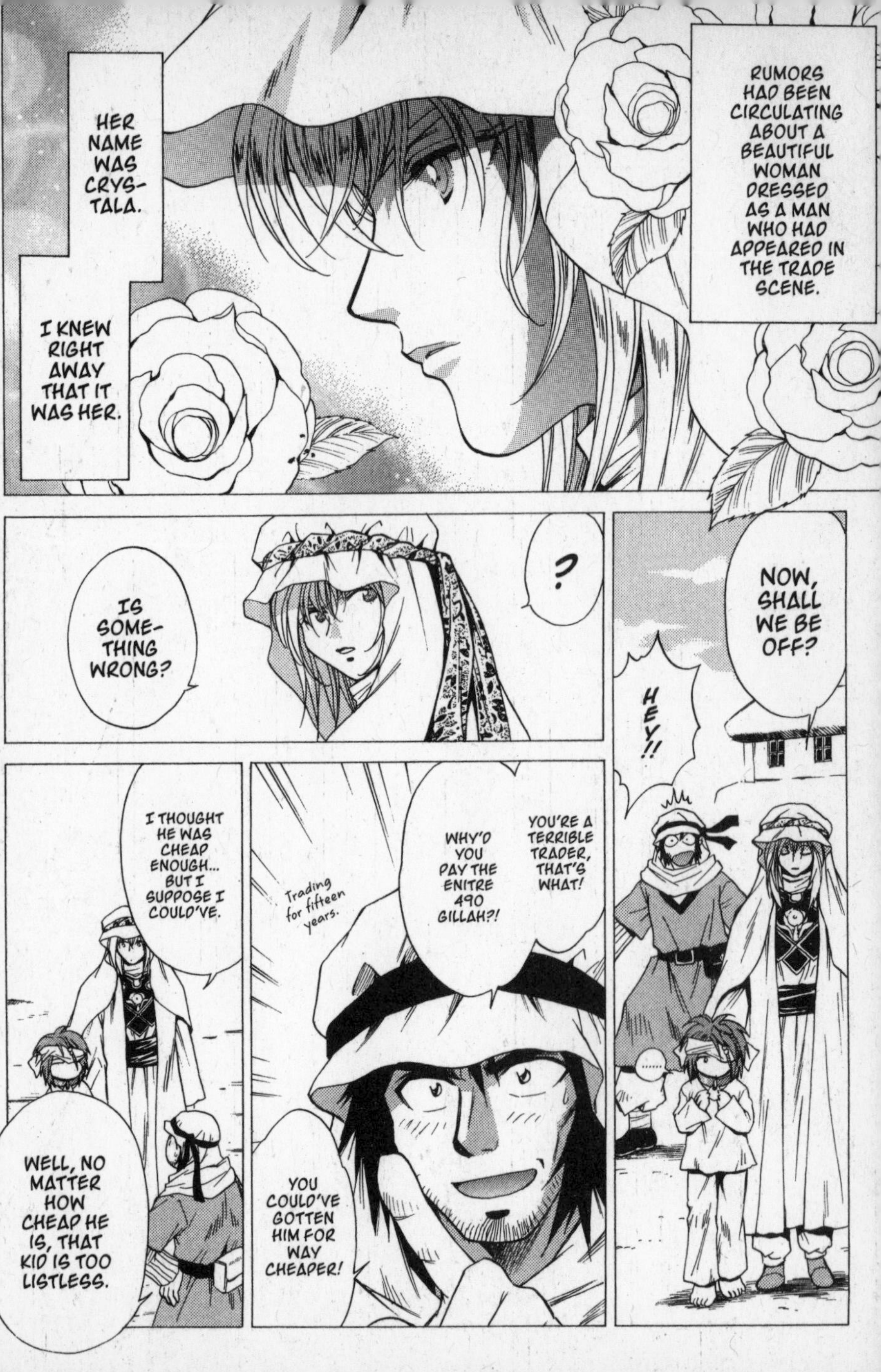
RUMORS HAD BEEN CIRCULATING ABOUT A BEAUTIFUL WOMAN DRESSED AS A MAN WHO HAD APPEARED IN THE TRADE SCENE.
HER NAME WAS CRYS-TALA.
I KNEW RIGHT AWAY THAT IT WAS HER.
NOW, SHALL WE BE OFF?
HEY!!
......
?
IS SOME-THING WRONG?
YOU'RE A TERRIBLE TRADER, THAT'S WHAT!
WHY'D YOU PAY THE ENITRE 490 GILLAH?!
Trading for fifteen years.
YOU COULD'VE GOTTEN HIM FOR WAY CHEAPER!
I THOUGHT HE WAS CHEAP ENOUGH... BUT I SUPPOSE I COULD'VE.
WELL, NO MATTER HOW CHEAP HE IS, THAT KID IS TOO LISTLESS.

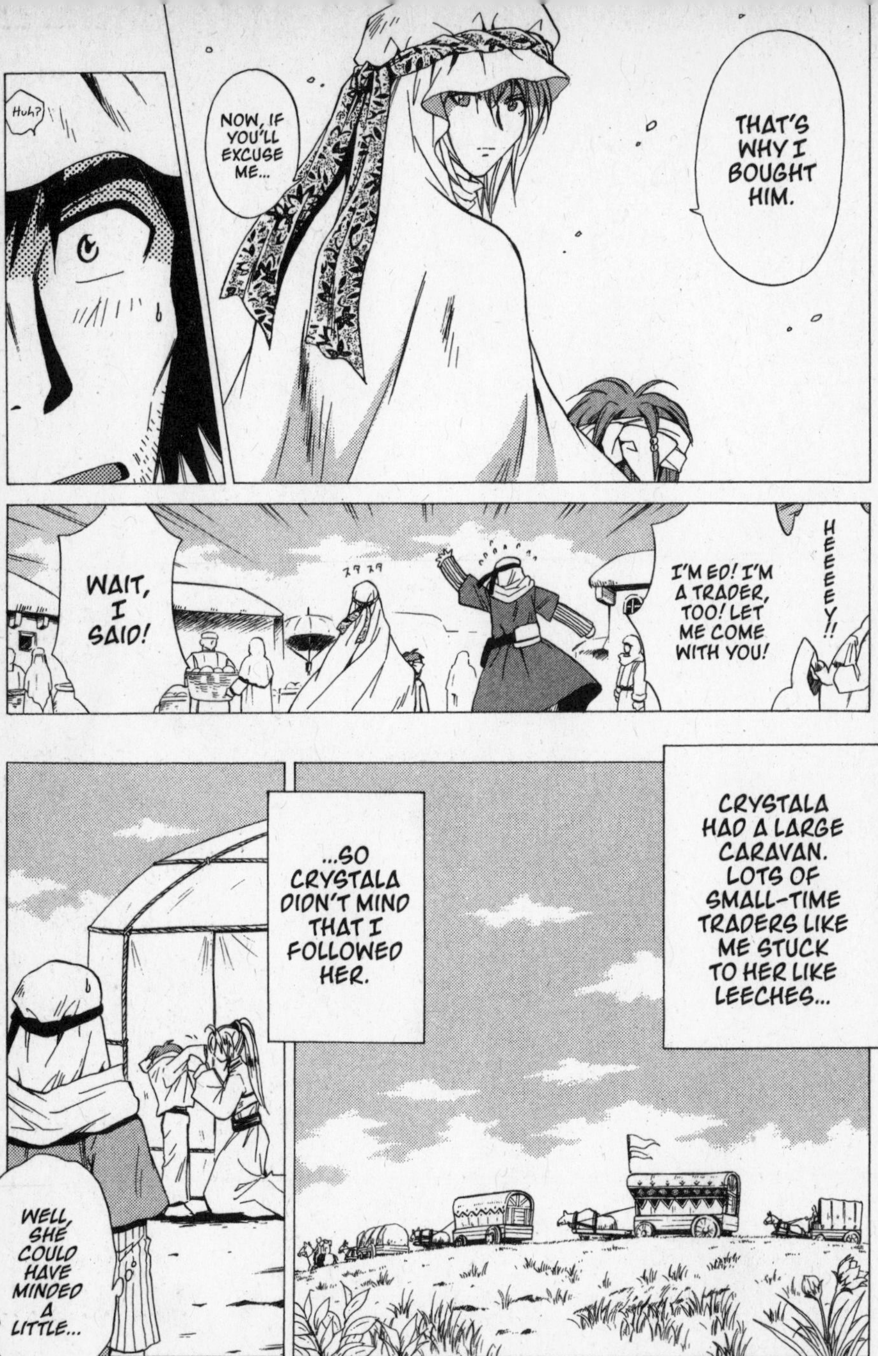
THAT'S WHY I BOUGHT HIM.
NOW, IF YOU'LL EXCUSE ME...
Huh?
HEEEEY!!
I'M ED! I'M A TRADER, TOO! LET ME COME WITH YOU!
WAIT, I SAID!
CRYSTALA HAD A LARGE CARAVAN. LOTS OF SMALL-TIME TRADERS LIKE ME STUCK TO HER LIKE LEECHES...
...SO CRYSTALA DIDN'T MIND THAT I FOLLOWED HER.
WELL, SHE COULD HAVE MINDED A LITTLE...

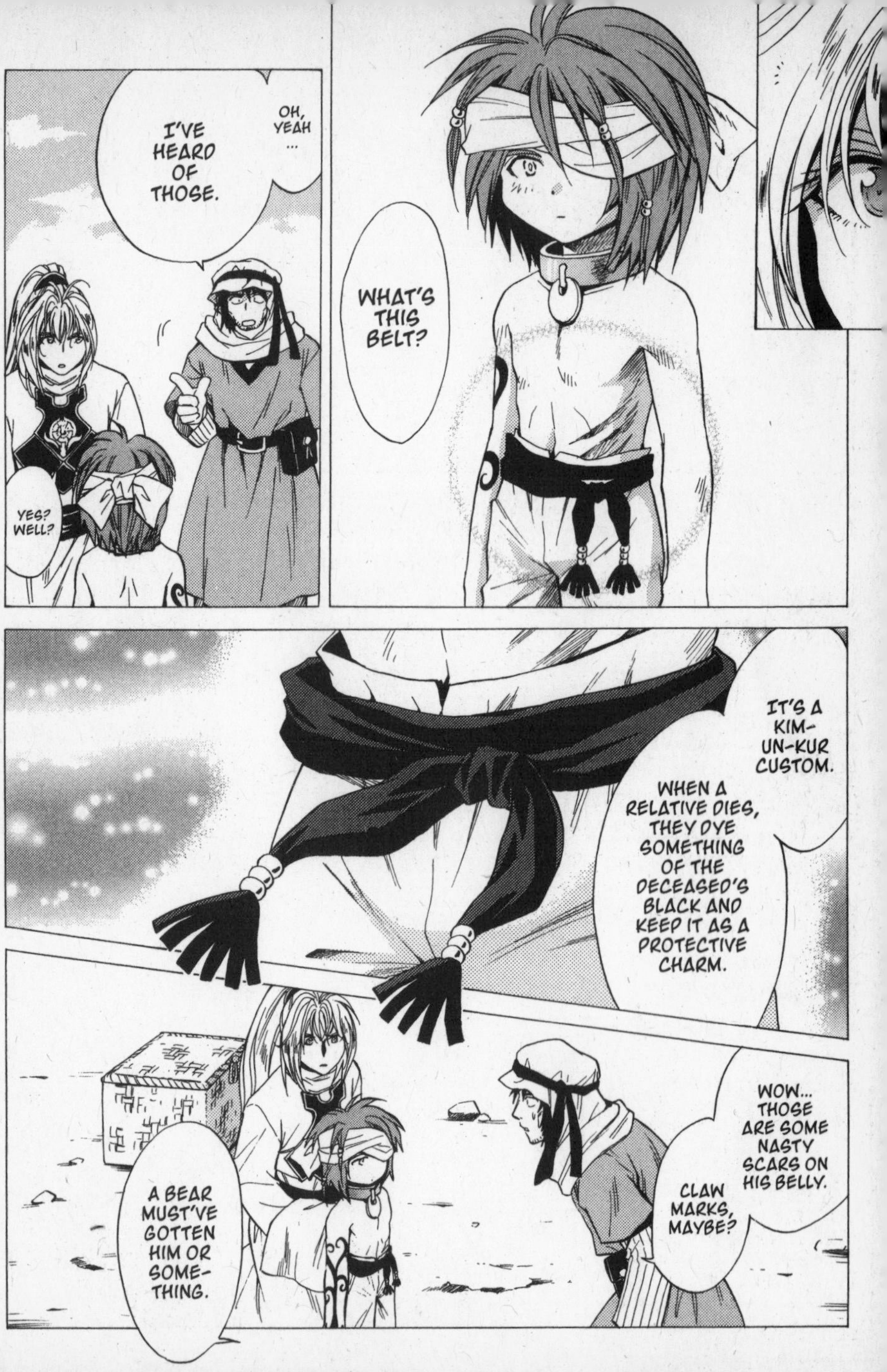
WHAT'S THIS BELT?
OH, YEAH...
I'VE HEARD OF THOSE.
YES? WELL?
IT'S A KIM-UN-KUR CUSTOM.
WHEN A RELATIVE DIES, THEY DYE SOMETHING OF THE DECEASED'S BLACK AND KEEP IT AS A PROTECTIVE CHARM.
WOW... THOSE ARE SOME NASTY SCARS ON HIS BELLY.
CLAW MARKS, MAYBE?
A BEAR MUST'VE GOTTEN HIM OR SOMETHING.

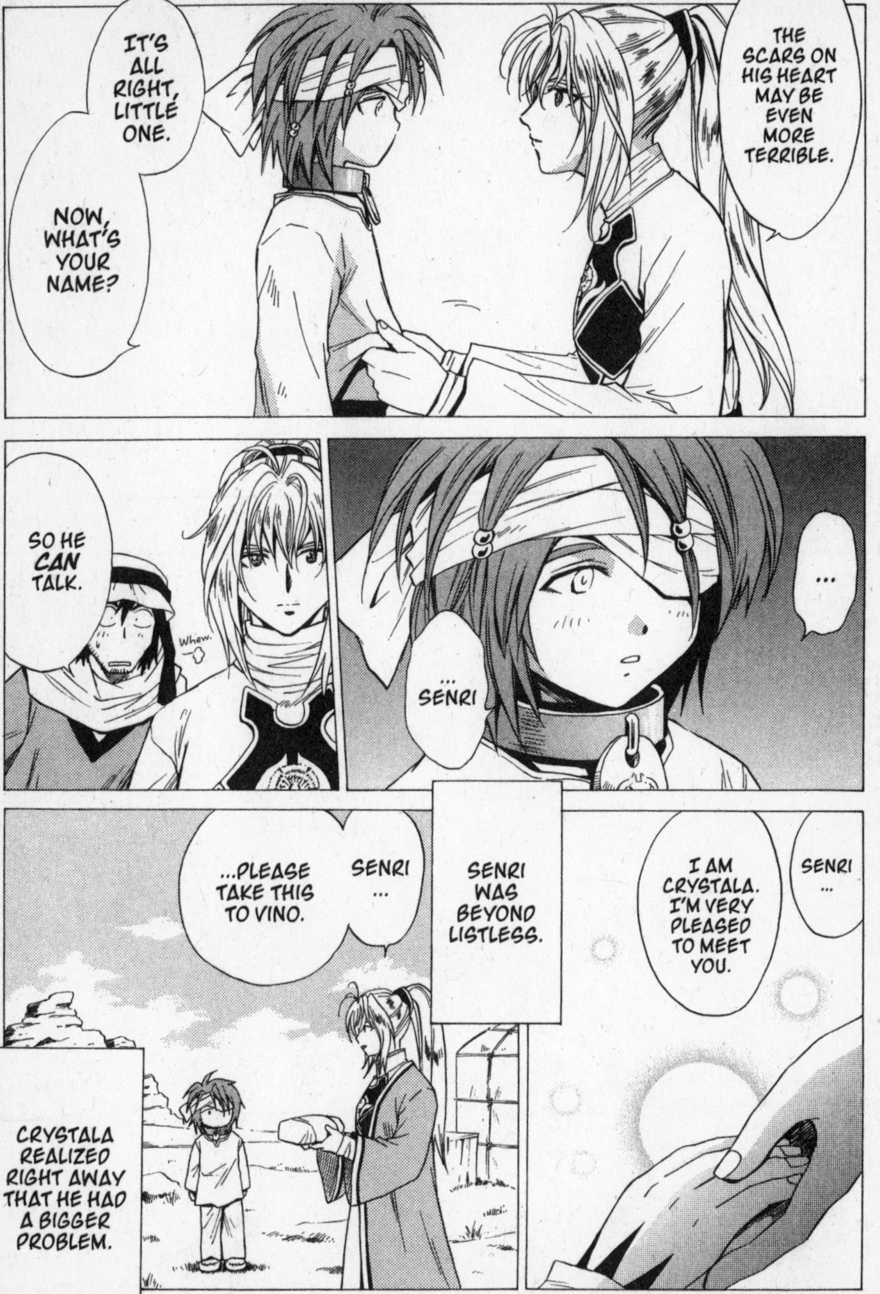
THE SCARS ON HIS HEART MAY BE EVEN MORE TERRIBLE.
IT'S ALL RIGHT, LITTLE ONE.
NOW, WHAT'S YOUR NAME?
...
... SENRI
SO HE CAN TALK.
Whew.
SENRI ...
I AM CRYSTALA. I'M VERY PLEASED TO MEET YOU.
SENRI WAS BEYOND LISTLESS.
SENRI ...
...PLEASE TAKE THIS TO VINO.
CRYSTALA REALIZED RIGHT AWAY THAT HE HAD A BIGGER PROBLEM.

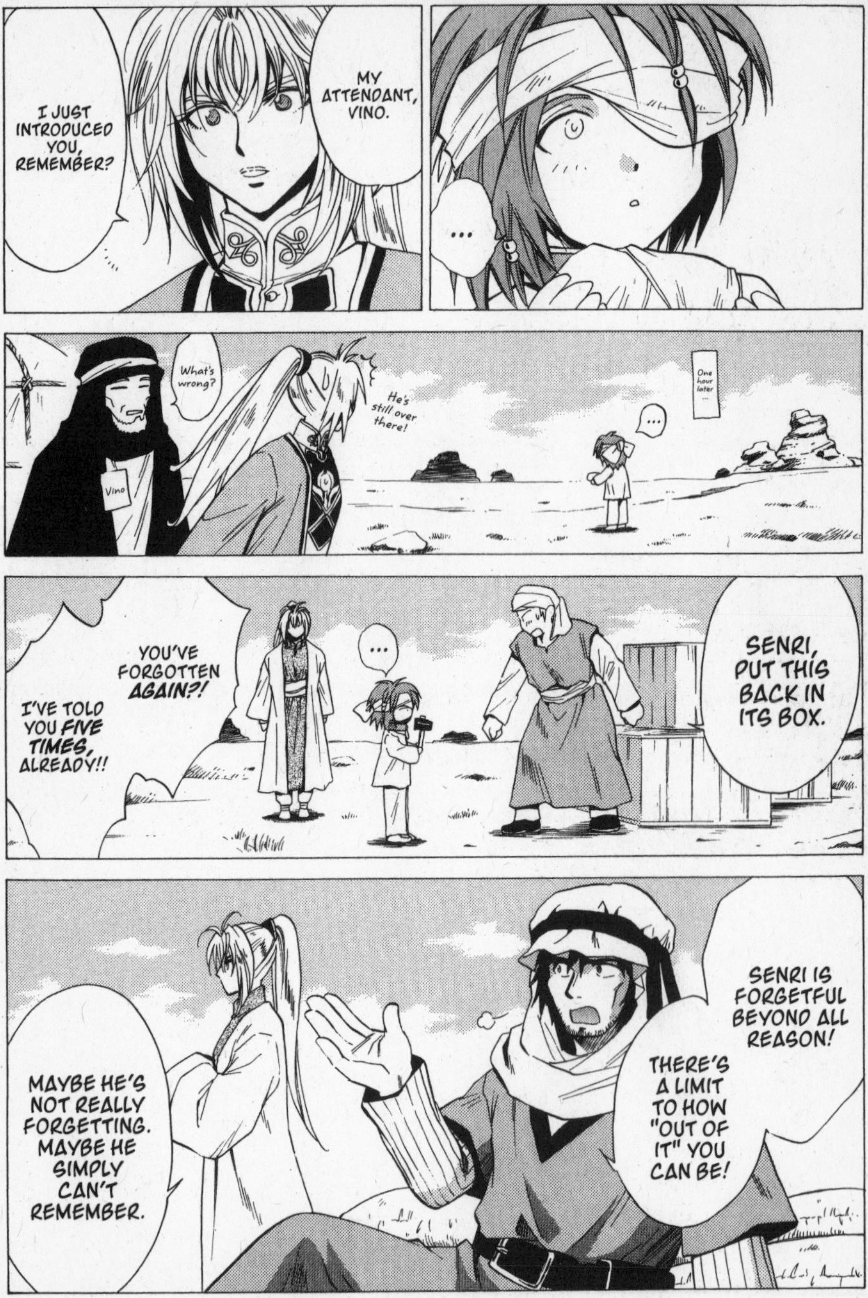
...
MY ATTENDANT, VINO.
I JUST INTRODUCED YOU, REMEMBER?
One hour later ...
...
He's still over there!
What's wrong?
Vino
SENRI, PUT THIS BACK IN ITS BOX.
...
YOU'VE FORGOTTEN AGAIN?!
I'VE TOLD YOU FIVE TIMES, ALREADY!!
SENRI IS FORGETFUL BEYOND ALL REASON!
THERE'S A LIMIT TO HOW "OUT OF IT" YOU CAN BE!
MAYBE HE'S NOT REALLY FORGETTING. MAYBE HE SIMPLY CAN'T REMEMBER.

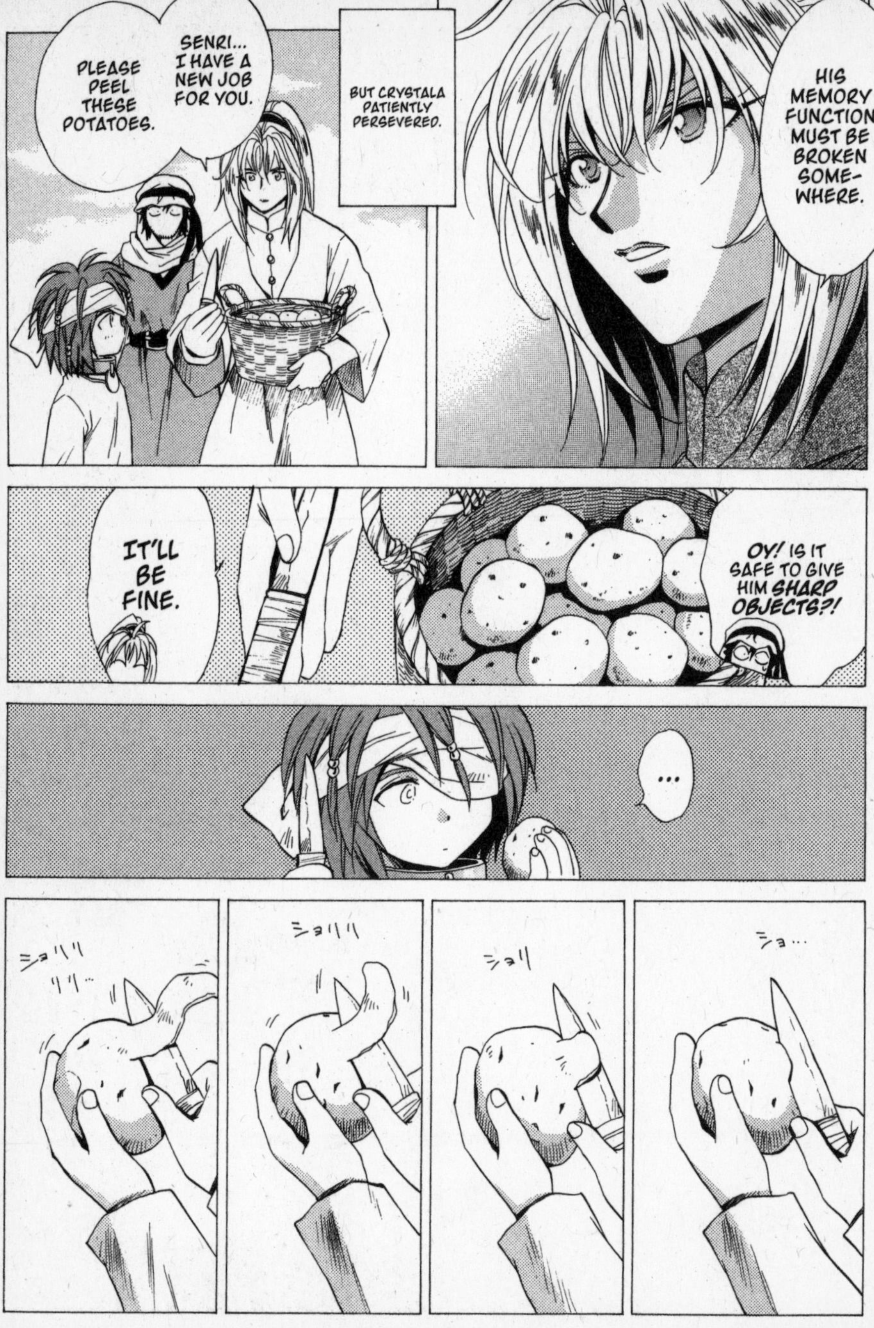
HIS MEMORY FUNCTION MUST BE BROKEN SOME-WHERE.
BUT CRYSTALA PATIENTLY PERSEVERED.
SENRI... I HAVE A NEW JOB FOR YOU.
PLEASE PEEL THESE POTATOES.
OY! IS IT SAFE TO GIVE HIM SHARP OBJECTS?!
IT'LL BE FINE.
...
ショ…
ショリ
ショリリ
ショリリ
リリ…

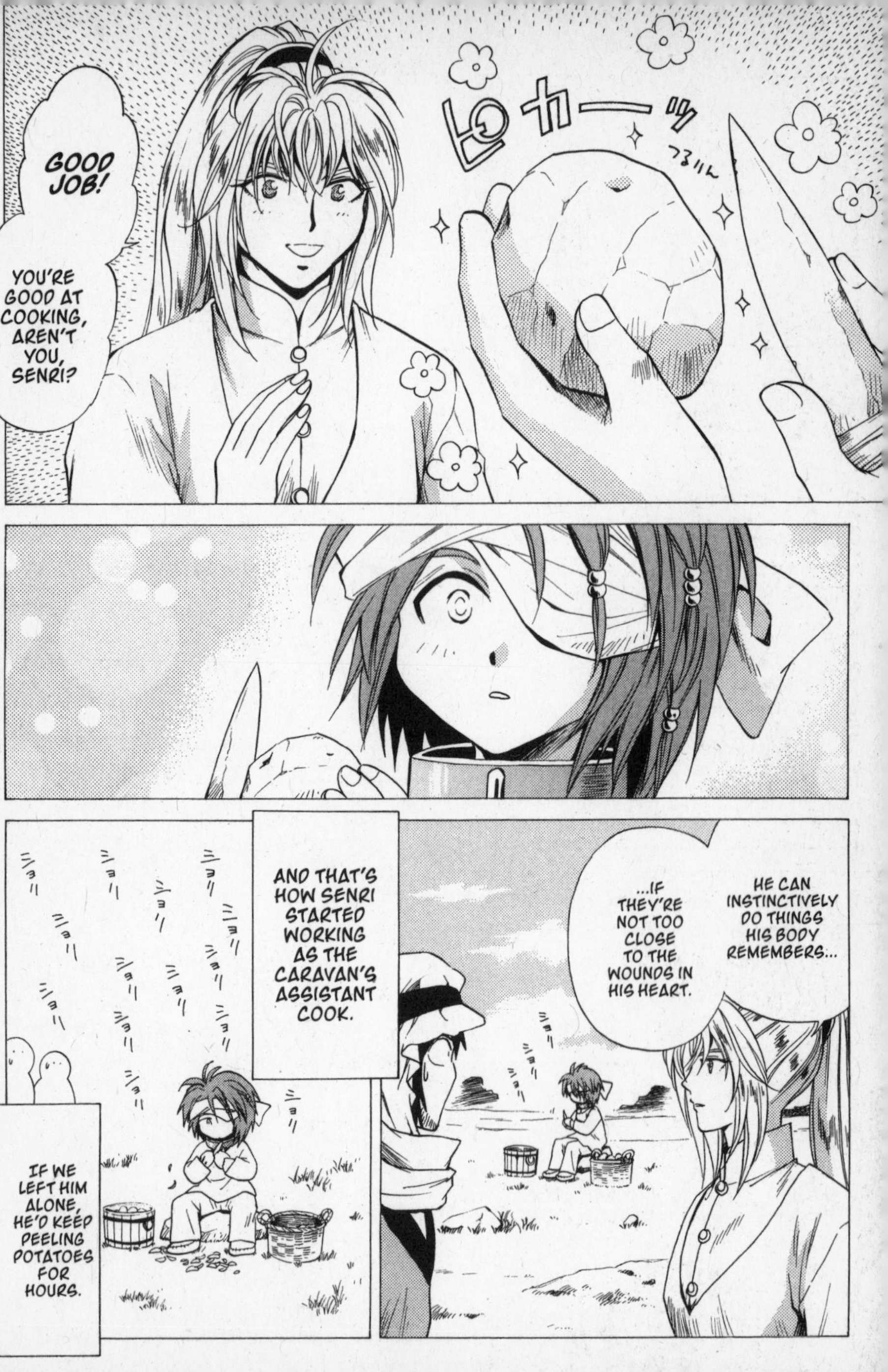
ピカーッ
つるん
GOOD JOB!
YOU'RE GOOD AT COOKING, AREN'T YOU, SENRI?
HE CAN INSTINCTIVELY DO THINGS HIS BODY REMEMBERS...
...IF THEY'RE NOT TOO CLOSE TO THE WOUNDS IN HIS HEART.
AND THAT'S HOW SENRI STARTED WORKING AS THE CARAVAN'S ASSISTANT COOK.
IF WE LEFT HIM ALONE, HE'D KEEP PEELING POTATOES FOR HOURS.

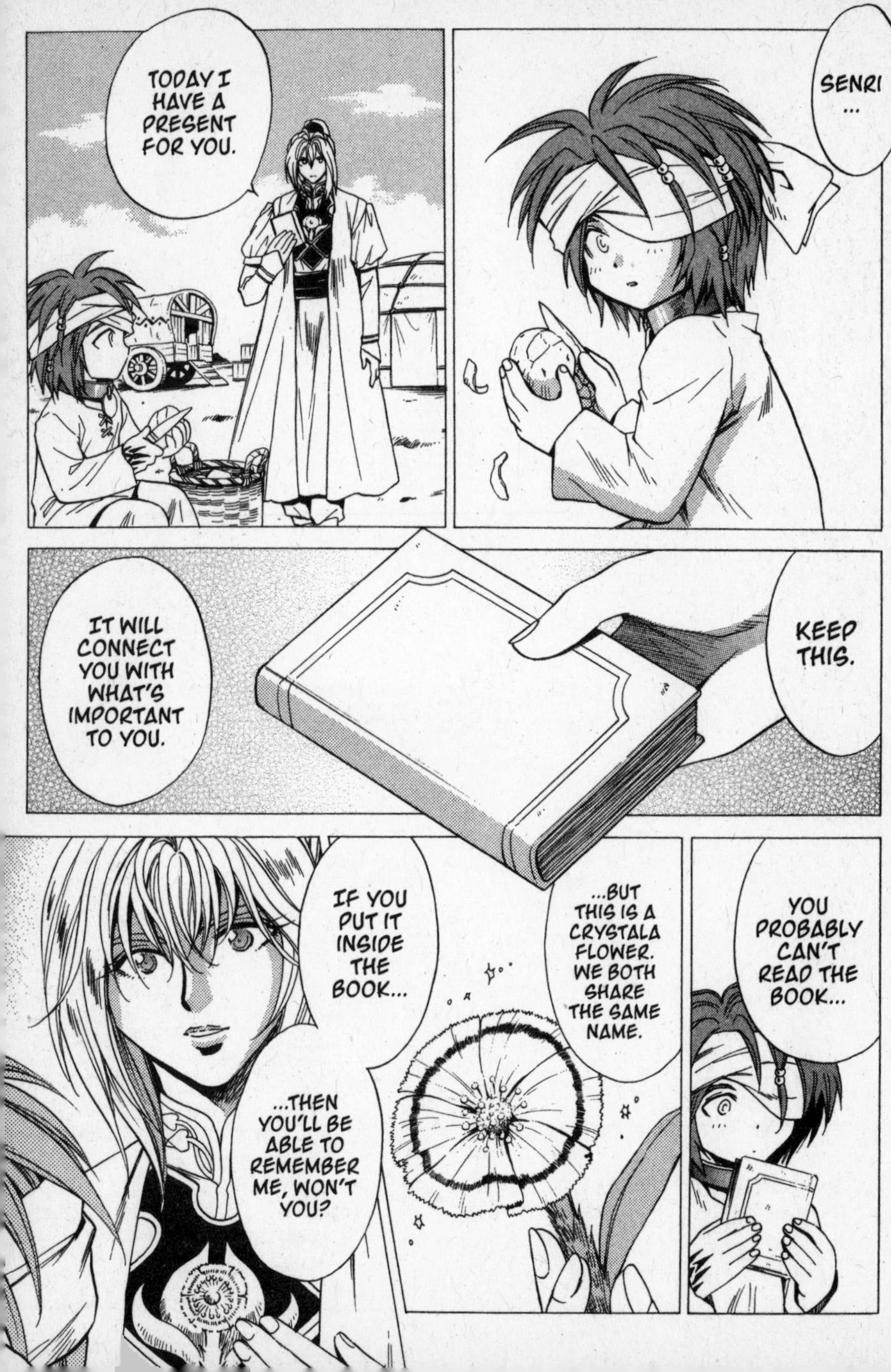
SENRI ...
TODAY I HAVE A PRESENT FOR YOU.
KEEP THIS.
IT WILL CONNECT YOU WITH WHAT'S IMPORTANT TO YOU.
YOU PROBABLY CAN'T READ THE BOOK...
...BUT THIS IS A CRYSTALA FLOWER. WE BOTH SHARE THE SAME NAME.
IF YOU PUT IT INSIDE THE BOOK...
...THEN YOU'LL BE ABLE TO REMEMBER ME, WON'T YOU?

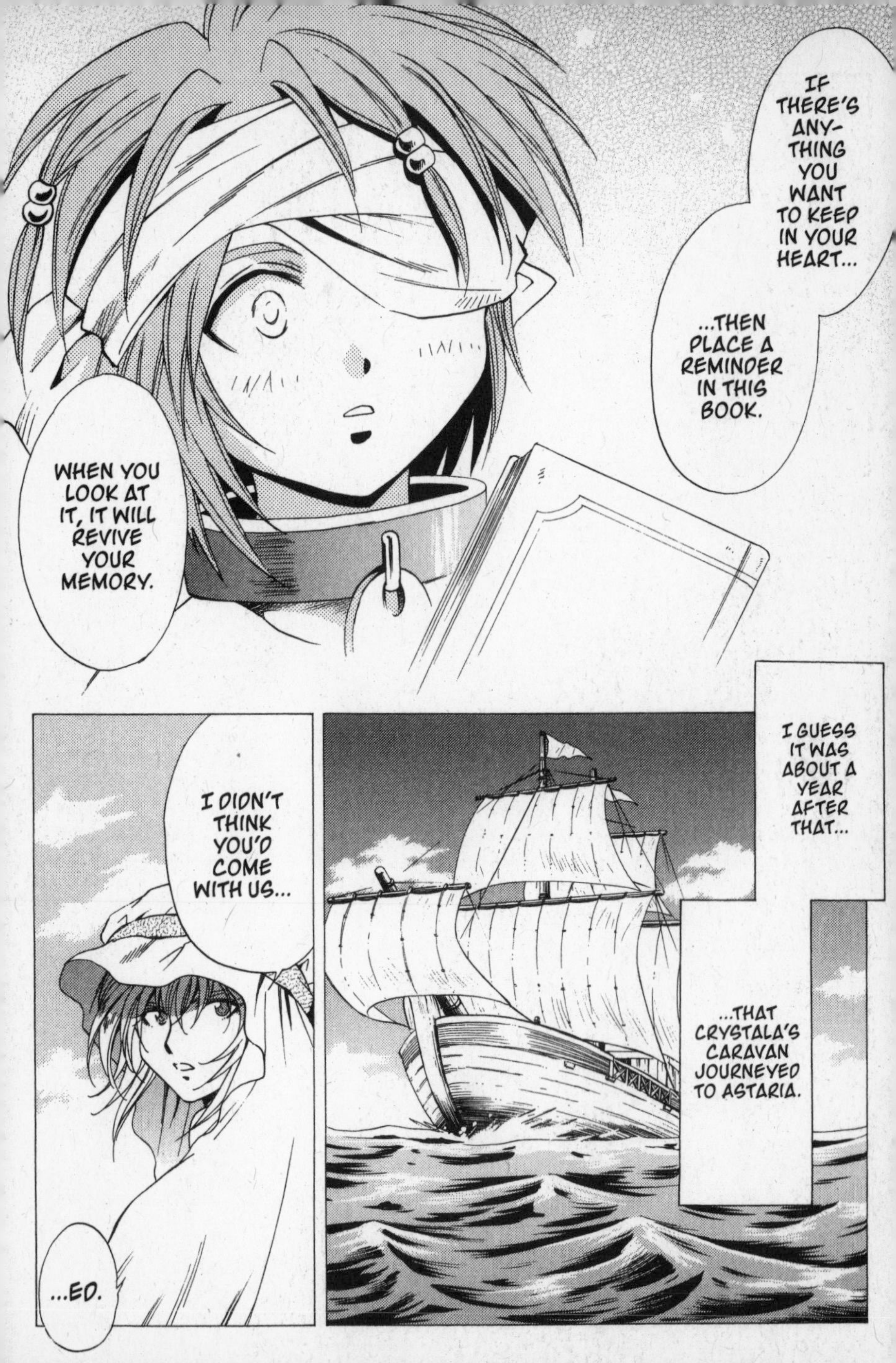
IF THERE'S ANY-THING YOU WANT TO KEEP IN YOUR HEART...
...THEN PLACE A REMINDER IN THIS BOOK.
WHEN YOU LOOK AT IT, IT WILL REVIVE YOUR MEMORY.
I GUESS IT WAS ABOUT A YEAR AFTER THAT...
...THAT CRYSTALA'S CARAVAN JOURNEYED TO ASTARIA.
I DIDN'T THINK YOU'D COME WITH US...
...ED.

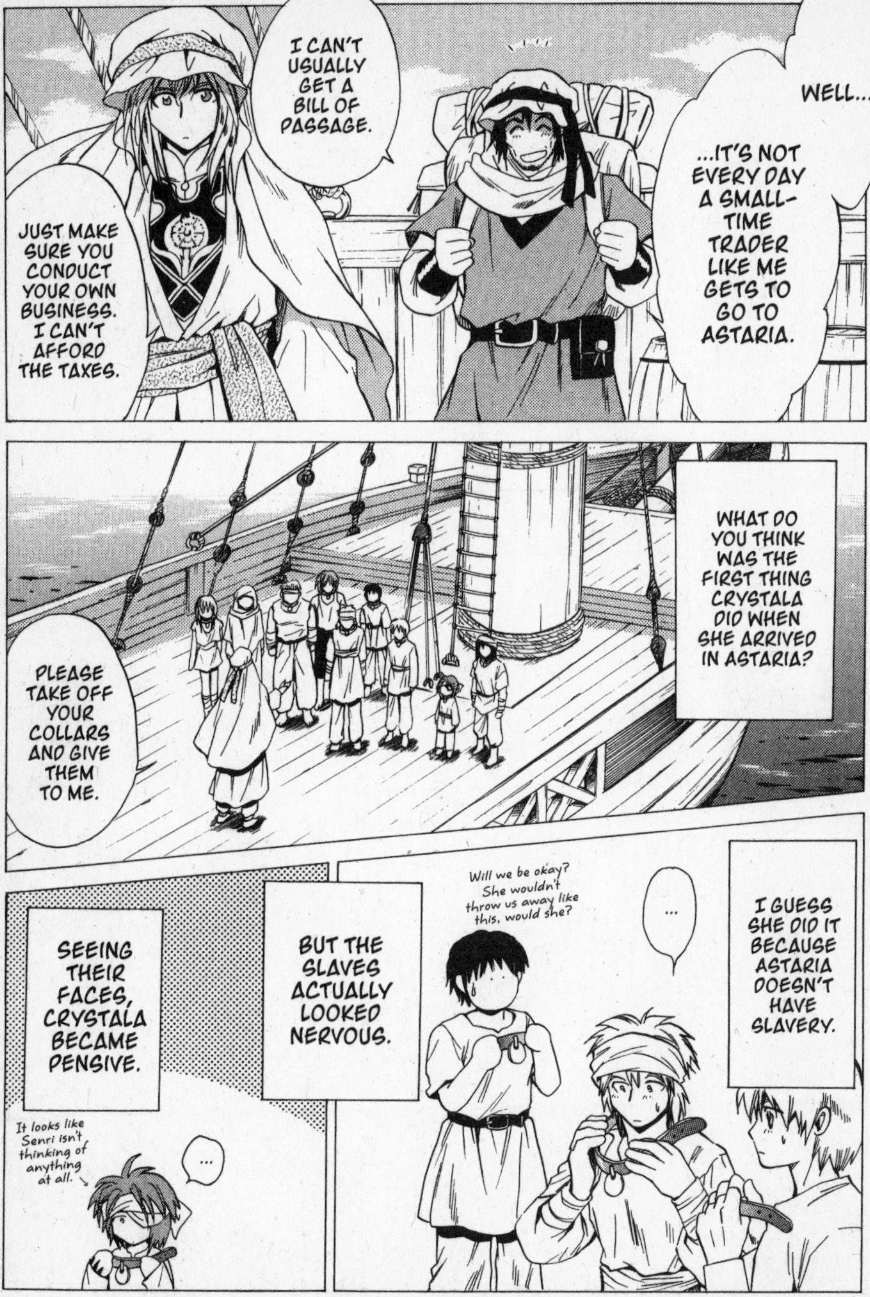
WELL...
...IT'S NOT EVERY DAY A SMALL-TIME TRADER LIKE ME GETS TO GO TO ASTARIA.
I CAN'T USUALLY GET A BILL OF PASSAGE.
JUST MAKE SURE YOU CONDUCT YOUR OWN BUSINESS. I CAN'T AFFORD THE TAXES.
WHAT DO YOU THINK WAS THE FIRST THING CRYSTALA DID WHEN SHE ARRIVED IN ASTARIA?
PLEASE TAKE OFF YOUR COLLARS AND GIVE THEM TO ME.
I GUESS SHE DID IT BECAUSE ASTARIA DOESN'T HAVE SLAVERY.
...
Will we be okay? She wouldn't throw us away like this, would she?
BUT THE SLAVES ACTUALLY LOOKED NERVOUS.
SEEING THEIR FACES, CRYSTALA BECAME PENSIVE.
It looks like Senri isn't thinking of anything at all.
...

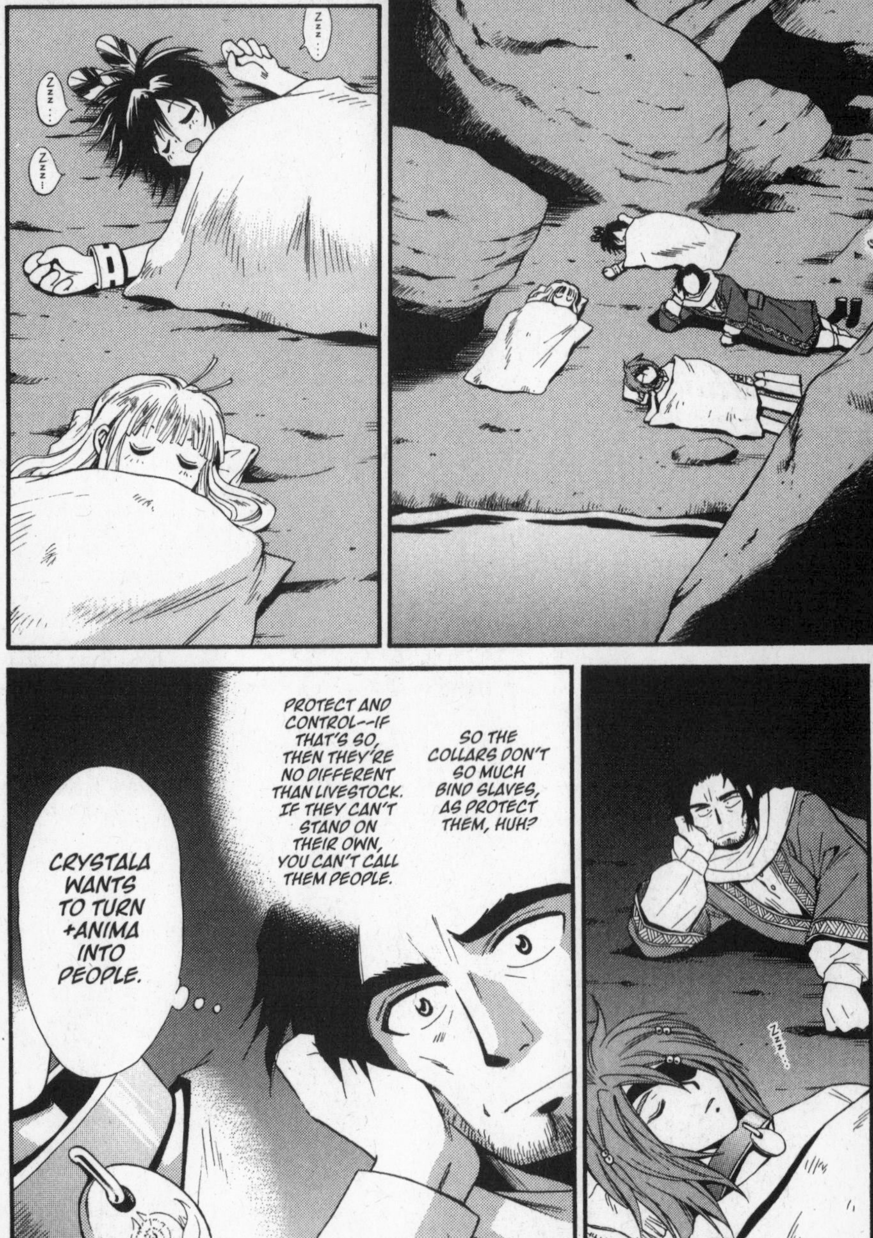
Zzz...
Zzz...
Zzz...
Zzz...
SO THE COLLARS DON'T SO MUCH BIND SLAVES, AS PROTECT THEM, HUH?
PROTECT AND CONTROL--IF THAT'S SO, THEN THEY'RE NO DIFFERENT THAN LIVESTOCK. IF THEY CAN'T STAND ON THEIR OWN, YOU CAN'T CALL THEM PEOPLE.
CRYSTALA WANTS TO TURN +ANIMA INTO PEOPLE.

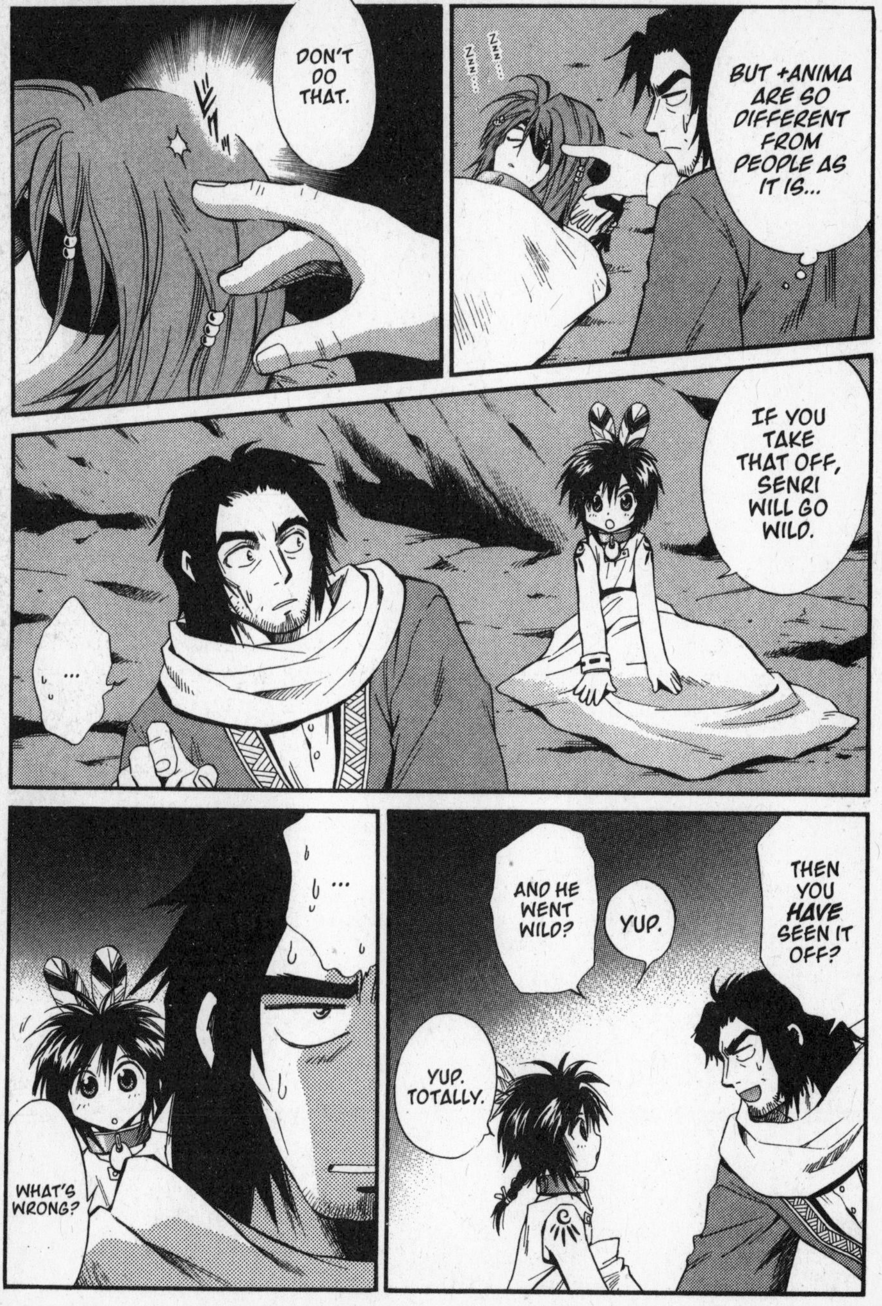
Zzz...
Zzz...
BUT +ANIMA ARE SO DIFFERENT FROM PEOPLE AS IT IS...
DON'T DO THAT.
IF YOU TAKE THAT OFF, SENRI WILL GO WILD.
...
THEN YOU *HAVE* SEEN IT OFF?
YUP.
AND HE WENT WILD?
YUP. TOTALLY.
...
WHAT'S WRONG?

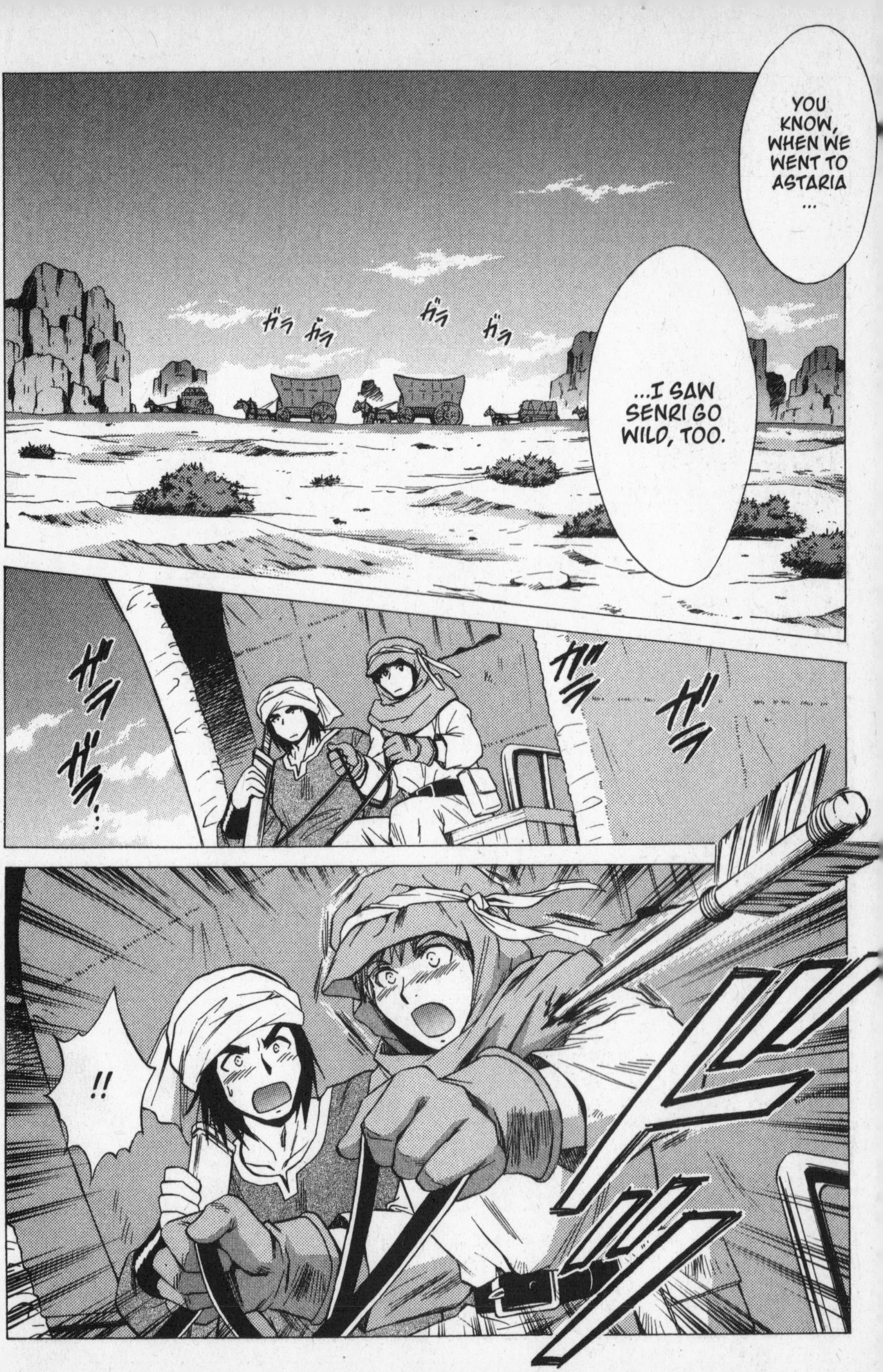
YOU KNOW, WHEN WE WENT TO ASTARIA ...
...I SAW SENRI GO WILD, TOO.
ガラ ガラ ガラ ガラ
ガラ ガラ
ガラ ガラ...
!!

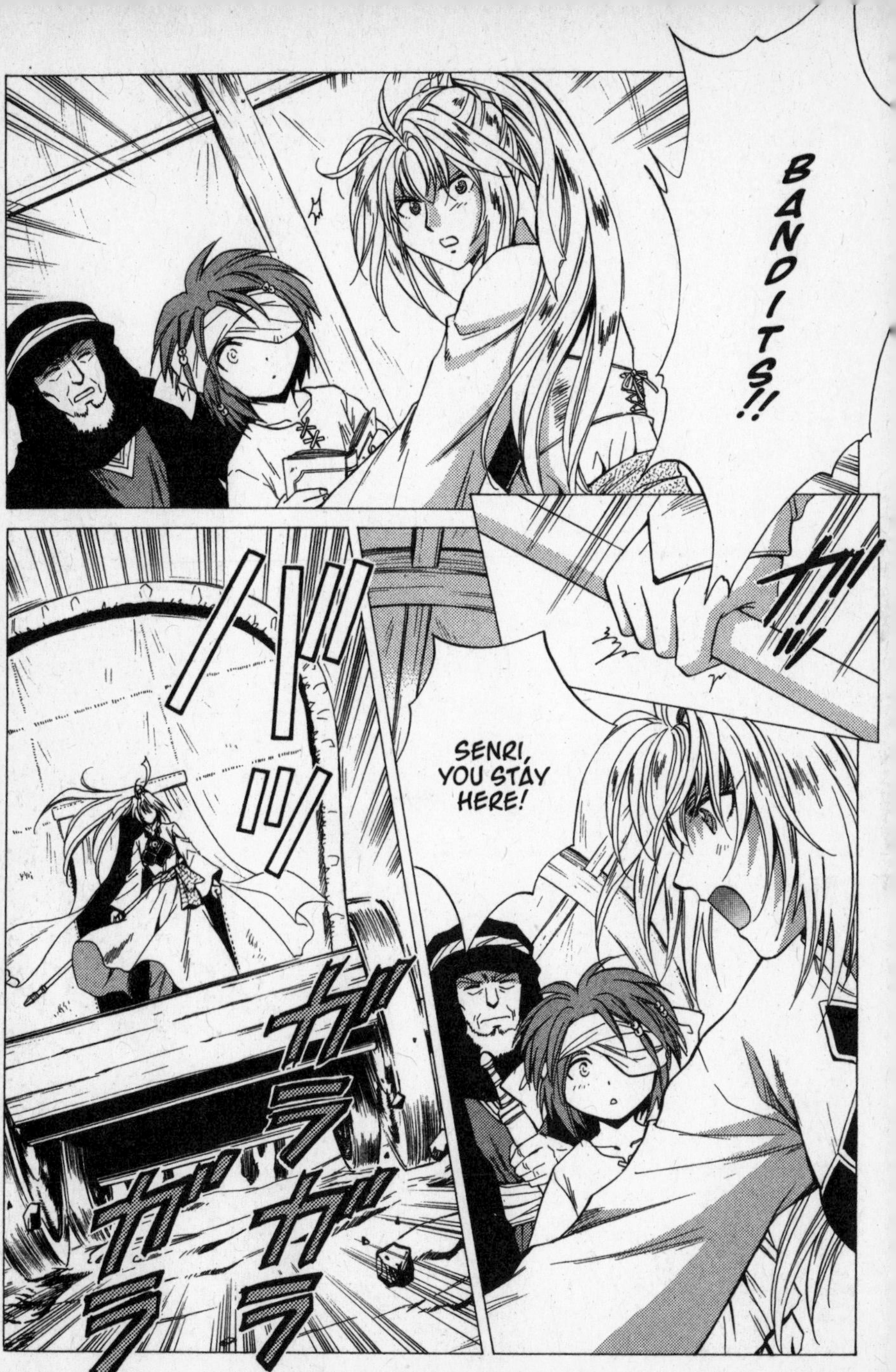
BANDITS!!
SENRI, YOU STAY HERE!
ガラガラ
ガラガラ

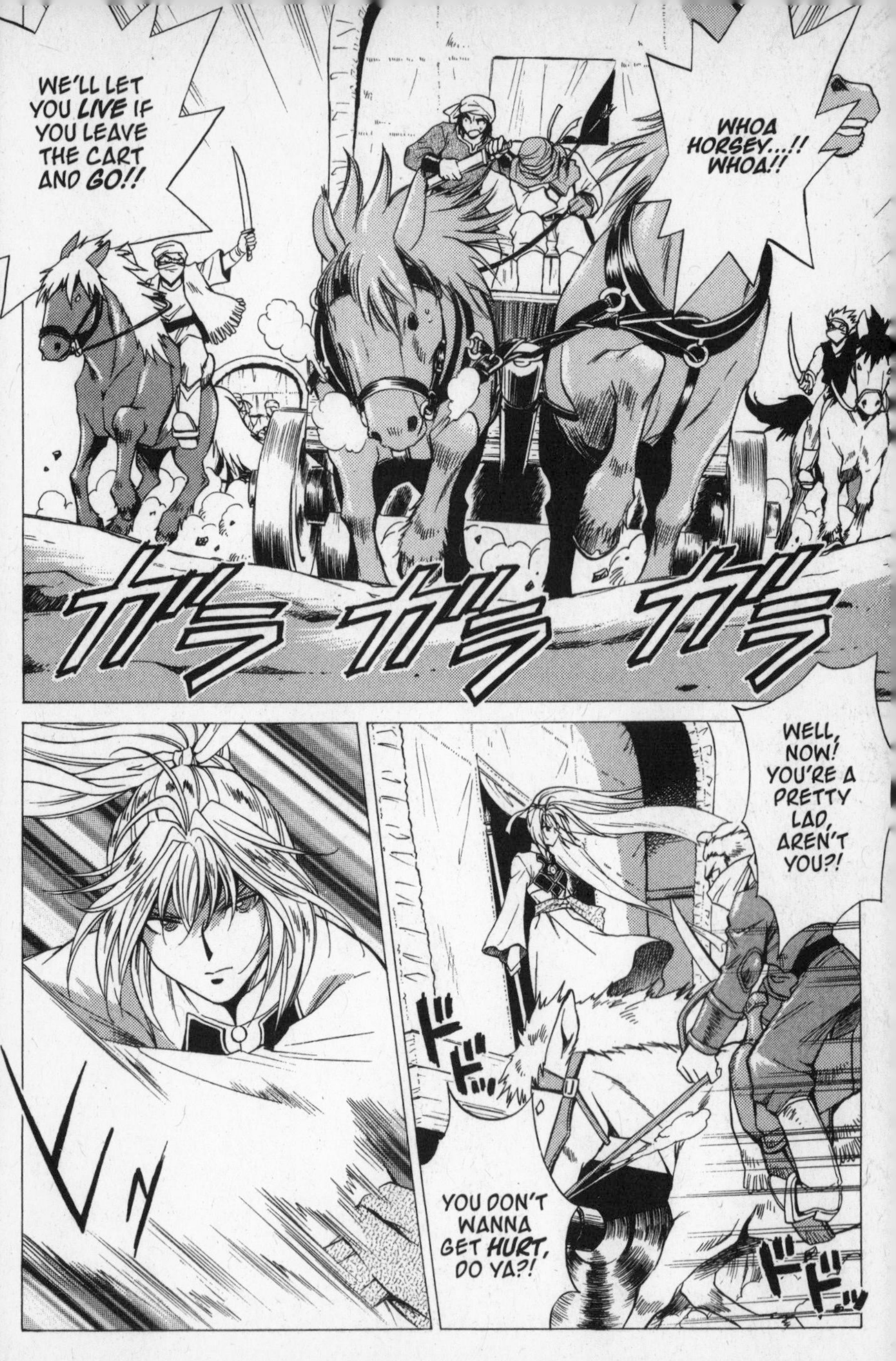
WHOA HORSEY...!! WHOA!!
WE'LL LET YOU LIVE IF YOU LEAVE THE CART AND GO!!
ガラ ガラ カラ
WELL, NOW! YOU'RE A PRETTY LAD, AREN'T YOU?!
ドドッ
YOU DON'T WANNA GET HURT, DO YA?!
ドドッ
VUN

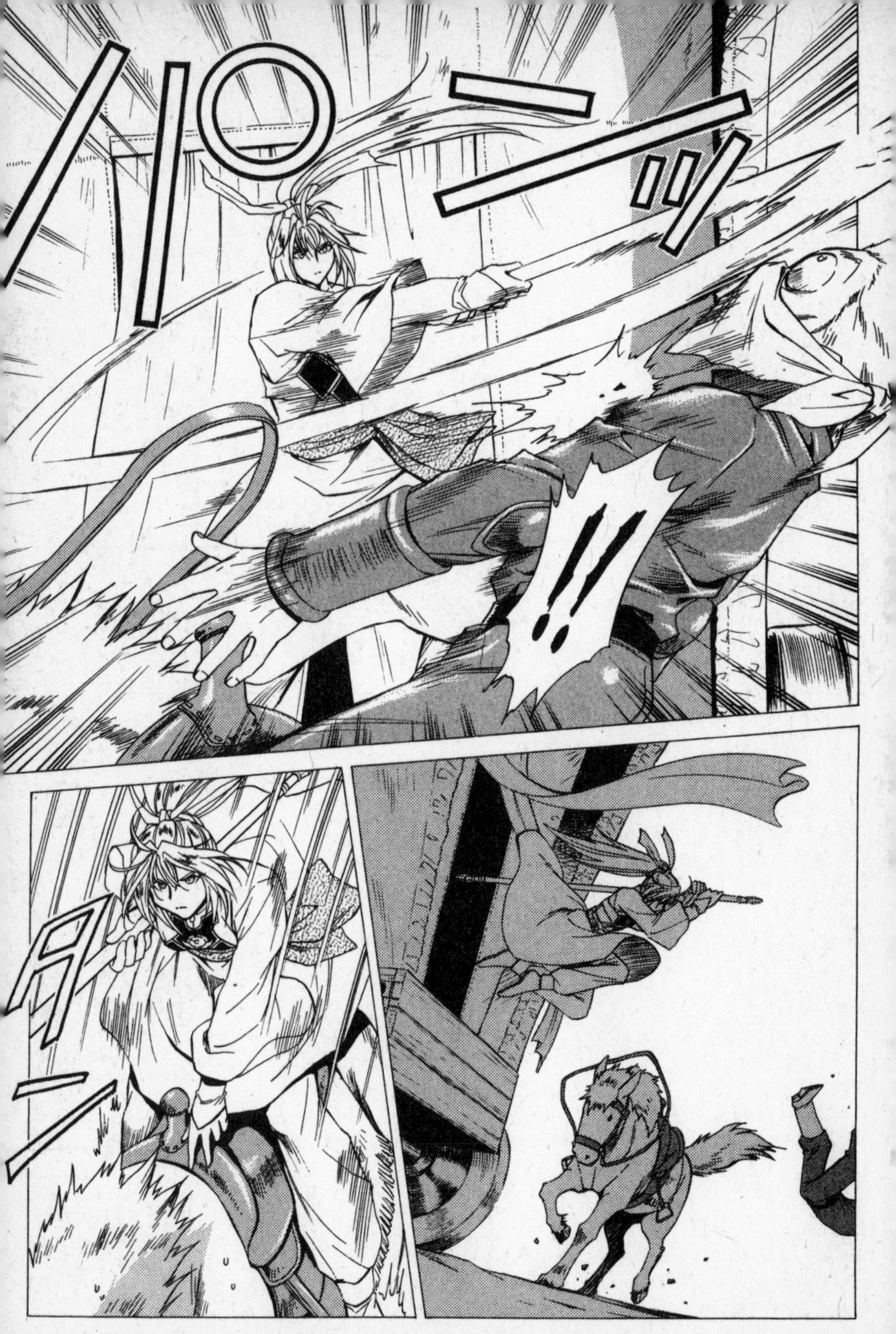
パーーッ
!!
タン

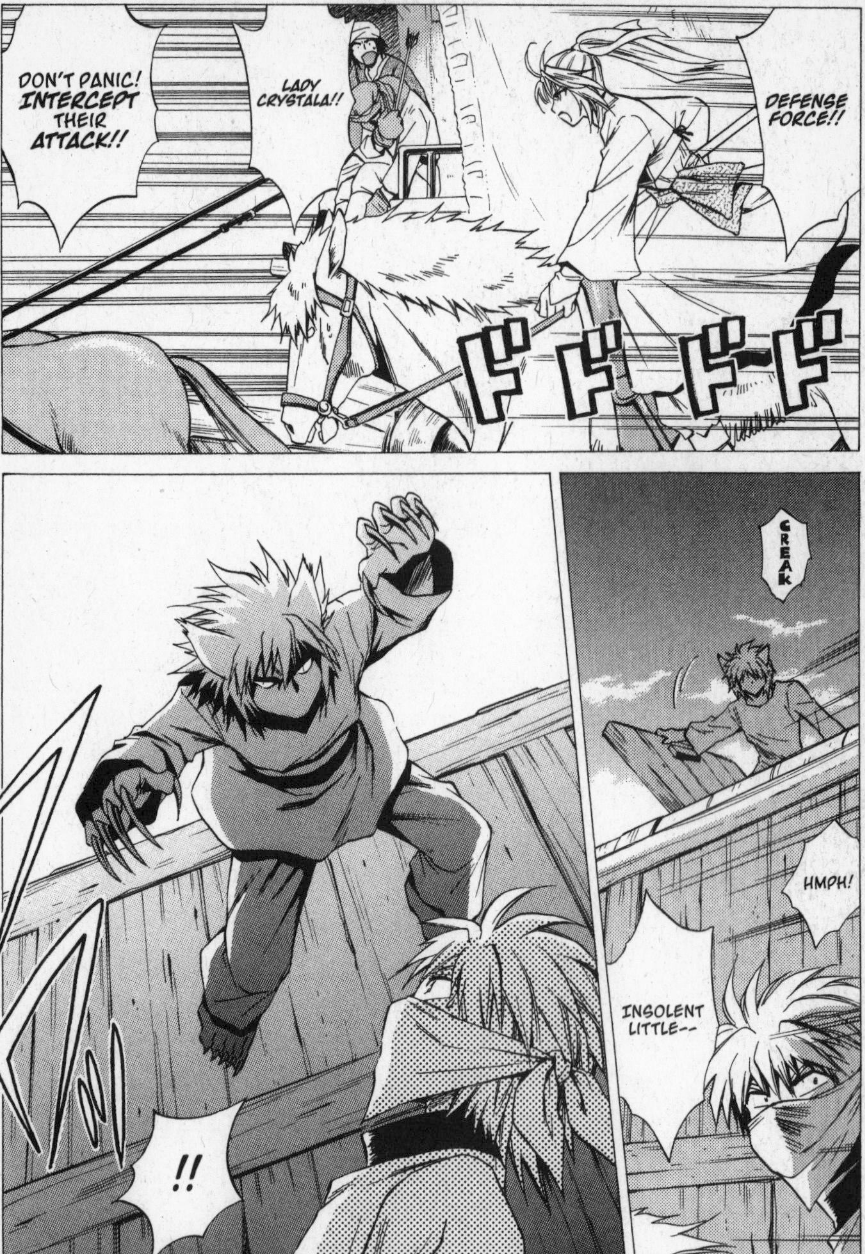
DEFENSE FORCE!!
LADY CRYSTALA!!
DON'T PANIC! INTERCEPT THEIR ATTACK!!
ドドドード
CREAK
HMPH!
INSOLENT LITTLE--
!!

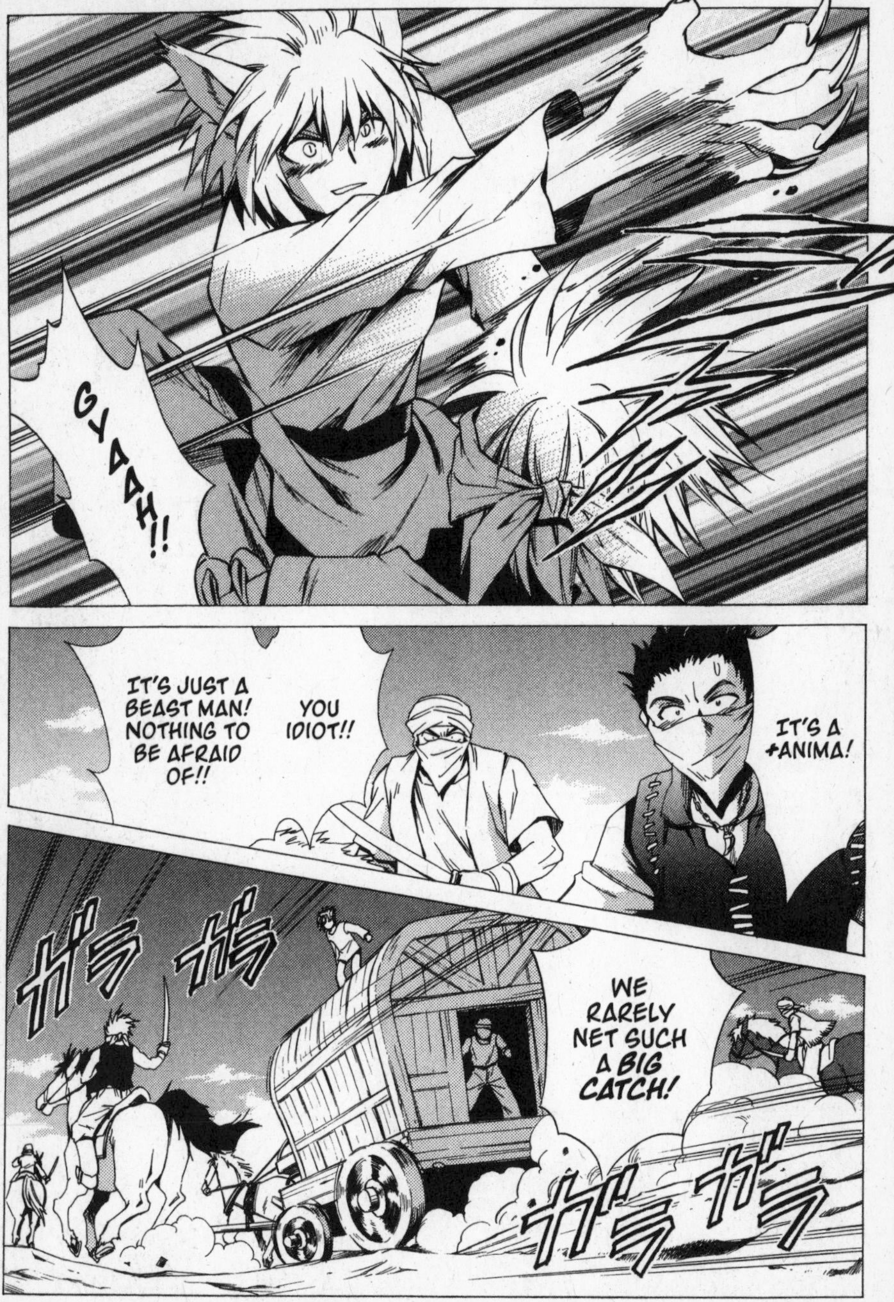
GYAAH!!
IT'S A +ANIMA!
YOU IDIOT!!
IT'S JUST A BEAST MAN! NOTHING TO BE AFRAID OF!!
ガラ ガラ
WE RARELY NET SUCH A BIG CATCH!
ガラ ガラ

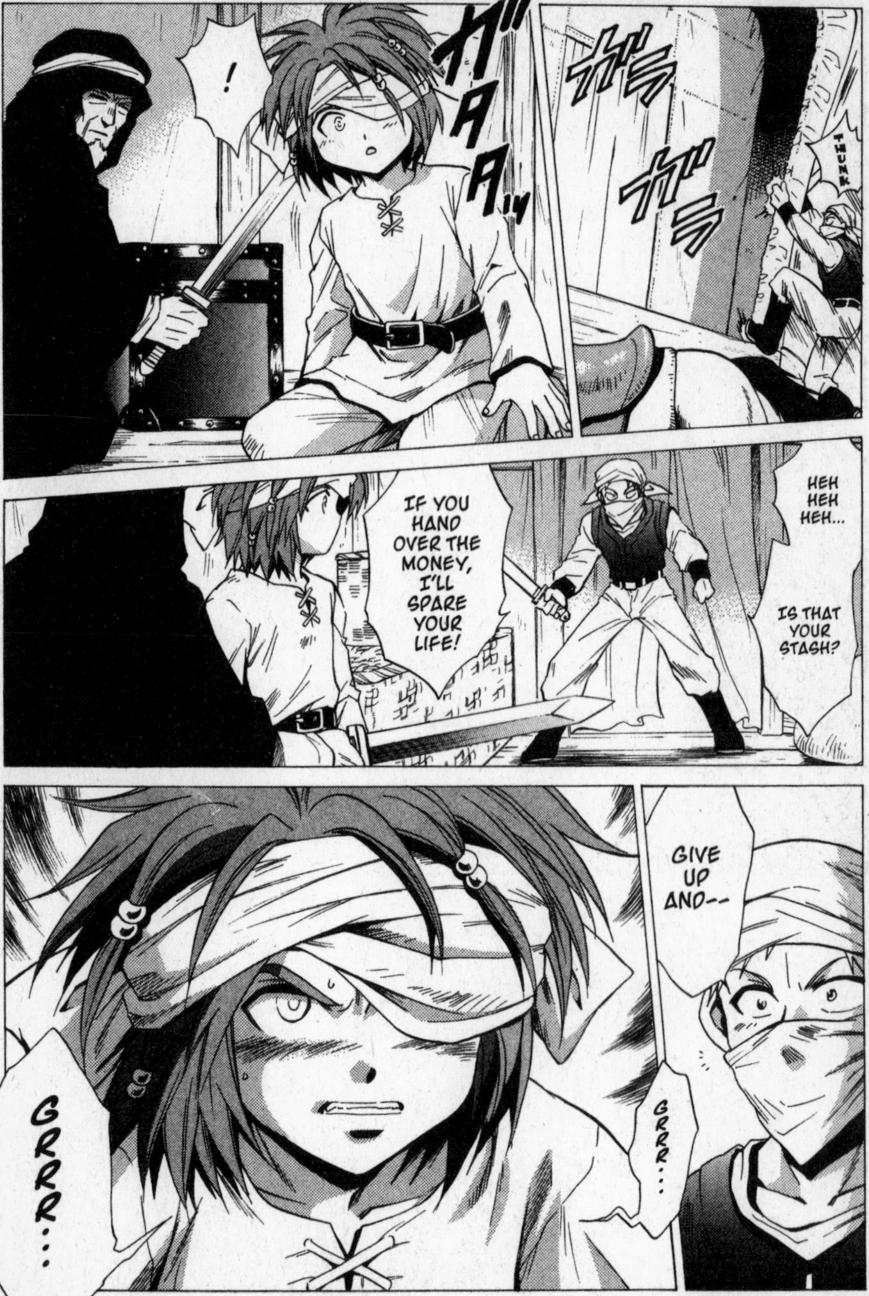
ガラ
ガラ
THUNK
ガタタッ
!
HEH HEH HEH...
IS THAT YOUR STASH?
IF YOU HAND OVER THE MONEY, I'LL SPARE YOUR LIFE!
GIVE UP AND--
GRRR...
GRRR...

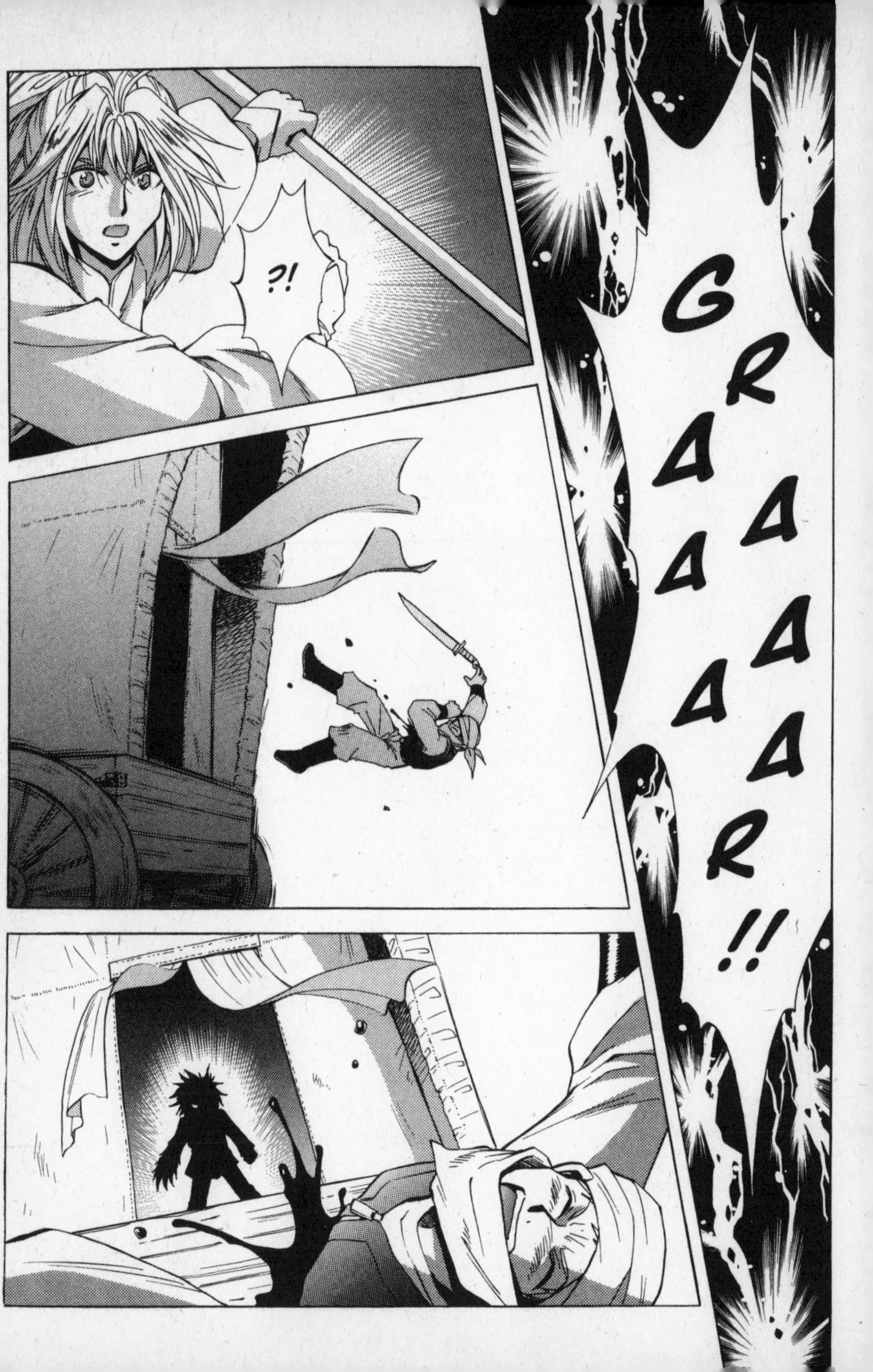
GRAAAAAAAR!!
?!

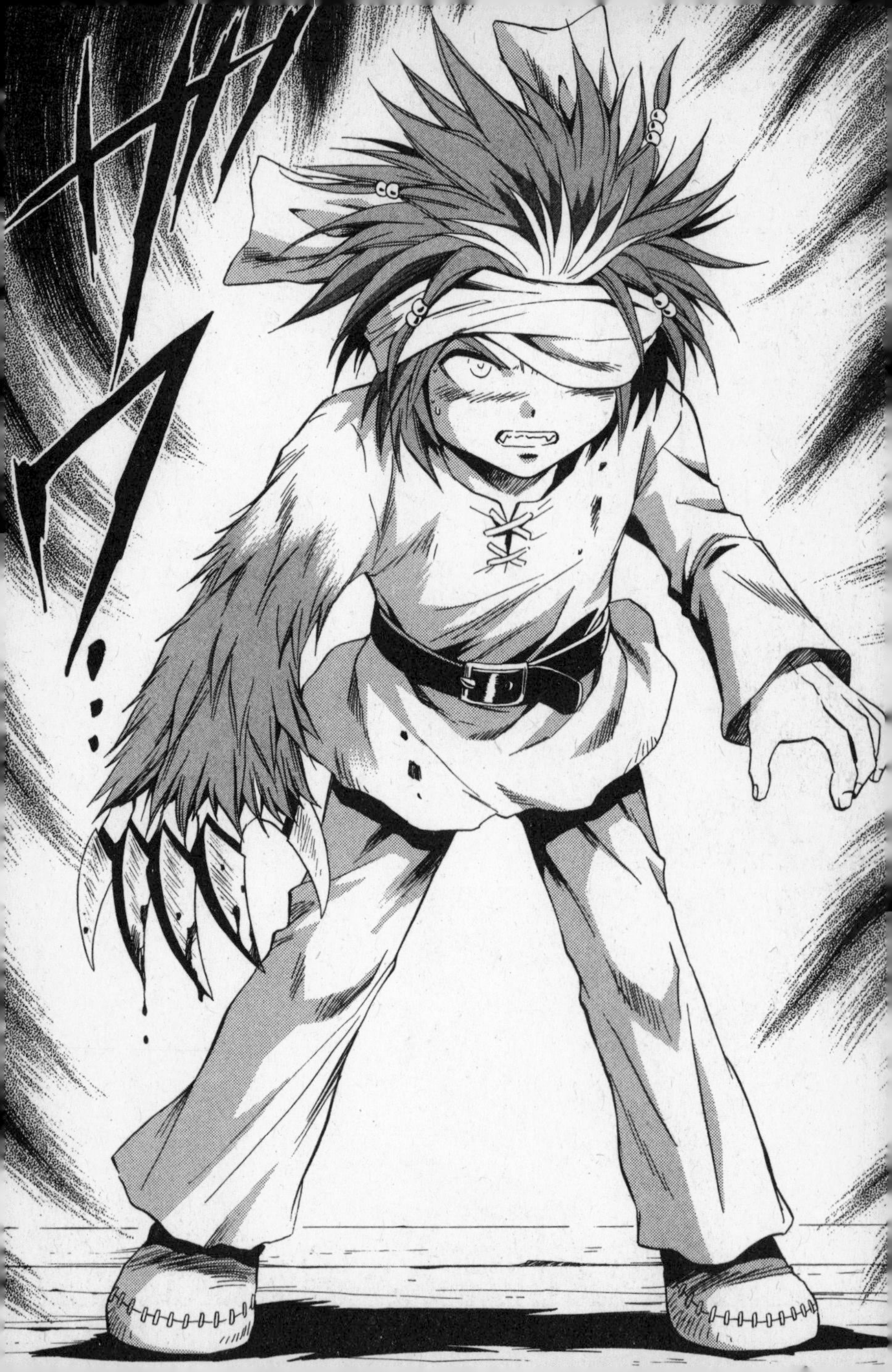

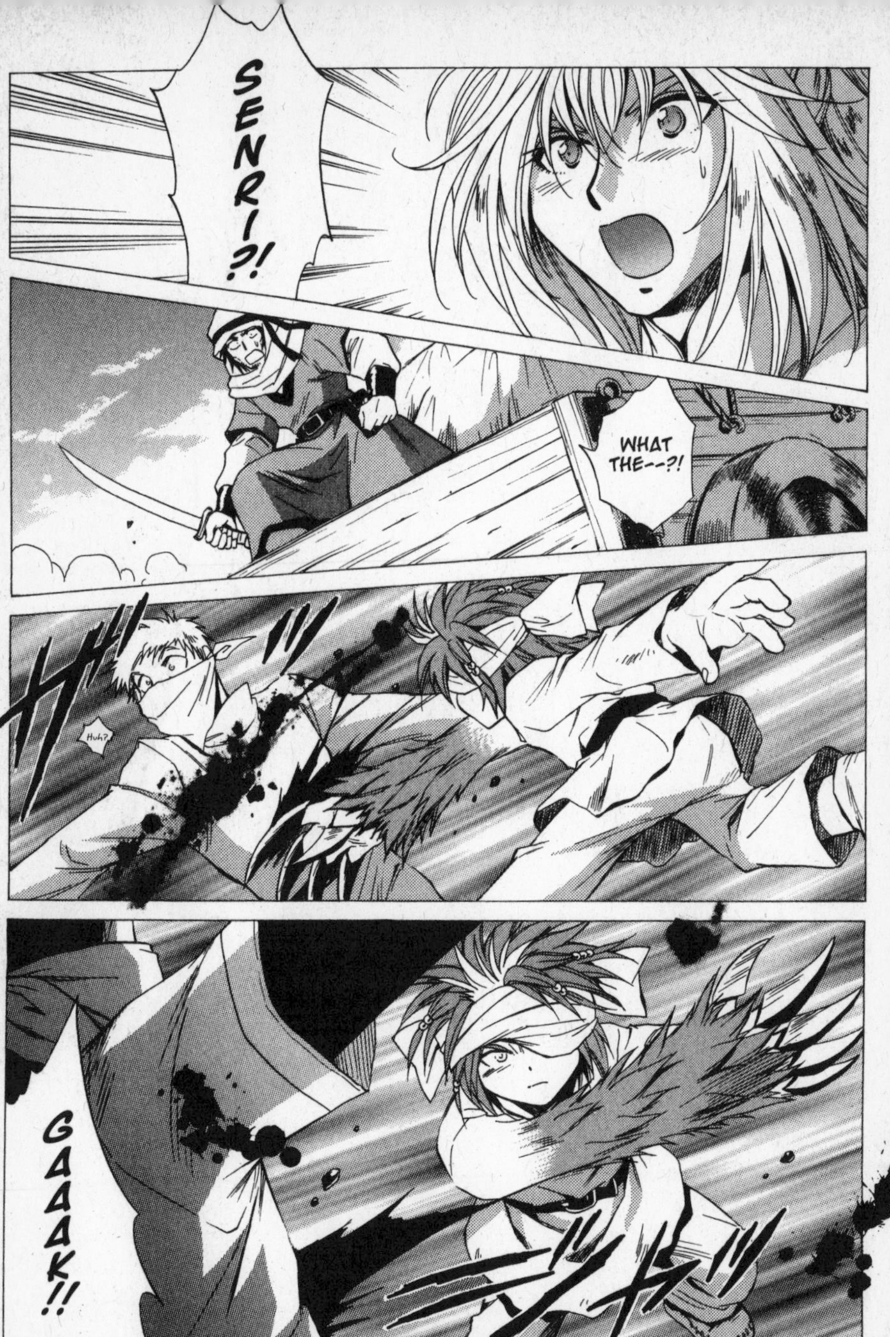
SENRI?!
WHAT THE--?!
Huh?
GAAAAK!!

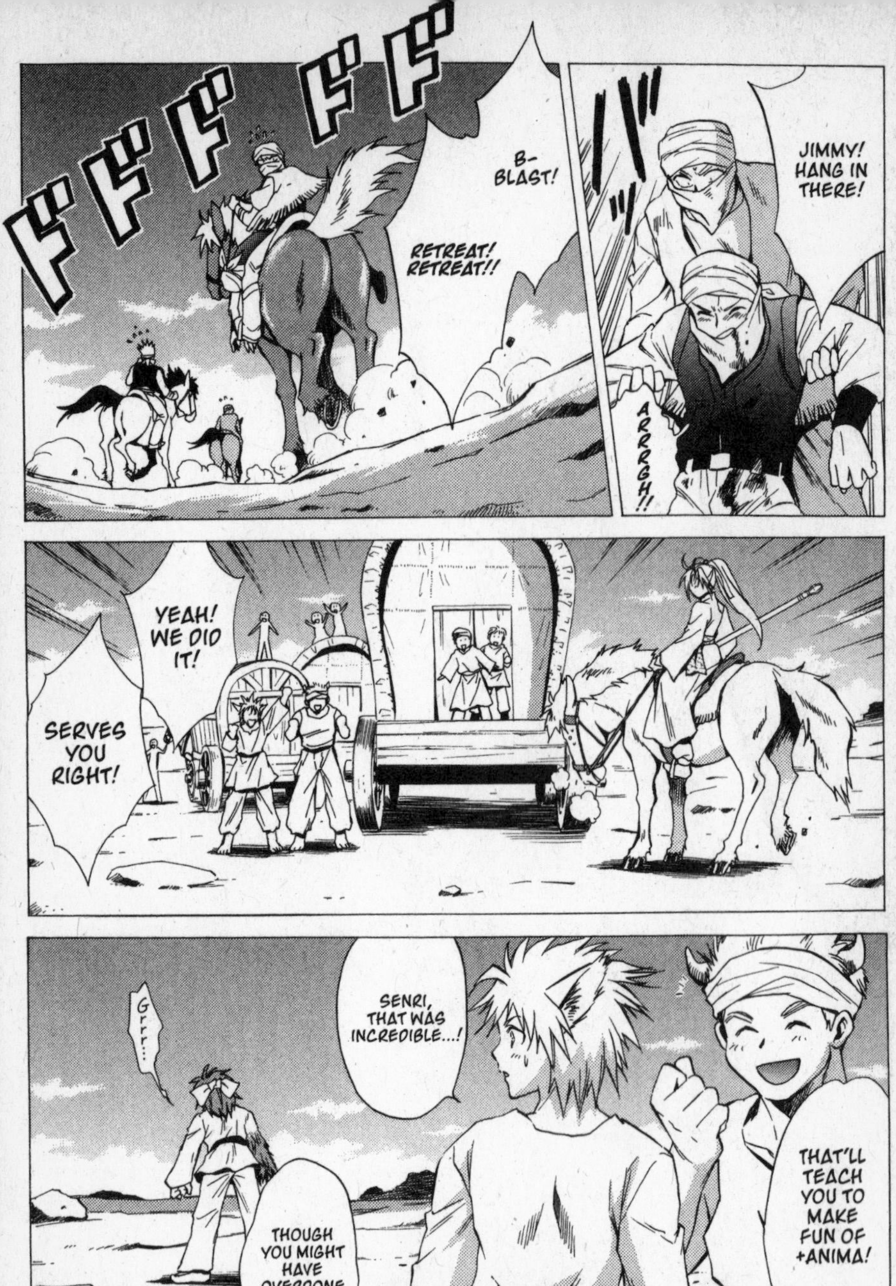
JIMMY! HANG IN THERE!
ARRRGH!!
ドドドドドド
B-BLAST!
RETREAT! RETREAT!!
YEAH! WE DID IT!
SERVES YOU RIGHT!
THAT'LL TEACH YOU TO MAKE FUN OF +ANIMA!
SENRI, THAT WAS INCREDIBLE...!
THOUGH YOU MIGHT HAVE OVERDONE IT A LIT--
Grrr...

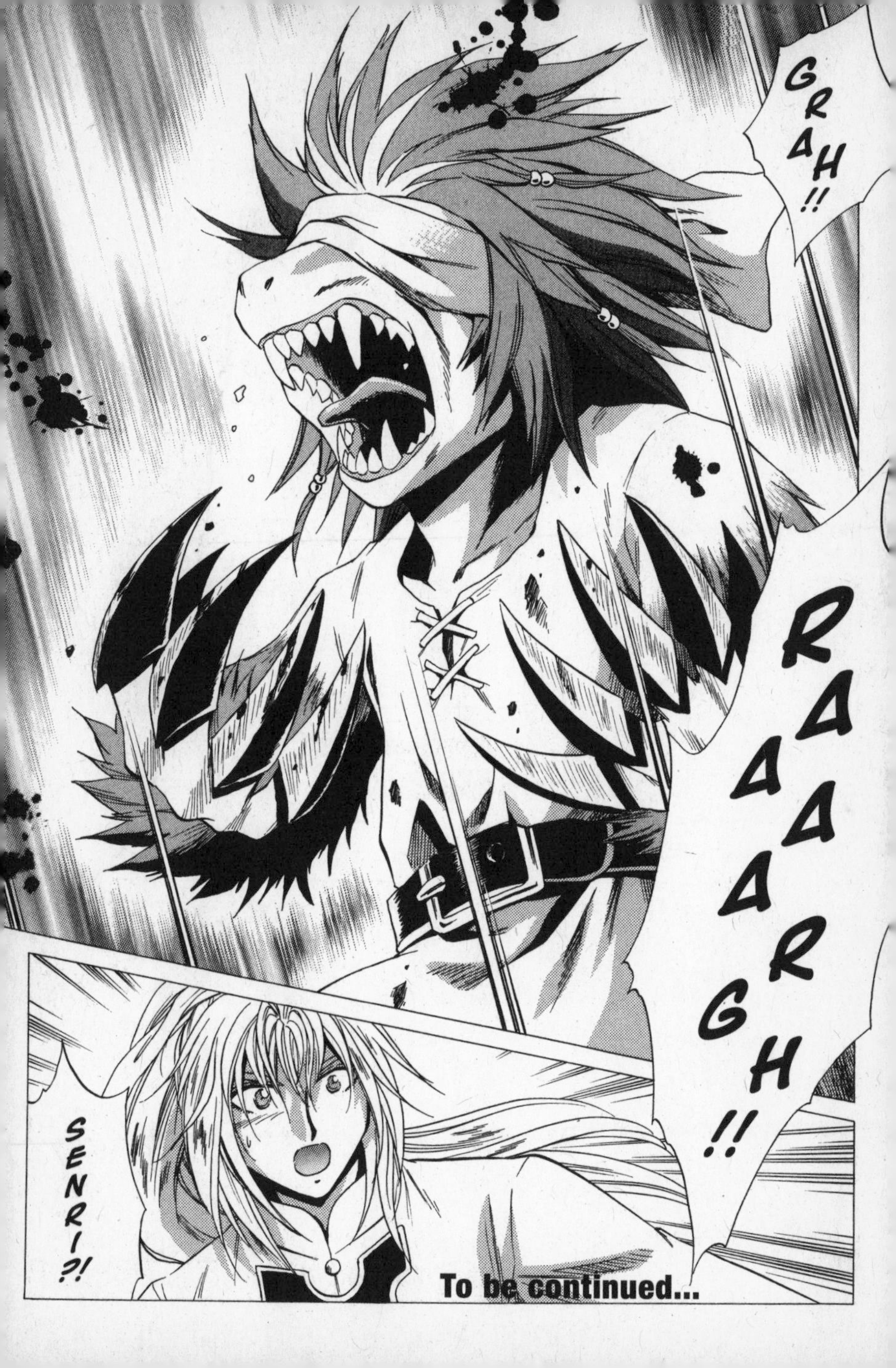
GRAH!!
RAAAARGH!!
SENRI?!
To be continued...

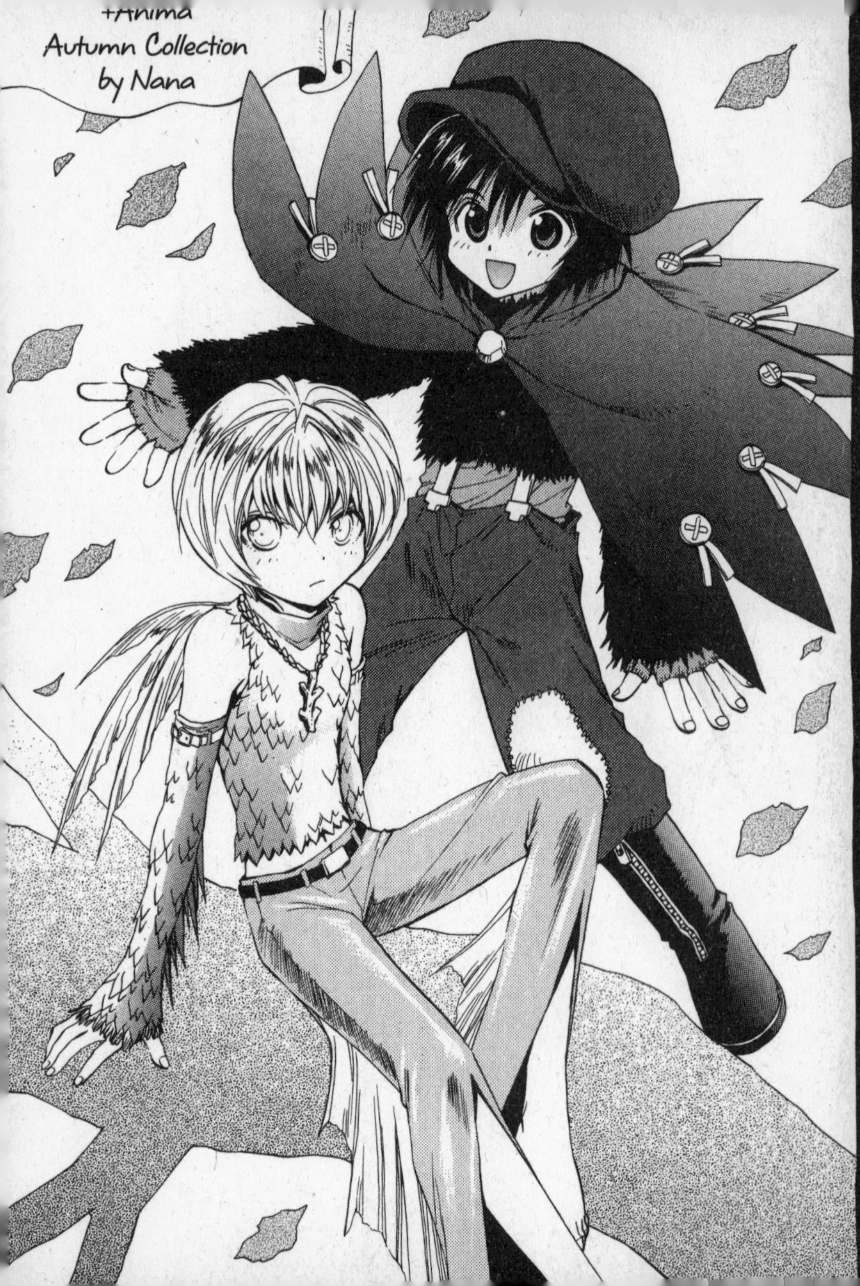
+Anima
Autumn Collection
by Nana

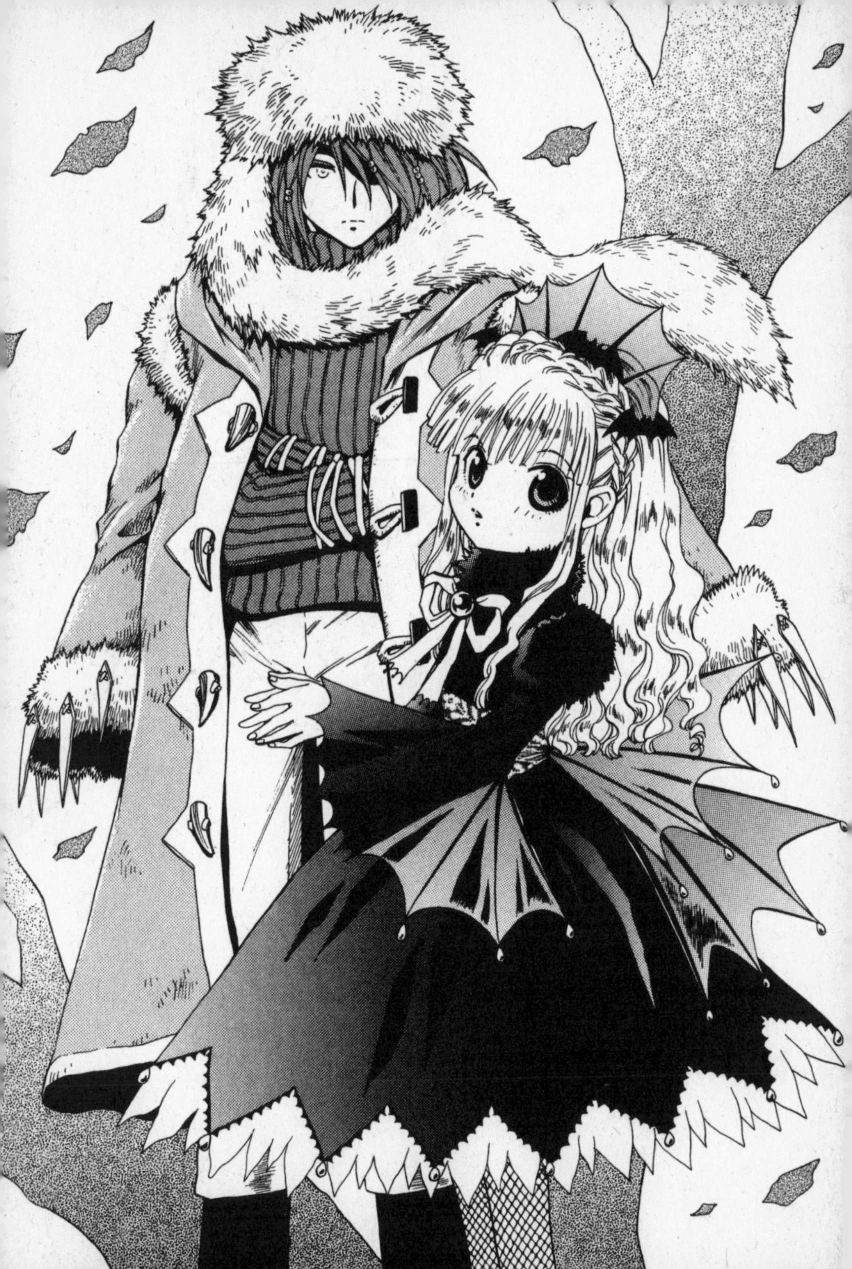

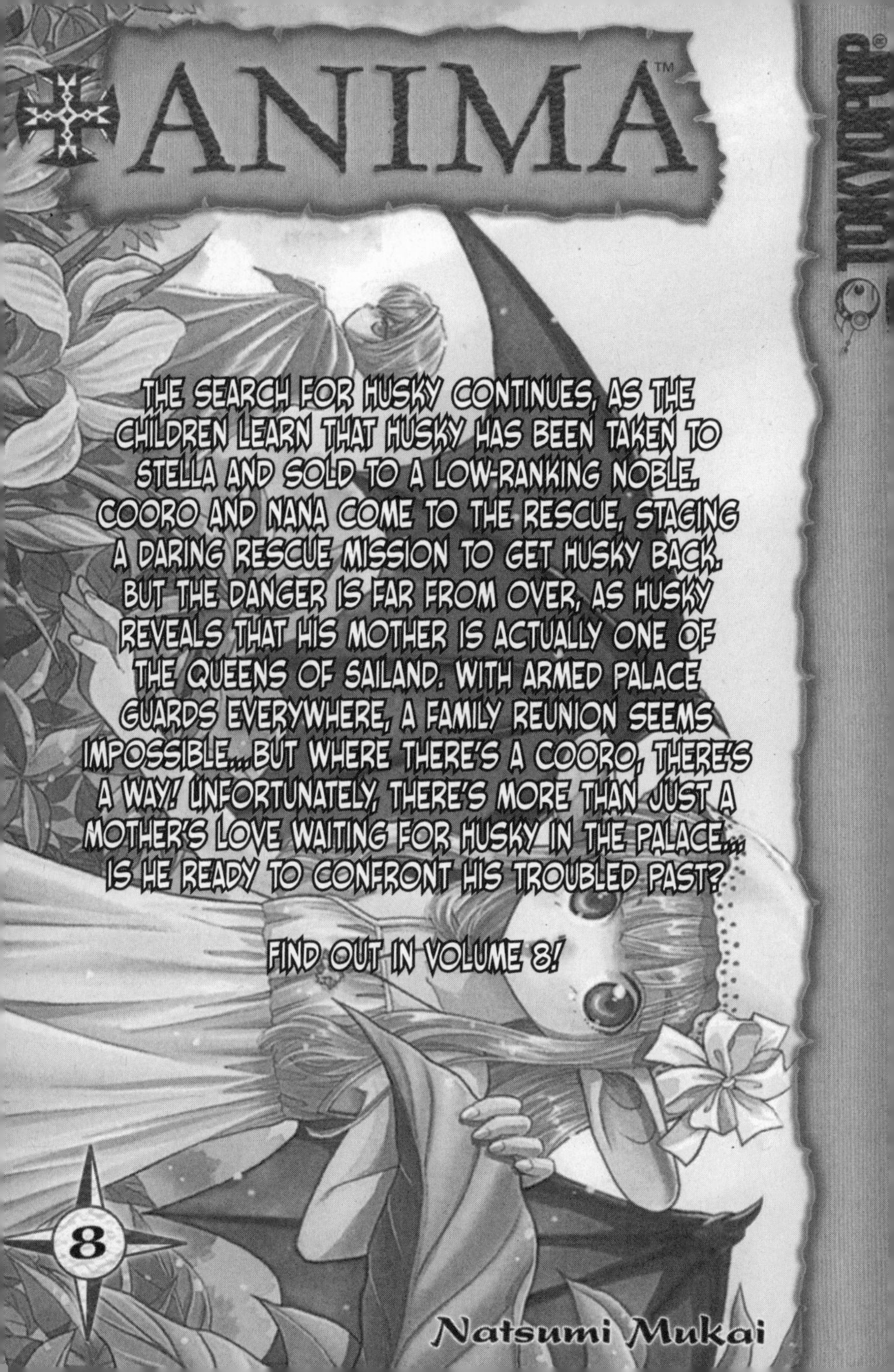
+ANIMA™
TOKYOPOP®
8
Natsumi Mukai

THE SEARCH FOR HUSKY CONTINUES, AS THE CHILDREN LEARN THAT HUSKY HAS BEEN TAKEN TO STELLA AND SOLD TO A LOW-RANKING NOBLE. COORO AND NANA COME TO THE RESCUE, STAGING A DARING RESCUE MISSION TO GET HUSKY BACK. BUT THE DANGER IS FAR FROM OVER, AS HUSKY REVEALS THAT HIS MOTHER IS ACTUALLY ONE OF THE QUEENS OF SAILAND. WITH ARMED PALACE GUARDS EVERYWHERE, A FAMILY REUNION SEEMS IMPOSSIBLE... BUT WHERE THERE'S A COORO, THERE'S A WAY! UNFORTUNATELY, THERE'S MORE THAN JUST A MOTHER'S LOVE WAITING FOR HUSKY IN THE PALACE... IS HE READY TO CONFRONT HIS TROUBLED PAST?

FIND OUT IN VOLUME 8!

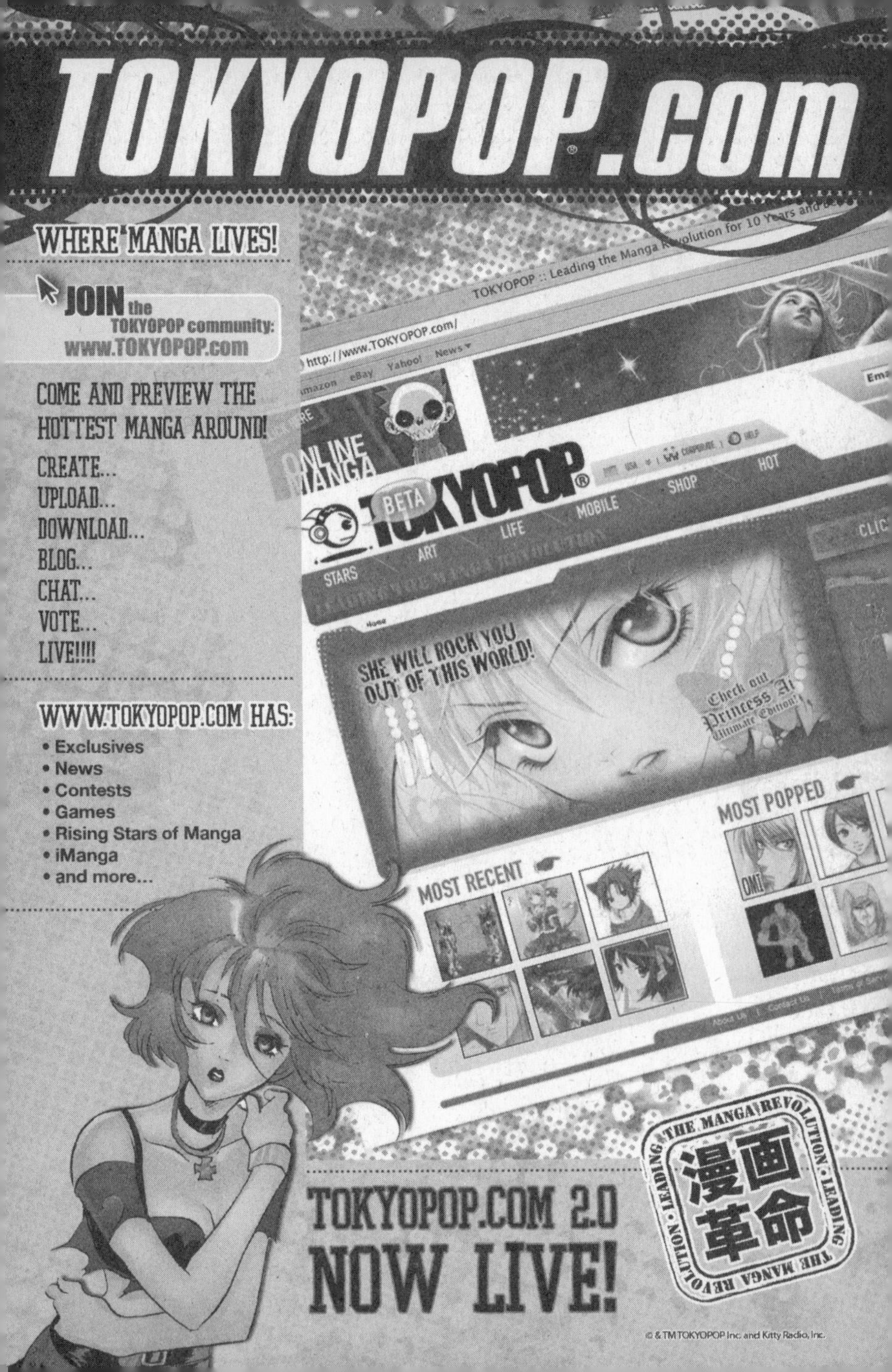

TOKYOPOP.com
WHERE MANGA LIVES!
JOIN the TOKYOPOP community: www.TOKYOPOP.com
COME AND PREVIEW THE HOTTEST MANGA AROUND!
CREATE...
UPLOAD...
DOWNLOAD...
BLOG...
CHAT...
VOTE...
LIVE!!!!
WWW.TOKYOPOP.COM HAS:
• Exclusives
• News
• Contests
• Games
• Rising Stars of Manga
• iManga
• and more...
TOKYOPOP :: Leading the Manga Revolution for 10 Years and Be
http://www.TOKYOPOP.com/
ONLINE MANGA
BETA TOKYOPOP
STARS
ART
LIFE
MOBILE
SHOP
HOT
SHE WILL ROCK YOU OUT OF THIS WORLD!
Check out Princess Ai Ultimate Edition!
MOST RECENT
MOST POPPED
TOKYOPOP.COM 2.0
NOW LIVE!
THE MANGA REVOLUTION • LEADING
漫画革命
© & TM TOKYOPOP Inc. and Kitty Radio, Inc.